Heinrich Spies

Studien zur Geschichte des englischen Pronomens im XV. und XVI. Jahrhundert

Heinrich Spies

Studien zur Geschichte des englischen Pronomens im XV. und XVI. Jahrhundert

ISBN/EAN: 9783337220204

Hergestellt in Europa, USA, Kanada, Australien, Japan

Cover: Foto ©Thomas Meinert / pixelio.de

Weitere Bücher finden Sie auf **www.hansebooks.com**

STUDIEN

ZUR

ENGLISCHEN PHILOLOGIE

HERAUSGEGEBEN

VON

LORENZ MORSBACH,
O. Ö. PROFESSOR AN DER UNIVERSITÄT GÖTTINGEN.

Heft I.
HEINRICH SPIES:
STUDIEN Z. GESCHICHTE D. ENGLISCHEN PRONOMENS
IM XV. UND XVI. JAHRHUNDERT.

HALLE A. S.
MAX NIEMEYER.
1897.

STUDIEN
ZUR
GESCHICHTE DES ENGLISCHEN PRONOMENS
IM XV. UND XVI. JAHRHUNDERT.

(FLEXIONSLEHRE UND SYNTAX.)

VON

HEINRICH SPIES,
DR. PHIL.

HALLE a. S.
MAX NIEMEYER.
1897.

Meinen Eltern.

Vorwort.

Indem ich hiermit die vorliegende Untersuchung der Oeffentlichkeit übergebe, bemerke ich, dass sie, auf Anregung des Herrn Professor Dr. Morsbach entstanden, in ihren wesentlichen Bestandteilen bereits der philosophischen Fakultät der Universität Göttingen als Dissertation vorgelegen hat, aber nur zum geringsten Teile (Flexionslehre) als solche gedruckt worden ist.

Ich hoffe damit einen nicht unwillkommenen Beitrag zur Methode und Geschichte der englischen Syntax geliefert zu haben, im weiteren auch zur Erklärung und zum Verständnis von Werken des 15. und 16. Jahrhunderts, insbesondere Shaksperes, beizutragen.

Der ganzen Arbeit liegt der Hauptgedanke zu Grunde, eine Reihe grammatischer Erscheinungen durch einen grösseren Zeitabschnitt hindurch zu verfolgen und in historischen Zusammenhang mit früheren und späteren Sprachepochen zu bringen. Vorläufig wird auf diese Weise gerade auf dem Gebiete der Grammatik des 15. und 16. Jahrhunderts mehr erreicht werden, als durch die Betrachtung des Sprachgebrauchs eines einzelnen Schriftstellers, die so lange lückenhaft bleiben muss, als wir nicht auf Grund historischer Untersuchungen einzelner Erscheinungen Individuelles vom Allgemeingültigen trennen können.

Leider macht sich der Mangel an kritisch wirklich zuverlässigen Ausgaben noch recht fühlbar; so habe auch ich eine Reihe von Texten (Dodsley-Hazlitt, Dyce, Fairholt's Lyly Ausgabe, sowie die von Sidneys Arcadia) benutzen müssen, die auf streng wissenschaftliche Genauigkeit keinen oder nur geringen Anspruch machen können und daher rein lautlichen oder metrischen Untersuchungen nicht zu Grunde gelegt werden dürfen. Auch kritische Ausgaben, die auf genauen Abdruck Anspruch erheben, sind nicht immer unbedingt zuverlässig; man vergl. zu diesem Punkte die interessante Bemerkung Habersangs inbetreff der Ausgaben Coopers und Arbers von Ralph Roister Doister, Beilage zum Progr. des Adolphinums zu Bückeburg 1875. Wenn ich nun auch das Gebiet des Lautlichen nicht ganz habe umgehen können, so sind doch die Ergebnisse meiner lautlichen Erörterungen, insbesondere die in § 1 angestellten Betrachtungen über die englische Orthographie des 15. und 16. Jahrhunderts durch die weit überwiegende Zahl der benutzten kritisch genauen Ausgaben hinreichend gesichert; auf den syntaktischen Teil, in dem ich den Kern meiner Abhandlung sehe, hat die Unzuverlässigkeit einzelner Texte so gut wie gar keinen Einfluss.

Dass uns selbst in den alten Drucken noch nicht eo ipso die sprachliche Form des Autors vorliegt, und dass wir ohne etwaige Zuhülfenahme anderer Kriterien nicht entscheiden können, was dem Verfasser und was dem Drucker angehört, möchte ich auch an dieser Stelle wie in § 1 Ende noch einmal betonen.

Bei der Wiedergabe von Belegstellen (über die Wahl derselben siehe Ende der Einleitung p. 2) habe ich mir mit Rücksicht auf den Raum eine gewisse Beschränkung auferlegen müssen; sollte sich für das eine oder andere Kapitel die Anführung weiterer Belege als wünschenswert herausstellen, so werde ich natürlich jederzeit aus meinem reichhaltigen etwa 14 000 Zettel umfassenden Material bereitwilligst weitere Mitteilungen machen.

Die Fülle des Materials hat mich auch bestimmt, manche

Erscheinungen, für deren Auffassung sich keine neuen Momente ergaben, doch durch Konstatierung des Thatbestandes im 15. und 16. Jahrhundert vorübergehend zu streifen.

Kleine Unebenheiten in der Orthographie deutscher Wörter erklären sich durch den Anschluss an die in der Druckerei geltenden Formen.

Zum Schluss ergreife ich mit Freuden die Gelegenheit, meinem hochverehrten Lehrer, Herrn Prof. Dr. Morsbach in Göttingen, auch an dieser Stelle meinen herzlichsten Dank auszusprechen für die vielseitigen Anregungen auf dem Gebiet der Anglistik, insbesondere ferner für das mir und meiner Arbeit entgegengebrachte Interesse und den stets in liebenswürdigster Weise erteilten Rat, sowie für die freundliche Uebernahme der 3. Korrektur.

Göttingen im Juni 1897.

Heinrich Spies.
Dr. phil.

Abkürzungen.

Fl. = Flügel, Neuenglisches Lesebuch.
Fox = Reynard the Fox, Transl. by Caxton.
Franz ohne römische Ziffer bezieht sich auf die Artikel in Engl. Stud. XVII.
M. = Malory, Morte Darthure.
P. L. = Paston Letters.
R. A. = Roger Asham.
Die übrigen sind bekannt oder ergeben sich von selbst.

Benutzte grammatische und lexikalische Werke.

Abbot, A Shakesperian Grammer, London 1891.
Baumann, Londinismen, Berlin 1887.
Blume, Die Sprache der Paston Letters, Progr. Bremen 1882.
Deutschbein, Shakespeare Grammatik für Deutsche, 2. Aufl. Coethen 1897.
Ellinger, Syntaktische Untersuchungen zu der Sprache der mittelenglischen Romanze von „Sir Perceval of Galles". Xenia Austriaca, Festschrift der österr. Mittelschulen etc., Wien 1893.
Flamme, Syntax der Blickling Homilies, Diss. Bonn 1888.
Franz, Die Dialektsprache bei Ch. Dickens, Engl. Stud. XII, 197 ff.
Franz, Zur Syntax des älteren Neuenglisch, Engl. Stud. XVII, 200 ff., 384 ff.
Günther, Edmund Spensers syntaktische Eigentümlichkeiten, Herrigs Archiv Bd. 55.
Hoelper, Die englische Schriftsprache in Tottels „Miscellany" (1557) und in Tottels Ausgabe von Brookes „Romeus and Juliet" (1562), Diss. Strassburg 1894.
Jespersen, Progress in Language, London 1894.
Kellner, Einleitung zu Blanchardyn and Eglantine, London 1890.
Kellner, Historical Outlines of English Syntax, London 1892.
Koch, Hist. Grammatik Bd. II, 2. Aufl. Cassel 1878.
Luick, Untersuchungen zur englischen Lautgeschichte, Strassburg 1896.
Lummert, Die Orthographie der ersten Folioausgabe der Shakspere'schen Dramen, Diss. Halle 1883.
Mätzner, Englische Grammatik, 2. Aufl. Berlin 1873—1875.
Morris, Historical Outlines of English Accidence, London 1895.
Morsbach, Mittelenglische Grammatik, Erste Hälfte, Halle 1896.
Morsbach, Shaksperes Leben und Werke, Sprache und Verskunst, Vorlesungen S. S. 1895.

Morsbach, Ueber den Ursprung der neuenglischen Schriftsprache, Heilbronn 1888.
Panning, Dialektisches Englisch in Elisabethanischen Dramen, Diss. Halle 1884.
Ritzenfeldt, Der Gebrauch des Pronomens, Artikels und Verbs bei Th. Kyd, Diss. Kiel 1889.
Römstedt, Die engl. Schriftsprache bei Caxton, Göttingen 1891.
Rost, Die Orthographie der ersten Quartoausgabe von Miltons Paradise Lost, Diss. Leipzig 1892.
Schmidt (Imm.), Grammatik der engl. Sprache, Berlin 1896.
Schmidt, Shakespeare Lexikon, Berlin und London 1874.
Sopp, Orthographie und Aussprache der ersten ne. Bibelübersetzung von William Tyndale, Anglia XII, 273 ff.
Storm, Englische Philologie I, 2, Leipzig 1896.
Sturzen-Becker, Some notes on the leading grammatical Characteristics of the principal early english dialects, Diss. Copenhagen 1868.
The New Testament, Parallel Versions of 1611 and 1881, Oxford 1881.
Wright, The Bible Word-Book, London 1884.
Wülfing, Die Syntax in den Werken Alfreds des Grossen, Erster Teil, Bonn 1894.
Würzner, Die Orthographie der beiden Quarto-Ausgaben von Shaksperes Sommernachtstraum, Xenia Austriaca, Festschrift der österr. Mittelschulen, Wien 1893.
Wunderlich, Unsere Umgangssprache in der Eigenart ihrer Satzfügung dargestellt, Weimar und Berlin 1894.
Zupitza, Archiv 84, 181 Besprechung von Barker's „Original English etc."

Auf andere Werke ist an der betr. Stelle verwiesen.

Inhalt.

	Seite
Einleitung	1
Quellenverzeichnis	3

Flexionslehre.

Allgemeines zur Orthographie § 1	8
Personalpronomen § 2—19	11
Personalpronomen der 1. Person § 2—5	11
I § 2	11
Me § 3, *we* § 4, *us* § 5	13
Personalpronomen der 2. Person § 6—9	13
Thou § 6, *thee* § 7, *ye* § 8	13
You § 9	14
Personalpronomen der 3. Person § 10—16	14
He § 10, *him* § 11, *she* § 12	14
Her § 13, *it* § 14, *they* § 15, *them* § 16	15
Verschmelzung des Personalpronomens mit anderen Wörtern § 17	16
Grossschreibung der Personalpronomina § 18	17
Verschiebung im Gebrauch der Personalpronomina § 19	17
Possessivpronomen § 20—33	18
Adjektivisches Possessivpronomen § 20—27	18
My, mine, thy, thine § 20	18
His § 21	19
Her § 22, *its* § 23, *our* § 24	20
Your § 25, *their* § 26	21
Grossschreibung der Possessivpronomina § 27	21
Substantivisches Possessivpronomen § 28—33	22
Mine, thine, his § 28	22
Hers § 29, *ours* § 30, *yours* § 31, *theirs* § 32	22
Formen ohne *s* § 33	22
Reflexivpronomen § 34—44	23
Vorbemerkungen § 34	23
Myself § 35, *thyself* § 36	23
Himself § 37, *herself* § 38, *itself* § 39, *one's self* § 40	24
Ourselves § 41, *yourselves* § 42, *themselves* § 43	25
Ourselfe und *yourselfe* als Majestätsplural § 44	26

XIV

	Seite
Demonstrativpronomen § 45—54	26
This § 45, *these* § 46	26
That § 47, *those* § 48, *such* § 49	27
Thilk § 50, *ilk* § 51, *self* § 52, *same* § 53	28
Yon, yond, yonder § 54	29
Interrogativ- und Relativpronomen § 55—66	29
Who § 55	29
Whose § 56, *whom* § 57, *what* § 58	30
Whether § 59, *which* § 60, *who so, who(so[m])ever* § 61	31
What so, what(so[m])ever § 62, *which(so[m])ever* § 63	32
That § 64, *at* § 65	32
Grossschreibung der Relativpronomina § 66	33
Indefinita § 67—88	33
One § 67	33
No, none § 68, *both* § 69	34
Aught, ought § 70, *naught, nought* § 71, *nothing* § 72, *some* § 73	35
Enough § 74, *few* § 75, *much* § 76	36
Any § 77, *many* § 78, *each* § 79	37
Every § 80, *either* § 81, *neither* § 82, *other* § 83	38
All § 84, *sundry* § 85	40
Divers § 86, *certain* § 87, *several* § 88	41

Syntax.

Personalpronomen § 89—153	42
Auslassung des Personalpronomens § 89—104	42
Vorbemerkung § 89	42
I. Auslassung des Personalpronomens als Subjekt § 90—101	43
A. Das Pronomen ist aus dem Zusammenhang zu ergänzen § 90—95	43
1. Auslassung von *thou* § 90—92	43
a) In Fragesätzen § 90	43
b) In Aussagesätzen § 91	44
Bemerkungen zu a und b § 92	45
2. Auslassung des Personalpronomens in koordinierten Sätzen § 93—94	45
a) Bei gleichem Subjekt in beiden Sätzen § 93	45
b) Bei verschiedenem Subjekt in beiden Sätzen § 94	47
3. Auslassung des Personalpronomens bei subordinierter Satzfügung § 95	48
B. Das Personalpronomen ist aus einem vorhergehenden Kasus obliquus zu ergänzen § 96	49
C. Pronomen beim Imperativ § 97	50
Formelhafte Wendungen und Besonderes § 98	52
D. Auslassung von *it* in unpersönlichen Sätzen § 99—101	53
1. Bei unpers. mit einem Objekt verbundenen Verben § 99	53
2. Bei unpers. mit keinem Objekt verbundenen Verben § 100	55
3. Bei *to be* § 101	56

	Seite
II. Auslassung des Personalpronomens als Objekt § 102	58
Sekundäre Fälle § 103—104	59
1. Bewusste Auslassung § 103	59
2. Auslassung in der Umgangssprache § 104	61
Pleonastischer Gebrauch des Personalpronomens § 105—112	63
Vorbemerkung § 105	63
1. Das Pronomen geht seinem Nomen voran § 106	64
2. Das Pronomen folgt seinem Nomen § 107—111	64
a) Unmittelbar § 107	64
b) Das Pronomen ist von seinem Nomen getrennt § 108—111	67
α) Durch einen oder mehrere Satzteile § 108—109	67
1. Als Subjekt § 108	67
2. Als Objekt § 109	70
β) Durch einen Nebensatz § 110	71
γ) Durch ein Partizip § 111	74
3. *It* als Objekt bei intransitiven Verben § 112	74
He und *she* zur Bezeichnung des Geschlechts § 113	76
Majestätsplural § 114	78
Kasusvertauschungen beim Personalpronomen § 115—140	78
Vorbemerkung § 115	88
I. Contamination § 116—126	79
Verschiedene Fälle § 116—119	79
Einfluss von Wörtern, die Präp. und Konj. sind § 120—126	81
Vorbemerkung § 120, *but* § 121	81
Save § 122	82
Except § 123	83
(Such) as § 124	84
Like § 125	85
Than § 126	86
II. Stellung § 127—128	87
III. Anakoluthe § 129	90
IV. Einfluss der Nomina § 130	91
V. Kasusvertauschungen in Sir Clyomon § 131	93
VI. Andere Fälle § 132	95
VII. *Me* für *I* in bewusster Absicht § 133	96
It is I § 134	97
You für *ye* § 135	101
Ye für *you* § 136—137	103
Erklärungsfälle § 138—140	109
Anhang — Unconnected Subject § 141	111
Gebrauch von *thou* (*thee* etc.) und *ye* (*you* etc.) § 142—150	114
Vorbemerkung § 142	114
I. Anrede an Gott und Maria § 143	114
II. Anrede an den Menschen § 144—146	114
a) An den Menschen im allgemeinen § 144	114
b) Im besonderen § 145—146	115

	Seite
α) Im gewöhnlichen Dialog § 145	115
β) In verächtlicher und Schimpfrede § 146	117
III. Anrede an leblose und vorgestellte Dinge § 147	119
Allgemeines Resultat § 148	120
Stimmungsübergänge § 149	120
Unterschiedsloser Wechsel von *thou* und *ye* § 150	121
Dativus comm. und incomm. § 151	122
Dativus ethicus § 152	123
To me ward § 153	124
Possessivpronomen § 154—171	126
Ersatz von *its* § 154	126
Possessive Beziehung auf ein unbekanntes Subjekt § 155	127
Analytische Umschreibung des Possessivpron. durch *of* + Personalpron. § 156	128
Das Possessivpron. in der ursprünglichen Bedeutung als Genitiv des Personalpron. § 157—159	131
1. Beziehung eines Relativpron. auf ein Possessivpron. § 157	131
2. *Both* + Possessivpron. § 158	131
3. Das Possessivpron. in Verbindung mit substant. gebrauchten Adj. § 159	134
My (*our*) in der Anrede § 160	136
Your im Sinne eines Dativus ethicus § 161	136
Stellung des adj. Possessivpron. § 162	137
Das Possessivpron. zur Bezeichnung des Genitivs § 163—164	138
Verwendung des subst. Possessivpron. anstatt des Adj. § 165—166	141
1. In der Poesie zur Erzielung eines feierlichen Tons § 165	141
2. Pseudo-partitiver Genitiv § 166	143
Wechsel und Verwechslung von Poss. und Personalpron., sowie von Poss. mit dem Artikel *the* § 167—171	145
1. Verwechslung von Poss. und Personalpron. a) *my* für *me* und b) *you* für *your* und umgekehrt § 167—168	145
2. Wechsel und Verwechslung von *thy* mit dem Artikel *the* § 169—170	148
3. Andere Fälle § 171	151
Reflexivpronomen § 172—197	152
Bezeichnung des refl. Verhältnisses durch Pron. § 172—184	152
I. Bei ursprüngl. Transitiven, die reflexiv gebraucht sind § 172—177	152
Entwicklung seit dem Ae., Zustand in den P. L. § 172	152
Zustand im Morte Darthure § 173	154
Chronologisches § 174	155
Erste Hälfte des 16. Jahrhunderts § 175	156
Zweite Hälfte des 16. Jahrhunderts § 176	157
Besonderes (*to recomand, advise, assure, content, bow, complain, endeavour, lay, remember, disport, ware*) § 177	160

II. Bei intr. urspr. mit refl. Dativ konstr. Verben § 178—182 ... 165
   Vorbemerkung § 178 .. , ... 165
     1. Verba der Ruhe § 179 166
     2. Verba der Bewegung § 180 167
   Allgemeine Bemerkungen zu 2. § 181 171
     3. Verba des Affekts § 182 172
     4. Andere Verba § 183 175
   Rückblick — Erklärung § 184 176
Bezeichnung des reciproken Verhältnisses § 185—191 179
   Vorbemerkung § 185 179
   I. Entwicklung seit dem Ae. § 186 179
   II, 1. Fortentwicklung im 15. Jahrhundert § 187—188 180
   II, 2. Fortentwicklung im 16. Jahrhundert § 189—190 ... 182
     Ersatz des reciproken Pronomens durch *together* § 191 ... 183
     Verstärkung von *myself* etc. durch *own* § 192 185
     Self als Substantivum § 193 186
     His self, their selves § 194 188
     Ersatz von *one's self* § 195 190
     Myself etc. als Subjekt § 196 190
     Self für *himself* etc. § 197 191
Demonstrativpronomen § 198—206 192
   Self im Sinne von *same* § 198 192
   This für *these* § 199—201 193
   Wechsel und Verwechslung von *this* und *thus* § 202—203 ... 197
   This many a hundred year, this many a day § 204 199
   Such + like § 205 200
   Gebrauch von *same* § 206 201
Interrogativpronomen § 207—228 203
   Who im Sinne von *any one* § 207—209 203
   Who für *whom* und umgekehrt § 210—215 207
   Whom für *who* § 210—212 207
   Who für *whom* § 213—214 209
   Zur Erklärung § 215 211
   What für *who* § 216, *what* als Ausruf § 217 213
   What a § 218, *what* im Sinne von *why* § 219 214
   What im Sinne von *how* § 220, *what* (etwas) § 221 215
   What — what (and) § 222 216
   Gebrauch u. Verbreitung von *whether* § 223, *who so, what so* § 224 217
   Who that, what that, which that § 225 218
   Whichsoever 226, *whatso(m)ever, what that ever, which so ever*
     in adj. Funktion § 227 219
   Whosoever, whatsoever in erweiterndem Sinne § 228 220
Relativpronomen § 229—233 221
   Auslassung des Relativs § 229 221
   Relative Anknüpfung § 230—231 222

XVIII

	Seite
1. Vermittelst eines Pronomens § 231, 1	222
2. Vermittelst relativer Adverbien § 231, 2	225
Pleonastisches Relativum § 232—233	226
Indefinita § 234—244	228
Bezeichnung des unbestimmten „man" § 234	228
No als Negation § 235	231
Stellung von *none* am Ende des Satzes § 236	232
None in neutralem Sinne § 237	233
Both a) Stellung von *both* § 238	234
b) *both two* § 239	236
Nothing als verstärkte Negation § 240	237
Few 1. *In few*, 2. *Fewer* und *fewest* § 241	237
Many § 242	239
Each und *every* § 243	239
All § 244	239
Schlussbetrachtung und Folgerungen § 245—259	241
Vorbemerkung § 245	241
I. Dialektisches (zur Entwicklung der ne. Schriftsprache) § 246	241
II. Analytische Tendenzen § 247	244
III. Kürze des Ausdrucks — Sparsamkeit § 248	244
IV. Verschwenderische Züge der Sprache § 249	245
V. Contaminationen § 250	245
VI. Einfluss des Traditionellen § 251	246
VII. Einwirkung fremder Sprachen § 252	246
VIII. Erscheinungen, die im 15./16. Jahrhundert aufhören oder entstehen § 253	247
IX. Eigentümlichkeiten einzelner Schriftsteller § 254	249
X. Eigentümlichkeiten einzelner Literaturgattungen § 255	250
XI. Umgangssprache des 15. und 16. Jahrhunderts § 256	251
XII. Stellung Shaksperes u. Spensers zur Sprache des 16. Jahrhunderts § 257	252
XIII. Bibelsprache § 258	253
XIV. Textkritisches § 259	254
Anhang I. Zum Uebergang von unpersönlichen Verben in persönliche § 260—294	257
Vorbemerkung § 260	257
1. Eigentliche Verben § 261—288	257
a) Verba im Aktivum § 261—285	257
To ail § 261	257
To chance § 262	258
To delight § 263, *to desire* § 264	259
To forthynk § 265, *to fortune* (*mysfortune*) § 266	260
To grieve § 267, *to happen* (*myshappen*) § 268	261
To joy § 269, *to lack* § 270	262
To like (*dislike, mislike*) § 271, *to list* § 272	263

To long § 273, to marvel § 274, to myster § 275, to need § 276   265
To owe § 277 266
To pity § 278, to please § 279 267
To repent § 280, to rue (rew) § 281 269
To seme § 282 270
To shame § 283 271
To think § 284 272
As it rehercoth, sheweth, telleth etc. § 285 273
   b) Verba im Passivum § 286—288 273
     α) Das Verbum regiert urspr. den Dativ, hat aber kein
       Akkusativobjekt § 286 273
     β) Das Verbum ist mit einer Präposition verbunden § 287   275
     γ) Das Verbum regiert einen Akkus. und einen Dativ § 288   275
2. To be in Verbindung mit einem Adjektiv § 289 276
Zur Erklärung des Uebergangs unpers. Verba in persönl. § 290—294   278
1. Unklarheit ob persönl. oder unpersönl. Konstruktion § 290 . . 278
2. Einfluss begrifflich gleicher oder ähnlicher Verben und Wendungen § 291—293 280
   a) Begrifflich gleiche oder ähnliche Verben § 291 280
   b) Verbindung ursprüngl. unpers. Verben mit pers. § 292 . . 281
   c) Begrifflich gleiche oder ähnliche Wendungen § 293 . . . 281
3. Verbindung urspr. unpers. Verben mit anderen persönl. § 294 .   283

Anhang II. Zum Bau der Relativsätze im 15. u. 16. Jahrh. § 295—302   284
Vorbemerkung § 295 284
1. Der ganze Hauptsatz geht voran, der Relativsatz folgt § 296—297   284
   a) Das Relativum steht im Nominativ § 296 284
   b) Das Relativum steht in einem Kasus obliquus § 297 . . . 285
2. Der Hauptsatz wird durch den Relativsatz in zwei Hälften ge-
   teilt § 298—299 287
   a) Das pleon. Pers. steht im Nom. § 298 287
   b) Das pleon. Pers. steht in einem Kasus obliquus § 299 . . 288
3. Der Relativsatz geht dem Hauptsatz voran § 300—301 289
   a) Das Personalpronomen im Nominativ § 300 289
   b) Das Personalpronomen in einem Kasus obliquus § 301 . . 291
   Bemerkungen zu a und b § 302 292

Anhang III. Einzelne Kapitel aus der Syntax des Satzes § 303—305   293
Rückbeziehung auf das im Sg. stehende Subjekt vermittelst eines
Pers. oder Poss. im Plural § 303 293
Zur Kongruenz des Prädikats mit dem einfachen Subjekt, wenn
dieses ein Relativum ist § 304 295
Kongruenz des Prädikats in Beziehung auf mehr als ein Subjekt
§ 305 296
Anhang IV. Apposition statt partitiver Genitiv § 306 298
Sachregister 301
Wortregister 305
Berichtigungen und Nachträge 310

Einleitendes über Anlage der Arbeit, Methode, Quellen etc.

Da es uns in unserer Untersuchung vor allen Dingen darauf ankam, darzulegen, wie sich die Formen und die einzelnen syntaktischen Erscheinungen des Englischen im 15. und 16. Jahrhundert in der Sprache des Volkes und in der der Gebildeten zeigten, so haben wir uns zunächst an diejenigen Quellen gehalten, welche Gerber seiner Arbeit über die Substantivierung des Adjektivs (Diss. Göttingen 1895) zu Grunde gelegt hat, und die teils ein durchaus volkstümliches Gepräge tragen, weil sie entweder für weite Kreise der Bevölkerung bestimmt oder direkt dem Borne der Volkssprache entsprungen waren, teils die Ausdrucksweise der damaligen gebildeten Stände, teils auch endlich die gehobene Sprache der Poesie wiederspiegeln.

In dem Glauben jedoch, dass diese allein nicht genügen würden, ein wirklich deutliches Bild der pronominalen Verhältnisse im 15. und 16. Jahrhundert zu geben, haben wir zur Vervollständigung unseres Materials weitere Quellen verschiedener Art und Zeit in den Kreis unserer Betrachtung gezogen und konnten dadurch teils in manchen und nicht unwesentlichen Punkten die Sicherheit unserer Resultate erhöht finden, teils für einzelne Erscheinungen weiteres schätzbare Material beibringen.

So haben wir denn noch, abgesehen von den sämtlichen von Dodsley-Hazlitt veröffentlichten (Bd. I—VII) Erzeugnissen der dramatischen Literatur des 16. Jahrhunderts, die sich ja überhaupt wegen der dialogischen Form für die Eigenheiten der Umgangssprache als fruchtbar erweisen musste, besonders solche Texte der Camden Society benutzt, die, weil fast ausschliesslich nicht zum Drucke bestimmt und nur den Zwecken der Gegenwart dienend, als direkter unverfälschter Ausdruck der gesprochenen Volkssprache des 15. bezw. 16. Jahrhunderts angesehen werden dürfen.

Für die Regierungszeit Heinrichs VIII. boten uns ferner die gerade edierten Texte Flügels willkommenen Stoff aus allen Gebieten der Literatur.

Von den bedeutenderen Dramatikern haben wir auch die lyrischen Sachen, von Marlowe auch dessen Uebersetzungen aus dem Lateinischen berücksichtigt, zu denen, wie auch zu Th. More's Utopia das lateinische Original so weit als ratsam zur Vergleichung herangezogen wurde.

Inbetreff der Anlage der Arbeit mag weiter bemerkt werden, dass es uns nicht wünschenswert erschien, in der Syntax nur den Zustand im 15. und 16. Jahrhundert zu schildern, dass wir vielmehr so weit als tunlich und möglich auf die älteren Sprachperioden des Englischen zurückgegriffen haben, da ohne sie an ein gründliches Verständnis der Sprache unseres Uebergangszeitraumes nicht gedacht werden kann. Vom Jahre 1600 ab haben wir alsdann in der Regel bei jeder einzelnen Erscheinung, um ein in sich geschlossenes Gesamtbild derselben zu geben, die weitere Entwicklung bis heute, wenn auch meist nur mit knappen Worten, angeknüpft und hierbei insbesondere die Sprache Shakspere's, in geringerem Masse die des archaisierenden Spencer, berücksichtigt.

Was die Belege anlangt, so sind stets alle (wenn auch oft nur durch Seitenangabe) dann gegeben, wenn dieselben recht gering an Zahl und daher durch ihre Seltenheit wertvoll, oder so wichtig waren, dass auch trotz ihres grösseren Umfanges eine Wiedergabe sämtlicher Belege wünschenswert erscheinen musste. Wo wir nur einzelne Belege oder eine Auswahl geben, ist das stets besonders vermerkt. In der Regel wird nach Seiten (und Zeilen) zitiert, in den P. L. nach Briefen (und Seiten), in Sidney's Astrophel and Stella nach Sonetten, in Bale's Thre Lawes, Gorboduc, Marlowe's Tamburlaine, Doctor Faustus, Jew of Malta nach Versen.

Verzeichnis
der für vorliegende Arbeit untersuchten Quellen.

(Die mit * bezeichneten gehören zur Gruppe II [cf. § 1].)

* The Paston Letters 1422—1509, ed. James Gairdner, Birmingham 1872—75.
* Plumpton Correspondence 1460—1551, ed. Camden Society Nr. 4, London 1839.

Malory: Le Morte Darthure 1469—70, ed. Sommer, Lond. 1889.

* The Digby Mysteries 1480—1490 (?), ed. Furnivall, New Shakspere Society, London 1882.
* Ancient Mysteries described etc. ed. Hone, London 1823.

The History of Reynard the Fox. Transl. and printed by William Caxton, June 1481, ed. Arber Engl. Schol. Libr. Nr. 1.

Caxton's Englishing of Alain Chartier's Curial 1484, ed. E. E. T. S., London 1888.

* Rutland Papers 1487—1553, ed. Camden Society Nr. 21, London 1842.
* The Egerton Papers 1499—1600, ed. Camden Society Nr. 12, London 1840.

(*) Flügel: Neuengl. Lesebuch Bd. I. Die Zeit Heinrichs VIII., Halle 1895.

The Four Elements 1517 (?), ed. Dodsley-Hazlitt I, 1 ff.

The Tragi-Comedy of Calisto and Melibaea, ed. D. H. I, 51 ff.

Hickscorner, ed. D. H. I, 143 ff.

Everyman, A Moral Play, ed. D. H. I, 93 ff.

John Heywood: 1. The Pardoner and the Friar vor 1521, ed. D. H. I, 197 ff; 2. The Four P. P. ed. D. H. I, 323 ff.

The World and the Child 1522, ed. D. H. I, 239 ff.

William Tyndale: The first printed English New-Testament, 1525 oder 1526. (Ausgabe von 1536).

Simon Fish: A Supplicacyon for the Beggers 1529.
A Supplication to Kynge Henry VIII. 1544.
A Supplication of the Poore Commons 1546.
The Decaye of England 1550—53.
} ed. E. E. T. S. Nr. XIII, London 1871.

George Joy: An Apology to W. Tindale 1535, ed. Engl. Schol. Libr. Nr. 13.

Thersites 1537, ed. D. H. I, 389 ff.

John Bale: 1. God's Promises 1538, ed. D. H. I, 277 ff.; 2. Comedy concernynge thre Lawes ed. Schroeer, Halle 1882; * 3. Kynge Johan, ed. Camden Society, London 1838.

* Roger Asham: 1. Toxophilus 1545, ed. Arber Engl. Repr. Nr. 7; 2. The Scholemaster 1570, ed. Arber Engl. Repr. Nr. 23.

Hugh Latimer: 1. Seven Sermons before Edward VI. 1549, ed. Arber Engl. Repr. Nr. 13;
   2. The Ploughers, ib. Nr. 2.

* The Diary of Henry Machyn 1550—63, ed. Camd. Soc. Nr. 42, London 1848.

Kleine Mitteilungen zur Litteratur des 16. Jahrh. von E. Flügel, Anglia XIII, 455 ff.

Nicholas Udall: Ralph Roister Doister 1551, ed. Arber Engl. Repr. Nr. 17.

Lusty Iuventus by R. Wever, ed. D. H. II, 41 ff.

Interlude of Youth 1554 (?), ed. D. H. II, 1 ff.

* The Private Diary of Dr. John Dee 1554—1601, ed. Camd. Soc. Nr. 19, London 1842.

Sir Thomas More: Utopia. Transl. into English by Ralph Robinson 1556, ed. Arber Engl. Repr. Nr. 14.

The History of Jacob and Esau 1557—58, ed. D. H. II, 185 ff.

John Knox: The first Blast of the Trumpet 1558, ed. Arber Engl. Schol. Libr. Nr. 2.

The Disobedient Child vor 1560, ed. D. H. II, 265 ff.

Gorboduc or Ferrex and Porrex. A Tragedy by Thomas Norton and Thomas Sackville 1561, ed. Toulman Smith, Heilbronn 1883.

Cambyses by Th. Preston 1561, ed. D. H. IV, 157 ff.

Jack Juggler, ed. D. H. II, 103 ff.

A Pretty Interlude, called Nice Wanton, ed. D. H. II, 159 ff.

Appius and Virginia 1563 (?), ed. D. H. IV, 105 ff.

John Still: Gammer Gurton's Needle 1566, ed. D. H. III, 163 ff.

The Trial of Treasure 1567, ed. D. H. III, 257 ff.
Like Will to Like 1568, ed. D. H. III, 303 ff.
The Marriage of Wit and Science vor 1569, ed. D. H. II, 321 ff.
Damon and Pithias vor 1571, ed. D. H. IV, 1 ff.
New Custom vor 1573, ed. D. H. III, 1 ff.
Philip Sidney: 1. Astrophel and Stella 1591, ed. Flügel, Halle 1889; 2. Arcadia 1590—93, Sonnets and Translations, The Lady of May, A Masque, London 1724.
3. An Apologie for Poetrie 1595, ed. Arber. Engl. Repr. Nr. 4.
John Lyly 1554(?)—1606:
Euphues 1579—81, ed. Arb. Engl. Repr. Nr. 9.
Dramatic Works, ed. Fairholt, London 1858.
1. Campaspe 1584.
2. Sapho and Phao 1584.
3. Woman in the Moone vor 1584.
4. Endimion 1591.
5. Mydas 1592.
6. Mother Bombie 1594.
7. Love's Metamorphosis vor 1601.
The Conflict of Conscience 1581, ed. D. H. VI, 29 ff.
* Letters of Queen Elizabeth and King James VI. of Scotland 1582—1602, ed. Camd. Soc. Nr. 46, London 1849.
The Three Ladies of London 1584, ed. D. H. VI, 245 ff.
Christopher Marlowe 1564—93:
1. Tamburlaine 1587, ed. Wagner, Heilbronn 1885.
2. Doctor Faustus nach 1587, ed. Breymann und Wagner, Heilbronn 1889.
3. Jew of Malta 1589—90, ed. Wagner, Heilbronn 1889.
4. Edward II. 1589—90.
5. Massacre of Paris 1592.
6. Tragedy of Dido.
7. Hero and Leander.   Vor   ed. Alex. Dyce,
8. Ovid's Elegies.   1593   London 1850.
9. The First Book of Lucan.
* Correspondence of Robert Dudley, Earl of Leycester 1585—86, ed. Camd. Soc. Nr. 27, London 1844.
The Misfortunes of Arthur 1587, ed. D. H. IV, 249 ff.

John Udall: 1. The State of the Church of England 1588, ed.
Arb. Engl. Schol. Libr. Nr. 5;
2. A Demonstration of Discipline, ib. Nr. 9.
Martin Marprelate: The Epistle 1588, ed. Arb. Engl. Schol.
Libr. Nr. 11.
Thomas Kyd 1557(?)—1594 (?):
1. The First Part of Jeronimo um 1588, ed. D. H. IV, 345 ff.
2. The Spanish Tragedy um 1588, ed. D. H. V, 1 ff.;
3. Cornelia 1594, ed. D. H. V, 175 ff.
An Introductory Sketch to the Martin Marprelate Controversy 1588—90, ed. Arb. Engl. Schol. Libr. Nr. 8.
George Puttenham: The Arte of English Poesie 1589, ed.
Arb. Engl. Repr. Nr. 15.
The Rare Triumphs of Love and Fortune 1589, ed. D. H.
VI, 143 ff.
Robert Greene 1550(?)—92:
Menaphon 1589, ed. Arb. Engl. Schol. Libr. Nr. 12;
Dramatic Works, ed. Alex. Dyce, London 1831.
1. Friar Bacon and Friar Bungay 1591.
2. Orlando Furioso 1591.
3. A Looking-Glass for London and England vor 1592.
4. George-a-Greene, the Pinner of Wakefield vor 1592.
5. James the Fourth 1592.
6. Alphonsus, King of Arragon 1592.
Kleinere Dichtungen, Bd. II, 215 ff.
George Peele 1552(?)—1598(?):
Dramatic Works, ed. Alex. Dyce, London 1829.
1. The Arraignment of Paris 1584.
2. The Battle of Alcazar 1591.
3. The old Wives Tale 1592.
4. The Chronicle of Edward I., 1593.
5. David and Bethsabe 1598.
Kleinere Dichtungen, Bd. II, 147 ff.
Sir Clyomon and Sir Clamydes (früher Peele zugeschrieben),
ed. Alex. Dyce, London 1883.
The Three Ladies of London 1584, ed. D. H. VI, 245 ff.
The Three Lords and Three Ladies of London 1590,
ed. D. H. VI, 371 ff.
Tancred and Gismonda (1568) 1591, ed. D. H. VII, 27 ff.

Soliman and Perseda 1592(?), ed. D. H. V, 253 ff.
Life and Death of Jack Straw 1593, ed. D. H. V, 375 ff.
A Knack to Know a Knave 1594, ed. D. H. VI, 503 ff.
Thomas Lodge: The Wounds of Civill War 1594, ed D. H. VII, 97 ff.
Mucedorus 1598, ed. D. H. VII, 199 ff.
The two angry women of Abington 1599, ed. D. H. VII, 261 ff.
Richard Barnfield, Poems 1594—98, ed. Arb. Engl. Scholar's Library Nr. 14.
Look about You 1600, ed. D. H. VII, 385 ff.
* The Diary of Philip Henslowe, ed. Collier, Sh. Soc. London 1845 (p. 1—181 i. e.—1600).
* The Alleyn Papers, ed. Collier, Sh. Soc. London 1843 (p. 1—22 i. e.—1598).

Flexionslehre.

Allgemeines zur Orthographie.
§ 1.

Bei der Darstellung einer Flexionslehre aus dem Gebiete der älteren Sprachperioden des Englischen, wie jeder anderen Sprache, spielt die Orthographie eine nicht unbedeutende Rolle. Das darf wie für das Ae. und Me. in gleichem Masse auch für das 15. und 16. Jahrhundert gelten,

Die Orthographie dieser Zeit ist so wenig oder noch weniger einheitlich (wenn sich auch Caxton um eine Sichtung und Sonderung der überlieferten Schriftzeichen bemüht hatte, Römstedt, Schriftspr. bei Caxt. p. 53), als es die des heutigen Englisch ist, und doch können wir in den uns erhaltenen Denkmälern in Bezug auf die Orthographie einen wesentlichen Unterschied wahrnehmen und diese mit Rücksicht hierauf in zwei grosse Gruppen zerlegen.

Während nämlich diejenigen Erzeugnisse der Literatur des 15. und 16. Jahrhunderts, welche zur Zeit ihrer Entstehung oder kurz darauf durch Drucke allgemein verbreitet wurden, (wir bezeichnen sie mit Gruppe I), eine im Ganzen ziemlich geregelte (soweit überhaupt von einer Einheitlichkeit die Rede sein kann) Orthographie aufweisen, zeigen umgekehrt die erst in unserer Zeit auf Grund handschriftlicher Aufzeichnungen buchstabengetreu veröffentlichten Schriften (Gruppe II) eine in den mannigfachsten Variationen wechselnde, oft bis zur Unkenntlichkeit die Wörter verstümmelnde und daher nicht selten sinnentstellende Orthographie. Diese letztere Gruppe steht an Umfang der ersteren bedeutend nach, sie setzt sich fast durchweg aus Schriftwerken zusammen, die allein privaten, vielfach nur momentanen, Interessen dienen sollten und bei denen daher noch weniger als bei anderen von ihren Verfassern an einen Druck gedacht worden ist. Dazu kommt, dass sie wegen ihres Stoffes für die Allgemeinheit in damaliger Zeit meist von keinem oder so geringem Interesse waren, dass sich hier ein etwaiger „Raubdruck", der bei Erzeugnissen besonders des Dramas meist auf einen pekuniären Erfolg rechnen durfte, keineswegs gelohnt hätte.

Erst unsere Zeit hat, angeregt durch Interessen mancherlei Art, solches handschriftliche Material, dass sich besonders aus der Brief- und Tagebuchliteratur des 15. und 16. Jahrhunderts zusammensetzt, weiteren Kreisen durch den Druck zugänglich gemacht. (Um eine doppelte Aufzählung zu vermeiden, haben wir diese Texte der Gruppe II im Quellenverzeichnis mit einem * bezeichnet).

Was nun den Unterschied der Orthographie in beiden Gruppen anlangt, so können wir uns einen eingehenderen Beweis ersparen: ein vergleichender Blick auf je eine Seite beider sowie die Betrachtung unserer Flexionslehre, wo wir stets schon der Uebersicht halber diese Unterscheidung machen mussten, wird von der Richtigkeit dieser Tatsache überzeugen.

Im Uebrigen vergleiche man als besonders charakteristisch bei Peele II, 259 „The Hunting of Cupid", sowie bei Marlowe II, 336f. die in der Anmerkung wiedergegebene zweite Version einer Szene aus „The Massacre at Paris", welche beide auf Grund einer Handschrift gedruckt sind, mit der auf alten Drucken beruhenden Umgebung. Gerade das letztere ist besonders deshalb lehrreich, weil es sich um zwei verschiedene Versionen ein und derselben Szene, also zum Teil auch um die gleichen Worte in der gleichen Materie handelt, welche die Verschiedenartigkeit der Orthographie zeigen.

Schliesslich mag noch als weiterer charakteristischer Beleg auf die vielfach wechselnde Schreibung der Dramentitel in Henslowe's Diary (z. B. 84 Joranymo, 87 Jeronymo, 88 Joronymo, 89 Joronemo, 90 Jeronemo, 91 Jeroneymo) gegenüber der einheitlichen in der Druckausgabe (Jeronimo) hingewiesen werden. Ganz ähnlich steht es mit dem Namen Shaksperes.

Also eine im ganzen ziemlich geregelte Ortho-

graphie in Gruppe I, grösste Unsicherheit und Regellosigkeit in Gruppe II.
Wie ist das zu erklären?
Der Grund liegt auf der Hand. Er kann kein andrer sein, als der, dass in elisabethanischer Zeit Drucker oder Verleger, die oft auch in einer Person vereinigt waren, die zum Druck bestimmten Werke in der handschriftlichen Vorlage, welche zweifellos ebenso wie unsere Texte der Gruppe II die durch mancherlei Einwirkungen phonetischer und analogischer Art beeinflusste Naivität und Individualität des einzelnen Schreibers (Autors) haben zu Tage treten lassen, in Bezug auf ihre Orthographie normalisierten.

Wenn nun dieses der Fall ist, so ergiebt sich daraus als nächste Folge eine weitere erhebliche Stütze für die von Morsbach (Verhdlg. des Philologentages zu Bonn 1895, neuphilol. Sektion, p. 105 ff.) aufgestellte Ansicht, dass in elisabethanischer Zeit Verleger und Drucker, nicht aber der Autor, die Gestalt des Druckes bestimmten, dass also die Schriften dieser Zeit nicht in der ihnen vom Autor gegebenen sondern vielfach entstellten und mit Fremdem vermischten, daher durchaus unzuverlässigen Gestalt auf uns gekommen sind.

In der nun folgenden Flexionslehre wird sich, wie gesagt, der von uns aufgestellte Satz im Einzelnen bestätigt finden. Es mag jedoch bemerkt werden, dass wir nicht alle kleinen graphischen Varianten der Gruppe II anführen werden, die sich nur als lautlich bedeutungslose Schreibfehler dokumentieren und daher für unsere Zwecke und auch die anderer auf keinen Wert Anspruch machen können. Dagegen sind ethymologisch verschiedene Formen von blossen Schreibungen durch Hinzusetzung der betreffenden me. Form unterschieden worden, wie es denn auch wünschenswert erschien, auf die Schreibungen der beiden Quarto-Ausgaben von Shaksperes Sommernachtstraum, der ersten Folio-Ausgabe der Shakspere'schen Dramen und der ersten Quarto-Ausgabe von Milton's Paradise Lost, soweit wir sie bei Würzner, Lummert und Rost belegt fanden, zu verweisen.

Personalpronomen.

Personalpronomen der 1. Person.
§ 2. *I.*

Als Regel gilt *I.*

Anm. 1: Häufig im 15. Jahrhundert in den P. L., vereinzelt auch sonst (Digby Myst. 65, 292, Fox 53, 84), und im 16. Jahrhundert (Fl. 113/49, 145, 7, 223/4) also fast ausschliesslich bei Gruppe II, findet sich die ältere Schreibung *y*, *i*, die meist mit *I* wechselt.

Anm. 2: Im 16. Jahrhundert tritt, vornehmlich in der dramatischen Literatur und hier wieder besonders an solchen Stellen, wo Bauern oder den unteren Ständen angehörige Personen auftreten, zumeist auch offenbar, um eine komische Wirkung zu erzielen, die südliche Form *ich* auf; vgl. hierzu Panning 37 ff.

Und zwar als *ich*: Cambyses 218, 223, Nice Wanton 169, 178, Damon and P. 58, 69, 81, Calisto and Mel. 73 etc., überaus häufig in G. G. Needle 175, 176, 177 etc., Sir Clyomon 518a;

als *ych*: Bale, Thre Lawes 399, 423;

als *iche*: Puttenham 213 (Citat aus seinem nicht erhaltenen Interlude „The Woer");

als *cha*: Sir Clyomon 515b (4 mal), 516a (2 mal), 516b etc.;

als *che*: Trial of Treasure 272, Greene, Look. Glass 96.

In zahlreichen Fällen wird (wie schon me. cf. Morsb. me. Gr. § 51) dieses *ich* mit dem folgenden Worte, welches meist das Verbum ist, falls dieses mit einem Vokal oder den Konsonanten *h*, *w* beginnt, unter Verlust des anlautenden *i* von *ich* und (doch nicht ausnahmslos s. u.) des *h*, *w* verschmolzen.

So entstehen die Verbindungen:

chever für *ich ever*: G. G. Needle 241;

cham für *ich am*: Cambyses 219, 223, G. G. Needle 175, 176, 179 etc. (als *chim*. ib. 192), Trial of Treasure 280, Like Will to Like 313, Damon and P. 70, 81, 84, Rare Triumphs 203, Sir Clyomon 515b, 518a etc., Knack to Know a Knave 547;

chwas für *ich was*: Damon and Pithias 73;

chwere für *ich were*: G. G. Needle 179;

chave für *ich have*: Cambyses 219, 221, G. G. Needle 181, 185, Damon and P. 81, Sir Clyomon 515b, 516a etc.;

ch'ave für *ich have*: G. G. Needle 221;
cha für *ich have*: Bale, Thre Lawes 397, G. G. Needle 196, 212 etc.,
Like Will to Like 314, 327, Damon and P. 69, 70, Greene, Look. Gl. 96,
wieder aufgelöst in *'Ch'a*, (*Ch'a*): G. G. Needle 224, 226, (254);
chad für *ich had*: G. G. Needle 178, 179, 192 etc., Like Will t. L. 331;
cheard für *ich heard*: G. G. Needle 205, 220;
chope für *ich hope*: G. G. Needle 205;
chall für *ich shall*: G. G. Needle 192;
chill für *ich will*: Cambyses 222, G. G. Needle 178, 184, 195 etc., Trial of Treasure 280, Damon and P. 60, 72, 73 etc., Sir Clyomon 515 b, 516 b etc.;
chould für *ich would*: Cambyses 221, G. G. Needle 194, 212, 219 etc.,
(als *chold* G. G. Needle 180, 219, als *chud* Like Will to L. 327), Damon and P. 58, (als *chuld* ib. 79), Sir Clyomon 516 a, 518 b (mit den Uebergangsformen *ch'would* G. G. Needle 177, *chwold* ib. 176, 195, *ch'ould* ib. 183, 214).

Diese Verschmelzung führte, da sie vielfach nicht verstanden wurde, weiter dazu, dass man durch nochmaliges Vorsetzen von *I* das Pronomen doppelt ausdrückte: Cambyses 219 *I chil*, 220 *I chould*, G. G. Needle 178 *ich chave*; sogar in der Frage: G. G. Needle 255 *Cham I not a good son, gammer, cham I not?*

Enclisis von *ich* wurde nur einmal in einer Handschrift von Calisto and Mel. (cf. ib. 73 *karych*) beobachtet.

Anm. 3: In Trial of Treasure 277 *Ick en can ghene english spreken von waer*. erweist sich *ick* als aus dem Niederländischen herübergenommen zur Erreichung einer komischen Wirkung.

Anm. 4: Die Schreibung *ay* für *I* Confl. of Consc. 73 bezeichnet (wie ib. 73 *may*, 75 *taym* etc.) die schottische Form an einer beabsichtigten Dialektstelle; dieselbe Schreibung zeigt sich Greene, James IV, aber nur im Vorspiel 73, 76; wenn auch umgekehrt die Schreibung *I* für *ay(e)* „ja" vorkommt (cf. Anm. 5), so haben wir doch in Anbetracht der redenden Person, eines Schotten, sowie der Schreibung *ay* für *i(y)* in anderen Wörtern wie *whay*, *may*, *thay* lautliche Geltung anzunehmen; vgl. Luick § 29, Panning 32f.; dass diese Schreibung sich nur im Vorspiel, nicht aber in den Zwischenspielen (94 ff., 110 f., 122 f., 135 f.), wo der Schotte weiterhin auftritt, findet, ist wohl dem mangelhaften Druck zur Last zu legen; vgl. ib. die Anmerkung zu p. 70 und 94.

Anm. 5: *I* wird infolge gleicher Aussprache (cf. Shakspere's Wortspiel von *I* und *ay* [Warth, Das Wortspiel bei Shakspere, Wien u. Leipzig 1895, p. 116 f.]) auch für das um 1575 (Oxf. Dict.) plötzlich auftauchende *aye* = ja geschrieben; charakteristisch ausgeprägt ist das bei Lyly, besonders bei Antithesen im Euphues.

Vgl. z. B. Euphues 183,
But she was amiable, but yet sinful, but she was young and might haue liued, but she was mortall and must haue dyed. I but hir youth, made thee often merry, I but thine age shold once make thee wise. I but hir greene yeares wer vnfit for death, I but thy hoary haires should dispyse life, ferner 57, 59, 316, 337 etc.; zahlreich auch bei Marlowe, aber nur im

Jew. 218, 356 etc.; Tamb. 681 etc., Faust 73, 79 etc., Edw. II 199, (dagegen 280 *ay*), Lyly, Mydas 10, 17, 21, Bombie 73, 78 etc. etc.; Kyd, Jer. 363; Sidney, Arc. 611, 621; Greene, Menaphon 40, 48, 56 (hier wohl auf Kosten d. Druckers zu setzen, da die anderen, dramatischen Werke keinen Beleg aufweisen).

NB. Auffallender Weise giebt das Oxf. Dict. für diese Schreibung erst einen Beleg aus dem Jahre 1598.

§ 3. *me* (Dat. und Acc.).

Als Regel gilt *me*; daneben im 15. und 16. Jahrhundert die Schreibung *mee*, besonders bei Gruppe II; Würzner p. 149, Lummert p. 11 und Rost 18 f. *me* und *mee*.

§ 4. *we*.

Als Regel gilt *we*; daneben im 15. und 16. Jahrhundert die Schreibung *wee*, besonders bei Gruppe II; Würzner p. 149, Lummert p. 11 und Rost 18 f. *me* und *mee*.

§ 5. *us*.

Als Regel gilt *us*. In den P. L. graphische Varianten *ws* (238, 681/24), *ous* 517, 560/291, welch letzteres schwerlich mehr die alte Länge (me. *ous*) als satzbetonte Form bezeichnet.

Personalpronomen der 2. Person.

§ 6. *thou*.

Als Regel gilt *thou*; daneben in den P. L. häufiger, im 16. Jahrhundert selten nur in Gruppe II die Schreibung *thow*, ausserdem in den P. L. zahlreiche graphische Varianten mit ʒ für *y*, in den Digby Myst. häufig *þou*, *thu*, letzteres auch Bale, Thre Lawes und Kynge Johan.

§ 7. *thee* (Dat. und Acc.).

Als Regel gilt *thee*; daneben in den P. L. und Flügels Texten häufiger, später seltener *the*, in den Digby Myst. auch *þe*; Würzner p. 139, Lummert p. 11 und Rost 18 f. *the* und *thee*.

Anm.: Inbetreff *dee* für *thee* R. R. Dolster 52 cf. § 45, Anm. c.

§ 8. *ye* (Nom. und Acc.).

Als Regel gilt *ye*; daneben im 15. und 16. Jahrhundert die Schreibung *yee* (noch in Marl. Tamb. und Faust). In den P. L.

auch graphische Varianten mit ȝ für y; Würzner p. 149, Lummert
p. 11 und Rost 18 f. ye und yee.

§ 9. you (Nom. und Acc.).

Als Regel gilt you; daneben seltener yow, vereinzelt nur
in Gruppe II (Egerton Pap., Diary of M., Leycester Corr., Henslowe's Diary) youe. Graphische Varianten in den P. L.: yowe,
yw, yu sowie Schreibungen mit ȝ.

Anm.: Die Uebergangsstufe zwischen God be with you (ye) z. B. Sir
Clyomon 500 a (Bale, Kynge Johan 56) und dem jetzigen Goodby(e) haben
wir Angry Women 349 God be w' ye, sir, Knack to know a Knave 592, 553
God b' w' y'.

Personalpronomen der 3. Person.

§ 10. he.

Als Regel gilt he; daneben im 15. und auch noch im 16. Jahrhundert nicht selten die Schreibung hee (Euphues, Marprelate,
Putt., Sidney, Leyc. Corr. etc.); Würzner p. 140, Lummert p. 11
und Rost 18 f. he und hee.

Anm.: Bisweilen in den P. L. (216/302, 396/20, 527/234), vornehmlich
jedoch bei den Dramatikern der zweiten Hälfte des 16. Jahrhunderts findet
sich die me. nur südlichem Dialekt (Sturzen-Becker 39) angehörende Form
ha, 'a, a, z. B.:

G. G. Needle 241, Rare Triumphs 177, Three Ladies 300, Marl., Edw.
II 239, Greene, Bacon 162, Knack to Know a Knave 548 und schliesslich
ganz besonders häufig bei Peele, Edw. I 98, 142, 157, 164, 177, Arr. 21, 22,
38 etc., Sir Clyomon 515 b, 518a, meist in satztieftoniger Stellung bei Anlehnung an das Verb., bisweilen jedoch auch an gehobenen Stellen, man vgl.:

Mucedorus 240, *What manner of man was a?* Lodge, Wounds 190,
faith, a pretty fellow is a., sowie Peele, Arr. 48.

Dieses auch zahlreich bei Shakspere; cf. Deutschbein § 40.

§ 11. him.

Als Regel gilt him; daneben im 15. Jahrhundert und in
der ersten Hälfte des 16. Jahrhunderts häufig die Schreibung
hym, in den P. L., Texten Flügels vereinzelt, zahlreich in Henslowe's Diary hyme, Digby Myst. 171/3 hymm, im Diary of
Machyn ym (21, 36), im (221) wie ys, is für hys, his (§ 21, Anm. 1).

§ 12. she.

Als Regel gilt she; daneben seltener shee. In den P. L. zahlreich, in den Digby Myst. sowie im 16. Jahrhundert mehrfach,

aber nur bei Gruppe II *sche*; Würzner p. 149, Lummert p. 11 und
Rost 18f. *she* und *shee*. Graphische Variante in den P. L. auch
che (197, 428/73, woselbst auch *chall* für *shall* etc.).

Anm.: Die me. (nördl.) *sho* entsprechende Form *sho* fand sich zahllos
in den Digby Mysteries.

§ 13. *her*.

Als Regel gilt *her*; daneben vielfach im 15. Jahrhundert
und häufiger als im 16. (entspr. me. *hire*) *hir*, *hyr*. Graphische
Varianten in den P. L. auch *here*, *herr(e)*, *hire*, *hyre*; Digby
Myst. 68/378, 75/550 etc., Myst. ed. Hone 73, 94 sowie Fl. 138/II
auch *hur* (ebenfalls als poss. s. d. § 22), was sich me. zuweilen
im südlichen Dialekt findet; cf. Sturzen-Becker 42.

§ 14. *it*.

Als Regel gilt *it*; daneben im 15. Jahrhundert, im 16. Jahrhundert besonders bei Gruppe II vielfach *yt(t)*, sowie Formen
mit noch erhaltenem h: *hit*, *hyt*. Graphische Varianten in den
P. L. *itt*, *hitt*, *hytt*, *hyte*.

§ 15. *they*.

Als Regel gilt *they*; daneben im 15. und im 16. Jahrh. vorwiegend bei Gruppe II die Schreibungen *the*, *theie*, in den P. L.
auch *theye*. In Gruppe II einschliesslich der P. L. und Digby Myst.
fand sich die me. (nördl.) *thai* entsprechende Form *thai*, *thay*.

Anm. 1: Inbetreff P. L. 68/65, 428/73 *dey*, cf. § 45 Anm. b., inbetreff
Three Ladies 307 *day* für *thay* = *they* cf. ib. Anm. a.

Anm. 2: Confl. of Consc. 71 (2 mal), 72, 73, 74 *thea* erweisen sich
als beabsichtigte schottische Dialektformen.

§ 16. *them*.

Als Regel gilt *them*; daneben im 15. Jahrhundert vornehmlich bei Gruppe II die Schreibung *theme*, sowie die Formen
theim, *theym* (P. L. auch *theyme*) = me. (Orrm) *þeʒm*; *thaym*,
thaime, *tham* (P. L. auch *thayme*) = me. (nördl.) *thaim*, *tham*.

Anm. 1: Die dem alten *heom*, *hem* entsprechende südliche Form
hem erscheint noch zahlreich im 15. Jahrhundert in den P. L. als *hem*,
ham, *hym*, im M. als *hem*, in den Digby Myst. als *hem*, vereinzelt *heym*,
seltener im elisabethanischen Drama in der Kürzung '*em*, z. B.: Marl., Jew
1439, Edw. II 211 (Lesart), Three Ladies 313; vgl. Panning 41.

Anm. 2: Confl. of Consc. 71, 74 *tham*, 71 *theam* sind beabsichtigte
schottische Dialektformen.

Anm. 3: Inbetreff Three Ladies 305 *dem* für *them* cf. § 45 Anm. a.

Allgemeines zum Personalpronomen.

§ 17.

1. Verschmelzung des Personalpronomens mit anderen Wörtern (proclisis, enclisis), vielfach verbunden mit Elisionen und Apokopen, ist in den P. L. nichts ungewöhnliches und im 16. Jahrhundert in hervorragender Weise im Drama zu finden.

Wir führen zur Veranschaulichung dessen die hauptsächlichsten an:

Inbetreff *ich* s. § 2 Anm. 2;

Ile für *I will* (Lyly, Myd. 24), *I'll* desgl. (Peele, Edw. I 95, Greene, Orl. 10), *I'am* für *I am* (Marlowe, Verm. 306), *I'sh* für *I shall* (Heywood, Pard. and Friar 232);

thou'rt für *thou art* (Ovid 187, 197), *th'art* desgl. (G. G. Needle 176, Peele, Edw. I 86, Greene, Bacon 150), *thou'st* für *thou hast* (Angry Wom. 298, Look ab. you 447), *th'hast* desgl. (Greene, James 93, Looking Glass 63), *th'adst* für *thou hadst* (G. G. Needle 230), *thou'lt* für *thou wilt* (Marlowe, Verm. 307, Greene, Orl. 33);

h'hath für *he hath* (Look. ab. you 505), *h'ath* desgl. (Damon and P. 83), *h'had* für *he had* (Marl., Jew 25),

he's (Three Ladies 288, 293), \
hees (Udall, State IX), } für *he is*, \
hys (P. L. 396/20), \
so erklärt sich Fox 9 *his is*

he'll für *he will* (G. G. Needle 241, Greene, Orl. 33);

sh'ath für *she hath* (Peele, Arr. 48), *sh'ase* desgl. (G. G. Needle 221), *she's* für *she is* (Greene, Orl. 40), *sch'was* für *sche was* (Myst. ed. Hone 63), *she'll* für *she will* (Greene, Bacon 148);

we'd für *we would* (Marl., Edw. II 176);

we'll für *we will* (G. G. Needle 184, Peele, Edw. I, 94);

let's für *let us* (G. G. Needle 191, Greene, Orl. 12), *shall's* für *shall us* (Kyd, Jer. 363);

ye're für *ye are* (Angry Wom. 347), *y'are* desgl. (Misf. of Arthur 267, Greene, Orl. 51, *y'have* für *ye have* (Misf. of Arthur 275), *you've* für *you have* (Myst. ed. Hone 95), *ye'ad* für *ye had* (G. G. Needle 213), *you'll* für *you will* (Peele, Edw. I 133, Greene, Orl. 42);

they're für *they are* (Jac. and Esau 229), *th'are* desgl. (Misf. of Arthur 306), Barnfield, Poems 19), *they'd* für *they had* (Marl., Edw. II 234), *they'll* für *they will* (Misf. of Arth. 325, Greene, Bacon 164);

ageynstem für *ageynst hem* (P. L. 207/292);
'tis (G. G. Needle 176, Peele, Arr. 36, Greene, Orl. 32), *'twas* (G. G. Needle 193, Peele, Arr. 7), *'twere* (G. G. Needle 214, Marl., Edw. II 266), *'T'ath* für *it hath* (Damon and P. 76), *'twill* (G. G. Needle 219, Peele, Alc. 120), *'twould* (Greene, Orl. 42, Marl., Edw. II 208), *'t must* (Marl., Edw. II 241);

be't (Marl., Lucan 283), *is't* (Greene, Pinner 183), *wert, wer't* (Heywood, P. P. 377, Greene, Orl. 11), *ha't* (Peele, Arr. 25), *do't* (Jac. and Esau 219), *may't* (Marl., Edw. II 212), *wilt* (Greene, Orl. 37), *an't* (Marl., Edw. II 199), *in't* (Angry Women 341), *to't* (Peele, Verm. 202);

payed für *pay it* (P. L. 491/162), *to byit, seydyt, makyt, takyt* (P. L. 809/214 f.), insbesondere bei unpersönlichen Verben *plesyt, plesid* (graphische Verwechselung mit dem Praet.), infolge davon, weil formelhaft geworden und nicht mehr verstanden, (wie bei *cham* § 2 Anm. 2) doppelte Bezeichnung des Pronomens: P. L. 442/92 *Pleasyt it you to understond the grete expens* ... ib. 457/108 *Lekit it ʒow to wethe* ...;

sonst P. L. 502/186 ... *to tell hym all mater howt it was;*
schliesslich findet fast regelmässig enclisis statt bei der den elisabethanischen Dramatikern sehr geläufigen Wendung *I prythee* für *I pray thee* (cf. § 104 Anm. 1).

§ 18.

2. **Grossschreibung der Anfangsbuchstaben der Personalpronomina** findet, aber durchaus nicht konsequent, dann statt, wenn sich dieselben auf Gott (z. B. P. L. 609/350, Everyman 131, Hickscorner 181), Christus (z. B. World and Child 274), vereinzelt auch, wenn sie sich auf **Fürstlichkeiten** beziehen (Fl. 350 f., Sidney, Astr. XCVI, II).

§ 19.

3. Eine nicht unbeträchtliche, sich teilweise jedoch wieder ausgleichende Verschiebung im Gebrauch der einzelnen Personalpronomina tritt insofern ein, als

a) durch den Uebergang von unpersönlichen zu persönlichen Verben (cf. Anhang I) die früheren Dative (formell = acc.) durch die entsprechenden Nominative,

b) die Accusative durch den steigenden Gebrauch der verstärkten Formen des Personals bei reflexiven Verben,

c) ye durch you und umgekehrt you durch ye verdrängt werden.

Von geringerer Bedeutung sind die anderen Fälle von Vertauschungen des Nom. mit dem Acc. und umgekehrt, für unseren Zeitraum auch die Verdrängung von thou durch you.

Possessivpronomen.

I. Adjektivisches Possessivpronomen.

§ 20. *my, mine, thy, thine.*

In Gruppe I gelten die noch jetzt üblichen Formen als Regel; daneben vereinzelt Schreibungen mit *i* bezw. *y* und umgekehrt oder mit Apokope des *e*, die bei Gruppe II, wo überhaupt starkes Schwanken herrscht, zahlreicher sind.

Anm. 1: Ueber den Gebrauch der längeren (älteren *mine, thine*) und der kürzeren (jüngeren *my, thy*) Formen ist folgendes zu sagen:

Im 15. Jahrhundert werden *mine, thine* ausser vor Vocalen auch noch vor jedem folgenden Konsonanten gebraucht. Jedoch nehmen sie in letzterem Falle in den P. L. etwa seit dem Jahre 1461 (Brief 390—410) stark ab und zählen Ende des Jahrhunderts schon zu den Seltenheiten. Die mit dem Jahre 1460 einsetzende Plumpton Correspondence zeigt niemals *mine* oder *thine* ausser vor *h* und Vokalen, woraus wir mit Sicherheit den Schluss ziehen können, dass dies in der Umgangssprache des Volkes schon in den letzten Jahrzehnten des 15. Jahrhunderts zur Regel geworden war. Daran ändert auch die Tatsache nichts, dass der sprachlich ziemlich konservative Morte Darthure überwiegend die volleren Formen aufweist, wenn auch nicht (wie Sommer II, 34 fälschlich behauptet) ausschliesslich; denn kurze Formen finden sich: *my* 133/28, 232/23, 513/11, *thy* 100/11, 108/8, 775/20 etc.

Die weitere Entwicklung in der Volkssprache ergiebt sich aus folgendem:

Im 16. Jahrhundert sind *mine, thine* vor Konsonanten ausser *h* sehr selten (Heywood, P. P. 347, Joy, Ap. 30). Nur Tyndale's Bibelübersetzung hat auch in diesen Fällen vielfach die volleren Formen, welche die Auth. Vers. und die Rev. Vers. meist beibehalten haben; geändert z. B. Matth. 22/37, Rom. 10/6).

Vor stummem *h* sind *mine*, *thine* noch bei den Dramatikern vor Shakspere (so besonders bei Marlowe) nicht ungewöhnlich, vor anderem *h* im Ganzen selten.

Vor Vokalen zeigen sich auch im 16. Jahrhundert noch vielfach die volleren Formen. Einen Unterschied zwischen beiden Arten je nach der Betonung konnten wir jedoch nicht wahrnehmen; vgl. Abbot § 237.

Anm. 2: In der Verbindung *myn own* flossen beide Worte in der Rede in eins zusammen, und indem das *n* von *myn* silbenanlautend und nicht mehr silbenauslautend gesprochen wurde, entstand aus *myn own* — *my nown*: P. L. 310 *my nown comyng*, Joy, Ap. 28 (35) *my nowne translacion (pleasure)*, R. R. Doister 21 *my nowne Annot Alyface*, Leyc. Corr. 236 (417) *my none self* etc. Diese Erscheinung erhält dadurch eine interessante Beleuchtung, dass *nown* für *own* nun auch bei anderen Possessiven eintrat: R. R. Doister 12
For what he sayth or doth can not be amisse,
Holde vp his yea and nay, be his nowne white sonne.
Das *n* von *myn* wächst ebenso an andere vokalisch anlautende Worte, z. B.: P. L. 716/78 *my nawnte*, 780/167 *my nowncle*, G. G. Needle 243 *my narse*.

Anm. 3: Der Fall P. L. 600/339 *To myght' well belovyd brother* ... kann als eine über *myryth* (P. L. 809/214) gehende und eine flüchtige Aussprache darstellende Schreibung von *my ryght* angesehen werden, ist aber wohl so aufzufassen, dass der Schreibende, als er *my* schrieb, in Gedanken schon bei *ryght* war, ein Vorgang, der noch heutigentags zu beobachten ist.

Anm. 4: Verkürzung von *my* findet sich in Ausrufen: G. G. Needle 194, 217 *By m' father's soul*, ib. 226 *By m' fay*. So erklären sich weiter: *Bum troth = by my troth* (Damon and P. 62, 73, Cambyses 219); *Bum vay = by my vay*, (Cambyses 219, 220, 222), *Bom fay = by my fay* (Trial of Tr. 272).

Anm. 5: Lodge, Wounds 140 *dy* ist nach § 45 Anm. a zu beurteilen.

Anm. 6: Confl. of Consc. 75 *may* ist schottische Dialektform, desgl. *may*, *thay* (Greene, James IV 73); cf. § 2 Anm. 4.

§ 21. *his*.

Als Regel gilt *his*; daneben vornehmlich bei Gruppe II die Schreibung *hys*. Graphische (s. jedoch Anm. 2) Varianten in den P. L. noch: *hise, hyse, hyz, hiis, hes(e)* (auch Myst. ed. Hone 40), *is, ys, yss*, im 16. Jahrhundert herrscht *ys* fast durchweg im Diary of Machyn.

Anm. 1: Die Schreibung *is* (*ys*) ist, auf eben solcher Aussprache beruhend, durch Satztieftonigkeit bei enclisis an ein vorhergehendes Wort entstanden, und zwar zeigt sie sich besonders in den Fällen, wo *his* zur Bezeichnung des Genitivs steht. Doch treten diese Schreibungen in grösserem Umfange allein in den P. L. auf (vereinzelt sonst M. 257/31), im 16. Jahrhundert sind sie nur im Diary of Machyn (105, 110 etc.), einmal auch in einem Drucke von Lusty Iuventus 101 belegt.

Anm. 2: *Hise*, welches me. als Plural zu *his* vorkommt, kann im 15. Jahrhundert, wo es allein in den P. L. belegt ist, nicht mehr als Plural gelten, da es mehrfach (84, 87 etc.) auch als Singular erscheint. Diese Vertauschung erklärt sich durch das Verstummen des auslautenden *e*; cf. Morsb., Me. Gr. § 4, 3 c.

§ 22. *her*.

Als Regel gilt *her*; daneben besonders bei Gruppe II aber auch sonst *here*; sowie *hir, hyr*, in den P. L. auch noch *hire, hyre, hier* = me. *hire*; Digby Myst. und Fl. 138/II das südliche *hur* (auch als Personalpronomen s. d. § 13).

Anm.: *Hers* für *her* in einer Lesart Marl., Hero 98 erklärt sich nach § 25 Anm. wie *yours* für *your* etc.

§ 23. *its*.

Das erste bisher bekannte Beispiel stammt aus dem Jahre 1598. In den von uns untersuchten Denkmälern findet es sich nicht, doch dürften folgende Belege auf ein schon damaliges Vorkommen von *its* hindeuten, zumal da *self* in dieser Zeit allgemein als Substantiv gefasst wurde: Sidney, Arcadia (1590 bis 1593) 253

since my heart cannot persuade its self to part from it.

ib. 798 *Time ever old, and young it still revolved Within it's self, and never tasted end:*

§ 24. *our*.

Als Regel gilt *our*; daneben besonders bei Gruppe II *oure, owr(e), ower(e), ouir*, in den P. L. auch *howr* (325/439, 428/73) und *howur* (804/203); vgl. zu letzterem die Bemerkung betr. *heny* für *eny* § 77.

Anm. 1: In dem Ausrufe *By our Lady* wird *our* nicht selten zu '*r* verkürzt oder fällt auch als Folge dieser Verkürzung ganz weg (Umgangssprache!), z. B.: Trial of Treasure 261

By'r Lady, I am glad I have gotten thus clear.

ib. 298, Mucedorus 217, Damon and P. 25, 78; Sir Clyomon 503 a, 526 b *by'rlady*;

Peele, Edward I 100

By Lady, my lord, you go near the matter.

Marl., Faust II 1163
By Lady sir, you haue had a shrewd iourney of it,
Cambyses 218 (*by lakin*), Angry Women 337, 343, Jack Straw 394.
Anm. 2: Confl. of Consc. 70 *awer*, 70, 71 *awr*, 71 *aur*, 76 *awre* erweisen sich als beabsichtigte (schottische) Dialektformen.

§ 25. *your*.

Als Regel gilt *your*; daneben vereinzelt *youre*. Bei Gruppe II vielfach *youre, yowr, yower*. Die P. L. bieten ausserdem, abgesehen von Schreibungen mit z für *y*: *iowr, yowýr, ywr(e), youer, ywyr, yor(e)*; zu *yowyr* vgl. *fowyr = four* und *owyr = hour* (P. L. 422).

Anm. 1: *Yours* für *your* P. L. 156 *yours goode cosynes and frendes* erklärt sich durch das häufige Vorkommen von *your* für *yours* (§ 33, 2).

Anm. 2: *Ye* für *your* (ein Beleg Hoelper 48) bemerkten wir nicht.

§ 26. *their*.

Als Regel gilt *their*; daneben (bei Gruppe I nur vereinzelt) *theyr(e), theire; thair = me. þair; ther, there* (satztieftonige Form daher graphische Verwechselung mit *there = dort*, so umgekehrt *their* für *there* P. L. 920), *thir*.

Anm. 1: In den P. L. finden sich noch mehrfach Reste des ae. *hiera hira, heora*, mc. *her(e), hir* und zwar als *her* 46/59, 77/107, als *here* 4/13, als *herr* 38/48, als *herre* 502/185, als *hir* 557; ganz vereinzelt später Peele, Arr. 32 *her*, vgl. auch Marl., Dido 426 (Lesart); bei Shakspere 3 mal als *her* (Deutschbein § 51).

Anm. 2: *Theirs* für *their* P. L. 254/347 *and thei seyd right shrewedly ... that he hath thers herts.*, erklärt sich nach § 25 Anm. wie *yours* für *your* etc.

Allgemeines.

§ 27.

Adjektivische Possessivpronomina werden zuweilen mit grossen Anfangsbuchstaben geschrieben, wenn sie sich auf Gott (z. B. P. L. 363, Four El. 11, Jac. and Esau 262), Christus (z. B. P. L. 332/459, New Custom 34) oder die Dreieinigkeit (z. B. P. L. 856/277), vereinzelt auch wenn sie sich auf Fürstlichkeiten (Fl. 350 f.) beziehen; besonders interessant ist der Fall P. L. 804/204 *Hour Lord* (vgl. § 77).

II. Substantivisches Possessivpronomen.

§ 28. *mine, thine, his.*

Hierfür gelten ohne wesentliche Abweichungen dieselben Formen wie für die entsprechenden adjektivischen Formen (§ 20 f.).

§ 29. *hers.*

Als Regel gilt *hers*; daneben vereinzelt *hyrs, hirs.* Die P. L. bieten noch *herys, hyrrys.*

§ 30. *ours.*

Als Regel gilt *ours*; daneben vereinzelt *oures, owris,* in den P. L. auch *owr(e)s, owyrs*; *howrys* (vgl. Bemerkung zu *heny* für *eny* § 77).

§ 31. *yours.*

Als Regel gilt *yours.* Vereinzelt in Gruppe II *youres, youris, yowrs, yowers.* Die P. L. haben ferner, ausser Schreibungen mit ʒ, *youres, yowres, yourez, yors*; zu *Your ys* P. L. 819/215 vgl. § 164.

§ 32. *theirs.*

Als Regel gilt *theirs*; daneben vereinzelt *theires, theyres.* In den P. L. ferner (entspr. *ther*) *thers,* das sich auch in Tyndale's Bibelübersetzung, Bale's Johan 51 und in den Briefen Elizabeths 24 findet.

§ 33. Allgemeines. Formen ohne *s.*

Häufig im 15. Jahrhundert in den P. L., vereinzelt im 16., zeigen sich noch Formen ohne das (seit me. Zeit) an die substantivischen Possessivpronomina angefügte *s.* Ihr zahlreiches Vorkommen in den P. L. deutet darauf hin, dass diese Formen im 15. Jahrhundert noch in der Volkssprache (ausser *their?*) lebendig waren.

1. *her* für *hers.*

P. L. 71/90 .. *if ʒe may se .. that his childern and hire may enheryten ..* ib. 400/26, 681/23.

2. *your* für *yours.*

P. L. 362/533 ... *his pore presoner and your ...,* ib. *his wurchippfull counsaill and youre ...* ib. 502/189, 670/8, 697/50 etc., Heywood, P. P. 374.

Help me to speak with my lord and your ...
3. *their* für *theirs*.

Tyndale, Matth. 5/3 *for their is the kyngdome of heauen*
(Auth. Vers. und Rev. Vers. *theirs*); *their* kann aber auch
Druckfehler sein, da Vers 10 steht: „*for theirs is the kyngdom of heuen.*"

Reflexivpronomen.

§ 34. Vorbemerkungen.

1. Soweit für das Reflexiv noch die einfachen Formen des Personalpronomens gebraucht werden, ist natürlich auf dieses zu verweisen.

2. Da bei den verstärkten Formen des Reflexivs stets die Möglichkeit der Schreibung in éinem Worte oder in zwei vorliegt, werden wir im folgenden der Einfachheit halber nicht jede sich hieraus ergebende Variante verzeichnen.

3. Aus demselben Grunde werden wir die sich ja von selbst ergebenden me. Entsprechungen von *self* (*self, silf, selve, selven*) nicht jedesmal wiederholen.

§ 35. *myself*.

Als Regel gelten *my self(e)*, vereinzelt *miselfe*; daneben in Gruppe II *my selff(e), my silf(e), my sylf(e), my sealf(f)e* (Henslowe's Diary), *my selve* (Digby Myst. 146/185), in den P. L. ausserdem *my silff, my sylff*.

Anm. 1: P. L. 327/441 ... *and elles J wold a labored theder myn self*. Da wir sonst *myn self* in unseren Quellen nicht belegt fanden, können wir die Ansicht Blume's (d. Sprache d. P. L. Progr. Bremen 1882, p. 17) acceptieren, dass es sich aus der Eigentümlichkeit des Schreibenden erklärt, der stets *myn* für *my* braucht.

Anm. 2: Das ae. Dativ entsprechende *me* + *self* begegnet im 15. und 16. Jahrhundert nicht so ganz selten; da es sich in Denkmälern verschiedenster Art findet, war es wohl sehr verbreitet:

P. L. 419, *as for me self*.

Fl. (Skelton) 55/41 *I will me selfe discharge*, Egerton Pap. 292... *well known to me self ... und ... I wishe you all helth and happines as to me self*, Utopia 13, 14, Three Ladies 276, Leyc. Corr. 319.

§ 36. *thyself*.

Als Regel gelten *thy self(e)*; daneben (vorwiegend bei Gruppe II) *thi(e) self, thy silfe, thy sylfe*, Myst. ed. Hone 35 *thi selph*.

Anm.: Entsprechend *me self* findet sich *the self*: More, Utopia 109 *Contrary wyse to withdrawe somethinge from the selfe to geue to other* ...

§ 37. *hymself.*

Als Regel gelten *himself(e)*, neben seltenerem *hymself(e)*; daneben vereinzelt in Gruppe I, häufig in Gruppe II *hým(e) sýlf(e)*, *hymsylff, hym selve, hymsellve, hime selfe, ym selffe, ym seylff*, in den P. L. ausserdem noch *hymselve*, sowie infolge graphischer Verwechselung mit dem Plural *hem self(e)* im Impeachment of the Duke of Suffolk, P. L. 76/99 ff., aber hier überwiegend.

§ 38. *herself.*

Als Regel gelten *her self(e)*; daneben selten in Gruppe I, häufiger in Gruppe II Formen mit *hir, hyr*, in den P. L. ausserdem alle erdenklichen Variationen mit *y, i* für *e* in *her* und *self*, *ff* für *f* etc.; im Diary of Machyn auch *here seylff, yr seylff*.

§ 39. *itself.*

Itself, das in den P. L. überhaupt nicht vorkommt (dafür *the self* cf. Anm.), erscheint im 16. Jahrhundert in der Regel als *itself* seltener *ytself*, vereinzelt als *its self* (cf. *its* § 23), in Gruppe II auch als *yt selffe, hit selfe*.

Anm.: Für *itself* erscheint in den P. L. (analog einem zuerst 1340 belegten *the own* für *its own* cf. Morris § 185) einige Male *the self*:

P. L. 144/189 ... *thow summ maters ben not presentable, or peraventure in seche forme not corigyble ther, yet so that the mater in the self be orible and fowle* ...

P. L. 520/221 *And I told hym that as for such mony that shuld come from hym for that lond, I wold take it of hym and ley it up by the self, that I myght purchase other lond therwith* ...

P. L. 612/357 ... *he supposyd as well that it myght fall downe by the self as be plukyd downe* ...

§ 40. *one's self.*

Das zur Bezeichnung einer unbestimmten Person dienende *one's self* ist erst aus Sidney zu belegen:

Arcadia 102 ... *there is no wisdom but in including both heaven and earth in ones self*;

ib. 724 *What an inward discountenance it was to master Dametas ... nothing can describe, but either the feeling in one's*

self the state of such a mind Dametas had, or at least, the bethinking what was Midas's fancy ...
ib. 755 *And truly my Pyrocles, I have heard my father, and other wise men say, that the killing of ones self is but a false colour of true courage ..*
Sidney, The Lady of Mai p. 172
Who in one's self these divers gifts can plant:

§ 41. ourselves.

Als Regel gilt für das 16. Jahrhundert *ourselves* (vereinzelt *our selfes*), in der ersten Hälfte noch zahlreich *our self(e)*, während der Morte Dartbure nur *our self(e)*, die P. L. *our self(e)*, *owre selff, oure silffe*, die Digby Myst. *our self* aufweisen; gruppe II zeigt im 16. Jahrhundert *our self(e), oureselves, owreselves, our seallves*.

§ 42. yourselves.

In den P. L. nie Formen mit *s*; dagegen *your self(e), yow̆r(e) sylf(e), yowyr sylfe*. Im Morte Darthure *your(e) self(e)*, Digby Myst. *your silf, yower selfe (sylfe), yowre self, your Selff*.

In der 1. Hälfte des 16. Jahrhunderts herrschen, wenn mehrere Personen gemeint sind, neben selterem *yourselves (yourselues* vereinzelt *your selfes) your self(e)*; die Formen mit *s* sind in der 2. Hälfte Regel.

§ 43. themselves.

Die P. L. haben *them self(e), theym(e) self* und nur einmal (883/319, 1485) *themselfs*.

Im 16. Jahrh. gilt als Regel *themselves*, in der 1. Hälfte noch zahlreiche Formen ohne *s* = *them self(f)(e)*. In Gruppe II, vereinzelt sonst finden sich als weitere Schreibungen bezw. Formen (cf. § 16 und § 34, 3) *themself(f)es, them sellŭys, thaimselfis, theimselfes, theymeselves*.

Anm. 1: Die Formen mit *hem* finden sich mehrfach in den P. L. (27/41, 181/245 etc.), vereinzelt im Morte Darthure (57/5), Fox und bei Flügel (10/27).

Anm. 2: Eine schwache Form zeigte sich in unseren Texten nur Fl. (hist. Volkslieder) 157/3 *the are standards of the stanleys: that stands by them seluen*.

§ 44. Allgemeines zum Reflexivpronomen.

Ourself(e) und *yourself(e)* in Beziehung auf éine Person.

Als Majestätsplural erscheint *ourselves* nur in Formen ohne *s*, *our self(e)* (Kyd, Jer., Span. Trag., Briefe Elizabeths, Leyc. Corr.); ebenso *yourselves* in den P. L. als wie unter *yourselves* angegeben, im 16. Jahrhundert in Gruppe II als *yourself(e)*, *your(e) selff*, *your sellff*, in Gruppe I als *yourself(e)*.

Demonstrativpronomen.

§ 45. *this.*

Als Regel gilt *this* neben selteuerem *thys*. Vereinzelt in den P. L. und Fl. *thes* entspr. me. *thes.*

Anm.: a) Die Schreibung *dis* für *this* Three Ladies 277, 304, 346 bezeichnet, wie *day, dem, dat, dese* für *thay = they, them, that, these* (s. d.) und *ting, tink, tank* für *thing, think, thank* ib. 305 bezw. 307, 331 etc. eben diese (noch jetzt im Negerenglisch [cf. Harrison, Negr. English, Anglia VIII, 247; XIV, 37 ib. auch Grade, Negerenglisch der Westküste von Afrika] vorhandene) Aussprache des italienischen Mercators, Rare Triumphs 208 *dis* die eines anderen Italieners, Lodge, Wounds 140 die eines Franzosen; der Zweck der Komik ist unverkennbar.

b) Dagegen haben wir P. L. 36/48 (und wohl auch Fl. 206/8, wenn hier nicht Druckfehler) einfach dialektische Formen wie *toder, moder* (ib.) anzunehmen, ebenso P. L. 68/85 (ib. *hydder* für *hither*) und 428/73 (ib. *togeder*) für *dey*.

c) Eine komische Absicht liegt zweifellos *dem, dis, dee* R. R. Doister 52 zu Grunde, wie sich auch aus der Form *lub* für *love* ergiebt:

Canst thou lub dis man which coulde lub dee so well?

§ 46. *these.*

Als Regel gilt *these*; daneben in Gruppe II (vereinzelt nur in Gruppe I: Utopia *thies, thees*, R. A., Toxophilus *theise, thies*), *thes, theis(e)*, einmal (Plumpt. Corr. 244) *theas*, in den P. L. auch noch *thees(e), theyse.*

Anm. 1: Inbetreff *dese* für *these* Three Ladies 307 cf. § 45 Anm. a.

Anm. 2: Die me. (Orrm, Chaucer etc., vgl. auch Morsb., Schriftsprache p. 128) Pluralform *thise* (über *this* als pl. cf. § 198 ff.) findet sich noch im 15. und 16. Jahrhundert konsequent für den Plural, nie vor einem Sg., was bei der sonst so schwankenden Orthographie der hier vornehmlich in Betracht kommenden Denkmäler der Gruppe II einigermassen bemerkenswert ist; vgl. z. B.:

P. L. 173/240 *thise partyes* neben *this schir* u. zweimaligem *this contre*.
P. L. 283/389 *thise deies* neben *this my poor letter* p. 388 etc. etc.
Thise ferner: Rutl. Pap. 15, 16, 22, M. 520/15, 763/26, Fox zahllos, cf.
z. B. p. 39, Fl. 2/13, 8/19, Briefe Elizabeths 15, 102.

§ 47. that.

Als Regel gilt *that*. In den P. L. ausserdem *thet* (= me.
þet), *thatt*, sowie Schreibungen mit *y* für *th* (diese letzteren
auch vereinzelt im 16. Jahrhundert).

Anm.: Inbetreff *dat* für *that* Three Ladies 275, 346 etc., sowie Rare
Triumphs 202, 203, 207 cf. § 45 Anm. a.

§ 48. those.

Als Regel gilt *those*; daneben, vornehmlich in Gruppe II,
thos. Andere Schreibungen der P. L. *thoos(e)*, *thoes*, *thois*,
Digby Myst. auch *thoys*.

Anm.: Neben *those* findet sich noch bis in die erste Hälfte des
16. Jahrhunderts die auf ae. *þā*, me. *tho(o)* zurückgehende Form *tho*.
So in den P. L. 18/32, 71/89, 108/146, 348/510 etc., Digby Myst. 3 69,
4/87, 29/46 etc. als *tho*, *thoo*, *thoe*, desgl. M. 3/22, 49/12, 59/26 etc.,
mehrfach in Tyndale's Bibelübersetzung, Rom. 6/21, 14/19, Hebr. 6/19,
Rev. 2/10, 20/12, wo die Auth. Vers. und die Rev. Vers. *tho* teils in
those, teils in *the* ändern oder ganz weglassen.

§ 49. such.

Folgende me. Formen kommen für uns in Betracht, aus
denen sich die unten angeführten Formen des 15. und 16. Jahrhunderts erklären: *such*, *soch*, *swich(e)*, *sich*, *sech*.

Als Regel gilt in gruppe I *such*, seltener ist *suche*; Joy,
Ap. *soch(e)*, *siche*; gruppe II hat ausserdem *sooche*, *sutch*; *shuche*,
shyche auch im Diary of Machyn.

Die P. L. weisen ausser *such(e)*, *soch(e)* noch folgende Formen (s. o.) bezw. Schreibungen auf:

shuch, *souche*; *swich(e)*, *swyche*, *swhyche*, *suych(e)*, *syyche*,
sych(e), *siche*; *swech(e)*, *swheche*, *suech*, *sech(e)*; die Digby Myst.
haben *soch*, *sich*, *sych*, *swyche* je 2 mal.

Anm. 1: Die nördliche (schottische) Form *sike* fand sich nur
Greene, James IV 95; cf. Panning 50.

Anm. 2: Die Schreibung *shush*, *sush* (Three Ladies 274, 307) giebt die
(als komisches Element verwertete) mangelhafte Aussprache von *such*
im Munde eines Italieners wieder; cf. *sh in mershant*, *mush*, *grush* für
ch ib. 275 etc.; *much* ib. 276, sowie *such* ib. 277 beruhen auf Inkonsequenz
des Druckers, der die Bedeutung der Schreibung nicht erkannte.

§ 50. thilk.

Als einziger Beleg für diese durch Mischung aus ae. *þyllic, þylc* und *se ilca* entstandene (cf. Pabst, Robert of Gloucester, Diss. Berlin 1889, § 21) und noch bei Spenser mehrfach (Günther, Archiv 55, p. 63) vorkommende Form fand sich in unseren Quellen

Damon and Pithias 74
A murrain take thilk wine, it so intoxicate my brain,
That to be hanged by and by I cannot speak plain.

§ 51. ilk.

Ae. *se ilca*, me. *ilk(e)* entsprechend begegnet es mehrfach im 16. Jahrhundert nur in der Poesie, darunter vereinzelt im Drama:

Fl. (Balladen) 174/81 *But he come this ylke day*
ib. 177/29 *That they wolde be with Robyn*
That ylk same [nyght] (Pleonasmus!)
ib. 181/59 *And for that ylke lordes loue*
ib. 184/54 *And for this ylke tydynge*
Blyssed mote thou be
Heywood, Pardoner and Friar 200
And if that house be worthy and elect,
Th'ilk peace there then shall take effect;
And if that house be cursed or pervert,
Th'ilk peace then shall to yourself revert.
World and Child 264 *By that ilk truth ...*
Confl. of Consc, 74 an einer (schott.) Dialektstelle.

§ 52. self.

Soweit es in Verbindung mit Personalien das Reflexivum darstellt s. d. (§ 34 ff.).

Sonst Sg. *self(e)*, Pl. *selves* wenn substantivisch, ersteres allein, wenn adjektivisch gebraucht.

§ 53. same.

Als Regel gilt *same*; vereinzelt ist *sam*.

§ 54. *yon, yond, yonder.*

Sie sind im 15. und 16. Jahrhundert doch ziemlich volkstümlich, da sie nicht weniger der Lyrik als der Dramatik angehören in den Formen

yon: Myst. ed. Hone 67, 68, Jack Juggler 119, Peele, Arr. 33, Greene, James IV, 136, Marl., Dido 379, Verm. 303, Lodge, Wounds 149;

yone: Digby Myst. 20/486, Briefe James 15, 46, 106;

yonne: Fl. (Balladen) 195/37;

yond: Marlowe, Jew 772, Greene, James IV 108, Lodge, Wounds 168;

yonder: (die häufigste Form): P. L. nur 916/361 als *yondyr,* Myst. ed. Hone 68, M. 38/36, 61/10, Fl. (Jagdlieder) 152/16, Tyndale, Matth. 17/20, Bale, Johan 69, R. A., Toxophilus 64, Interl. of Youth 77, Lyly, Galathea 231, Marl., Edward II 234, Kyd, Jer. 370, Puttenham 201, Look about You 484 etc. etc.

Anm. 1: Der bei neueren belegten Schreibung *yon'* (Koch § 335, Mätzner I, 324) entspricht im 16. Jahrhundert etwa: Lodge, Wounds 119
His beardless face and wanton, smiling brows,
Shall, If I catch him, deck yond' capitol.

Anm. 2: Die auf altem *i*-Umlaut beruhende Form *yender* ist in unseren Quellen nur Digby Myst. 109/1438, 122/1785, 125/1865, 126/1859 als *ʒendyr*, sowie Fl. (Gedicht auf die Schlacht bei Otterburne) 194/13 als *yender* belegt.

Interrogativ- und Relativpronomen.

Vorbemerkung.

Der Einfachheit halber behandeln wir beide gemeinsam, da sie ja in der Form meist übereinstimmen; auf etwaige Unterschiede werden wir im Einzelnen hinweisen.

§ 55. *who* (Interr. und Rel.).

Als Regel gilt *who*; daneben vereinzelt in Gruppe I, häufig in Gruppe II *whoo, whoe, wo*, in den P. L. ausserdem *ho, hoo, howe*, als Relativ auch *how* (cf. Anm. 1).

Anm. 1: Wie in den P. L. *how* für *who* geschrieben wird, so auch umgekehrt *who* für *how* (P. L. 161), was auf gleiche Aussprache hinweist; cf. Luick § 112, 139, Morsb., Me. Gr. § 135, Anm. 4, Panning p. 35 unten.

Anm. 2: Im elisabethanischen Drama spiegelt die zuweilen (Lyly, Bombic 98, Marl., Faust 680) vorkommende und über *who's* (Marl., Faust II 1075) gehende Schreibung *whose* für *who is* die dem Genitiv *whose* gleiche Volksaussprache des täglichen Lebens von *who is* wieder.

Anm. 3: Gelegentliche Verdoppelungen von *who* (Puttenham 290, Marprelate, Epistle 12) sind als Fehler des Druckers anzusehen; ebenso findet sich M. 492/15 *one one*, 806/39 *be be* (Lesart), Greene, Orl. 50 *the the* (Lesart) etc.

Anm. 4: Die me. im nördlichen Mittellande und weiter nördlich belegte Form *quho* findet sich P. L. 521 (als *qwo*), in den Briefen James 21, als *quha* neben *quho* Fl. (Lieder Wedderburn's) 131 ff.

Anm. 5: Confl. of Consc. 76 *whe* ist schottische Form an einer Dialektstelle; cf. § 56, Anm. 2.

§ 56. *whose* (Interr. und Rel.).

Als Regel gilt *whose*; daneben vereinzelt, meist bei Gruppe II, *whoes, whos, whoys, whoos, whosse, wos*. Andere Schreibungen der P. L. *hos*, für das Relativ auch *whois, whows, hose, hoose, hoes, hois, hows*.

Anm. 1: Verdoppelung von *whose* (Digby Myst. 205/995) ist Schreibfehler; vgl. auch § 55 Anm. 3.

Anm. 2: Confl. of Consc. 70 *whese* ist beabsichtigte schottische Form (cf. ib. 75 *hely* für *holy* etc.)

§ 57. *whom* (Interr. und Rel.).

Als Regel gilt *whom*, seltener ist *whome*.

Schreibungen der P. L. *whom(e), hom*; als Relativ auch *whem*, mehrfach *wham* (schott.), *hwm*, Digby Myst. ferner *wom*.

Anm. 1: Die Form *quhom(e)* (cf. § 55 Anm. 4) findet sich P. L. 27/41 (als *qwm*), Fl. (Wedderburn) 131/30 sowie in Briefen James 19, 126, 143.

Anm. 2: Zuweilen wird *whom* mit der es regierenden Präposition zu einem Worte verschmolzen, analog zu *wherewith, whereby, whereto, wherfrom*:
More, Utopia 136
For them whomewyth they be in wayges they fyghte hardelye...

Briefe James 14 ... *of such a prince as ye are; quhomto I am ... in so manyfold wayes beholden.*

ib. 126
... *my seruande, quhomby ye shall be informed...*

ib. 143 *Quhomby I haue in deid receaued a letter of his maisteris owin hande...*

§ 58. *what* (Interr. und Rel.).

Als Regel gilt *what*; Suppl. for the Beggers nur *whate*. Gruppe II hat auch die Schreibungen *whatt, whate*; die P. L.

bieten *what(t)(e)*, *wat*, *whath* *whet* für Interr. und Rel., für letzteres auch *wathc*.

Anm. 1: Die Form *quhat* (cf. § 55 Anm. 4) findet sich als *qhat* P. L. 78/112 (nur interr.), 56/67, 67/83, als *qwat* ib. 419, 818/231, 625, als *qwhat* ib. 829/245, als *quhatt* ib. 78/110 (und Interr.), Fl. (Schäferkalender) 95/9 (cf. Anm. Flügels), Briefe James 21; in den Digby Myst. als *qwat, quat*.

Anm. 2: Dialektisches (südliches) *vat* für *what* Rare Triumphs 208, Three Ladies 305, 330 im Munde von Italienern, wie *vell* ib. 208 bezw. 357 für *well* (komische Absicht!); cf. Panning 36.

Anm. 3: Verdoppelung von *what* M. 378/16 ist nach § 55 Anm. 3 zu beurteilen.

§ 59. *whether*.

Stets *whether* ausser Fl. (Briefe) 338/6 *whither* (lautliche Geltung des *i* nicht unwahrscheinlich; cf. Morsb., Me. Gr. § 109).

Anm.: *Whethersoever* begegnete in unseren Texten nur: R. A., Toxophilus 59
... *eyther to goodnesse or badnesse, to whether soeuer they liste*:

§ 60. *which* (Interr. und Rel.).

Als Regel gilt *which(e)*, seltener ist *whych(e)*. Gruppe II bietet für das Rel. auch *wych(e), weche*; die P. L. zeigen ausserdem folgende Variationen für das Rel.: *whishe, wyche, whech(e), wech, whesch(e)*; die Digby Myst. haben *whych, wiche, whech(e)*.

Anm. 1: Die nördliche Form *whilk* (*quilk*) findet sich an folgenden Stellen, wo sie sich teils durch die Heimat des Verfassers bezw. Schreibers erklärt, teils als beabsichtigte Dialektstelle erweist:
Fl. (Briefe) 331/21, Plumpt. Corr. 37, J. Knox 57 ... *quilk conteaneth in few and sempill wordes my confession*..., Confl. of Consc. 71, 74 (zahlreich), Greene, James IV 95, Briefe Elizab. und James nur in Briefen James 5, 52, 148 (Sg. *quhilk*, Pl. *quhilkis*).

Anm. 2: Die Form *quhich* (cf. § 55 Anm. 4) findet sich: in den P. L. als *qwych(e) quych, ghyche, qwhych, qweche, queche, gheche*, Fl. (Barclay) 94/35 als *qwych*, Briefe James 15 als *quhich*.

§ 61. *whoso, whos(o)(m) ever* (Interr. und Rel.).

Als Regel gelten *who so, whoever, whosoever* bezw. mit getrennten Bestandteilen. Vereinzelte Schreibungen *whosoe, whosoe*, besondere in den P. L. *whoo so, whoo so evyr, wo so ever, ho so ever*.

Anm. 1: Die schon bei Orrm belegte Form mit *summ* für *swa* „*who somever*" treffen wir auch bisweilen, z. B.: P. L. 506/197 (als *whosome ever*), M. 176/35, Fl. (Rhetorik) 301/52, Greene, Alph. 56 etc.

Anm. 2: Der Acc. *whomsoever* ist nicht so selten:
Tyndale, Rom. 6/16 *whom so ever* (Auth. Vers. und Rev. Vers.
nur *whom*), Fl. (More) 262/40, Disob. Child 309, Heywood, Pard. and Friar
204, Three Ladies 336, Rare Triumphs 229 etc. *whomsoever* bezw. mit getrennten Bestandteilen.

§ 62. *what so, what(so)(m) ever* (Interr. und Rel.).

Als Regel gelten *whatso, whatever, whatsoever* oder mit getrennten Bestandteilen, daneben im Drama Formen mit synkopiertem *v „what(so)e'er"*. Andere Schreibungen, besonders bei Gruppe II, *what evere, what so evyr, wat so ever*.

Anm. 1: Die *whosomever* entsprechende Form *whatsomever* findet sich in Gruppe I selten (M. 219/8, Fox 31, Hickscorner 192, Thersites 427, Greene, Alph. 53, 59), zahlreich in Gruppe II einschliesslich der P. L. und Digby Mysteries.

Besondere Schreibungen: P. L. *w(h)at som ever, whatsomevyr, wat swm ever, wathe some ever*; Fox 31 *what somme euver*, Diary of Machyn *whatsumever, wat somover*.

Anm. 2: Nördliche (schottische) Formen in den P. L. 338/494 *qwat som ever*, 521/223 *qwat sum ever*, ausserdem nur in Briefen James 15, 16, 22 etc. als *quhatsumever*.

§ 63. *which(so)(m)ever* (Interr. und Rel.).

Es erscheint als *whichso(o)ever*, auch getrennt, ferner als *whichever*, P. L. auch *whiche sum ever*.

§ 64. *that* (Rel.).

Als Regel gilt *that*. Gelegentlich finden sich auch noch im 16. Jahrhundert Schreibungen mit *y*.

§ 65. *at*.

P. L. 63/78 ... *and qwat at evyr ʒe pay in this matir, I schal truly ... repay ageyn to ʒow*.
ib. 72/91 ... *in that at longeth to my party* ...
ib. 132/171 ... *in that at y can or may* ...
ib. 329/442 ... *y wold be glad to doo that at might please yonre good Lordship* ...
ib. 437/87 *Yf ye will any thyng atte I may do* ...
Plumpt. Corr. LXV ... *those trew men att sall pas thereupon* ...
Joy, Ap. 12 ... *desyering all that be able to mende that at was amysse in it* ...
ib. 29 ... *that at is amysse* ...

Ob wir hier die im nördlichen Dialekt selbständig oder unter an. Einfluss entwickelte, um 1300 zuerst belegte, Form *at* (cf. Oxf. Dict. sowie Sturzen-Becker p. 56) vor uns haben, muss dahin gestellt bleiben; denn da in den meisten Fällen ein Pronomen mit auslautendem *t* vorausgeht (*qwat at, that at*) kann das *t* hier Produkt der Assimilation von *t* und *th* sein, wie in dem häufigen me. *thatte = that the* etc.; cf. Morsbach, Me. Gr. § 51 b; einigermassen unanfechtbar wären die beiden Fälle P. L. 437/87 und Plumpt. Corr. LXV (s. o.), wenngleich man diese wieder als analogische Uebertragungen deuten könnte

Allgemeines zum Relativpronomen.

§ 66.

Wie das pers. und poss. Pronomen, so werden auch die Relative *who* und *which*(e) bei Beziehung auf Gott bisweilen mit grossen Anfangsbuchstaben geschrieben, doch nur in den P. L.:

697/50 ... *with Godes grace, Who preserve yow.*
813/221 ... *God, the Wheche mot preserve yow at all oures.*

Indefinita.

§ 67. one.

Als Regel gilt *one*; daneben in Gruppe II *on, oon(e)*, zuweilen auch (= me. *ō*) *o, oo* P. L. 765/142, 862/290, Myst. ed. Hone 66, Fl. (Balladen) 169/25, Puttenham 213, auch in *eachoo*, cf. § 79, Anm.

Anm.: Mehrfach begegnen im 15. wie im 16. Jahrhundert die Formen *the tone* (cf. Morsbach, Me. Gr. § 51 a aus *thet one* für *the one* wie *the tother* aus *thet other* § 83, Anm. 3), *t'one, tone* (aus *the tone*, indem *t* als Artikel angesehen wurde), sowie *th'one, thone* (infolge Apokope des *e*):
P. L.716/79 ... *ther ye shall not fayill of the tone of of both ...*
Fl. (Balladen) 194/45 *For thys trespasse thou hast me done*
The tone of vs schall dye.
Fl. (Briefe) 342/50 (343/58) ... *to say precisely the tone way, or elles precisely the tother.*
New Custom 30 *But of th'one she is able a solution to make,*
Misfortune of Arthur 322 (302, 323)
Nor t'one nor t'other side that can destroy
Her foes so fast, as 'tis itself destroyed.
Marl., Faust 995
Wel, tone of you hath this goblet about you.

Angry Women of Ab. 378 *I coulde please tone,*
Look about You 485;
Lyly, Loves Metam. 219 . . . *th'one as ready to execute mischiefe as the other . . .*
Puttenham 80, 131 etc., Three Lords 410;
Jacob and Esau 211
For thone is but a fool, and thother a stark knave.
Leyc. Corr. 108 *thone by provokinge a minister of ours . . .*

§ 68. *no, none.*

Als Regel gelten *no*, *non(e)*; daneben in Gruppe II *noo, noe, noon(e)*; in den P. L. ausserdem *nonne, noun, nowne*.

Anm. 1: Dialektische (nördliche) Formen fanden sich nur Fl. (Wedderburn) 131/35 *na*, 132/18, 21 *nane*.

Anm. 2: Mehrfach bis in die 2. Hälfte des 16. Jahrhunderts begegnet die Schreibung *no nother* für *non(e) other*, veranlasst durch die silbenanlautende Aussprache des zweiten *n* wie in *a nother*, (cf. auch *my nown* § 20, Anm. 2):
P. L. 512/186 . . . *in thys mater nor in no nothyr;*
Fl. (Tyndale) 231/40, (Fabyan 268/25)
I know one that departed the courte for no nother cause than . . .
Four Elements 22, 31;
Diary of Machyn 14 . . . *they thought no nodur butt . . .*

Anm. 3: Ueber die Frage, ob *no* oder *none* in attributiver Beziehung, ist folgendes zu sagen:
Die P. L. brauchen noch vielfach *none* auch vor Konsonanten, z. B. P. L. 621/375 *non dyreccion*, im 16. Jahrhundert ist das nur vereinzelt zu beobachten, z. B. Fl. (Anekdoten) 327/52 *none man*; mit Ausnahme von *none such* (G. G. Needle 236, Lyly, Mother Bombie 146, Greene, James IV 92 etc.). *None* vor Vokalen, seltener vor *h* ist noch bis Ende des 16. Jahrhunderts üblich, wenn auch überwiegend *no* eintritt, z. B.: Tyndale, Vorwort zu Mark. 6 *none honoure*, Leyc. Corr. 63 *none other scope*.

Anm. 4: Verbindungen mit *no*:
no one, subst. und adj. (*none* für *no* in diesem Fall P. L. 862/290 *non oo man*, Fl. [Elyot] 253/19 *none one autour*), wofür wohl ebenso oft *not one* vorkommt; *no body*, noch häufig getrennt.

Anm. 5: Das von Morris § 232 angeführte *noddy* (Damon and P. 17, 78), das sich ferner Heywood, P. P. 383, Jacob and Esau 209, Nice Wanton 177, Confl. of Consc. 76 findet, ist keine Kontraktion aus *nobody*, sondern Ableitung von *to nod*.

§ 69. *both.*

Als Regel gelten *both(e)*; vereinzelt findet sich *bocth, booth*. Die P. L bieten *bo(o)th(e)*, daneben mehrfach *bothen* (342/499, 931/379), *bothyn* 229, 689/37.

Anm.: Eine Pluralform *boths* fand sich nicht, dagegen M. 98/7 *to our bothes destruction* mit Genitiv-*s*; P. L. 42/55 *to your bothenerys pleaser* (*botheres* + *bothen?*).

§ 70. *aught, ought.*

Als Regel gelten nebeneinander *aught* und *ought*; in den P. L. findet sich auch *owght*; Rost 35 f. *aught* neben viel seltenerem *ought*.

§ 71. *naught, nought.*

Nought findet sich mehr als *naught*; daneben vereinzelt in Flügels Texten *noght, nocht, nowght*, in den P. L. ausserdem *nougght, nott*; *not* 281/385 (Verwechselung mit *not*, umgekehrt *nowth* für *not* ib. 36/48, *nought* für *not* ib. 739/111); Rost 36 *nought*.

Anm.: Einen Plural *noughts* hat nur Greene entwickelt:
Never to late, Bd. II, 307
  Needless noughts, as crisps and scarfs, worn a la morisco,;
dagegen liegt wohl adverbiales *s* vor:
Menaphon 89
  Leauing behinde nought but repentant thoughts
  Of daies ill spent, for that which profit noughts.
Never to late, Bd. II, 269
  My feeble wit, that then prevailed noughts,
  Perforce presented homage to his ill:

§ 72. *nothing.*

Als Regel gilt *nothing*, seltener ist *nothyng*. Die Schreibung in zwei Wörtern fast nur bei Gruppe II, sehr häufig in den P. L. und hier mit Varianten von *no* (s. d. § 68).

Anm.: Confl. of Consc. 72 *nething* ist schottische Form an einer Dialektstelle.

§ 73. *some.*

Als Regel gilt *some*; daneben zuweilen *som, somme*, in Gruppe II (vereinzelt in Gruppe I) *sum(m)(e)*. Andere Schreibungen der P. L. *soom(e), swm, sum(me), soumme*.

Anm. 1: Im 15. Jahrhundert scheint zum Teil noch ein (wenn auch wohl nur traditionell graphischer) Unterschied zwischen *sum* als Sg. und *summe* als Pl. (wie me. besonders bei Piers Ploughman, cf. Mätzner I, 333) gemacht zu sein. Man vgl. P. L. 18/34 ... *he hath be stured by summe from his lernyng...*, dagegen ib. *sum persone*, während wieder 18/35 ... *summe come to the Kinges presence*...

807/212 ... *sum write of trespas*, dagegen ... *these arn summe of ther namys of Scrowby*.
Aber 806/207 auch *by soumme well disposed brother*.

Anm. 2: Verbindungen mit *some*:
some one stets getrennt } mit graphischen Varianten beider Bestandteile,
some body meist getrennt
some thyng(e) noch oft getrennt,
sometyme(s) seltener getrennt,
sŏme(e)what (*qat* P. L. 428/73, cf. § 59, Anm. 1) seltener getrennt;
Rost 51 *somthing, somtimes, somwhat, somwhere* meist ohne *e*.

§ 74. *enough*.

Als Regel gilt im 16. Jahrhundert *enough*, daneben jedoch (wie meist im 15. Jahrhundert) noch vielfach, vorherrschend bei Gruppe II, *ynough(e)* (me. *enogh, inoh[e]*), *anough(e)*; *ynow(e)* (me. *inow[e], inou*), bei dieser allein *ynowghe, anowghe, y(i)nough*, letzteres recht zahlreich in den P. L., wo auch *ynoghe, i nowge*, abgesehen von offenbaren und unwesentlichen Schreibfehlern; Rost 20 über das auch bei Milton mehrfach vorkommende *anough*.

§ 75. *few*.

Als Regel gilt *few*, vereinzelt ist *fewe*. Diary of Machyn 74 einmal *fuwe*, in den P. L. und Digby Myst. (162/661) auch mit dem bekannten *ff*.

Als Komparativ und Superlativ erscheinen stets *fewer* und *fewest*.

Anm.: Für Tyndale's Testament ist charakteristisch *feawe* (z. B. Matth. 7/14, 15/34 etc., wo die Auth. Vers. und die Rev. Vers. stets *few* haben), das sich auch bei Roy Fl. 76/49 findet; cf. Sopp 292. Lummert p. 6 und Würzner p. 150 *eaw* für *eu(ew)* in *deaw*.

§ 76. *much*.

Als Regel gilt *much(e)*; daneben vereinzelt in Gruppe I (z. B. Four Elements 22, 43, Calisto and Mel. 75), mehrfach in Gruppe II *moch(e)* = *moch(e), mych(e)* = me. *miche*, in letzterer auch *mutch(e), motch*.

Anm.: Die nördliche Form *mykel, mickle* ist im 15. und 16. Jahrhundert gar nicht so selten, wie sich aus folgendem Verzeichnis der in unseren Texten vorkommenden Belege ersehen lässt:

P. L. 363/534 ... *I thank you mekel of that ye have doone for me or seide;*

Digby Myst. 31/109 (*mykyll*), 55/22 (*mykyl*), 210/1140 (*mekill*), Myst.
ed. Hone 74 (*mykel*[*l*]), M. 37/3 (*mykel*), 262/3, 371/22, 434/2, Fl. (Book of
St. Albans) 10/27, 10/41 (*mekyl*), 195/46 (Balladen *mykkel*), 199/7 (desgl.
mickle), World and Child 249, 255, R. R. Doister 32, Appius and Virg. 140,
Peele, Verm. 173, 157 (2 mal), Greene, Alph. 27, 28, 44 (2 mal), 52, 62,
Look. Glass 98, James IV 81, 156, Pinner 189, Verm. 281, Marl., Edw. II
253, Dido 401, Sidney, Arcadia 411, 706, Lodge, Wounds 119.

§ 77. *any.*

Me. ēni, āni, ōni.

Als Regel gilt im 15. und 16. Jahrhundert *any*; daneben
in Gruppe II *anie, anye, annie, annye* (vereinzelt in Gruppe I);
ony, eny, einmal (Fl. [Briefe] 346/3) *heny* mit analogischer Uebertragung des verstummten (cf. Greene, James IV 114 *this ten ours*)
anlautenden *h* (wie *hothyr* für *othyr* § 83, cf. *Hynglond* Fl.
(hist. Volkslieder) 161/16, P. L. 424/68 *helder* für *elder*, ib. 452, 103
a hothe für *an oathe* etc.), in den P. L. *any, ony*(*e*)*, eny.*

Anm.: Verbindungen mit *any*:
any one, subst. und adj., stets getrennt,
any body, meist getrennt,
any man ist selten,
any thing, meist getrennt (NB. auch in adverbiellem Sinne, z. B. R. A.,
Toxophilus 95 ... *yf he be any thyng learned at al* ...).

§ 78. *many.*

Me. *meni*(*e*)*, mani*(*e*)*, moni*(*e*).

Als Regel gilt für das 15. und 16. Jahrhundert *many*, vereinzelt ist *manie*. In Gruppe II auch *meny, mony* (letzteres
me. charakteristisch für nördlichen besonders schottischen
Dialekt, cf. Morsb., Me. Gr. § 89, Anm. 2, hier im Diary of
Machyn 54, 63 etc., sowie in den P. L. (s. u.) wohl nach *ony*);
in den P. L. *meny, manÿ, mony, måney.*

Anm.: Verbindung mit *many*: *many a one* (*many one*, cf. § 238,
Anmerkung).

§ 79. *each.*

Als Regel gilt im 16. Jahrhundert *each*. Zahlreich im 15.
selten im 16. Jahrhundert sind *eche, ich*(*e*)*, ych*(*e*).

Anm.: Verbindungen mit *each*:
each one, meist getrennt (auch *ech*(*e*) *on, echo*, ausser Variationen mit
each), im 15. und 16. Jahrhundert noch recht gebräuchlich,
each man, stets getrennt, ist seltener,
each body, stets getrennt, ist selten (R. R. Doister 81, Sidney, Arc. 513),
each thing, stets getrennt, nicht ungebräuchlich.

§ 80. *every*.

Als Regel gelten *every, euery, everie*, vereinzelt mit Synkope *eu'ry, eury*, in den P. L. auch *hevery* 428/73 (cf. *heny* für *eny* § 77); Rost 15 *every*, einmal *everie*.

Anm. 1: *eberych(e)* findet sich mehrfach in den P. L., vereinzelt sonst im 16. Jahrhundert, zuletzt bei Kyd, Cornelia 242 als *ever-each*.

Anm. 2: *everychon(e)*, auch getrennt *every(-)chon(e)* ist häufiger, z. B.: P. L. 526/233, 856/277, M. 76/33, Fl. (Balladen) 174/94, Digby Myst. 13/313, 16/396, Everyman 138, Hickscorner 170, Heywood, P. P. 358, Interl. of Youth 12, zuletzt in unseren Quellen J. Juggler 137.

Anm. 3: Die entsprechende nördliche Form ist in unseren Texten einmal (P. L. 918/362) belegt:

The Rebels' Proclamation, die beginnt „*To be knowyn to all the northe partes of England*..."

and thys to be fulfyllyd and kept by every ylke comenere upon peyn of dethe.

Anm. 4: Verbindungen mit *every*:
every on(e), stets getrennt, am häufigsten,
every body, e'rybody, meist getrennt, häufiger als
every man, stets getrennt,
every thing(e), noch zahlreich getrennt.

§ 81. *either*.

Als Regel gilt *either* neben seltenerem *eyther*. Vereinzelt *ether* (Joy, Ap. 23, Fl. [Balladen] 196/32), *ethar* (Fl. [Balladen] 200/43), im M. öfter *eider*, in den P. L. auch *owther* = me. *auther, other*).

§ 82. *neither*.

Als Regel gilt *neither* neben seltenerem *neyther*. Gelegentlich findet sich *nother* = me. *nother*: Fl. (Briefe) 332/22, 26, Heywood, P. P. 368, J. Juggler 114, vereinzelt *nether* = me. *nether*: Plumpton Correspondance 210, Joy, Ap. 7.

§ 83. *other*.

Als Regel gilt *other*; daneben in Gruppe II *othir, hothyr* (cf. *heny* für *eny* § 77), *othre, odur*; in den P. L. *other, othir, othyr, othre, (h)oder, odir, (h)odyr*, im Plural auch *otherys*.

Anm. 1: Die Schreibung *nother* in der ersten Ausgabe von Heywood, P. P. (s. ib. p. 344 Anm.) gegen *no other* der übrigen stellt sich als eine Verwechselung mit *nother* für *neither* (ib. 368) seitens des Druckers dar.

Anm. 2: In Bezug auf die Pluralbildung sind die Formen ohne *s* noch während des ganzen 16. Jahrhunderts üblich, wenn sie auch in der

2. Hälfte stark abnehmen. Nach 1600 scheinen sie schon nicht mehr als volkstümlich gegolten zu haben, denn die Ausgaben von Marlowe's Edward II aus den Jahren 1612 und 1622 haben z. B. p. 197 das *other* der Ausgabe von 1598 in *others* geändert; doch kommt *other* als Plural nach Franz 397 f. noch „häufig" im 17. Jahrhundert vor.

Der Wechsel von *other* und *others* erklärt *others* für *other*: Plumpt. Corr. 162 und R. A., Schoolemaster 41.

Anm. 3: Die aus *thet other* (wie *the tone* aus *thet one*, cf. § 67 Anm.) entstandene Form *the tother* (Mätzner I, 338), sowie das mit Apokope des *e* über *th'other* entstandene *thother* sind zahlreich im 15. Jahrh. in den P. L., seltener, aber immerhin noch ziemlich häufig im 16. Jahrh. zu finden, z. B.:

the tother: P. L. 72/94 ... *I have hit lever than the tother*;, ib. 678/20, Myst. ed. Hone 24, Fl. (More) 218/17, Joy, Ap. 7, 12, 13 etc., Latimer Sermons 113;

th'other: P. L. 941/392, Nice Wanton 171, New Custom 30, Greene, Verm. 304, Puttenham 44, Lyly, Loves Metam. 239, Three Lords 410;

thother: M. 179/18, Leyc. Corr. 218. Eine Weiterbildung von *thother* durch nochmalige missverständliche Vorsetzung des Artikels, also *the thother*, findet sich nur im Diary of Machyn als *the thodur*: ib. 5 ... *and the thodur parte was the yerle of Harfford*... (124, 238, 287).

Anm. 4: Für *other* erscheint eine (noch jetzt dialektisch in Somerset als *wither* lebendige [cf. Nicolai, Herrigs Archiv 55, 386]) Form *wother* (Luick § 85):

Fl. (Roy and Barlowe) 72/4
    Prestes also they have in reverence
    With all wother persones of the spretualte
ib. 75/25   *Oure master also I dare saye*
    With many wother prestes gaye,
ib. 76/38   *Celarius, Symphorian, and wother mo,*
ib. 76/49   *the wother syde,* ib. 82/10 *none wother thinge,* ib. 89/27 *in none wother vse,*

Fl. (Tyndale) 224/43 *The one axeth and requyreth, the wother perdoneth and forgeveth. The one treateneth, the wother promyseth.*

ib. 225/39 ... *many wordes, which are wother wyse onderstonde of the commen people*:

Joy, Ap. 26 *then eny wother before,* ib. 31, 32, 47, 48; 49 *by wother men.*

(Dagegen liegt für die von Sopp 300 angeführten Fälle zum Teil ein Irrtum vor; Matth. 6/15 heisst es *other*, Joh. 7/46 hat überhaupt kein *other*; 1. Cor. 11/34 und 2. Cor. 8/13 hat nur die Ausgabe von 1525 *wother*.)

Hieraus können wir nun mit Sicherheit schliessen:

Der (schon me. vorhandene, cf. Luick § 85) *w*-Vorschlag ist, obwohl ursprünglich örtlich beschränkt, mit der ersten Hälfte des 16. Jahrhunderts in die Schriftsprache eingedrungen, und dass er allgemein verstanden wurde, dürfte zweifellos aus der Volkstümlichkeit der Werke Joy's und Tyndale's, die für weite Schichten der Bevölkerung bestimmt waren, hervorgehen.

Anm. 5: Verbindungen mit *other*:
another, das infolge der silbenanlautenden Aussprache des *n* missverständlich *a nother* geschrieben wird (cf. P. L. 60/74 *a nold debate*, Diary of Machyn 35 *a nold man; a nowre tür an hour* ib. 39), zahllos in den P. L. 99/134, 150/202 etc. etc., sonst bei Joy, Ap. 11, 24, Suppl. to Henry VIII 55, R. A., Toxophilus 56, 101, Schoolemaster 41; P. L. 705/61, 62 *an nother messenger*, Leyc. Corr. 174 *by an nother meanes*.

Besonders charakteristisch sind 3 Fälle aus Machyn's Diary, die, mit gänzlicher Unterdrückung des *a*, wohl auf solche Aussprache in der damaligen Umgangssprache des Volkes hindeuten:

p. 4 *...and she was burnyd at Canturbury...and on at Hospryng, and nodur in the he way to Canturbury...*

ib. 45 *...and at Ledyne-hall was nodur pagant hangyd with cloth of gold...*

ib. 87 *The XVIII day of May was nodur lad wypyd at the same post in Chepe...*

otherwise (wofür übrigens im 15. wie im 16. Jahrhundert das einfache *other* nicht selten gebraucht wird, z. B.: P. L. 862/290, Fl. [poet. Volksbücher] 202/9, Marl., Hero 49, Puttenham 56, Leyc. Corr. 57) in wechselnder Schreibung von *other* und *wise*,
other wáy(e)s, zusammen oder getrennt.

§ 84. *all*.

Als Regel gilt *all*; daneben, seltener in Gruppe I, häufiger in Gruppe II, *al, alle*.

Anm.: *All thing(e)(s)* steht im 15. und 16. Jahrhundert zahlreich im Sinne von *everything*, z. B.: P. L. 297, 775/161, Calisto and Mel. 53, Marl., Jew 2199, Kyd, Jeronimo 356 etc. etc.

§ 85. *sundry*.

Als Regel gilt *sundry*, vereinzelt ist *sundrye, sondry(e)*, in den P. L. auch *sondery*.

Anm.: *Sundry* ist besonders beliebt auf Titeln von Dramen, z. B.: Lyly, Mother Bombie 71,
Mother Bombie. As it was sundry times played by the children of Pauls, ferner Greene, Alph. 2
The Comicall Historie of Alphonsus, King of Aragon. As it hath bene sundrie times acted.
Greene, James IV 70
As it hath bene sundrie times publikely plaide.
Marlowe, Tamburlaine 1
Deuided into two Tragicall Discourses, as they were sundrie times shewed vpon Stages in the Citie of London.
etc. etc.

§ 86. *divers*.

Als Regel gilt *divers(e)*, *diuers(e)*; Fl. (Caxton) 1/2, 2/25 *dyuerce*, Diary of Machyn 110, 112 *dyver*, in den P. L. (5/21, 19/36, 310) auch ein Plural *diverseś*.

§ 87. *certain*.

Erscheint meist als *certain(e)*, aber auch als *certeýn(e)*, *certen*, Diary of Machyn und Bale, Thre Lawes auch *serten*, in ersterem ferner *sarten*.

§ 88. *several*.

Als Regel gelten die Formen mit *ll*, seltener sind die mit *l*; P. L. 239/330 *severelle places*.

Syntax.

Personalpronomen.

Auslassung des Personalpronomens.

§ 89. Vorbemerkung.

Wir behandeln zunächst diejenigen Fälle, die sich als Ueberreste eines alten Sprachzustandes darstellen. Solange Flexionsendungen zur Unterscheidung der Personen dienen, sind Personalpronomina, sofern nicht ein besonderer Nachdruck auf sie gelegt wird, überflüssig; sobald dieselben verfallen, treten Personalpronomina an ihre Stelle; dies gilt bereits für das Ae. als Regel. Daneben kommen jedoch, unterstützt und stets aufs neue wieder aufgefrischt durch den gerade in dieser Hinsicht recht sparsamen Zug der Umgangssprache, im Ae. wie im Me. noch zahlreiche Fälle der Auslassung vor, wenn sich das Pronomen aus dem Zusammenhang ergänzen lässt (Beispiele für das Ae. und Me. s. Kellner, Hist. Outlines, § 270 ff. sowie Wülfing § 223 ff.).

Diese Fälle der Auslassung nun nehmen im Laufe der englischen Sprachgeschichte infolge des Strebens nach möglichster Prägnanz und Genauigkeit des Ausdrucks in schriftlicher Darstellung fortgesetzt ab. Im 15. und 16. Jahrhundert sind jedoch noch mancherlei Reste des alten Sprachzustandes erhalten, die wir im folgenden näher betrachten wollen.

Allgemein müssen wir vorausschicken, dass wir der Ansicht Einenkels, Neuphil. Centralblatt III, 5 ff., der die Auslassung des Personalpronomens durch den Einfluss des afr. erklären will, durchaus nicht beipflichten können; die (sogen.) auslassung des Personalpronomens ist eben eine Erscheinung, die

sich durch die Geschichte der englischen Sprache
unter Berücksichtigung der Umgangssprache vollauf
erklärt, und zu deren Deutung wir des afr. nicht be-
dürfen.

Zur Erklärung und Rechtfertigung des Wortes „Auslassung" mag noch bemerkt werden, dass diese Bezeichnung
für das Fehlen des Personalpronomens nur der Zweckmässig-
keit halber gewählt wurde; in Wirklichkeit können wir nicht
eigentlich da von einer Auslassung des Pronomens reden, wo
dieses erst sekundär ist.

I. Auslassung des Pronomens als Subjekt.
A. Das Pronomen ist aus dem Zusammenhang zu ergänzen.

1. Auslassung von *thou*.
a) In Fragesätzen.
§ 90.

Digby Myst. 70/435 *Cum owzt, I sey! heryst nat what I seye?* Four Elements 23, Calisto and Mel. 67 *Wottest who is here?*, ib. 68 *How knowest all this?*, ib. 71, 72, 82,

Fl. (John Holt, Lac puerorum) 298/18

Howe knowest a partycyple of the present tens? By his englysshe and by his latyn.

Bale, Kynge Johan 95, Lusty Juventus 95,

G. G. Needle 184

Art deaf, thou whoreson boy? Cock, I say; why, canst not hear?

ib. 194, 204, 206,

ib. 218 *Com'st behind me, thou withered witch?*

Damon and Pithias 58

O Stephano, hast thou been so long with me,
And yet dost not know the force of true amity?

Sidney, Astr. and Stella 34/5 (36/8)

Art not asham'd to publish thy disease?

Peele, Arr. of Paris 8

Think'st, Faunus, that these goddesses will take our gifts in worth?, ib. 9,

Misfortunes of Arthur 266 *Why stayest? It must be done!*

Kyd, Spanish Tragedy 88
Dost see yonder boy with the box in his hand?
ib. 119 *Art a painter? canst paint me a tear or a wound?
A groan or a sigh? canst paint me such a tree as this?*
Lyly, Mother Bombie 127
why then did'st not bring a stoole with thee, that I might sit downe?
Greene, Bacon and Bungay 148
Sirrah Ned, wouldst fain have her? ib. Look. Glass 62, 126,
Marl., Tamburlaine 3277
*Villain, art thou the sonne of Tamburlaine,
And fear'st to die ...*
Faust 1174, Jew 598 *What wast, I prethe?*
ib. 847 *What, hast the Philosophers stone?* ib. 1199, 1698, 1930,
Ovid 117 *Why enviest me?* ib. 151 *What dost?*
ib. 158 *Ungrate, why feign'st new fears, and dost refuse?*

b) In Aussagesätzen.
§ 91.

G. G. Needle 205
Durst swear of a book, cheard him roar, straight after ich was gone;
ib. 206 *To-morrow, Hodge, if we chance to meet, shall see what I will say.*
Lyly, Euphues 325
If he loue not, then stretchest out lyke a Wyre-drawer ...
Lyly, Endimion 10
Loth I am Endimion thou shouldest die, because I love thee well; and that shouldest live, it grieveth me ...
Sidney, Astrophel and Stella 6/1
Some Louers speake ... of wot not what desires,
Peele, Arr. of Paris 7
Peace man, for shame, shalt have both lambs and dams and flocks and herds ...
ib. 8 *Say'st truly, Faunus;*
Greene, Looking Glass 85
Fear not; let's go; I'll quiet her, shalt see.
Cf. ib. 66 die zwei Lesarten teils mit, teils ohne *thou* etc.

Bemerkungen zu 1, a und b.
§ 92.
Die Auslassung von *thou* beruht auf altem Brauche; cf. Mätzner II, 30.

Diese Fälle erlangen im 16. Jahrhundert besonders seit dem Aufblühen des Dramas eine ausserordentliche Verbreitung in der Literatur. Wir dürfen daraus schliessen, dass sie besonders der Umgangssprache eigen waren; gerade der schnell dahineilende Dialog der Umgangssprache war es, der die Auslassung des Personalpronomens in einem Falle begünstigte, wo überdies die erhaltene Flexionsendung die Person noch deutlich bezeichnete.

In einer nicht geringen Anzahl von Fällen ist der Wohlklang für das Fehlen des Pronomens mit massgebend geworden, man vergleiche:

Calisto and Melibaea 83
What say'st thou, what say'st, thou shameful enemy?
Heywood, Pardoner and Friar 222
But I say, thou lewd fellow thou,
Haddest none other time to show thy bulls but now?
Heywood, P. P. 377
What callst her, quoth he, thou whoreson? etc.

Einzelne der gegebenen Belege können auch unter 2a gerechnet werden.

2. Auslassung des Personalpronomens in coordinierten Sätzen.

a) Bei gleichem Subjekt in beiden Sätzen.
§ 93.

Die Satzverbindung kann eine mehrfache sein; um den Gesamteindruck jedoch nicht zu verwirren, teilen wir in dieser Hinsicht nicht weiter.

In paratakischen Sätzen wird das Pronomen bekanntlich auch jetzt nicht bei jedem neuen Verbum wiederholt; solche noch heute möglichen Fälle aus damaliger Zeit sind z. B.:

M. 111/10 ... *syre Tor prayed the heremyte to pray for hym, he sayd he wold and betooke hym to god, and so mounted vpon horsbak* ...

R. A., Toxophilus 142
Therfore seyng I wyll be glad to folowe your counsell in chosynge my bowe and other instrumentes, and also am ashamed that I can shote no better than I can... (jetzt nur mit Aenderung der Stellung ... *and am also ashamed...*).
R. A., Schoolemaster 147
This booke was so liked, that it had few to read it, but none to folow it: But was presentlie contemned:
Conflict of Conscience 36
*I said to Eve: tush, tush, thou shalt not die,
But rather shalt as God know everything;*
Lyly, Endimion 76
Divine Cynthia, by whom I receive my life, and am content to end it;
Marlowe, Massacre 329
*Fain would I find some means to speak with him,
But cannot, and therefore am enforc'd to write,*
Puttenham 172
...which thing peraduenture I deny not in part, and neuerthelesse for some causes thought them not so necessarie:
etc. etc.
Andere Fälle würden jetzt anders (Partizipialkonstr. etc.) gewendet werden, so:
P. L. 520/220
I recomaund me to yow, and have reseyvid II lettirs...
ib. 950/401 *Cousyn Paston I recommaunde me unto you, and have received your letter...*
Dagegen sind zu den im jetzigen Englisch nicht mehr möglichen Fällen folgende zu rechnen:
P. L. 178/236
And the seid Chirche seyth as for that he hath seyd of hem that he hath appelyd befor this tyme, he woll awow itt and abyd therby; and seyth that he woll appele one that hath mor nobelys than they have all...
Heywood, P. P. 345
*Wherefore I went myself to the self thing
In every place and without saying:
Had as much pardon there assuredly,
As ye can promise me here doubtfully.*

Lyly, Euphues 426
Manye dayes hee vsed speach with the Ladyes, sundrye tymes with the Gentle-women, with all became so familyar, that he was of all earnestly beloued.

Puttenham 279
The French king neither liking of his errant, nor yet of his pompous speech, said somewhat sharply, I pray thee good fellow clawe me not where I itch not with thy sacred maiestie, but goe to thy businesse, and tell thine errand in such termes as are decent betwixt enemies, for thy master is not my frend, and turned him to a Prince of the bloud, who stoode by saying...
etc. etc.

Hieraus ergiebt sich:
Auslassung des Personalpronomens in koordinierten Sätzen bei gleichem Subjekt findet im 15. und 16. Jahrh. noch in Fällen statt, wo es im jetzigen Englisch nicht mehr möglich ist, d. h. in solchen, wo das den Satz einleitende Subjekt vom Verbum des zweiten Satzes durch eine Reihe von Satzteilen, oft auch durch einen oder mehrere Sätze getrennt ist. Je nach der Länge dieser erscheinen die einzelnen Fälle vom Standpunkt des ne. Sprachgefühls aus mehr oder weniger **auffällig.**

b) Bei verschiedenem Subjekt.
§ 94.

P. L. 36/48
My fader Garneyss senttee me worde, that he xulde ben her the nexch weke, and my emme also, and pleyn hem her with herr hawkys, and thei xulde have me hom with hem;

M. 67/14 *... and so the kyng mounted on his hors and Merlyn on another and so rode vnto Carlyon...*

ib. 109/30 *... thenne ther cam one armed on horsbak, and dressyd his shelde, and cam fast toward Tor, and he dressid hym ageynst hym, and so ranne to gyders that...*

ib. 403/12 *And kynge Mark rode ageynst hym, and smote eche other ful hard...*

Dieser Fall, der also nur im 15. Jahrhundert zu belegen ist, ist in unseren Belegen insofern recht begreiflich, als die in dem ausgelassenen *they* liegenden Personen stets unmittelbar vorher genannt sind; die beiden letzten Fälle berühren sich zum Teil mit den unter B. mitgeteilten.

2. Auslassung des Personalpronomens bei subordinierter Satzfügung.

§ 95.

P. L. 18/33 ... *till that he shal mowe have speche with ... to that ende that, the defaulte of eny suche persone knowen unto him, shal mowe ordeigne therupon as theim shel thenke expedient and behovefull.*

ib. 179/238 *and when they had kepte hym as long as they lyst, lete hym goo.*

ib. 437/86 *Perys of Legh come to Lynne opon Cristynmesse Even in the fresshest wise, and there he dyned so as was.*

R. A., Toxophilus 19
Yf any man wyll applye these thynges togyther, shal not se the one farre differ from the other.

Lyly, Euphues 383
Consider we are in England, where our demeanour will be narrowly marked if we treade a wrie, and our follyes mocked if vse wrangling.

Egerton Pap. 293
Being arrived, not as a marchant but as a messenger to the Emperour with letters, was, accordinge to the custome of the countrey, received ashore by certaine gentlemen...

Kyd, Span. 99 zwei Fälle schon bei Ritzenfeldt, p. 7.

Rare Triumphs 205
uplandish, now, cham worse than ever was.

Bemerkungen hierzu:
Bei gleichem Subjekt im Haupt- und Nebensatze, wobei die Aufeinanderfolge beider belanglos ist, hat Auslassung des Personalpronomens in einem von beiden im 15. und 16. Jahrhundert noch bisweilen statt. Für den Nebensatz kann auch ein Partizipium eintreten.

Anm.: In dem von Ritzenfeldt p. 7 angeführten Fall Span. 113/10 liegt nicht Auslassung des Personalpronomens, sondern des Relativs vor, ebensowenig in dem Falle Span. 122/15, wo *find* vielmehr Imperativ ist.

B. Das Pronomen
ist aus einem vorhergehenden Casus obliquus zu ergänzen.

§ 96.

P. L. 36/48 *I pray yow hertely that wol wochesaf to sende me a letter as hastely as ʒe may...*

P. L. 58/71 *Yt happyd hym to have a knavys loste, in pleyn termes to swhyve a quene, and so dyd in the Konyneclosse.*

P. L. 65/80 *And as to the tytyll of rigth that I have to the Lordship of Gressam schal with in short tyme be knoweyn...*

ib. 522/224 *...the wiche reknyng greved the seide Nicholas his fadir, and seide...*

ib. 829/245 *As for your son Water, his labor and lernyng hathe be, and is, yn the Faculte of Art, and is well sped there yn, and may be Bacheler..*

Malory 709/21 *...and thenne sawe they a knyghte armed al in whyte and was rychely horsed...*

Caxton, Eneydos 12/30
And thys comen to the knowleche of plasmator, thoughte in his minde, and conspyred the deth of the sayd polydorus.

Fox 53 *...it repenteth hym and is sory that he euer hath don spoken or trespaced ayenst you...*

Fl. (Caxton) 3/36 *Therfor I haue practysed and lerned at my grete charge and dispense to ordeyne this said book in prynte after the manner and forme as ye may here see, and is not wreton with penne and ynke...*

Lyly, Euphues 317 *Thou broughtest me into Englande Euphues to see and am blynde, to secke aduentures, and I haue lost myself, to remedy loue...*

Peele, Edw. I 176
Bind fast the traitor and bring him away, that the law may justly pass upon him, and receive the reward of monstrous treasons and villainy...

Bemerkungen hierzu:

Diese Fälle, die ihren Grund in dem Nachklang des sich mehr der Umgangssprache anschliessenden Ausdrucks einer weniger geregelten Sprachperiode finden, werden zum Teil dadurch recht begreiflich, dass das durch das ausgelassene

Pronomen bestimmte Subjekt das logische Subjekt des ersten Satzes bildet; P. L. 65/80 ist eine Konstruktion ἀπὸ κοινοῦ.

Anm. 1: In dem Falle Fox 100
My lord was not this ynough sayd and warned, who so wold vnderstonde it, that al that he fonde he shold saye the contrarye ist „My lord" zugleich als Dativ und Nom. gefasst.

Anm. 2: Zur Erklärung von Fällen wie:
P. L. 132/175 *Whych I trust to God shall better have hys cours then it hath beforn;*
ib. 787/175 *and I prey to Jesu preserve yow und yours.*
ib. 49/62 *...I beseche the blissed Trinite, preserve you in honor and prosperite.*
ib. 515,212 *And I pray God hertely send us good tydyngs of yow...*
R. A., Schoolemaster 61
which, I praie God, kepe out of England...
P. L. 411/42 *...ʒour welfar and good prosperite the qwyche I pray God encresse to His plesur and ʒowr herts hesse;*
P. L. 812/220 *What so ever it menyth, I prey God send us good tydynges...*
Fl. (Skelton) 64/77
I pray God saue the kynge
Gorboduc 57
And so I pray the Goddes requite it them, etc., die in dieser oder ähnlicher Form eine ständige Briefflos kel in den P. L. bilden und von Kellner, Outl. § 274 mit Recht als eine Konstruktion ἀπὸ κοινοῦ aufgefasst werden, bieten sich besonders die letzten 5 Fälle dar, wo *I pray* auch als absolut ohne Objekt aufgefasst werden kann, cf. P. L. 53/65 *I preye write to myn modre...*
P. L. 56/70 *I pray ye that ʒe wyl vwche save...*
etc. etc.

C. Pronomen beim Imperativ.

§ 97.

Im Ae. wird der Imperativ nur dann mit dem Pronomen verbunden, wenn dasselbe nachdrücklich hervorgehoben werden soll. Sonst genügen die Flexionsendungen zur Bezeichnung der Person. Im Me. tritt ein allmälicher Umschwung der ae. Verhältnisse ein. Insoweit die Flexionsendungen zur Unterscheidung der Personen genügen, zeigt sich der ae. Zustand erhalten. Da aber Sg. und Pl. des Imperativs in der Form schon vielfach zusammenfielen, musste die Sprache nach einem anderen Unterscheidungsmerkmal suchen, und was war natürlicher, als dass der Gebrauch der Personalpronomina,

der früher nur in besonderen Fällen beim Imperativ eintrat,
der in den übrigen Modi zum grössten Teile durchgeführt war,
nun beim Imperativ auf alle Fälle ausgedehnt wurde — das
Pronomen konnte auch in solchen Fällen zum Imperativ treten, in denen keine nachdrückliche Hervorhebung beabsichtigt war.

Wie steht es nun im 15. und 16. Jahrhundert?

Für das 15. und 16. Jahrhundert ist die Zusetzung
des Pronomens zum Imperativ besonders charakteristisch. Das zeigen, von den Paston Letters anfangend bis
zum Jahre 1600, fast alle untersuchten Denkmäler, mögen sie
der Epik, Lyrik, Dramatik (und zwar sowohl der Hofdichter
Lyly als auch Volksdichter wie Marlowe, Peele, Greene) oder
der Prosa angehören; ausgenommen sind natürlich solche
Werke, die ihrem Charakter gemäss Imperative überhaupt
nicht aufweisen, wie das Diary of Dr. Dee und das von Machyn.
Was die Ausdehnung dieser Erscheinung innerhalb der beiden
Jahrhunderte anlangt, so ist sie sich im allgemeinen bis etwa
1550 ziemlich gleich geblieben. In der 2. Hälfte des 16. Jahrhunderts zeigt sich eine erhebliche (relative) Zunahme in den
untersuchten Quellen — das Drama spielt die führende Rolle
in der englischen Literatur.

Im übrigen lassen sich keine genauen Grenzen ziehen.
Beide Ausdrucksweisen, Imperativ mit Pronomen und Imperativ
ohne Pronomen, waren stets nebeneinander üblich, und wenn
wir im elisabethanischen Drama besonders zahlreiche Belege
finden für den Imperativ mit Pronomen, so zeugt das eben für
den Zustand in der Umgangssprache. Im übrigen war
die Frage, welches von beiden, vielfach teils von der
unbewussten Laune des Augenblicks (sozusagen „wie es
einem gerade in den Sinn kam"), teils von dem Zusammenhang der Rede, teils auch endlich, und nicht zum mindesten, in der Poesie von den Erfordernissen des
Verses abhängig.

Da Beispiele fast auf jeder Seite anzutreffen sind, beschränken wir uns auf einige wenige:

P. L. 758/136 *And send ye me word...*

M. 73/16 *...go ye into yonder barge...*

Fl. (Balladen) 182/119 *Lye thou there thou proud sheryf*

Gorboduc 1454
>In the meane while, make you in redynes
>Such band of horsemen as ye may prepare.

Marl., Faust 326
>Learne thou of Faustus manly fortitude,.

NB. Das nebenbei das Pronomen wie früher, so auch jetzt eines wirkungsvolleren Nachdruckes wegen gesetzt wurde, bedarf wohl keiner besonderen Erwähnung.

§ 98.

Im einzelnen ist noch folgendes zu bemerken:

1. Eine Reihe formelhafter Ausdrücke und Redewendungen weist verschiedene Entwicklung auf:

Die Wendung *wete ye (you, thou) well* wird stets mit dem Pronomen verbunden, z. B.: M. 422/6, (585/34, 450/21), Everyman 114. Ebenso die vor allem im Drama vorkommende Wendung *be ye sure* mit vereinzelten Ausnahmen, z. B.:

Pl. Corr. 179 *For be ye sure, Sir, that...*
Digby Mysteries 6/121
>*My lord, be ye sure accordyng to your will,*

Heywood, P. P. 347 *But be ye sure I would be woe,*
Greene, Alph. 22 *But be thou sure that...*
dagegen ib. 58 *No, no, be sure that...*
Trial of Treasure 292 *Be sure you shall want no kind of wealthiness.*

Ferner *know(e) ye*, das besonders dem Briefstil angehört (z. B. Egerton Pap. 142, 158), aber auch sonst (Gorb. 605, Sidney, Arcadia 117) belegt ist. Hierher ist auch zu rechnen *marke ye well* (Digby Myst. 215/1327).

Das ebenfalls formelhafte *farewell* steht fast ausnahmslos in Begleitung des Pronomens, also *fare thou (ye, you) well*. Niemals dagegen findet sich das G. G. Needle zahlreich (z. B. 227) vorkommende *see now* mit dem Pronomen.

2. Eine Art Imper. praet. entbehrt stets des Pronomens, z. B.:

Marl., Edw. II 232 *Away! tarry no answer, but begone!*
Greene, James IV 146 *My friends begone...*

Fl. (Barclay) 94/25 *Haue done now Faustus, laye there a strawe and rest*
Marl., Edw. II 250 *Madam, have done with care and sad complaint:* etc. etc.

3. Tyndale verwendet in seiner Bibelübersetzung meist den Imperativ mit Pronomen. Die Auth. Vers und Rev. Vers. haben dasselbe teils beibehalten wie
Matth. 6/33 *But rather seke ye fyrst the kyngdome of heauen ...*
Luk. 9/13 *Giue ye them to eate*, teils geändert 2. Cor. 13/11 *Fynallye brethren fare ye well ... (farewell).*

4. In der Anrede vor dem Vokativ ist das Pronomen (seit dem Ae., cf. Mätzner II, 169) im 15. Jahrhundert, und im 16. besonders in der dramatischen Literatur ganz gewöhnlich, z. B.
P. L. 697/50 *Thow prowd prest. Thow prowd sqwyer.*
G. G. Needle 205 *Ye foorlish dolt ...*
Tindale, Ap. 13/26 *Ye men and bethren ...* (Auth. Vers. und Rev. Vers. lassen *ye* weg).
Lyly, Woman 188 *Ascend, thou winged pursevant of love.*
Marl., Tamb. 1367
Awake, ye men of Memphis!
Lodge, Wounds 143
You men of Rome, my fellow-mates in arms,.
Vergl. auch § 135 (*you* für *ye*) Ende.

D. Auslassung von *it* in unpersönlichen Sätzen.

1. Bei unpersönlichen mit einem Objekt verbundenen Verben.

§ 99.

Im Ae. und Me. gilt die Auslassung von *it* geradezu als Regel; cf. Mätzner II, 32 f.

Im 15., weniger (s. u.) im 16. Jahrhundert fehlt *it* fast immer, wenn der oblique Pronominalkasus vor dem Verbum (aus euphonischen Gründen erklärlich, das Zusammentreffen zweier Personalpronomina wird also hart vermieden), seltener, wenn er nach demselben steht.

Doch werden diese Fälle schon seit dem 15. Jahrhundert von einer anderen Richtung her eingeschränkt, durch den Uebergang von unpersönlichen zu persönlichen Verben (Anhang I).

a) Das Objekt steht vor dem Verbum.

to avail: Everyman 105
> Thee availeth not to cry, weep, and pray:

Tancred and Gismonda 34

to behove: M. 187/4 (Fox 110)
> ...and therfore the behoueth now to chese...

to beseem: Misfortunes of Arthur 266
> but thee beseems more high revenge.

to happen: M. 200/2
And at the laste by fortune hym happend ageynst a nyghte to come to a fayr courtelage..., Fox 33, Fl. (Balladen) 177/61.

to long: Fl. (Balladen) 185/126 (ib. 192/24)
> Me longeth sore to bernysdale

to lyke: M. 74/3 *me lyketh* (ib. 182/10) Fl. (Skelton) 65/111 *as hym lykys*.

to lyst: P. L. 201/278 ...*and kepte hym as long as them lyst*... ib. 348/510, M. 90/27, Fox 16, Fl. (Skelton) 64/112, Joy, Ap. 50, R. R. Doister 12, Marriage of Wit 333, Peele, Arr. 17.

to nede: P. L. 255/348 ...*than me nedith*, Fl. (More) 41/27 *Me nedeth not to bost*...

to owe: M. 694/6 ...*he bere me as truly as my oughte to be born.*
Fox 13, 47.

to pertain: Greene, Looking Glass 92
> To thee pertains to do the Lord's command.

to please: P. L. 203/287 *as hym plesith*, R. R. Doister 31 *when him please*, Peele, Alcazar 140 *as him pleaseth best*.

to seme: P. L. 71/90 ...*me semeth he were good*... ib. 423/67 *And as you semeth best*... M. 409/27, 576/33, 740/10, Fl. (Balladen) 169/26, J. Juggler 116, Sidney, Ap. 32.

me thinks, me thought: im 15./16. Jahrhundert wie heute üblich, Beispiele unnötig. Dagegen erscheinen *thinks* und *thought* im 15. und 16. Jahrhundert auch in Verbindung mit *him, us, them*, z. B.:

P. L. 18/34 ...*into what place him thenketh necessarie*...

M. 661/22 *And at the laste hym thoughte they of the castel were putte to the werse.*

M. 806/20 *Syre vs thynketh best that*...
M. 620/3 ... *that hem thought*...
Fl. (Balladen) 189/116
> *Them thought they herd a woman wepe*
> etc. etc.

b) Das Objekt steht nach dem Verbum.
Peele, Edw. I 106
> *Honour and love him, as behoves him best,*

Fl. (Skelton) 67/121 *Neuer half the paine*
> *Was betwene you twayne*
> *Pyramus and Thesbe*
> *As then befel to me*

P. L. 317/429 *And haped me, at the fyrste abordyng of us, we toke a schippe*...
Kyd, Span. 158 *Behoves thee there, Hieronimo, to be revenged:*
Kyd, Corn. 185
> *What helps thee now t'have tam'd both land and sea?*

aber *What helps it thee, that*...
P. L. 135/180 *Like you to witte that*...
ib. 626/382 ... *to goo in to what place shall like theim*...
Appius and Virg. 144 ... *as liketh thee best.*
M. 606/30 ... *and that caused yow to haue moche more labour for my sake than nedeth yow.*
Fox 71 ... *and preue it as ought to be to a noble man*...

P. L. 135/181 *Plese you that ye remembr* ib. 150/204, 205, Plumpt. Corr. 5, 15, Fl. (Briefe) 346/36, 350/1, More, Utopia 44 *as please them,* Jacob and Esau 226 *if please you,* Camb. 212, Damon and P. 81, Soliman and Pers. 340, Peele, Edw. I 83, Marl., Faust II 1331, Greene, Looking Glass 99.
> etc. etc.

NB. Dass bei *to please* die Fälle so zahlreich sind, erklärt sich aus der weitverbreiteten Verwendung dieses Verbums in Höflichkeitsformeln.

Anm.: Besonders mag hier das bei Shakspere so häufige (Abbot § 37) *how chance,* das formelhaft ist, bemerkt werden:
G. G. Needle 231, Soliman and Perseda 279, Sir Clyomon 518 b, Greene, Bacon and Bungay 195
> *How chance you tary so long.*

Marl., Jew 123 *How chance you came not*..., Edw. II 191 etc.
Doch haben wir hier wohl keine Auslassung von it, sondern persönliche Konstruktion verbunden mit einer solchen ἀπὸ κοινοῦ anzunehmen.

2. Bei unpersönlichen mit keinem Objekt verbundenen Verben.

§ 100.

Dieser Fall ist besonders (noch jetzt, cf. Mätzner II, 32 f.) in Komparativsätzen häufig; einzelne Fälle (*may happe*, cf. G. G. Needle 243 *Yea, Master Baily, there is a thing you know not on, mayhap:* sowie *sufficeth* (s. Anm.) sind formelhaft.

P. L. 42/54 ... *and therfore may happe it shall be makid newe...*

Joy, Apol. 6 *If Christ be preached to haue rysen, how happeneth that some of you saie there is no ressureccion?*

G. G. Needle 194 *Boots not, man, to tell,*

Lyly, Euphues 219 ... *if by some more curious then needeth, it shall be tolde hym...*

Kyd, Span. 28
Yet what avails to wail Andrea's death,
From whence Horatio proves my second love?

Peele, Edw. I 141, Marl., Mass. 349, Edw. II 230, Sidney, Arc. 683 ... *accusing Zelmane of more curious stay than needed...*

Jack Straw 393 *Here's a stir more than needs;*

Hensl. Diary 8 ... *as apereth by his bell...*

Alleyn Papers 17 etc.

Anm.: Als besonderen Fall finden wir Auslassung von *it* bei *sufficeth*:
Peele, Arr. 60
Sufficeth me, it shall be none of mine.
Kyd, Span. 143
Sufficeth thee that poor Hieronimo
Cannot forget his son Horatio;
ib. 169 *Sufficeth, I may not, nor I will not tell thee.*
Greene, Bacon and Bungay 166
Suffice to me he is England's paramour.
Looking Glass 79 *therfore suffice, the Usurer hath done me wrong;*
Menaphon 58
Sufficeth at this instant to vnfolde...
Rare Triumphs 229
Enough sufficeth to confirm your might.

3. Bei *to be*.

§ 101.

Hierfür gilt im ganzen das für 2 gesagte.

P. L. 177/235 ... *and never was spokyn of ther.*

P. L. 263/362 ... *as he hath had in commanndement, and was his part to doo;*

P. L. 357/525 ... *and the Quene and the Prynce byth in Walys alway. And is with hir the Duc of Excestre and other* ...

Digby Myst. 111/1499
þat day he satt vp-on wateris,
As holy wrytt berytt wettnesse.

Fox 8 *Therof hym had be better to haue hold his pees* ...

Fl. (Caxton) 3/13 ... *as a fore is sayd*. .

M. 80/33 ... *and ther was told hym the aduenture of the swerd* ...

M. 800,22 ... *for loue that tyme was not as is now adayes.*

Latimer, Sermons 144
and euen so is possible he maye haue ryghte ...

J. Knox 38 ... *as is before declared* ...

Gorb. 57 *And so I pray the Goddes requite it them,*
And so they will, for so is wont to be.

G. G. Needle 207
Good lord! shall never be my luck my nee'le again to spy?

Misfortunes of Arthur 270
Look back in time: too late is to repent,
When furious rage hath once cut off the choice.

Introductory Sketch 154
The ancient Councils and Synods, as is noted by the Ecclesiastical Story ...

Puttenham 25 ... *as is sayd before* ...

Leycester Corr. 322 ... *I beseech you to hast awaie the monie as soone as may be* ...

etc. etc.

Anm. 1: Die schon me. (z. B. Chaucer, Knightes Tale 759, 1108) belegte Wendung *if so be* ist als eine halb erstarrte zu betrachten, daher meist ohne Pronomen (doch kommen daneben Fälle mit Pronomen vor, z. B.: P. L. 768/148, Plumpt. Corr. 68, Lyly, Euphues 196, Marlowe, Greene etc.):

P. L. 674/12 ... *I tryst to se yow, if so be that eny of the Kynges hows com in to Norwyche.*

ib. 739/109 ... *alweys reservyng that if so be that Mastresse Eberton wyll dele with me, that ye shold not conclude in the other place* ...

M. (373/31), 412/1 *And yf so be ye can descryue what ye bere*...
Plumpt. Corr. 30 *and as for your awne, if so be ye will that*... (ib. 204)
Tyndale, Eph. 4/21 *But ye haue not so learned Christ, yf so be ye haue hearde of him*... (Auth. Vers. und Rev. Vers. ebenso),
ib., 1 Peter 2/3 (Auth. Vers. und Rev. Vers. andere Wendung).
Latimer, Sermons 29
R. A., Toxophilus 95, More, Utopia 65.
etc.

Wahrscheinlich wurde der Auslassung in diesen Fällen auch durch die Anlehnung an *al be it, how be it* entgegengewirkt, cf. Lyly, Euphues 50 *if so be it* (Stellung von *it*!) *they thought not one too many;* in der zweiten Hälfte des 16. Jahrh. bemerkten wir nur: Disob. Child 285, 304.

Dasselbe nun auch im praeteritum ist nur im 15. Jahrhundert zu belegen, doch war es da eine sehr populäre Erscheinung:

P. L. 733/104 ... *and iffe so weer that a good mariage myght be had*...
P. L. 739/109 ... *thow so wer that Eberton wold not geve so moche*...
P. L. 780/167 ... *and (= if) so were that myn uncle and Herry Heydon made none ende in therin*...
M. 807/26 ... *yf soo were that the quene were on that morne broughte to the fyre*...

Anm. 2: Eine sonst nicht beobachtete Erklärungsformel, die eine Eigentümlichkeit Puttenhams bildet, möge an dieser Stelle Erwähnung finden; „*and is*" *(was)* steht in diesen Fällen für *and that (which) is (was)*; cf. ib. 213 *and this is by the figure Prosonomata*... und weiter *which is when ye turne and translace a word into many sundry shapes*...

91 ... *a maner of speach ... which they called ὁμοιοτέλευτον, and was the nearest that they approched to our ryme:*
(Uebergangsbeispiel, *which* als Objekt zu *called* und als Subjekt zu *was* gefasst).

121 *one other pretie conceit we will impart vnto you and then trouble you with no more, and is also borrowed primitiuely of the Poet*...

178 *Ye haue another auricular figure of defect, and is when we begin to speake a thing*...

214, 226, 228, 244, 300,

274 *so as when they heare or see any thing tending that way they commonly blush, and is a part greatly praised in all women.*

II. Auslassung des Personalpronomens als Objekt.

§ 102.

Für diesen Fall ist schon von Kellner, Outl. § 275 B., der zwei Belege aus Gower und Caxton beibringt, eine plausible Erklärung gegeben; wir können hier nicht eigentlich von einer Auslassung reden, vielmehr gilt das zu *as for* etc. gehörige

Substantiv infolge Wechsels der Konstruktion zugleich als Objekt (ein analoger Fall für das Subjekt ist P. L. 813/221 *Towchyng the cause of my wrytyng to yowr masterschep is…*) des folgenden Verbs. Aus den Belegen ergiebt sich, dass diese Fälle nicht auf das 15. Jahrhundert beschränkt, wenn auch äusserst selten sind.

P. L. 672/11 *As for pardon, I can never get, withowght I schold paye to myche money for it.*

M. 433/25 *As for my name they shalle not wete, but telle hem …*

Introductory Sketch 129
And touching the Author of the Booke, he knoweth not, unless yt were Penry:

Andere Fälle der Auslassung des Personalpronomens.

Hieran schliessen wir diejenigen Fälle der Auslassung des Personalpronomens, welche sich erst sekundär, zum Teil vielleicht in Erinnerung an den noch in Resten vorhandenen alten Sprachzustand, entwickelt haben, und die ihre Entstehung teils einem bewussten Streben nach Kürze, teils dem schnellen Dialog der Umgangssprache verdanken.

§ 103.

1. Auslassung des Personalpronomens (bez. Subjekts überhaupt) zum Zweck der Erzielung eines knappen, gedrungenen Stils.

Das Personalpronomen (bez. Subjekt überhaupt) kann fehlen bei Inhaltsangaben bez. Auszügen aus anderen Werken, ferner im Protokoll eines Verhörs, wenn die betr. Person bekannt ist oder als bekannt vorausgesetzt wird. Im ersteren Fall ist Werk (und Verfasser) oft am Rande vermerkt.

Fl. (theol. Schriften) 243/43
Teacheth in a few leeues shortly all the poyson that …
ergänze Frith.

Udall, Demonstr 31
When he appoynted Eradius to succeed him, sayth, it was the approoued right and custome, that …
Am Rande: *Augustine.*

ib. *In an Epistle to Damasus, Ambrose etc. sayth, we have ordayned Nectarius Bishopp of Constantinople* ...
Am Rande: *Concil. constan. text. tripart. hist. lib.* 9 *cap.* 14.
ib. 57 *Speaking of these Deacons, lamenteth that* ...
Am Rande: *P. Mart. rom.* 12.
ib. *Describing the Deacons of the Apostles time, sayth, that* ...
Am Rande: *Caluin Insti. lib.* 4 *cap.* 3. *sect.* 9.
ib 62 *Lamenteth, that some were found* ...
Am Rande: *Bucer de reg. Christ.* 15.
Introductory Sketch 82
The examinacion of Walter Rogers. *Saith, that about the Moneth of September last ... the said Perkes did open, and declare to this Examinate that* ...
(Es folgen 8 Druckzeilen.)
Sayth further, that ... (es folgen 5 Druckzeilen.)
And further sayth, that ...
ib. 85 The examinations of Nicholas Tomkins. *And being asked of whome he could have had them, sayth he might have had them of Waldegrave* ... (ebenso Egerton Pap. 169, 170).

Diesen Fall, der zu den in § 95 genannten gehört, führen wir hier an, um die nahe Berührung dieser mit den folgenden zu zeigen.

ib. 89 Examination of Udall.
Being asked whether he were not acquainted with the makinge of the demonstracion of Discipline and of Diotrephes. Saith that he desireth to be pardoned ...
ib. noch ein Beleg, ebenso 90 2 Fälle (einmal für *saith-desireth*); 92, 93, 129, 131 sind dem Fall von 82 ähnlich.

ib. 103 Verhör des Buchbinders.
Being demanded, whether Master Pigot of Coventry was privy to the printing of any of those Bookes, which were there printed. Answereth that of certain knowledge he is not able to charge him ...

Leycester Corr. 21
Wondereth and complaineth that the queen will not seale his booke of assurance.

Der Grund der Auslassung ist in den meisten dieser Fälle in der Absicht zu suchen, eine möglichste Kürze zu erreichen, bei den ersteren auch wohl der Uebersicht wegen,

indem man Werk (und Verfasser) behufs schnellerer Orientierung
aus dem Text heraus an den Rand setzte.

Anm.: In den Bühnenanweisungen steht das Pronomen regelmässig, wenn es die Deutlichkeit verlangt, also häufig im Plural, z.B.:
Heywood, P. P. 355
    Here they sing.
  Lyly, Woman 155 *They draw the curtains from before Natur's shop . . .*
(Dagegen Cambyses 180 *Draw their swords*, wo *their* die Person andeutet.)

Im Sg., wo zwar die erhaltene Flexionsendung die Person bezeichnet, herrscht grosse Inkonsequenz auch in ein und demselben Stücke, cf. z. B.:
  Marl., Jew 1760 *He writes.*
  ib. 1819 *Throws it on the flour.*
  ib. 1820 *Kisses him.*
  Greene, Orlando 38 *He beateth him out:*
  ib. 41 *Lies down and sleeps.*
  ib. 44 *He lieth down again.*
                etc. etc.

§ 104.

2. Auslassung des Personalpronomens, auf dem schnellen Dialog der Umgangssprache beruhend.

Diese Fälle treten in unseren Texten erst mit dem Beginn des 16. Jahrhunderts auf, wenn sie auch höchstwahrscheinlich in der Volkssprache schon früher vorhanden waren.

  Fl. (Balladen) 189/89
    Haue here your keys sayd adam bel
  Heywood, The Four P. P. 345
    Had as much pardon there assuredly,
    As ye can promise here doubtfully.
  R. R. Doister 19 *Where good stale ale is will drinke no water I trust.*
  G. G. Needle 208
    Gammer: Why, know you any tidings which way my nee'le is gone?
    Diccon: Yea, that I do, doubtless, as ye shall hear anon,
'A see a thing this matter toucheth within these twenty hours,
  Damon and Pithias 80
    By'r Lady, you are of good complexion,
    A right Croyden sanguine, beshrew me.
  Greene, Orlando 49
    Beshrew you, lordings, but you do your worst;

Peele, Arr. 16
Dare say no nymph in Ida woods hath more:
Conflict of Conscience 92
For though I lack instruments to put him to smart,
Yet shall he abide in a hellish black dungeon:
As for blocks, stocks and irons, I warrant him want none.
Marl., Mass. 302
Nav.: Doth not your grace know the man that gave them you?
Old Queen of Nav.: Not well; but do remember such a man.
etc. etc.

Anm. 1: Die beiden Wendungen *I pray* und *I would* sind besonders zu betrachten. Auslassung von *I* ist hier erst im 16. Jahrhundert (der Fall P. L. 256/349 *and pray you* gehört unter die Fälle § 94) zu beobachten.

I pray: Auslassung findet sich zahlreich im Drama, war also in der Umgangssprache recht gewöhnlich. Als erster Beleg fand sich R. R. Doister 49 *May not folks be honest, pray you, though they be pore?*

Dann G. G. Needle 181, Lyly, End. 52, Kyd, Span. 105, Greene, Pinner 184, Peele, Edw. I 86, Marl., Jew 1350. etc. etc.

Weitergehender Einfluss der Umgangssprache zeigt sich in Fällen wie: Kyd, Jer. 356 *Pr'y-thee, let him go.*, Greene, Alph. 12 *But, prithee, tell me...*, Marl., Faust 945 *Robin, prethe come away...*

I would und *I woulde to God.* Auslassung von *I* findet sich seit Anfang des 16. Jahrhunderts vorwiegend im Drama. Erster Beleg: Four Elements 19
Now would to God I had that man now here.

Dann Fl. (More) 40/4, R. A., Schoolemaster 54, 132, 140, R. R. Doister 53 zuerst bei *I would*:
Woulde I might for your sake, spende a thousand pound land.

Gorb. 1091, Kyd, Jer. 373, Peele, David and Beths. 11, Marl., Jew 1721 etc. etc. Besonders häufig bei Lyly, sowohl im Euphues 62, 63, 64 etc., wie in seinen Dramen Camp. 119, Woman 186, Galathea 222 etc.

Auf die Volkstümlichkeit der Auslassung weist hin: Knack to Know a Knave 561
Honesty: Sirrah, tell me who hath most poor men in suit at this Sizes?
Clerk: That hath Walter Would-have-more:

Auch hier waren in manchen Fällen Gründe des Wohlklangs für das Fehlen des Pronomens massgebend, z. B.:
Sidney, Astr. p. 51/2
...ô would I then had lied;

Marl., Ovid 156
Would I were culpable of some offence!

Durch Contamination von *I would to God* und *would God* entsteht *I would God*, das in unseren Texten Latimer, Sermons 35, Leycester Corr.

256, 259, 339 (nur in Briefen des Earl of Leycester), als *'Would God* auch bei Peele, David and Bethsabe 77 belegt ist.

Anm. 2: *Advise you and assure you.*
Eine genaue Grenze zwischen den Fällen, wo wir Auslassung des Personalpronomens annehmen oder *you* als Reflexivum fassen können, ist nicht zu ziehen; vgl. jedoch § 176, 2 und 3.

Dagegen haben wir natürlich zweifellos Auslassung von *I* in Fällen wie:
Peele, Edward I 89 *Assure your grace we shall have great supply*
Marl., Edward II 241 *Yet have we friends, assure your grace, in England.*

Anm. 3: Niemals fand sich Auslassung von *I* bei *I thank you* (z. B. Four Elements 36, Interl. of Youth 19, Marl., Edw. II 220), für das übrigens im 15. und 16. Jahrhundert meist andere Wendungen gebraucht werden, so:

godamercy, z. B.: Digby Myst. 127/1920, Peele, Edw. I 128, Greene, Pinner 203;

gramercy, z. B.: Four Elements 34, Peele, Edw. I 83, Greene, Pinner 169;

thanks, (am gebräuchlichsten in elisabethanischer Zeit) z. B.: Peele, Edw. I 55, Greene, Alph. 21, Marlowe, Edw. II 195, Soliman and Pers. 349, Mucedorus 224, oder ähnliches.

Weiterentwicklung.

Solche und ähnliche Fälle der Auslassung des Personalpronomens sind auch im Ne. noch zum Teil gebräuchlich (cf. Foelsing-Koch III, § 168).

Pleonastischer Gebrauch des Personalpronomens.

§ 105. Vorbemerkung.

Der durch die Hinzufügung eines Personalpronomens bewirkten Verdoppelung des Subjekts (oder Objekts) kann eine doppelte Ursache zu Grunde liegen:

Einmal kann es sich darum handeln, das Subjekt bezw. Objekt mit stärkerem Nachdruck hervorzuheben, indem es aus dem Satze absolut herausgestellt und in diesem durch das Personalpronomen ersetzt wird; das ist zweifellos bei den in § 107 f. mitgeteilten Beispielen der Fall, zum Teil auch bei denen in § 109 f.

Andrerseits dient zum Teil bei diesen letzteren, wie bei denen in § 111 f. die Hinzufügung des Personalpronomens dazu, das Subjekt bezw. Objekt wieder in der Erinnerung des Hörers, besonders bei langem Zwischensatz, wachzurufen

(Anakoluth). Fast in allen Fällen haben wir es mit einer Erscheinung zu thun, die ursprünglich und vor allem der Umgangssprache angehört, die aber auch, und, wie wir sehen werden, im 15. und 16. Jahrhundert noch in hervorragendem Masse, in der Schriftsprache zu finden ist, aus der sie verschwindet, je mehr das Streben nach Korrektheit des Ausdrucks in der Sprache an Einfluss gewinnt.

§ 106.

1. Das Pronomen geht dem Nomen, zu dem es gehört, voran.

Aus unseren Belegen ergiebt sich, dass dieser Fall für das 15. und 16. Jahrhundert auf die Poesie beschränkt ist, der im Ae. und Me. weitere Ausdehnung auch in der Prosa hatte (cf. Wülfing § 235 a sowie Mätzner II, 18).

Fl. (Balladen) 178/25
They wente vp to the sayles
These yemen all thre

ib. 186/74 *The were outlawed for Venyson*
These thre yemen evere chone.

§ 107.

2. Das Pronomen folgt dem Nomen, zu dem es gehört.

a) Unmittelbar.

Dieser Brauch ist im Ae. (Wülfing § 235 a, Belege aus Beda, Engl. St. XX, 458 f.) und Me. (Ellinger 124, sowie Mätzner II, 19) recht verbreitet.

P. L. 273/375 ... *Maister Scrope he shall be beneficed yn the ryʒt of it.*

ib. 357/526 *And the Duc of Somerset he is in Depe...*

ib. 406/32 *The preests of Castyr they be streytely take hede at þe Roberd Harmerer and hoder...*

ib. 462/119 *Othyr tydings the were come to London...*

ib. 582/313 *A ryche juelle yt ys at neede for all the cuntre...*

P. L. 617/364 *On Fryday the Bysshope he sent for her...*

M. 257/31, ib. 508/26 *And syr Percynale he fought...*

ib. 814/19 *...but my lord he sayd...*

ib. 857/7 *...my lord kyng Arthur he shal berye me...*

Fox 81 ... *but maister abrion of tryer he is a wyse man*
Anc. Myst. ed. Hone 17
    And, in the lyke wyse, Anne, thy blyssyd wyff,
    Sche shal ber' a childe, schal hygth Mary,
Fl. (Vaux) 35/20 *My lustes they do me leeue,*
ib. 35/26 *And lusty life away she leapes,*
ib. (Skelton) 62/22 *Her lewde lyppes twayne*
            The slauer men sayne
ib. 66/81 *And yet this proude Antiochus*
        He is so ambicious
ib. 70/90 *My pen it is vnable*
        My hand it is vnstable
ib. (Liebeslieder) 134/1 *My loue she morneth for me.*
ib. 135/32, 145/62,
ib. (Jagdlieder) 153/2 *The Birds they sing*
              The Deare they fling
              hey nony nony nony no.
              The Hounds they crye,
              The Hunters they flye.
ib. (historische Volkslieder) 158/24
        The Earle he hathe a wryting made
ib. 197/25, 197/31, 201/9, Bale, Kynge Johan 43,
World and Child 247
        A new name I shall give thee here:
        Love-Lust, Liking, in fere;
        These thy names they shall be,
Tyndale, Luk. 1/36
And(,) beholde, thy chosyn Elizabeth(,) she hath also conceaued a sone in her age.
(Auth. Vers. und Rev. Vers. ebenso, nur 2 Kommata mehr).
    Latimer, Sermons 174
        ... the Byshoppes they coulde laughe at it.
Gorboduc 1350
    The mother she hath died her cruell handes
    In bloud of her owne sonne...
ib. 1484
    The people are in armes and mutynies,
    The nobles they are busied how to cease.

Cambyses 228
>   *My Lord and Knyght, of truth I speak,*
>   *My heart it cannot choose;*

G. G. Needle 186
And Hodge he hied him after, till broke were both his shins:
ib. 203 *O gracious God, my heart it bursts!*
ib. 205, 207, 208, 209,
ib. 235 *The women they did nothing…*
ib. 242, 244, 247.

Marriage of Wit 359
>   *My life it stays on you alone…*

Lyly, Mother Bombie 130
>   *The Hackneyman hee whiskes with his wand…*

Kyd, Span. 14 *When he was taken, all the rest they fled,*
Peele, Arr. 12
>   *Fair Venus she hath let her sparrows fly,*

Peele, Edward I 129
>   *the Friar he shall instruct us in this cause…*

Peele, Verm. 182
>   *And, as ye wot, this war and tragic sport*
>   *It was for Helena.*

Marl., Faust 772 *O, but my godmother, she was a iolly gentlewoman…*

Greene, Looking Glass 74
My hairs surpass they not Apollo's lock's? (Franz. Konstruktion).

Greene, Verm. 267 *Dian she*
>   *Scap'd not free,*

Puttenham 191
Thy hands they made thee rich, thy pallat made thee poore.
ib. 222 *Rich, poore, holy, wise, all flesh it goes to ground.*
Mucedorus 231 *My father he may make…*
>   etc. etc.

Bemerkung hierzu:

Aus der grossen Zahl unserer Belege ergiebt sich, dass die pleonastische Verwendung des Personalpronomens in dieser Stellung eine allgemein verbreitete Erscheinung war, die vor allem der gesprochenen Volkssprache (man beachte die zahlreichen Fälle in der im Volkston geschriebenen Komödie

G. G. Needle) angehörte, aber auch in der Schriftsprache als nichts Ungewöhnliches galt, ja in der Lyrik sogar eine ausserordentliche Verbreitung fand.

Anm.: Morte Darthure 665/20
Sir Gawayn hym semed he came in to a medowe...
haben wir ein in diesem Falle seltenes Beispiel, dass das Pronomen im obliquus steht.

§ 108.

b) **Das Pronomen ist von seinem Beziehungsworte getrennt.**

α) Durch einen oder mehrere Satzteile.

1. Als Subjekt (schon ae., Wülfing § 235 b)

P. L. 527/234 *And thes he thynkyth it were a gret urt to my master tytyll.*

P. L. 870/302 *My lyfe, alas! it servyth of no thing* (Gedicht einer Dame).

M. 143/15 *... they name me wrongfully tho that gyue me that name ...*

ib. 391/17 *Thenne kyng Arthur with a grete egre herte he gate a spere in his hand ...*

ib. 465/22 *And thenne the good prynce Boudwyne at the landynge he areysed the countrey ...*

Fl. (Balladen) 199.8 *the dougheti dogglas on A shede he Rode alle his men beforne*

J. Juggler 115
His mistress, I know, she woll him blame,

Peele, Edw. I 121
this hot weather how it makes me sweat!

Puttenham 176
Faire maydes beautie (alack) with yeares it weares away.

Sidney, Arcadia 707
Th'epistle self such kind of words it had;

Hieraus ersehen wir, dass diese Fälle ungleich seltener sind als die unter a) behandelten und im 16. Jahrhundert mehr der Poesie angehören.

Anm. 1: M. 830/1
Thenne sir Lanncelot auaunced alle his noble knyghtes, and fyrste he auaunced them of his blood, that was syr Blamor, he made hym duke of

Lymosyn in gyan, and sir Bleoberys he made hym duke of poyters, and sir Gahalantyn he made hym duke of Ouerne etc. etc.
liegt kein Pleonasmus vor, vielmehr ist jedesmal *that was* zu ergänzen.

Anm. 2: P. L. 497/173 *Item, and yf it please it you* ... erklärt sich durch Kontamination von *yf it please you* und *please it you*; M. 204/16 *Thenne he dressid he is sheld* durch die Möglichkeit, Inversion eintreten zu lassen oder nicht; vgl. P. L. 543/263 ... *the cause why yt was nate endossed was* ...

Anm. 3: Durch die Schwierigkeit der Konstruktion bei relativer Anknüpfung erklärt sich: Sidney, Arcadia 732 *which* (welche) *he although he took to be Pamela, yet thinking no surety enough in a matter touching his neck, he went hard to the bedside of these unfortunate lovers* ...

Anm. 4: Wiederholung des Personalpronomens bei besonderer Hervorhebung:

Four Elements 95
    What, art thou here? I see well, I,
    The mo knaves the worse company.
Calisto and Melibaea 69
    Come hence, Parmeno, I love not this, I;
Heywood, Pardoner and Friar 222
    But I say, thou lewd fellow thou,
Bale, Thre Lawes 1569
    Tush, I heare them I, and that maketh me full sad.
R. R. Doister 80
    For about this houre is the tyme of likelyhood,
    That Gawyn Goodlucke by the sayings of Suresby,
    Would be at home, and lo yond I see hym I.
Jacob and Esau 210   *I reckon it best, I,*
    To bind your hands behind you, even as ye lie.
ib. 211 *He and Jacob are agreed, I dare say, I,*
ib. *Yea, and take vengeance, when I am dead too, I.*
ib. 232, Marriage of Wit 968,
Cambyses 215
    If it were to doo again, man, I durst do it, I.
ib. 230 *Four counsel theirs I mean not, I,*
ib. 247 *We can but thank you therefore, we can do no more, we.*
New Custom 39
    I force not, I, so the villain were dead.
Misfortunes of Arthur 309
    Condemn not mine attempts; he, only he,
    Is sole in fault that makes me thus thy foe.
G. G. Needle 196 *Cha no book, I.*
Kyd, Spanish Tragedy 26
    She, she herself, disguis'd in armour's mask
    Brought in a fresh supply of halberdiers,

ib. 47 *I doubt not, I, but she will stoop in time*: ib. 101, Cornelia 241
> *We fight not, we, like thieves, for others' wealth:*
> *We fight not, we, t'enlarge our xant confines:*

Lyly, Mother Bombie 82
Tush! spit not you, and I'le warrant I, my beard is as good as a handkerchieffe.

Peele, Edward I 161 *Ay, farmer, if you had been robbed of it; but if you be a gamester, I'll take no charge of you, I.*

Peele, David and Bethsabe 70
> *She, she, my dearest Bethsabe...*
> *Is fled the streets of fair Jerusalem,*

Rare Triumphs 202 *I can spose him, I.*
Tancred and Gismonda 91 *I, I the author of this tragedy.*
Marlowe, Faust 375
How, how, knaues-acre! 1, I thought that was al the land his father left him:
ib. 488 *I Mephastophilus, I giue it thee.*
Jew 28, 751; Jew 1677
> *The Law shall touch you, we'll but lead you, we:*

Edward II 189
> *I'll rather lose his friendship, I, then grant.*

Dido 376 *We come not, we, to wrong your Libyan gods,*
ib. 435 *I know not what you mean by treason, I;* Hero 32, Ovid 109; Lucan 277
> *He, he afflicts Rome that made me Rome's foe.*

Marprelate, Epistle 19
What i, I should report abroad, that cleargie men come vnto their promotions by Simonie?

Greene, Friar Bacon 201
> *Nay, Ned...I care not, I.*

Looking Glass 87 (Verschiedene Lesarten der Quartos), Orlando 49. Soliman and Perseda 344, 353,
Lodge, Wounds 135
> *I talk not, I, to please or him or thee,*

Mucedorus 210 *I know not, I;*
Barnfield, Gedichte 49
> *I meane, I, Pallas, and the Queene of Loue.*
> etc. etc.

Bemerkungen hierzu:

Dieser Fall ist, wie sich aus unseren Belegen, die zugleich ein Bild der zeitlichen Ausdehnung geben, fast ausschliesslich der dramatischen Literatur eigen und in Denkmäler anderer Art erst spät von dort aus eingedrungen. Er charakterisiert sich also als ein, und zwar beliebtes, rhetorisches Hilfsmittel in pathetischer Rede; zuweilen mag auch die Rücksicht auf den Reim auf seine Anwendung von Einfluss gewesen sein. Naturgemäss überwiegen die Fälle mit *I*.

Shakspere macht hiervon weitgehendsten Gebrauch (Deutschbein § 33, Schmidt 565 Sp. 1).

§ 109.

2. Als Objekt (schon ae., Wülfing § 236).

P. L. 779/166 *Item, where I tolde yow that the gowne clothe off olde chamlott, I wolde have it hoome for my suster Anne;*

M. 38/31 *...and this lord sir ector lete hym be sent for...*

M. 106/32 *...and the remenaunte he chaced hem...*

M. 148/6 *And alle she doth hyt for to cause hym to leue this countreye...*

M. 229/37 *...but alle that I dyd it for to preue...*

M. 284/9 *...and that pyece of the swerd the quene his syster kepte hit for euer.*

M. 442/33
And the eyght knyghtes he made them to swere...

Fox 113
And the debate bytwene yow I holde it on me.

Fl. (Barclay) 94/2
This wyse to labour, they count it for no payne

Fl. (Balladen) 172,3
*These bysshoppes and thyse archebysshoppes
Ye shall them bete and bynde*

Heywood, P. P. 343
Also your pain I not dispraise it;

Tyndale, Vorwort p. 1

R. A., Toxophilus 103 *And therfore this same hyghe and perfite waye of teachyng let vs leue it to hygher matters...*

Kyd, Spanish Tragedy 173
*False Pedringano, for his treachery,
Let him be dragg'd through boiling Acheron,*

G. G. Needle 183 (253)
My nee'le, alas, ich lost it, Hodge...

Lyly, Endimion 80
My unspotted thoughts, my languishing bodie, my discontented life, let them obtaine by princely favour, that...

Puttenham 174
And therfore al your figures of grammaticall construction, I accompt them but merely auricular...

Bemerkungen hierzu:
Diese Fälle sind also im 15. Jahrhundert ziemlich häufig, im 16. können wir einen Rückgang konstatieren, wenn sie auch in der Volkssprache noch entschieden lebendig waren.

§ 110.
β) Durch einen Nebensatz.

Das Personalpronomen nimmt ein vorangegangenes Subjekt wieder auf; je länger der Nebensatz ist, um so erklärlicher ist die Verwendung des Personalpronomens.

Im Ae. und Me. finden sich zahlreiche Fälle dieser Art (Wülfing § 235 d, Mätzner II, 19 ff.).

1. Durch einen Relativsatz.

P. L. 56/69 *and all that have don and seyd agens hym, they xul sore repent hem.*

ib. 132/172 *Wherfor such persones as have founde... they most effectuelly labour to my Lord Oxford...*

M. 199/29 *And the lorde that is owner of this castel I wold he receyued it as is ryght.*

M. 302/26 *Thenne it felle that sire Bleoberys and sire Blamore de ganys that were bretheren they hadde assomoned the kyng...*

M. 366/34 *The meane whyle the damoysel that syre Palomydes sente to seke sir Tristram she yede vnto sir Palomydes...*

M. 514/27 *And he that reuenged my dethe I wille that he haue my rede Cyte...*

M. 694/16
...he that shal prayse me moost, moost shalle he fynde me to blame...

M. 790/23 *And thenne sir Baraunt le apres that was called the Kyng with the honderd Knyghtes he assayed and fayled...*

Latimer, Sermons 55
All thinges yat are written in Gods boke, in the holye Byble, they were written before oure tyme...
ib. 130 *Al thinges yat are wrytten, thei are written, to be oure doctrine.*
ib. 177 *...my Lorde Chauncelour and suche other, what so euer they be, they do not all wayes seale...*
Tyndale, Matth. 21/42
The stone which the bylders refused, the same is set in the principall parte of the corner...
(Auth. Vers. und Rev. Vers. ebenso.)
Joh. 12/49 *but the father which sent me, he gaue me a commaundement.*
(Auth. Vers. und Rev. Vers. ebenso.)
G. G. Needle 175
She that set me to ditching, ich would she had the squirt.
ib. 247 *The tale I told before, the self-same tale it was his;*
Kyd, Cornelia 231
 Now Scipio, that long'd to show himself
 Descent of African... He durst affront me...
Udall, Demonstr. 60 *That whose seuerall parts is perpetuall...that same must be perpetuall:*
Lyly, Endimion 32
and therefore hee that began without care to settle his life, it is a signe without amendement he will end it.
etc. etc.

Bemerkung hierzu:
Diese Fälle sind also im 15. Jahrhundert häufiger wie im 16., wo sie aus der Schriftsprache mehr verdrängt werden. In einigen Fällen haben wir zur besonders starken Hervorhebung *the same* statt des einfachen Personalpronomens.

2. Durch Sätze anderer Art.
M. 459/19 *But at the last Kynge Mark and sir Dynas were they neuer soo lothe they withdrewen hem to the castel of Tyntagyll...*
Joy, Ap. 25
... that himselfe (though he wolde) yet can he not reuoke it and restore it me agene.

R. A., Toxophilus 104
And thus perfitnesse it selfe bycause it is neuer obteyned, euen therfore only doth it cause...

ib. 124 *These wooddes as they be most commonly vsed, so they be mooste fit to be vsed:*

ib. 150 *Wyse maysters whan they canne not winne the beste hauen, they are gladde of the nexte:*

Damon and Pithias 30
*Which virtue always though worldly things do not frame,
Yet doth she achieve to her followers immortal fame:*

Conflict of Conscience 66
Lyly, Endimion 8 ... *whose fall though it be desperate, yet shall it come by daring.*

Lyly, Euphues 130 (58)
The Grecians when they saw any one sluttishly fedde, they would say euen as nursses:

ib. 299 *so my minde though it could not be fired, for that I thought my selfe wise, yet was it almost consumed to ashes...*

Marlowe, Faust 227
... as this wine if it coulde speake, it would cuforme your worships,

Puttenham 280
The same translatour when he came to these wordes: Insignem... compulit. Hee turned it thus...

Wir sehen hieraus, dass diese Konstruktion noch im 16. Jahrhundert eine recht verbreitete war.

Anm.: Eine besondere Erwähnung verdienen hier diejenigen Fälle, wo bei relativer Anknüpfung das Relativum von einem Personalpronomen wieder aufgenommen wird. Wir beobachteten sie nur im 16. Jahrhundert, also in der Zeit, wo die relative Anknüpfung im Englischen ihren Höhepunkt erreicht (cf. § 229 f.):

Fl. (Barcl. Sallustübersetzung) 308/1
whiche after he had obtayned victory ouer Iugurth with greate glorye, triumph and fauoure of the commentie, he supported them in suche wyse agaynst the noble men:

Tyndale, Ap. 17/10 (23/33)
Which when they were come thyther, they entred into the synagoge of the Jewes.

(Auth. Vers. und Rev. Vers. *who — went.*)

R. A., Toxophilus 86
...which, as he is one, and hateth al diuision, so is he best of all pleased, to se...
ib. 99 ...the best shoter, which yf he be neuer so good, yet hath he many faulte...
Damon and Pithias 25 (38)
Which when it is spied, it is laugh'd out with a scoff,
Lyly, Euphues 297 (358)
...which though it merit no mercy to saue, it deserueth thankes of a friend...
Marlowe, Massacre 316
Which, as I hear, one Shekius takes it ill,
Sidney, Astr. XCIX (Vorrede des Druckers Nash)
Which although it be oftentimes imprisoned in Ladyes casks, and the president bookes of such as cannot see without another man's spectacles, yet at length it breakes foorth...
Sidney, Arcadia 87
which if it had been over-vehement, yet was it to be borne withal...
ib. 261 ...that virgin wax, Which while it is, it is all Asia's light.

§ 111.

γ) Durch ein einen Nebensatz vertretendes Partizip.

Nach den zahlreichen unter β mitgeteilten Fällen können diese nicht mehr auffallen, wenn sie auch vom ne. Sprachgefühl aus als recht hart empfunden werden:

Latimer, Sermons 123
He beynge a father vnto vs, he wyll heare vs soner...
ib. 154 *And afterwarde I beynge in the Tower, hauynge leaue to come to the Lieuetenauntes table, I hearde hym saye...*
Lyly, Euphues 378
...whereof one pient being mingled with fiue quartes of water, yet it keepeth his old strength and vertue...
Sidney, Arcadia 241 *But this matter being thus far begun, it became not the constancy of the princes for to leave it;*
ib. 770 *...with one blow struck it so clean off, that it falling betwixt the hands, and the body falling upon it, it made a shew as...*

§ 112.

3. *It* als Objekt bei intransitiven Verben.

Indem wir im übrigen für diese Erscheinung auf Kellner, Outl. § 283 und Koch § 306, für Kyd auch auf Ritzenfeldt p. 10

verweisen, geben wir im folgenden eine Reihe markanter Belege aus unseren Quellen, die zeigen, dass diese Erscheinung im 16. Jahrhundert — in unseren Quellen des 15. Jahrhunderts begegneten uns keine Beispiele — doch ziemlich verbreitet war.

Four Elements 47
>And I can dance it gingerly,
> „ „ „ foot it by and by,
> „ „ „ prank it properly,
> „ „ „ countenance comely,
> „ „ „ croak it courtesly,
> „ „ „ leap it lustily,
> „ „ „ turn it trimly,
> „ „ „ fisk it freshly,
> „ „ „ look it lordly.

Trial of Treasure 274
>I, Sturdiness, will face it out

Marriage of Wit 357
Nay, you must stout it, and face it out with the best:

Misfortunes of Arthur 294
>...we agreed, To war it out...

Greene, Friar Bacon 165
>Faith, Ned, and I'll lord it out till thou comest:

Orlando 18 Bid him come forth, and dance it if he dare,
Look. Glass 74 Madam, unless you coy it trick and trim,
Pinner 183
>Than I will trip it till I see my George.

Marlowe, Edward II 195
>Now let us in, and feast it royally.

Jew 1046
>For they themselues hold it a principle,
>Faith is not to be held with Heretickes;

Peele, Arr. 9
>Yea, jest it out till it go alone;

Edward I 132
>But she should court it with the proudest dames,

Jack Straw 404
>Neighbours and friends, never yield,
>But fight it lustily in the field:

4. Greene, Looking Glass 78
He thrusts the king out, and so they exeunt.
In dieser Bühnenanweisung soll sich *they exeunt* augenscheinlich auf den König und sein Gefolge beziehen, sodass kein Pleonasmus vorläge.

Weiterentwicklung.
Inbetreff der bei Sh. vorkommenden Fälle des pleonastisch verwandten Personalpronomens cf. Abbot § 242 f., Deutschbein § 32 f.

Fälle wie die in § 108, 109, 110 mitgeteilten gehören jetzt allein der Poesie an, solche wie in § 111 sind bei langem Zwischensatz noch möglich.

§ 113.
He und *she* zur Bezeichnung des Geschlechts.

Die durch den substantivischen Gebrauch (Koch § 308) veranlasste Verwendung der allein geschlechtlich unterschiedenen Personalpronomina (ausser *it*) zur Bezeichnung des Geschlechts scheint in Anlehnung an Ausdrücke wie *wretched I* (Kyd, Cornelia 191), *wretched we* (Marl., Edward II 252), *that other I* (J. Juggler 144), besonders unter Einfluss von Fällen wie *she-ape* (Fox 3), *hee-diuell* (Marlowe, Faust 416), *she devil* (Greene, Bacon 154), *she-chirurgeon* (Jests of Peele 276) etc. vor der Mitte des 16. Jahrhunderts entstanden zu sein. Frühere Beispiele aus dem 15. Jahrhundert bemerkten wir nicht.

Bale, Thre Lawes 422
Infid.: What, sumtyme thu wert an he.
Idol.: Yea, but now ych am a she,
Sidney, Astrophel and Stella 1/1
Louing in trueth, and fayne my loue in verse to show,
That the deere Shee, might take some pleasure of my pain:
ib. 91/1
And whiles faire you, my Sunne thus ouerspred
With absence vale I liue in sorrowes night,
Peele, Edward I 172
Follow! pursue! spare not the proudest he
That havocks England's sacred royalty.

Peele, Arr. 23, 24
   The only she that wins this prize am I.
Dieser Fall zeigt, dass bei der Entstehung dieser Erscheinung auch Fälle von Einfluss waren wie:
Rare Triumphs 151
               ... I am not she,
   That seeks with Venus to compare in her supremacy.
(Weitere Belege siehe § 125 Anm. 2.)
Peele, Arr. 30 *And I appoint which is the fairest she,*
ib. 58 *Who is the fairest she...*
Kyd, Jeronimo 357
   I'll be the he-one then, and rid thee soon
   Of this dull, leaden, and tormenting elf.
Soliman and Perseda 197
   But truth is a shee, and so alwaies painted.
Greene, Alphousus 54
         Let Amurack himself,
   Or any he, the proudest of you all,
   But offer once but to unsheath his sword,
Greene, James IV 93
   Ill warrant thee her virtues may compare
   With the proudest she that waits upon your queen.
Greene, Verm. 247
         Bright she was, for 'twas a she
   That trac'd her steps towards me:
Sidney, Arcadia 406
   And think she is a she that doth thee move.
Sidney, Sonn. and Transl. 137
         Alas! a lovely She no pity taketh
   To know my miseries;

Weiterentwicklung.

Diese Erscheinung ist ebenso bei Shakspere (Abbot § 224, Deutschbein § 38) üblich, wie im 17. und 18. Jahrhundert (Franz a. a. O. 213), heute meist mit dem Beigeschmack des Humors oder der Ironie; vgl. auch Koch, Archiv 91, 2.

§ 114.
Majestätsplural.

Ueber die Verwendung des erst im Me. (Koch § 209) auftretenden und noch heute üblichen Plur. maj. während des 15. und 16. Jahrhunderts ist nichts besonderes zu sagen; es mag jedoch betont werden, dass Fürstlichkeiten denselben **nur in offizieller Redeweise** verwenden. Dieses wird am besten durch die Briefe der Königin Elizabeth an König James illustriert. Briefe, die einen **offiziellen** Charakter tragen, beginnen z. B. p. 67

Right high right excellent and mighty prince, our deerest brother and cousin, we greete you well; oder p. 74

Right high right excellent and right mightie prince, our dearest brother and cousin, in our hartiest manner we commend us unto you.

Dagegen Briefe **vertraulichen** Charakters:
I am greatly satisfied, my deare brother, that I find...
Ebenso James an Elizabeth p. 147 gegen 5, 14.

etc. etc.

Kasusvertauschungen beim Personalpronomen.

§ 115. Vorbemerkung.

Was diese Erscheinung der englischen Sprachgeschichte anlangt, so ist es das Verdienst Jespersens gewesen, auf diesem Gebiete einmal grundsätzlich und gründlich aufzuräumen mit der beliebten Methode, in „wissenschaftlichen" Arbeiten einfach den Tatbestand zu konstatieren, anstatt die Erscheinungen auch zu erklären. Das Verdienst Jespersens ist allgemein anerkannt, wir wollen versuchen, auf dem von ihm vorgezeichneten Wege weiterzuschreiten und unter Anwendung und Vertiefung seiner Methode die in Frage stehende Erscheinung für eine Zeit behandeln, die diese Fälle wohl nicht gerade herausgebildet, wohl aber zum grossen Teil zum Eigentum der Schriftsprache gemacht hat — das 15. und 16. Jahrhundert, in dem der Einfluss der Umgangssprache auf die Literatursprache überhaupt von ganz erheblichem Einflusse gewesen ist.

Von dem für § 116—132 gesammelten Material kam uns einiges abhanden, das jedoch das Gesamtbild nicht wesentlich beeinträchtigt hätte. Die bereits von Jespersen mitgeteilten und genügend erklärten Fälle bleiben natürlich so wie so aus dem Spiele. Alle anderen (abgesehen von *ye, you* und *it is me*) führen wir im folgenden nach Erklärungsgründen geordnet vor.

I. Contamination.
§ 116.

Kyd, Jeronimo 363
And.: Prince Balthezar, shall's meet?
Bal.: Meet, Don Andrea? yes, in the battle's bowels;

Schon Jesp. § 186 deutet die Erklärung an; es sei gestattet, dieselbe hier vollkommen durchzuführen.

In diesem Falle liegt Contamination vor: *shall's meet* bildet ausser einer Frage zugleich eine Aufforderung; eine Aufforderung wird, wenn der Sprechende sich mit einschliesst, im 16. Jahrhundert teils, und zwar vorwiegend in der 1. Hälfte, durch die 1. Pl. pr. gegeben (z. B. Fl. [theol. Schriften] 213/21, Four Elements 47, R. R. Doister 65, Lyly, Euphues 72, Kyd, Span. 46, Jer. 373, Peele, Edw. I 185, Greene, James IV 118, Marl., Tamb. 2483 etc.), in der 2. Hälfte jedoch meist durch die Umschreibung mit *let* (z. B. Marl., Tamb. 324 *Come, let vs martch.*, Edw. II 279 *Let us assail his mind another while.*), wobei häufig das *u* von *us* syncopiert wird (z. B. Greene, Look. Glass 137 *Come, let's draw him away perforce.*, Peele, Edw. I 97 *Good, my lord, let's hear a few of his lines...* Kyd, Jeronimo 386 *Let's meet*).

So entsteht nun in unserem Falle, infolge Vermengung von
let's meet! (Aufforderung) und
shall we meet (Frage),
shall's meet!? durch den Gedanken an Aufforderung + Frage.

§ 117.

1. Tancred and Gismonda 91
   Let him with me, and I with him, be laid
   Within one shrine...

Dieser Fall entsteht durch den Gedanken an die Aufforderung *Let him with me be laid within one shrine* und den Wunsch *I with him will be laid within one shrine.*

    2. Calisto and Melibaea 84
*Wherefore, fair maid, let thy pity repair:
Let mercy be thy mother, and thou her heir.*

Wir haben hier Contamination von zwei Möglichkeiten der Aufforderung, von *Let mercy be thy mother, and thee her heir* und *Let... and be thou her heir.*

    3. Sidney, Astrophel and Stella p. 51/5
*Since she disdaining me, doth you in me disdaine,
Suffer not her to laugh, and both we suffer paine:*

Hier liegt nur scheinbar eine Kasusvertauschung vor; von *suffer* sind zwei Konstruktionen abhängig, ein Infinitiv und ein dass-Satz, in dem *that* unterdrückt ist (cf. z. B. Look about You 483 *But if I know she yield, faith, I'll defy her.*).

    4. Ebensowenig können wir in dem Fall Digby Myst. 30/89
*I am non hosteler nor non hostelers kynne,
But a Jentylmanys seruuant, I thou dost know;*

eine Kasusvertauschung erblicken, wie es vielleicht in Anbetracht der Interpunktion des Herausgebers scheinen möchte. Das zweite *I* ist hier nichts als eine rhetorische Wiederholung (cf. § 108 Anm. 4).

    5. Desgl. Marlowe, Massacre 302
*That those which do behold them may become
As men that stand and gaze against the sun.*
                    Old. ed. they

Wohl einfach Fehler des Schreibers, der *they (them)* als Subjekt zu *may become* fasste.

    6. Kyd, Spanish Tragedy 116
I know thee to be Pedro, and he Jaques.

erklärt sich durch Kreuzung von *I know (that) thou art Pedro and he Jaques* und *I know thee to be Pedro, and him Jaques.*

    7. Peele, Arr. of Paris 11
*That trust me, sirs, who did the cunning see,
Would at a blush suppose it to be she.*

Contamination von *...suppose it to be her* und *it be she* unter Einfluss des Reimes.

Bei den beiden letztgenannten Fällen (5 und 6) kann ausserdem auch Einwirkung der Formen auf *e(e)* nach Jesp. § 196 angenommen werden.

§ 118.

P. L. 725/92 *Item, as ffor the Bysshop and I, we bee nerrer to a poynt than we weer*...

Hier ist „*the Bysshop and I*", als Subjekt betrachtet, an *we* (dessen einzelne Teile sie ja bilden) angelehnt. Aehnliche Fälle siehe Jesp. § 156 Ende.

§ 119.

Marlowe, Tamburlaine 433
Thyselfe and them shall neuer part from me

Einen ganz analogen Fall bei Shakspere deutet Abbot § 214 durch den Gedanken an *Thyself and them[selves]*, was nicht unwahrscheinlich ist; doch können wir hier auch die in der damaligen Volkssprache ziemlich verbreitete Unsicherheit in der Kasusunterscheidung, sowie Fälle wie in § 132 zur Erklärung heranziehen.

Einfluss von Wörtern, die zugleich Präp. und Konj. sind.

§ 120. Vorbemerkung.

Fälle dieser Art behandelt Jespersen, dessen Ausführungen wir im wesentlichen zustimmen können, wenn auch im einzelnen noch einige neue Momente hinzukommen, in den §§ 158—161.

Es handelt sich hier hauptsächlich darum, dass, da bei der zweideutigen Natur dieser Wörter ein Schwanken in der Richtung eintritt, ob der Sprechende sie in dem einzelnen Falle (natürlich unbewusst) als Präposition oder als Konjunktion fasst, es in einer Reihe von Fällen zu einer wirklichen Kasusverschiebung kommt.

§ 121. *but.*
a) Mit dem Nominativ.

P. L. 383/493
...*and no body schall know of it but we thre.*

Heywood, P. P. 347
*Who should but I then altogether
Have thank of all their coming thither?*
Bale, Kynge Johan 57
who shuld defend her but I?
Jacob and Esau 226
Is none here but we?
Greene, Looking Glass 60
Rasni is God on earth, and none but he.
Orlando 33
...there was nobody at home but I, and I was turning of the spit...
Pinner 191
Which none but he in England should have gotten.
Marlowe, Dido 395
But tell them, none shall gaze on him but I,
Edward II 252 *...if none but we
Do wot of your abode.*
Jack Straw 383
It shall be no other but he

b) Mit dem Accusativ.

Marlowe, Dido 409
Never to like or love any but her!
Edward II 211
Poor Gaveston, that hast no friend but me!

c) Kyd, Spanish Tragedy 119 (cf. auch § 122 Ende)
Alas! sir, I had no more but he. (desgl. ein Fall mit *who* cf. § 174).

Hier bilden die unter a) und b) verzeichneten, völlig einwandfreien, Fälle den Uebergang zu c), wo sowohl Konjunktion wie Präposition den Accusativ verlangen würden.

§ 122. *save.*

Im allgemeinen tritt (wie bei Chaucer und Shakspere) der durch den Sinn bedingte Kasus ein.
So der Nominativ: Three Lords 450
Whom all the world admires, save only we,

So der Accusativ: Four Elements 41
> *Yea, I have slain them every man,*
> *Save them that ran away.*

Durch solche und ähnliche Fälle erklärt sich nun:
Sir Clyomon and Sir Clamydes 505 b
Were ever seen such contraries by fraudulent goddess blind
To any one, save only I, imparted for to be?

Dagegen ist *save* als Präposition gefasst:
Udall, State IX
...he sweetly aunswered him, saying: if it had bin any of the company saue him, he would haue graunted the suite...

Marlowe, Verm. 344
> *What creature liuing liues in griefe...*
> *Save me, a slaue to spoyle?*

Anders erklärt sich folgender Fall:
P. L. 338/493
...and this day we have grant to have the good owthe of Barmundsey with owthe avyse of any man, sawyng Worseter, Plomer, and I my selff...

Hier hätte *my selff* ohne *I* genügt, *me my selff* war unmöglich, *I my self(f)* in anderen Fällen allgemein üblich (z. B. P. L. 108/146 *as weel as I my self*, ib. 410/40, 619/369 etc.), und so verwandte der Schreiber des Briefes dieses (sozusagen schon zu Eins verschmolzene) *I my self(f)* auch hier.

Genau denselben Fall mit *but* haben wir über 100 Jahre später bei Greene, Alphonsus 60
> *For Amurack's stout stomach shall undo*
> *But he himself, and all his other crow.*

welcher zeigt, dass wir es nicht nur mit einem einzelnen und vielleicht zufälligen Belege zu tun haben.

§ 123. *except.*

Greene, Alphonsus 50
Whose captain is slain, and all his army dead,
Only excepted me, unhappy wretch.

§ 124. (such) as.

P. L. 437/86
bot when my Lorde of Oxenforde herde hereof he with his feliship and suche as I and other your presoneres come rydyng unto Lynne...

M. 202/10
he weneth no knyght soo good as he, and the contrary is oftyme preued.

Nice Wanton 171
Yea, I thank that knave and such a whore as thou.

Sidney, Astrophel 94/13
*Thou maist more wretched be than nature beares:
As being plast in such a wretch as I.*

Greene, Orlando 11
*The worst of these men of so high import
As may command a greater dame than I.*

ib.
*Untaught companion, I would learn you know
What duty 'longs to such a prince as he.*

ib. 30
No, soldier, think me resolute as he.

Looking Glass 99
Should I... Embase myself to speak to such as they?

ib. 110
*It fits not such an abject prince a I,
To talk with Rasni's paramour and love.*

Alphonsus 52
*Why, proud Alphonsus, think'st thou Amurack,
... Can e'er be found to turn his heels and fly
Away for fear, from such a boy as thou?*

Sir Clyomon and Sir Clamydes 500 a
*For triple honour will it be to him that gets the victory
Before so worthy a prince as he and nobles all so publicly,*

Marlowe, Edward II 197
*While others walk below, the king and he,
From out a window, laugh at such as we,*

ib. 228
>   Commit not to my youth things of more weight
>   Than fits a prince so youny as I to bear:

Massacre 313
>   To speak with me, from such a man as he?

Jack Straw 381
The king, God wot, knows not what's done by such poor men as we,
>   Knack to Know a Knave 521
>   He told me straight he took it in great scorn
>   To be begot by one so base as I.

Lodge, Wounds 123
>   I fear me Pluto will be wrath me,
>   For to disdain so grave a man as he.

Dass bei diesen Fällen in damaliger Zeit zweifellos die betr. Formen von *to be* ergänzt gedacht wurden, sie also dadurch eine ebenso schnelle wie einfache Erklärung finden, mögen folgende Belege erweisen:

>   P. L. 571/301 ... *I fynde hym no thyng so weele disposid as his brother is;*

>   M. 548/11 ... *why dyd ye smyte dounc soo good a knyght as he is...*

R. R. Doister 17
>   Woulde Christ I had such a husband as he is.

Angry Women 337
>   Well, 'tis not time of night to hold out chat
>   With such a scold as thou art;

Briefe Elizabeths 14
>   ... of such a prince a ye are;

§ 125. *like.*

Der Dativ ist das Ursprüngliche.

Sidney, Astr. and Stella 22/9
>   Stella alone, with face vnarmed marcht,
>   Either to doe like him, as carelesse showne:

Fälle mit dem Nominativ fielen uns nicht auf.

§ 126. than.

Jesp. § 160 f. Fälle mit *than* schliessen sich besonders eng an die in § 124 (*such as, as*) besprochenen, mit denen sie sich zum Teil berühren, an.

a) Der grammatisch zu erwartende **Nominativ** tritt ein:

Greene, Bacon 147
> *But in the court be quainter dames than she,*

Marlowe, Edward II 262
> *Commend me to my son, and bid him rule*
> *Better than I:*

b) Der grammatisch zu erwartende **Accusativ** tritt ein:

Jacob and Esau 229
> *But ... they're fit for better men than me.*

Sidney, Astrophel and Stella 69/2
> *Oh blisse, fit for a nobler seat than mee,*

Fälle dieser Art bilden die Voraussetzung für wirkliche **Vertauschungen**:

a) Accusativ für Nominativ.

Marlowe, Ovid 187
> *Greater than her, by her leave, thou'rt, I'll say.*

b) Nominativ für Accusativ.

Greene, Orlando 11
> *The worst of these men of so high import*
> *As may command a greater dame than I.*

James IV 74
> *... this whinyard has gard many better men to lope than thou.*

Three Ladies 291
> *Faith, he might have richer fellows than we to take his part,*
> *But he shall never have better eating fellows, if he would*
> *swelt his heart.*

Für diese Belege lässt sich zu weiterer Erklärung auch noch das in § 124 Ende betonte Moment heranziehen.

II. Stellung.

§ 127.

Greene, Pinner 175
> for, master, bc it known to you, there is some good-will betwixt Madge the Sousewife and I; (Worte des Clowns!)

gegenüber ib. 188
> ...a league of truce was late confirm'd
> 'Twixt you and me (Worte King Edwards!)

sowie: Calisto and Melibaea 62
> I love not to hear this altercation
> Between Melibaea and me her lover.

Peele, Edward I 142
> She might have favour with my queen and me.

Man beachte bei den Belegen aus Greene den Unterschied der Sprecher: das frappante Beispiel ist einem Manne aus dem Volke in den Mund gelegt.

Zu Jesp. § 192, dessen Erklärung zweifellos zutrifft. Von massgebendem Einfluss ist in diesen Fällen die Wortstellung in Wendungen, die zum grossen Teil (nicht immer! man vergl. die Erklärungsbelege sowie das Beispiel aus M. unten) durch die Höflichkeit geboten ist. Von der enormen Verbreitung solcher Wendungen schon in der Umgangssprache elisabethanischer Zeit (denn auf die Zeit der Entstehung solcher Kasusvertauschungen kommt es an; Jespersen operiert in begreiflicher Ermangelung an Belegen aus damaliger Zeit etwas viel mit Rückschlüssen aus heutiger, die nicht immer notwendigerweise zutreffen müssen) kann man sich einen Begriff machen, wenn man erwägt, dass folgende Liste von Belegen die Materie nicht erschöpft:

a) Pronomen + *I*.

thou and I:
Bale, Kynge Johan 5, Interlude of Youth 11, Jack Juggler 123, Peele, Arr. 35, Alcazar 114, Marl., Dido 419, Look about You 468;

he and I:
Digby Mysteries 193/654, Four Elements 45, Hickscorner 150, Jack Juggler 141, Sir Clyomon 501 a;

she and I:
Plumpt. Corr. 124, Four Elements 35, Greene, Verm. 308, Look about You 421;
ye (you) and I:
P. L. 9/27, 277/380, Plumpt. Corr. 167, Lusty Juventus 70, 71, 77, More, Utopia 21, Peele, Edward I 135, Greene, Alph. 39, Bacon 155, Sir Clyomon 503 b; hierzu
yourself and I: Greene, James IV 148;
they and I: Plumpt. Corr. 167.

b) Substantiv (Name etc.) + *I*.

P. L. 36/48 *my moder and I*, ib. 558/290 *John Dam and I*, Calisto and Mel. 85 *This knight and I*, Heywood, P. P. 374 *This devil and I*, Thersites 426 *my mother and I*, Jack Juggler 114 *This Jenkin and I*, ib. 126 *my master and I*, ib. 174 *my brother and I*, Sidney, Astrophel 84/7 *My muse and I*, Peele, Edw. I 123 *Ned and I*, Old Wives Tale 207 *Fantastick and I*, Greene, Bacon 196 *Bungay and I*, Pinner 181 *king James and I*, Marl., Edw. II 217 *my son and I*, Dido 398 *This man and I*.
etc. etc.

§ 128.

Wie schon oben angedeutet, handelt es sich vornehmlich um Verbindungen mit *I*; wenn wir für solche mit anderen Pron. vorläufig nur éinen Beleg (aus M., s. u.) beibringen können, so werden doch folgende Erklärungsbelege für später etwa aufzufindende Fälle nicht unwillkommen sein; sie zeigen, wie sehr solche Verbindungen von Pron. mit Pron. oder Subst. mit Pron. zu fest geschlossenen Wendungen werden, sodass ihre Verwendung im Accusativ nicht mehr auffällig erscheinen kann, wie wir sie gerade in der volkstümlichen Umgangssprache finden, die im Dialog des Dramas, insbesondere im Volksdrama der 2. Hälfte des 16. Jahrhunderts ihre beste Verkörperung in der Literatur erhalten hat. (Der Dialog in theologischen Streitschriften, wie z. B. Joy's Apology, repräsentiert nicht den Zustand in der Umgangssprache in solch ausgesprochenen Masse, weil er, durchaus reflektierender Art, trotz aller Lebhaftigkeit in ruhigen Bahnen dahinfliesst.)

a) Pronomen + Pronomen.

thou and she: M. 312/4;

he and thou: Marriage of Wit 346; auch negativ: Greene, Orlando 12 *Nor he, nor thou;*

he and she: M. 91/25, Greene, Verm. 274.

b) Substantiv + Pronomen.

P. L. 827/241 *hyr moder and sche*, Hickscorner 167 *Sir John and she*, Lusty Juventus 67 *Knowledge and he*, Jack Juggler 115 *Jenkin and she*, ib. 116 *my mistress and thou*, Marlowe, Edw. II 216 *the king and he*, Dido 403 *the queen and he*, Hero 78 *His love and he*, Massacre 327 *Thy brother Guise and we*;

auch negativ: Marl., Hero 14 *Nor heaven nor thou.*
etc. etc.

Auf Grund der angeführten Belege sowie ähnlicher ergiebt sich nun weiter die Erklärung folgender Fälle:

1. Greene, James IV 82
    Let father frown and fret, and fret and die,
    Nor earth nor heaven shall part my love and I.

2. Look about You 477
    Prythee, Moll,
    Let thou and I, and she, shut up this matter.

3. ib. 478 *tut, make no brawl,*
    'Twixt thou and I we'll have amends for all.

4. M. 112/29 ... *that made hym passynge good chere and wel easyd bothe his horse and he* ...

Zu Fall 2 vergl. auch § 117, 2, zu Fall 4 Jesp. § 196 (Einfluss von *me* auf den Gebrauch von *he, we* etc.), wonach auch wohl zu erklären ist:

Kyd, Spanish Tragedy 171
    Set me with him, and he with woeful me,
    Upon the main-mast of a ship unmann'd,

wenn hier nicht der Gedanke vorschwebt: *and then he with woeful me shall sit upon* etc.

III. Anakoluthe.
§ 129.

Everyman 102
> *He that loveth riches I will strike with my dart,*

Greene, Looking Glass 138
> *For those that climb he casteth to the ground,*
> *And they that humble be he lifts aloft.*

Diese Fälle erklären sich leicht aus der Bildung der Relativsätze im 16. Jahrhundert derart, dass das Beziehungswort nicht, wie häufig, wieder durch ein Personalpronomen im Accusativ aufgenommen ist; vgl. hierzu Anhang II.

IV. Einfluss der Nomina.
§ 130.

Jesp. § 167 ff.

1. Den von Jespersen angeführten Fällen, wo das Pronomen aus dem Zusammenhang herausgenommen ist, mag hinzugefügt werden:

R. R. Doister 15
> M. Mery. *What is hir name?*
> R. R. *Hir yonder.*
> M. Mery. *Whom.*
> R. R. *Mistresse ah.*

2. Fälle, wo das Pronomen zur Bezeichnung des Geschlechts dient, siehe § 113.

3. Aus den § 192, 3 Anm. 2 mitgeteilten Fällen (mein anderes [zweites] Ich) geht hervor, dass, abgesehen von den Fällen mit *myself,* das Pronomen in dem durch die Konstruktion bedingten Kasus (Nom. oder Acc.) steht. Dasselbe findet nun statt, wenn ein Adjektiv dem Pronomen vorangeht.

a) Nominativ.

Damon and Pithias 17
> *Ere you came hither, poor I was somebody;*
> *The king delighted in me, now I am but a noddy.*

Kyd, Cornelia 191
> *O, then shall wretched I, that am but one,*
> *(Yet once both theirs) survive, now they are gone?*

Peele, Arr. of Paris 39
> Then had not I, poor I, bin unhappy.

Marlowe, Edward II 252
> We were embark'd for Ireland; wretched we,
> With awkward winds and with sore tempests driven,

b) Accusativ.

Sidney, Astrophel and Stella 42/7
> Doe not, doe not, from me, poor me, remoue

ib. 51/5
> On sillie me, doe not your burthen lay
> Of all the graue conceipts your braine doth breede:

ib. 93/4
> Through mee, wretch mee, euen Stella vexed is:

4. Auch in Ausrufen steht der Nominativ (Jesp., der § 169 behauptet „nur *me*" ist demnach zu berichtigen), zum Teil zweifellos in Anlehnung an die Umgebung.

Gorboduc 1231
> O sillie woman I, why to this houre
> Haue kinde and fortune thus deferred my breath,
> That I should liue to see this dolefull day?

Sidney, Astrophel and Stella 74/1
> I neuer dranke of Aganippe well...
> Poor Lay-man I, for sacred rites vnfit.

ib. 83/7
> Nay, (more foole I) oft suffred you to sleepe,

Arcadia 172
> And yet I am the same, miserable I, that I was.

ib. 568
> O miserable I, that have, only favour by misery;

Peele, Edward I 163
> No traitor, no potter I, but Mortimer, the Earl of March;

Marlowe, Massacre 352
> My brother [the] Cardinal slain, and I alive!

Verm. 342
> Vnhappie I, poore I, and none as I,
> But pilgrim he, poore he, that should be by.

Misfortunes of Arthur 333
>*O happy they,*
>*Whose spotless lives attain a dreadless death!*

Rare Triumphs 156
>*The more fool she, and she were my own brother?*

Mucedorus 214
>*If Amadine do live, then happy I: yea, happy I, if Amadine do live!*

Barnfield, Poems 11
>*But if that thou disdainst my louing euer;*
>*Oh happie I, if I had loued neuer.*

Aber auch der Accusativ:
Kyd, Jeronimo 391
>*O me ill-sted! valiant Rogero slain!*

Sidney, Arcadia 196
>*O me unfortunate wretch, said she...*

ib. 261
>*And shall, O me! all this in ashes rest?*

ib. 666 *O me, what say I more?*
ib. 667 *O me, contemned wretch;*

5. **In Verbindung mit** *ah, alas, aye* **etc. dagegen steht immer** *me*:

Digby Mysteries 210/1161 *alas, mee!*
Lyly, Endimion 57 (Sapho and Phao 184)
>*Aye me, but what doe I heere.*

Peele, Edward I 163 (197) *Aye is me!*
David and Bethsabe 40, Alcazar 135, Greene, Look. Glass 92, Marlowe, Dido 368, Edward II 204, Hero 17.

Kyd, Cornelia 214 (Jeronimo 378)
>*Ah me! what see I?*

Tancred and Gismonda 84, Sidney, Arcadia 602 etc.

Anm.: In Uebersetzungen aus dem Lateinischen giebt *aye me* folgendes wieder:
  Hei mihi! (Marlowe, Ovid 110, 138, 147, 179);
  Me miserum! (Marlowe, Ovid 115, 123, 151, 174, 176);
  Heu! (Marlowe, Lucan 268).
Bei Uebersetzungen aus dem Französischen:
Cornelia 214 *Ah me, what see I?* frz. Las qu'est-ce que ie voy!

V. Kasusvertauschungen in Sir Clyomon and Sir Clamydes.

§ 131.

Eine Reihe von Fällen in Sir Clyomon and Sir Clamydes, die bereits von Kellner, Outl. § 209 erwähnt, uns aber nicht genügend erklärt scheinen, behandeln wir gesondert, da sie in Anbetracht ihrer verhältnismässig grossen Zahl gerade für dieses Stück charakteristisch sind, und unseres Erachtens nach das Zusammenwirken mehrerer Erscheinungen ihre Entstehung bedingt hat.

1. Sir Clyomon 508 a

fie on fell Fortune, she
Which hath her wheel of froward chance thus whirled back on me!

2. ib. 497 a

Do never view thy father I in presence any more.

3. ib. 505 b

What greater grief can grow to gripe the heart of grieved wight
Than thus to see fell Fortune she to hold his state in spite?

4. ib. 507 b

Clamydes, ah, by Fortune she what froward luck and fate
Most cruelly assigned is unto thy noble state!

5. ib. 501 b

But shall I frame, then, mine excuse by serving Venus she,
When I am known throughout the world fainthearted for to be?

6. ib. 514 a

Neronis, daughter to the king, by the King of Norway he
Whithin a ship of merchandise convey'd away is she.

7. ib. 497 a

Sith that mine honour cowardly was stoln by caitiff he,

8. ib. 491 b

I mean by Juliana she, that blaze of beauty's breeding,
And for her noble gifts of grace all other dames exceeding;

9. ib. 511 a

Yet though unto Neronis she I may not show my mind,
A faithful heart, when I am gone, with her I leave behind,

10. ib.

Besides, here longer in this court, alas, I may not stay,
Although that with Clamydes he I have not kept my day,

11. ib. 515 a
As hare the hound, as lamb the wolf, as fowl the falcon's dint,
So do I fly from tyrant he, whose heart more hard than flint
Hath sack'd on me such hugy heaps of ceaseless sorrows here,

Alle diese Fälle haben das Gemeinsame, dass das (meist entbehrliche) Pronomen, das stets im Nominativ anstatt in dem zu erwartenden Accusativ steht, in engste Verbindung zu einem unmittelbar vor ihm befindlichen Nomen gesetzt ist. Sehen wir uns nun in dem Stücke um, so finden wir, dass der Verfasser (und das ist auch ein nicht zu unterschätzender sprachlich-syntaktischer Grund gegen die Verfasserschaft Peele's) eine entschieden ausgesprochene Neigung für das **pleonastisch verwandte Personalpronomen**, wie es in § 107 dargestellt ist, hat. Aus praktischen Gründen lassen wir die methodisch dorthin gehörigen Fälle hier folgen:

Sir Clyomon 506 a
Before that noble prince of might whereas Clamydes he
Will slow himself in combat-wise for to exclaim...

ib. 516 b
...your king he will be one.

ib. 520 a
Well, within ten days is the time, and King Alexander he
Stayeth till the day appointed the trial to see;

ib. 523 a
And Duke Mustantius he smiles in his sleeve...

ib. 525 b
The truth thereof, renowned king, thy servant he shall show.

ib. 527 b
But sore I fear to contaries th'expect thereof will hap,
Which will in huge calamities my woful corpse bewrap
For sending of so worthy a prince, as was Clamydes he,
To sup his dire destruction there for wretched love of me.

ib. 529 a
If case my son he be thy friend, with heart I thee embrace

Bei Berücksichtigung dieser Belege werden die oben verzeichneten Fälle um so eher erklärlich, wenn wir erwägen, dass für Fall 1. **Attraktion an das Relativum** hinzukommt, für

Fall 3. § 141 (unconnected subject), für Fall 7. und auch wohl 11. § 130, 2 und 3 in Betracht zu ziehen sind, und dass schliesslich auch bei 1, 5, 6, 7 die Erfordernisse des Reimes mitspielen.

VI. Kasusvertauschungen auf allgemeiner Unsicherheit in der Kasusunterscheidung beruhend.

§ 132.

Für einige Fälle von Kasusvertauschungen lassen sich — wenigstens vorläufig — keine direkten Parallelbelege anführen, die ihre Entstehung bedingt hätten. Wir müssen uns daher damit begnügen, den Grund in der zweifellos schon damals besonders in der Umgangssprache vorhandenen Unsicherheit in der Unterscheidung von Nominativ und Accusativ (Dativ) zu sehen.

1. Digby Mysteries 164/712
ye! who is hym shall hem offende?

Vgl. hierzu Sir Perc. 2041 (aus Ellinger p. 126)
Art thou hym that, saide he thane,
That slew Gollerothirame?

2. Greene, Looking Glass 96
What, son Radagon, i'faith, boy, how dost thee?

Vgl. hierzu § 139 (Wechselwirkung des Pronomens beim Imperativ § 97 f. und des ethischen Dativs § 152).

3. Rare Triumphs 237
Sir, and you'll have us carry her, here be them come of the carriers.

4. ib.
And you'll have us marry her, here by them come of the marriers.

5. Three Ladies 291
Here be them that will eat with the proudest of them;

Hier könnte an ein in unseren Texten zwar nicht belegtes aber höchstwahrscheinlich in der Volkssprache vorhandenes *it be (is) them* gedacht werden (cf. § 134, 2).

6. Calisto and Melibaea 57

... *I find, thou art without pity.*, wo Old copy *the* hat, könnte hierher gerechnet werden, wenn nicht hier gedankenloser Schreibfehler vorliegt.

VII. *me* für *I* in bewusster Absicht.

§ 133.

Einem ganz anderen Umstande als die unter I—V behandelten Fälle verdankt die Verwendung von *me* für *I* ihre Existenz in einer Reihe von Dramen des elisabethanischen Zeitalters. Hier haben wir es mit einer bewussten Vertauschung zu tun, die (wenn auch wohl nicht ganz grundlos, man vergl. eben diese Verwendung von *me* für *I* in einigen Negerdialekten heutiger Zeit [Harrison, Negro English, Anglia VII, 246, Grade, Negerenglisch, Anglia XIV, 380]) einzelnen Personen und zwar Ausländern, Franzosen (Greene, James IV, Three Lords, Lodge, Wounds) oder Italienern (Three Ladies, Rare Triumphs) vom Verfasser des betr. Dramas in den Mund gelegt wird, um durch diesen absichtlich hervorgerufenen Schein von Unkenntnis in englischer Sprache eine komische Bühnenwirkung zu erzielen; dass das ein Effektmittel ersten Ranges war, dürfte sich in unseren Quellen aus seiner Verwendung in fünf Stücken von verschiedenen Verfassern ergeben.

Belege:

Greene, James IV 114

en bonne foi, prate you against Sir Altesse, me maku your tete to leap from your shoulders...

ib. 116

me be at your commandment.

ib. 117

Me sweara by my ten bones...
By my sword, me be no baby, lord.

ib.

...me thrusta my weapon into her belly, so me may be guard par le roy. Me de your service: but me no be hanged pour my labour?

ib. 125 f., 131 ff., 140,
Three Ladies 273
> *I judge in my mind a, dat me be not vare far
> From da place where dwells my Lady Lucar.*

ib. 275
> *Madonna, me be a mershant...
> Me be, Madonna, an Italian.
> ... me come from Turkey.*

ib. 276
> *Me will lie and forswear meself for a quarter so much as my hat.*

ib. 303 ff., 306
> *Madonna, me dare go to de Turks...*

ib. 329 ff., 345 f., 355 ff.,
Rare Triumphs 202
> *If me no help him, me carry no head away.*

ib. 203 *me speak with you: me can tell...*

ib. 204 *me no diavolo, me very fury.*

ib. 209 *But me am vera lot' de same to bring;*
Three Lords 438
*Me lack — a de monish pour de feene...
me muss a make money to go over in my own countrey... etc.*

Lodge, Wounds 139 (140)
> *...me will make a trou...
> me will make a spitch-cock of his persona.*

Natürlich bildet dieses *me* für *I*, wie wir hieraus auch ersehen können, nur ein Glied in der langen Reihe von Verstümmelungen **lautlicher, flexivischer und syntaktischer Art**, die in ihrer Gesamtwirkung für den Bühnenerfolg massgebend wurden.

§ 134. *it is I.*

Ae. *ic hit eom* entwickelt sich über me. *it am I* zu ne. *it is I* und *it is me*. Wie steht es damit im 15. und 16. Jahrhundert?

1. Fälle mit dem Nominativ.

Im 15. und 16. Jahrh. ist der Nominativ nach *it (this) is (was* etc.) absolute Regel; die Fälle mit dem Accusativ sind dem gegenüber verschwindende Ausnahmen, wie sich aus folgenden Belegen ergeben wird.

it is I:
>Bale, Promises 310
>*O Lord, it is I which have offended thy grace,*
>Tyndale, Matth. 14/27, Joh. 6/20 (Auth. Vers. und Rev. Vers. ebenso)
>Latimer, Sermons 74 ... *it is euen I ...*
>Marlowe, Jew 657, Edward II 238,
>Greene, Bacon 212, 213, Looking Glass 131,
>Sidney, Arcadia 363, 374, 743, 771.

it was I (etc.):
>P. L. 747/118 ... *my mayde wende it had been I that she speke off;*
>M. 83/25 ... *it was I ... that slewe this knyght ...*
>ib. 504/4, Joy, Ap. 49, Disobedient Child 308 (5 mal), R. R. Doister 25,
>G. G. Needle 238 ... *she saith it was not I.*
>Damon and Pithias 70, Kyd, Jeronimo 376, Marlowe, Tamburlaine 2228, Jew 2335, Massacre 349, Greene, Bacon 177, Pinner 188, Three Ladies 361.

it is thou:
>Latimer, Sermons 70 *O Lorde God, it is thou that ...*
>Kyd, Cornelia 184, 212, Lyly, Woman 191.
>Peele, Edward I 201, Marlowe, Edward II 186.

it was thou:
>M. 402/9 ... *it were thou that ...*
>Joy, Ap. 50 *But yt was thou ...*
>Marlowe, Edward II 287,
>Massacre 315 *Was it not thou that ...*

it (this, that) is he:
>P. L. 350/516 *It is he that makythe William Wurceter so froward as he is.*
>M. 409/8 *that be he*, ib. 507/34 *is not that he ...*
>ib. 643/13 *I deme hit be he ...*
>Latimer, Sermons 108, 148, 177, Lyly, Euphues 336,
>Kyd, Jeronimo 376, Marlowe, Faust 1208 *this is he.*

Massacre 310, 329, Dido 380 *this is not he,*
Greene, Alph. 20, Peele, Edward I 96, Old Wives Tale 218.

it was (were) he:
    M. 265/6 ... *it was he that had slayne their lord.*
    M. 288/37, 399/23 ... *that was he that* ...,
    M. 480/1, 552/14, Latimer, Sermons 109,
    G. G. Needle 238 ... *this was not he?*
    Kyd, Jeronimo 365, Peele, Alcazar 143, Marlowe, Jew 2031,
        Marprelate Epistle 18, Greene, Orlando 33,
    Sidney, Arcadia 769.

it (this) is she:
    R. R. Doister 26 ... *this is not she.*, Marriage of Wit 338,
        Lyly, Mother Bombie 95 *it is she,*
    Peele, Arr. 63, Greene, Orlando 37, Old Wives Tale 217, 246
        this is she that ran madding in the woods ...

it was she:
    M. 345/11 ... *and that was she that* ...
    Sidney, Arcadia 636 ... *it was she.*

it is we:
    Angry Women 270
                             'tis we that are
        Indebted to your kindness for this cheer:

it is ye (you):
    M. 205/17 ... *I trowe hit be not ye that* ...
    Lyly, Euphues 287 ... *it is not you* ...
    Kyd, Jeronimo 375 *My lord, I think 'tis you:*
    Lyly, Mother Bombie 79 *it is you that* ...
    Marlowe, Edward II 238 *Is't you, my lord?*
    Greene, Pinner 200 *What, George-a-Greene, is it you?*

it was (ye) you:
    M. 231/1 ... *it was ye that* ...
    M. 757/37 *yf it were yow or syr Tristram* ...
    Damon and Pithias 70 *Was it you* ...
    Kyd, Jeronimo 377 *Was it not you* ...?

it is they:
    P. L. 386/7 ... *and thei it is that have to this acte.*
    M. 531/35 ... *it be they in certeyn* ...

Bale, Kynge Johan 30
>*Coks sowll, yt is they*:

Latimer, Sermons 85 (189) ...*it is they that*...

2. Fälle mit dem Accusativ.

Four Elements 19
>*It is even thee, knave, that I mean.*

(Marlowe, Jew 1034 schon bei Jesp.)

Look about You 448
>*In recompence, if it be him I seek,*
>*I'll give thee his whole head to tread upon.*

Marlowe, Edward II 216
>*What would you with the king? is't him you seek?*

Fälle dieser Art sind bereits von Jesp. § 154 durch Attraktion an das Relativum erklärt. Doch kann auch noch an Einwirkung von Fällen wie M. 134/1 ...*for it is hym self kynge Arthur*... sowie Greene, Bacon 191 *Let it be me;* gedacht werden; zur Stellung des Reflexivpronomens vgl. auch M. 839/34 ...*and on hir hym self kyng Arthur bygate you*...

Auf Grund alles dessen folgern wir nun weiter, dass der Nominativ nicht, wie Jespersen sich bei beschränktem Material vorsichtig ausdrückt „seems to have been the natural idiom" sondern im 15. und 16. Jahrhundert thatsächlich das Volkstümliche gewesen ist; die an sich zweideutigen Fälle mit *ye, you* sind daher wohl als Nominative anzusehen. Hiermit ist nun die Ansicht von Ellis (cf. Jesp. § 184) „the phrase *it is I* is a modernisme, or rather a grammaticism, that is, it was never in popular use" etc. völlig widerlegt.

Anm. 1: Selten begegneten noch Reste der ae. Ausdrucksweise:

Everyman 140
>*All fleeth save Good Deeds, and that am I.*

J. Juggler 127 *It I be not, I have made a very good voyage* —

Greene, James IV 88 *Truly, sir, that am I.*

Knack to Know a Knave 517
>*That am I, father, that use the word of God,*

Anm. 2: Neben *it is I* etc. ist im 15. und 16. Jahrhundert die schon bei Chaucer (Koch § 302) belegte Ausdrucksweise *I am he* etc. nicht so selten:

M. 36/18, M. 67/6 *I am Merlyn, and I was he in the childes lykenes.*
ib. 231/3 *Also I am sure that ye are he*...

ib. 299/29 ...*for ye are he that slewe marhaus*...
ib. 331/11 *And I am he that delyuerd*...
ib. 713/15 *And thenne they sayd alle O my lord sir launcelot be that ye and he sayd Truly I am he.*
Digby Mysteries 66/309
   And I am he þat lengest xal Induer.
Heywood, Pardoner and Friar 229
   ...I am even he —
World and Child 263
   thou art he that Conscience did blame,
Bale, Kynge Johan 37
   The best of them all shall know that I am he.
Tyndale, Matth. 14/28 *yf thou be he.*
   (Auth. Vers. und Rev. Vers. *if it be thou*)
R. R. Doister 31 ...*if I were thou.*
ib. 47 *If I wer you, Custance should eft seeke to me*...
J. Juggler 132
   And then I woll confess that thou art I.
Damon and Pithias 18
   Carisophus is he,
Which hath long time fed Dionysius' humour:
Lyly, Euphues 365
   I am not he Camilla that will leaue the Rose...
Peele, Arr. 23
   Let this unto the fairest given be,
   The fairest of the three, and I am she.
Rare Triumphs 151
   I am not she,
That seeks with Venus to compare in her supremacy.
Clyomon and Clamydes 530a
   ...you are not he.
Greene, Orlando 16, 17 *I am he,* ib. 28 *I am not he,* ib. 34
   Ay thou art she that wrong'd the Palatine.
Looking Glass 116
   O, thou art he that I seek for.
Three Ladies 273
   I am he, and what would you withal?
Für Kyd cf. Ritzenfeldt p. 10.
Ebenso bei Shakspere; cf. Deutschbein § 43.

§ 135.
you für *ye*.

Die ersten sicheren Beispiele stammen aus der Mitte des 14. Jahrhunderts (Ipomadon, cf. Kellner, Outl. § 212). Was unsere Texte anlangt, so werden in den P. L. (also bis 1509) *ye* als Nom. und *you* als Acc. im Ganzen streng geschieden, wenn auch in den späteren Briefen eine Zunahme von *you* als Nom. auf Kosten von *ye* sich feststellen lässt.

Z. B.: P. L. 62/77 *I pray yow if ye have an other sone that you woll lete it be named Herry*...; *also I pray yow that ye woll send me dats and syuamun as hastyly as ye may.*

P. L. 816 225 *I marvel soor that yow sent me noo word of the letter*...

ib. ...*the next masenger that yow kan have to me.*

P. L. 827/241 *And as for hyr bewte, juge yow that when ye see hyr*...

Dagegen noch P. L. 616/362 (1462)
Be ye avysed what answer ye wuld yeve.

P. L. 716/78 (1473) *therfor I pray you, doo ye als wele therein as ye canne;*

P. L. 829/245 (1479)
Therfor meve ȝe the executores...

P. L. 922/368 (1491) *Know ye that*...

Diesen Zustand bestätigt uns ferner der Morte Darthure, wo sich zahlreiche *you* als Nominativ finden, wenn auch die *ye* bei weitem überwiegen; schon bei Kellner, Blanch. p. 13.

Was das 16. Jahrhundert anlangt, so fällt der Uebergang zum Ueberwiegen von *you* als Nominativ gegen 1550; Kellners (Blanch. 13) etwas unbestimmt ausgedrückte Ansicht „the nominative holds its place on to the time of Henry VIII" ist damit genauer präzisiert.

Die Plumpton Corr. zeigt noch bis 1545 ein Ueberwiegen von *ye*; ebenso Tyndale's Bibelübersetzung. Doch zeigt die dramatische Literatur dieses Zeitraums einen unterschiedslosen Wechsel; bei Asham und Latimer darf *you* schon als Regel gelten. Die zweite Ausgabe von Heywood, P. P. aus dem Jahre 1569 hat zuweilen, aber nicht konsequent, die *ye* der ersten (1540) in *you* geändert, so p. 343 *as you can*, 382 *as you see*; ähnlich später bei Peele, Edw. I 187 *you* (4to of 1599) gegenüber *ye* (4to of 1593). In der 2. Hälfte des 16. Jahrhunderts finden sich noch zahlreiche *ye* im Nominativ, *ye* und *you* waren eben beide als Nom. in der Volkssprache lebendig. Dass *ye* um 1600 als Nom. noch ganz gewöhnlich war, zeigt

z. B. Greene, Orl. 34 *Speak as if you knew her not*, ib. 38 *Come, come, you do not use me like a gentlewoman*, wo die Quarto von 1599 gegen die von 1594 *ye* hat.

Auch in der Anrede vor dem Vocativ (vgl. § 98, 4) sind noch Ende des 16. Jahrhunderts *ye* und *you* nebeneinander ohne Unterschied üblich.

Man vergl.: Peele, David and Bethsabe 44
   Depart with me, you men of Israel,
Marlowe, Jew 1410
   And now, you men of Malta, looke about,
mit: Peele, David and Bethsabe 12
   Courage, ye mighty men of Israel,
Marlowe, Tamburlaine 1367
   Awake, ye men of Memphis!
    etc. etc.

Dagegen wird *ye* an offenbar betonter Stelle doch ziemlich gemieden, und durch das gewichtigere *you* ersetzt.

Man vergl.:
Lusty Juventus 83 *Who, you?*
Marriage of Wit and Science 393
   You, you, my faithful squires, deserve no less,
Greene, Bacon and Bungay 199
   How fares the lady Elinor, and you?
vgl. ferner *it is (was, were) you* § 134.

Sehr selten sind Fälle wie:
Peele, David and Bethsabe 15
   Let us, Abisai: — and ye, sons of Judah,
   Be valiant, and maintain your victory.

Eine besondere Stütze für *ye* als Nominativ musste auch die Wechselwirkung zwischen *ye* und *you* gewähren, indem beide am Ende des 16. Jahrhunderts für Nom. und Acc. verwandt werden.

§ 136.
ye für *you*.

Ye für *you* tritt, soweit bis jetzt diese Erscheinung zu übersehen ist, später auf als *you* für *ye* (§ 135), doch früher als im 16. Jahrhundert, aus dem bis jetzt, so weit wir sehen, die ältesten Belege gegeben sind (Mätzner I, 314, Morris § 171).

Das mögen die folgenden Belege zeigen:

P. L. 7/26 (1426) W. Paston.

I submitte me and alle this matier to your good discrecion; and evere gremercy God, and ye, who ever have yow and me in His gracious governance.

P. L. 42/55 (1444) Anonymus.

Sir, ther arn XV jurores abowe to certifie ye, as many as ye will:

P. L. 66/82 (1449) Marg. Paston.

My moder prayith ʒe that ʒe wil send my brother ...

P. L. 522/224 (1465)

... and how that I yaf ye X. acres of fre londe, and ... I have now yove ye other X. acres of fre londe ... I shal yeve ye Goddys curse and myn ...

P. L. 774/159 (1476)

... mastress, for syche pore servyse as I now in my mind owe yow, purposyng, ye not dyspleasyd, duryng my lyff to contenue the same, I beseche yow to pardon my boldness ...

Plumpton Corr. 37 (1476)

And if ye will have it to be made here, it will stand ye to 6 marks or more ...

ib. 101 (1490)

All such newes as I here, John Bell can shew ye by mouth ...

ib. 135 (1499)

And of the day that ye appoynt, I pray ye send me word by my servant.

Digby Mysteries 77/601

I am þe gost of goodnesse þat so wold ʒe gydde.

ib. 79/641 *symond, I thank ʒe speceally*

ib. 110/1477 *woman, I pray ʒe answer me.*

16. Jahrhundert.

Fl. (Wyatt) 25/16 *None of ye all there is that is so madde to seke grapes ...*

Fl. (Weihnachtslieder) 120/96

*Mary moder I pray ye
Take me vp on lest*

ib. (Balladen) 195/33
>For Ihesus love sayd Syr Haryc Perssy
>That dyed for yow and me
>Wende to my lorde my father agayne
>And saye thow sawe me not with yee

ib. (Volksbücher) 202/23
>I feare if ye use it, it wyll ye mar.

ib. (Briefe) 348/23 *no quod he I ame not chargid therby I warrant ye nor wol not be.*

Four Elements 48 *Then go, I pray ye, by and by,*
Hickscorner 151 *I thank ye heartily, Sir Perseverance*
ib. 161 ... *I warrant ye:*
Bale, Thre Lawes 178
>*Marry God geue ye good euen,*

ib. 180, 181, 220, 271, 337 etc. etc.

Bale, Kynge Johan 40
>*I lefte ye not here to be so lyberall.*

ib. 44, 46, 55, 67, 71, 72 etc. etc.

Heywood, Pardoner and Friar 201
>*God and Saint Leonard send ye all his grace,*

ib.   *Wherefore I require all ye in this presence,*
>*For to abide and give due audience.*

ib.   *Now here I shall*
>*To God my prayer make,*
>*To give ye grace.*

ib. 202 *Exhorting ye all to do to them reverence.*

ib. 202 (203, 217) *Firste here I show ye of a holy Jew's hip   A bone*

ib. 202 *I am comen hither ye to visit;*
ib. *Our Saviour preserve ye all from sin,*
ib. 216 *This is the pardon that to heaven shall ye bring —*
ib. 236 *Master Prat, I pray ye me to spare;*

Heywood, P. P. 343
>*I think ye right well occupied,*

ib. 384 *Then would some matter perhaps clout ye,*
>*But, as for me, ye need not doubt yee;*
>*For I had liever be without ye,*
>*Then have such business about ye.*

ib. *after ye,* ib. *I ... do discharge ye.*
ib. 387 *upon ye,* Interlude of Youth 26,
Thersites 419 *Son, ye be wise, keep ye warm!*
R. R. Doister 49 *Get ye home idle folkes.*
ib. (40) 67 *Dame Custance, god ye saue ...*
ib. 51 *I will keepe ye right well ...*
Disobedient Child 275 *... I hold ye a groat,*
ib. 277 *I pray ye,* ib. 309 *I warn ye all:*
Gorboduc 137 *This is in summe, what I woulde haue ye wey:* ib. 475 *... to spoyl ye thus.*
ib. 811 *I called ye nowe to haue your good aduyse.*
Cambyses 178
  If a man ask ye, ye may hap to say nay.
ib. 179
Ah, ye slaves, I will teach ye how ye shall me deride.
ib. *I will beat ye,* ib. *Now have at ye, afresh again even now:* ib. *I can ye not abide.,* etc.
ib. 190   *If faithful steward I ye find*
          The same I will requite.
ib. 201, 233, 234,
Appius and Virginia 119 *Have with ye, have at ye ...*
ib. 136 (2 Belege),
G. G. Needle 198, 240, 244, 251,
Trial of Treasure 267, 271, 272, 288, 289,
Damon and Pithias 59, 77, 78,
Lyly, End. 13 *Nay I tell yee my master is more than a man.* Woman 187, Galathea 253.
Peele, Arr. 30 *Fair Venus ... bears it from ye all.*
ib. 55 *I promise ye,*
Edward I 86 *Madam, content ye:*
David and Bethsabe 13
  Our angry swords shall smite ye to the ground,
Old Wives Tale 224
Marlowe, Tamburlaine 307 *Soft ye, my Lords ...* 1849, 2733, Faust 997, Jew 1226, Dido 378,
Hero 8 *I could tell ye,*
Greene, Menaphon 64 *Ile serue yee ...*
Orlando 13, Bacon 152,
  .

Alphonsus 44
*That we should cause you make as mickle speed
As well you might, to hear for certainty
Of that shall happen to your king and ye.*

James IV 122, Looking Glass 86, Pinner 186, Puttenham 281 ... *I saw ye not.*

Rare Triumphs 158 *Content ye both:*

Lodge, Wounds 192

... I hope a man may now call ye knave by authority.

Leycester Corr. 65 *Thus referring ye for the rest to Mr. Davyson at his comyng...*

ib. *I warrant ye* etc. etc. fast auf jeder Seite, desgl. in den Three Lords and Three Ladies, den Three Ladies of London und vor allem in The two angry Women of Abington (s. unten).

NB. Bis zu G. G. Needle (um 1566) sind alle Belege gegeben, später in Anbetracht der grossen Anzahl nur eine Auswahl.

§ 137.

Bemerkungen hierzu.

Wie unsere Belege ergeben, stammt unser erstes Beispiel aus dem Jahre 1426, die nächsten aus 1444, 1449 etc.

Wir können also, da alle drei Briefe verschiedene Personen zu Verfassern haben, schon in der ersten Hälfte des 15. Jahrhunderts eine ziemliche Verbreitung von *ye* als Accusativ mit Recht annehmen; da ferner stets erst eine gewisse Zeit zwischen dem Auftreten irgend einer grammatischen Erscheinung und ihrer schriftlichen Fixierung verstreicht, so dürfen wir, auch wenn wir beachten, dass diese Zeit in Anbetracht des Briefcharakters bei brieflicher Fixierung meist eine kürzere ist, doch wohl berechtigt sein, die Anfänge der Uebertragung von *ye* auf den Accusativ für die gesprochene Volkssprache in das 14. Jahrhundert zurückzuverlegen, zumal da umgekehrt *you* für *ye* schon Mitte des 14. Jahrhunderts sicher belegt ist (cf. p. 135). Dass wir es hier mit einer Erscheinung zu tun haben, die für das ganze 15. Jahrhundert mehr der Umgangssprache als der Literatursprache angehört, zeigen uns weiter vortrefflich unsere Belege aus der 2. Hälfte des 15. Jahrhunderts — kein einziges Beispiel in dem sonst überaus populären und vielgelesenen (vgl. als Beweis die Bemerkung Asham's im Schoolemaster, p. 80 „*In our forefathers tyme, whan Papistrie, as a standyng poole, couered and ouerflowed all England, fewe bookes were read in our tong, sauyng certaine bookes Cheualrie, as they sayd, for pastime and pleasure, which, as some say, were made in Monasteries, by idle Monkes or wanton Chanons: as one for example Morte Arthure:*") Morte Darthure, dagegen mehrere in der Briefliteratur der Zeit, den Paston Letters, der Plumpton Correspondence und, was am meisten beweist, in den Digby Mysteries. Erst mit dem Beginn des 16. Jahrhunderts geht *ye* als Accusativ, wie unsere Belege ergeben, ganz in die eigentliche Literatursprache über; besonders die dialogische Form des Dramas lässt die alte Form in neuer Geltung zu reicher Entfaltung gelangen. Demzufolge zeigt sich nun in der 2. Hälfte des 16. Jahrhunderts der Höhepunkt der Entwicklung. Wenn wir auch hierbei in Betracht ziehen, dass die grosse Zahl der Belege bei den Dramatikern wie Lyly, Peele, Greene, Marlowe nicht einer absoluten Mehrheit entspricht, so bleibt damit doch zunächst erwiesen, dass *ye* als Accusativ in der Schriftsprache allgemein üblich war. Dass nun aber weiter in der Umgangssprache des ausgehenden 16. Jahrhunderts *ye* als Accusativ thatsächlich das herrschende geworden war, zeigt der ganz bedeutende Prozentsatz in den „Three Ladies of London" und „Look about You" sowie das wirkliche Ueberwiegen der *ye* als Accusativ über die *you* in der Leycester Corr. sowie in der volkstümlichen Posse „The two angry Women of Abington (1599)"; es hat also an einem völligen Siege von *ye* als Acc. nicht sehr viel mehr gefehlt, einem Siege, der dann das Verhältnis von *ye* und *you* geradezu umgekehrt hätte.

Weiterentwicklung.

Bei Shakspere „steht für *you* sehr oft *ye*" (Deutschbein § 36). Das folgende 17. Jahrhundert zeigt uns eine rückschreitende (und damit in diesem Falle uniformierende) Bewegung, *ye* als Acc. wird durch *you* wieder aus der Literatursprache verdrängt und auf die Konversationssprache und auf den Briefstil (Franz 215) beschränkt; doch sind die Fälle von *ye* als Accusativ noch heute nicht völlig ausgestorben und (Mätzner I, 313 f.) in der Poesie wie in der Vulgärsprache noch zu finden.

§ 138.

Noch einige Worte über die Ursachen der Vertauschung von *ye* mit *you* und umgekehrt. Wenngleich Jespersen dieselben bereits eingehend und vielleicht auch schon erschöpfend behandelt hat, möge doch noch einmal kurz auf verschiedene Punkte hingewiesen werden.

Einfluss der Stellung des Pronomens (Jesp. 188). Vgl. hierzu § 97 f. Pronomen beim Imperativ und § 178—182, Bezeichnung des reflexiven Verhältnisses bei intransitiven Verben, insbesondere § 182, *to doubt* und *to fear*, wodurch Jespersens Ansicht bestätigt wird, dass diese Wechselwirkung zur Möglichkeit der Verwechselung enorm viel beigetragen hat.

Einfluss der unpersönlichen Verben.

Betreffs des Uebergangs von unpersönlichen zu persönlichen Verben cf. Anhang I.

§ 139.

1. Eine andere Art von Fällen des Pronomens beim Imperativ (§ 97 f.) in Wechselwirkung mit dem ethischen Dativ (§ 152) war ein weiteres Moment, das Gefühl für Kasusunterschiede zu verwischen. Man vergleiche folgende Fälle:

G. G. Needle 218 *Take thee this to make up thy mouth,*

Marlowe, Massacre 337

Hold the, tall soldier, take thee this and flye

wo auch *thou* einen (wenngleich anderen) guten Sinn geben würde; solche, diesen genau analoge Fälle sind z. B. folgende:

G. G. Needle 217

Take thou this, old whore, for amends...

Marlowe, Faust II 1448

Take thou this other...

Besonders bemerkenswert: Kyd, Spanish Tragedy 72

Here, for thy further satisfaction, take thou this.

Quarto von 1623, 1633 „*thee*".

Als ähnliche Fälle wären zu vergleichen:
Marlowe, Massacre 302
Hold, take thou this reward.
Peele, Edward I 171
Verssess, quoth he take thou King Edward's chain,
etc. etc.
Die Möglichkeit des Einflusses solcher Fälle ist unverkennbar.

2. Eine ähnliche Wechselwirkung findet statt bei Fällen wie:
Thersites 412
And so within a while I trow I make thee shall.
Hier ist ausser *thee* (Acc. c. Inf. abhängig von *make*) auch *thou* (dass-Satz mit ausgelassenem *that*, vgl. den § 117, 3 angeführten Beleg) möglich.

§ 140.

Inbetreff *him* und *them* für *he* und *they* kann auch folgende Möglichkeit als bedeutungsvoll angesehen werden: In § 196 wird gezeigt, dass *him self* und *them selves* im 15. und auch im 16. Jahrhundert noch ganz allgemein ohne hinzugefügtes *he, them* als Subjekt verwandt wurden. Wenn wir nun bedenken, dass das einfache *self, selves* für *himself, themselves* (cf. § 197) auch noch üblich waren, war da die Möglichkeit, *him* und *them* nicht mehr als Accusative zu empfinden, so ganz unwahrscheinlich?

Weiterentwicklung.

Inbetreff der bei Shakspere vorkommenden Fälle von Kasusvertauschungen siehe die betr. §§ bei Jespersen sowie Abbot § 207 ff., Deutschbein § 34.

Für die heutige Zeit vergl. ausser Jespersen auch Franz, Die Dialektsprache bei Ch. Dickens, Engl. Stud. XII, 223 f., Zupitza, Archiv 84, 180, John Koch, Archiv 94 (1893) p. 3 sowie Ellinger, Beiträge zur engl. Grammatik, Engl. Stud. XX, 399 f. und Baumann XCVI f.

Anhang. — Unconnected Subject.

§ 141.

Im Anschluss an die vorangegangenen Kasusvertauschungen müssen wir einer Erscheinung aus der Syntax des englischen Verbums gedenken, die aller Wahrscheinlichkeit nach von einem nicht unbedeutenden Einflusse auf diese gewesen ist, ein Nom. c. Inf., von Jespersen als „Unconnected Subject" bezeichnet.

Da wir diese Erscheinung nur mit Rücksicht auf unsere Zwecke zu behandeln gedenken, verweisen wir im einzelnen auf Jespersen § 164 ff., Kellner, Hist. Outl. § 399 f., für die P. L. auch auf die recht ausführliche, aber äusserlich wenig übersichtliche Darstellung Blume's, D. Sprache d. P. L. Progr. Bremen 1882 p. 38 ff.

Wir geben im folgenden zunächst eine Reihe von Belegen aus unseren Quellen, indem wir unter Verweisung auf Blume die dort erwähnten nicht wiederholen.

a) Der Infinitiv in Ausrufen.

Es tritt der grammatisch zu erwartende Kasus ein:
Peele, Edward I 167
Versses.: *Tidings to make thee tremble, English king.*
Longsh.: *Me tremble, boy!*
Marlowe, Edward II 288
Edw. Third.: *This argues that you spilt my father's blood,*
Else would you not entreat for Mortimer.
Isab.: *I spill his blood! no.*
Greene, Looking Glass 123
Away, vassal, be gone! thou speak unto the king!
Three Ladies 311
Diss.: *Simplicity, now of my honesty, very heartily well-met.*
Simpl.: *Thou have honesty now? thy honesty is quite gone:*

b) Der Infinitiv in anderen Fällen.

1. Der Nom. c. Inf. anstatt eines von mehreren dass-Sätzen.
P. L. cf. Blume p. 39.
M. 40/35 *But this is my counceill ... that we lete puruey X knyztes men of good fame, and they to kepe this swerd ...*

ib. 310/21 ... *hit was neuer the custome of no place of worship that euer I came in, whan a knyghte and a lady asked herborugh, and they to receyue hem, and after to destroye them that ben his gestes.*

Egerton Papers 9

That all monasteries ... shall alsoe gyve out theire Chaptures seales ... and they that wilnot so doo, to be taken as rebelles according to theire desertes, and that the saide writynges shalbe enrolled in the Kinges records as they be in Inglande.

ib. *That these articles shall extende to all orders of fryers, observantes as other, what so ever they be, and they to affyrme the same under their seales.*

ib. *That the said Archbusshop shall se a unitie and concorde amonges the Gray Friers, named de observancia et de communi vita, and they to stand at his arbitrament.*

Diary of Machyn 122

The XXII day of Desember was a proclamasyon thrugh London ... that they to be taken and browth a-for the mayre or shreyff, baylle, justus a pesse, or constabulle, or oder offesers, and thay to ley them in presun, tyll the quen and her consell, and thay to remayn ther plesur, and to stand boyth body and goodes at her grace('s) plesur.

Greene, Looking Glass 83

... that ... you have forfeited your recognisance, and he to have the land.

2. Der Nom. c. Inf. anstatt eines anderen (Haupt- oder Neben-) Satzes.

P. L. Blume p. 42.

P. L. 239/328 *Wherefore, gracyus Lord, plese it your hyghe Majeste to delyvere such as we wole accuse ... and ȝe to be honorabled ...*

ib. 405/31 *... and lat hym make wrytyng unto them what day they shall come, and they to make a new eleccyon accordyng unto the law.*

ib. 493/165

... to make and found a College of VII. prests and VII. pore folk at Caster, in Flegge in Norffolk, for the soule of Sir John Fastolf, Knyght; thei to be indued with certeyn rent ...

M. 237/16 ...*for she loueth none of thy felauship, and thou to loue that loueth not the, is but grete foly,*

ib. 453/3 ...*for thow hast putte me and my bretheren to a shame, and thy fader slewe our fader, and thow to lye by our moder is to moche shame for vs to suffre.*

ib. 774/2 ...*bethynke the how thou arte a kynges sone, and knyghte of the table round and thou to be aboute to dishonoure the noble kynge that made the knyghte...*

Heywood, P. P. 372
> *But when I bethought me how this chanced,*
> *And...(that I) could not keep my friend from dangers,*
> *But she to die so dangerously,*
> *For her soul-health especially;*

Egerton Papers 14
And where the inhabitants understand not the Englishe tongue, they to cause the Englishe to be translated truły into the Irishe tongue...

Everyman 108
> *If I my heart should to you break,*
> *And then you to turn your minde fro me,*

Latimer, Sermons 147
...*and rather geue them moncy to take the offyce in hande, then they to geue money for it.*

Der für uns wesentliche Punkt ist, wie sich hieraus ergiebt, der, dass vornehmlich in der Volkssprache des 15. und 16. Jahrhunderts, aber auch im Curialstil der Nom. c. Inf. eine ausserordentliche Verbreitung hatte, der jedoch als solcher nur zu erkennen ist, wenn das Subjekt des Infinitivs ein Pronomen bildet, dessen Kasus nicht zweifelhaft sein kann. Dieser Nom. c. Inf. tritt nun auch da ein, wo die streng durchgeführte grammatische Konstruktion den Accusativ verlangen würde (vgl. dazu auch Jesp. p. 207 f.); der Grund liegt teils in dem grossen Uebergewicht der Nominativ-Fälle teils in der mangelnden Kasusbezeichnung bei Substantiven.

Wenn wir nun weiter erwägen, dass auch der Acc. c. Inf. zum mindesten ebenso verbreitet war, wie der Nom. c. Inf.

(man vgl. nur Blume p. 33 ff.), so haben wir hier ein neues Gebiet von Fällen vor uns, das geeignet war, das Gefühl für Kasusunterscheidung zu trüben.

Gebrauch von *thou* (*thee, thy, thine*) und *ye* (*you, your*).
§ 142. Vorbemerkung.

Ueber den Unterschied im Gebrauch von *thou* und *you* in historischer Entwicklung haben vornehmlich gehandelt: Kellner, Hist. Outl. § 277 ff., Blanchardyn § 10 b; vgl. ferner Ellinger p. 130, für das 17. und 18. Jahrhundert auch Franz 216 ff., der speziell die Stellung und Stimmung des Anredenden eingehender in Betracht zieht.

Unsere Untersuchung für das 15. und 16. Jahrhundert hat die Resultate dieser in allen wesentlichen Punkten bestätigt. Wir wollen uns daher darauf beschränken, unsere Beobachtungen in möglichster Kürze vorzuführen.

I. Anrede an Gott und Maria.
§ 143.

Immer *thou* im Anschluss an die Bibel, z. B.:
John Knox 30, Greene, Looking Glass 131; Fl. 10/1 f.;
desgl. umgekehrt: Latimer, Sermons 27.

II. Anrede an den Menschen.
§ 144.

a) An den Menschen im Allgemeinen.

In diesem Falle steht ausnahmslos *thou*, zum Teil im Anschluss an die Bibel, wie sich aus dem häufigen Vorkommen in theologischen Schriften ergiebt, aber auch in sprichwörtlichen Redensarten sowie Orakeln, z. B.:
Fl. (Speculum Xristiani) 9
Thou schalt loue god with Herte entiere
With alle thy soule and alle thy might
Other god in no manere
Thou schalt not haue by daye ne nyght.
Latimer, Ploughers 30, More, Utopia 108, 111,

R. A., Toxophilus 155
Knowe thy selfe: that is to saye, learne to knowe what thou arte able, fitte, and apt vnto, and folowe that.
R. A., Schoolemaster 54
To laughe, to lie, to flatter, to face:
Four waies in Court to win men grace.
If thou be thrall to none of theise,
Away good Peek goos, hens John Cheese:
Marke well my word, and marke their dede,
And think this verse part of thy Creed.

John Knox 23
for this cause was woman put vnder thy power ... and thou wast pronounced Lorde ouer her, that she shulde obey the ...
Lyly, Midas 23 (Orakel)
In Pactolus goe bathe thy wish and thee,
Thy wish the waves shall have, and thou be free.
Mother Bombie 131 (Wahrsagung)
In studying to be over naturall,
Thou art like to be unnaturall,
And all about a naturall:
Thou shalt bee eased of a charge,
If thou thy conscience discharge,
And this I commit to thy charge.
Sidney, Ap. 54
With a sword, thou maist kill thy Father, and with a sword thou maist defende thy Prince and Country.

b) Im Besonderen.
§ 145. α) Im gewöhnlichen Dialog.

1. Eltern und Kinder.

In der Regel sprechen die Eltern zu den Kindern *thou*, die Kinder zu den Eltern *you*. So z. B.:

Gorboduc 68 Ferrex zur Mutter *you*,
umgekehrt 69 *thou*,
  ib. 1127 Gorboduc zu Porrex *thou*,
umgekehrt 1132 *you*,

Jacob and Esau 230 Rebecca zu Jacob *thou*, umgekehrt *you*, ib. 260 Rebecca zu Esau *thou*, umgekehrt *you*,

Rare Triumphs 213 Vater (Duke) zur Tochter (Fidelia) *thou*, umgekehrt *you*.

Doch finden sich Ausnahmen:

P. L. 522/224 Vater zum Sohn

Remember the that thou hast be the costlyest childe that evere I hadde, and how that I yaf ye X acres… And I have now yove ye other X acres… and me thynketh be the thou heldest the not lowest, but woldest have all. But on thing I shall sey to the; if thou trouble John, thy brother… I shal yeve ye Goddys curse and myn…

Fl. (Froissartübersetzung) 310/60 Vater zum Sohn *ye*.

etc. etc.

2. Vorgesetzter zum Untergebenen, der höher stehende zum niedriger stehenden.

In der Regel *thou*, umgekehrt *you*.

P. L. 612/356 (Worte des Königs an einen Unterthanen)

„*Brandon, thow thou can begyll the Dwk of Norffolk, and bryng hym abow the thombe as thow lyst, I let the wet thow shalt not do me so; for I undyrstand thy fals delyng well inow.*"

M. 38/27, 61/34 Arthur zu Merlyn „*thou*", ib. 102/9 (Bettler zum König) *Syr it was told me that at this time of your maryage ye wolde yeue any man the yefte that he wold aske…*

Damon and Pithias 22 Damon zu seinem Diener *thou*, umgekehrt *you*, ib. 27 Aristipp zu seinem Diener *thou*, umgekehrt *you*,

Lyly, Endimion 35 Tophas zu seinem Pagen *thou*, umgekehrt *you*, Introduct. Sketch 71 Erzbischof zu einem John Penry *thou*, umgekehrt *you*;

etc. etc.

Auch hier haben wir begründete Ausnahmen, so in feierlicher Rede:

M. 102/8 (Bettler zum König) … *I byseche Jhesu saue the* …

3. Die Anrede an den Leser

geschieht durch *thou* und *you*, ersteres stets, wenn der Autor (Drucker) sich mit dem Leser auf einen intimeren Standpunkt stellt, was sich auch durch die Beiwörter deutlich ausspricht (Einfluss der Bibelsprache!), z. B.:

Joy, Ap. IX (Vorrede Tyndale's zur 2. Aufl. des New Testament)
Thou shalt vnderstonde moost dere reader...
ib. 12 ... *wherby thou mayst se (good reader)*...
More, Utopia 167,
Udall, Dem. 12
to direct thee (good reader) vnto thy further instruction, in the points therof. Thou hast in euery chapter, diuers proofs ...wherewith thou mayest...informe thy conscience: ...I am to shew thee...

Introd. Sketch 24 (The Printer to the Reader)
But cease to muse good christian reader, whosoeuer thou art:
Udall, State 3
Gentle Reader...thou knowest that..., Marlowe, Ovid 107;
dagegen ye (you):

M. 286/5 *And wete ye wel...*, ib. 288/4, Fl. (Caxton 3/38, Joy, Apol. X *Moreover ye shall vnderstonde that...*, R. A., Schoolemaster 144, Puttenham 31 (das Buch ist Lord Burghley gewidmet).

4. Anrede an den Angeklagten im Verhör.
Immer *you*, z. B.: Introductory Sketch 86, 88 ff., 170—172.

§ 146. β) In verächtlicher und Schimpf-Rede.

Teils *thou*, teils *you*, teils beides nebeneinander, z. B. *thou*: M. 326/6
Fy vpon the said sir Andred fals traitour that thou arte...
Fl. (Caxton) 5/36
A felon trayttre, fro whens is comen to the so grete cruelte, that thou hast brought with the...
Fl. (Memoiren) 325/27
Thou hoorson, how wilt thow doe?
Tyndale, Luk. 4/34
...what hast thou to do with vs, thou Jesus of Nazareth?
(Auth. Vers. und Rev. Vers. ebenso).
Jack Juggler 137
For a man may see, thou whoreson goose,
Thou wouldest lese thine arse, if it were loose!

Disobedient Child 304
Slay me with thy knife, thou shitten dastard!
New Custom 44
Nay, thou stinking heretic, art thou there indeed?
Puttenham 189
Or as another said a mouthy Aduocate, why barkest thou at me so sore?
Udall, State 22
Awaye thou rayling hypocrite, I will talke with thee no longer, if I catche thee in London, I will make thee kiss the Clinke for this geare.

ye, you:
Bale, Kynge Johan 66
Holde your tunge, ye whore, or by the messe ye shall repent.
Interlude of Youth 8
Ye whoreson, trowest thou so?
Jacob and Esau 190
Up, or I shall raise you in faith, ye drowsy whoreson.
G. G. Needle 205
Ye foolish dolt, ye were to seek, ere we had got our ground;
Trial of Treasure 294
Will ye be packing, you ill-favoured lout?
Sidney, Astrophel and Stella p. 53, Strophe 15
You then vngrateful theefe, you murthering Tyrant you, You Rebel runnaway...
Rare Triumphs 231
ye whore, I am not for I am not for your diet.
Peele, Old Wives Tale 229 *You capon's face...*
Greene, Pinner 194 *You whoreson cowardly scab...*
ib. 202 *Peace, ye slave, see where king Edward is.*

thou und *you* nebeneinander:
Bale, Kynge Johan 4
Hold yowr peace, ye whore, or ellys by masse, I trowe, I shall cawse the pope to curse the as black as a crowe.
Jack Juggler 127
What, ye drunken knave, begin you to rage! Take that: art thou Master Bongrace's page?

New Custom 44
>   *Ye precious whoreson art thou there too?*

Damon and Pithias 60
>   *Ye slave, I will have my pennyworths of thee therefore,
> if I die.*

ib. 102
>   *Away, villain! away, you flatt'ring parasite!
>   Away, the plague of this court! thy filed tongue, that forged lies,
>   No more here shall do hurt: away, false sycophant, wilt thou not?*

G. G. Needle 243
>   *What, you foul beast, does think 'tis either pild or bald?
>   Nay, ich thank God, chill not for all that thou may'st spend,
>   That chad one scab on my narse as broad as thy finger's end.*

Hieraus ergiebt sich: *thou* sowohl wie *ye, you* waren in verächtlicher und Schimpf-Rede im 15. und 16. Jahrhundert üblich; wir haben uns das zum Teil wohl so zu denken, dass, wenn der Sprecher dem Angeredeten näher stand, *thou,* wenn er ihm ferner stand, *ye, you* gebraucht wurde; man vergl. jedoch auch § 150 (unterschiedsloser Wechsel von *thou* und *you*).

III. Anrede an leblose und vorgestellte Dinge etc.
§ 147.

Immer *thou*, z. B.:

Wyatt an die Laute Fl. 21/4 (Sidney, Arcadia 167), Howard an das Gefängnis Fl. 32/20, Latimer Ploughers 22

>   *Therfore I saye, repente O London. Repent, repente.
>   Thou heareste thy faultes tolde the, amend them amend them.*

ib. 27 an England, Marl., Tamb. 2130 an die Erde, Hero 55
>   *Dear place, I kiss thee, and do welcome thee,*

Sidney, Arcadia 734 an die Nacht;

an abstrakte Wesen: Fl. (More) 42/19 an das *flatering fortune,* Lyly, Euphues 180 *Beauty where is thy blaze?* Sidney, Astrophel 4/2 an *Vertue,* ib. 10/1 an *Reason,* insbesondere an den Tod: Fl. (Buleyn) 37/1 ff., R. R. Doister 13 *Come death when thou wilt I am weary of my life.*

Marlowe, Tamburlaine 3415
>   *Death, whether art thou gone, that both we liue?*

§ 148.

Fassen wir das in § 143—147 gesagte im allgemeinen zum Resultat zusammen, so ergiebt sich, dass im 15. und 16. Jahrhundert für die Frage, ob *thou* oder *you*, in der Regel die angeredete Person massgebend war, dass im einzelnen jedoch die Situation Abweichungen bedingte und herbeiführte.

(Als direktes Zeugnis für die Bedeutung von *thou* vergl. man Hickscorner 180
Avaunt, caitiff, dost thou thou me!
I am come of good kin, I tell thee!
My mother was a lady of the stews blood born,
And (knight of the halter) my father ware an horn;
Therefore I take it in full great scovn,
That thou shouldest thus check me.)

Zugleich sehen wir aber auch hieraus, worauf schon Franz a. a. O. aufmerksam macht, dass dasselbe *thou* eine ganze Reihe von Nuancen besitzt, dass die *thou* durchaus nicht gleichwertig sind; es ist eben auch hier zu bedenken, dass der Buchstabe uns die lebendige Sprache nicht wiederzugeben vermag, wo der Klang der Stimme und die Geberdensprache sehr oft wie hier die ausschlaggebenden Faktoren sind; so haben wir ein *thou* der Ehrfurcht vor Gott und Maria, ein *thou* der Verehrung und Achtung vor Eltern und Vorgesetzten, ein *thou* der Entrüstung und Verachtung etc., ähnlich bei *ye, you*.

§ 149.

Schon bei Erörterung der einzelnen Fälle haben wir gesehen, dass die gewöhnliche Regel, ob *thou* oder *you*, durch Sonderfälle durchbrochen wird, die aber der Begründung nie entbehrten. Gerade so nun, wie mehrere *thou* in ein und demselben Satze eine durchaus verschiedene Färbung haben können, also gewissermassen *thou* 1. mit *thou* 2. etc. wechseln kann, so verhält es sich auch mit *thou* gegenüber *ye, you*, je nach der den Sprechenden beherrschenden Stimmung.

Fälle von offenbaren Stimmungsübergängen sind vereinzelt schon oben erwähnt, ausserdem auch von Kellner behandelt. Man vergl. hierzu ferner:

M. 102/26 König zum Sohn eines Bettlers *thou*, 102/36, wo er ihn mehr achtet, *you*.

Lyly, Euphues 36
Anrede des Verfassers an den jungen Gentleman erst *you* dann moralisierend *thou*.

Introductory Sketch 41
Lord Treasurer zu Barrow erst *you*, dann in vertraulich herablassenden Tone *Thou arte a fantasticall fellowe*.

Marlowe, Massacre 345
Cousin, assure you I am resolute,
Whatsoever any whisper in mine ears,
Not to suspect disloyalty in thee:
And so, sweet coz, farewell.

§ 150.

Demgegenüber haben wir nun aber doch Fälle, wo *thou* und *you* tatsächlich unmittelbar nebeneinander gebraucht werden, ohne dass ein greifbarer Grund wenigstens für unsere jetzige Auffassung und Empfindung ersichtlich wäre.

Kellner (Abwechselung und Tautologie, zwei Eigentümlichkeiten des alt- und mittelenglischen Stiles, Engl. Stud. XX, p. 1 ff.) will unter anderem den Wechsel von *thou* und *you* als Stilmittel nachweisen. Ob das wirklich in dem ausgesprochenen Masse der Fall ist, möchten wir bezweifeln; der unterschiedslose Wechsel von *thou* und *you* scheint vielmehr doch der Umgangssprache entsprungen zu sein; man vergl. die folgenden Fälle, darunter besonders den ersten:

P. L. 75/97
Fals thefe, you shall be hanged, and as mony of thy maistre men as may be goten ...

NB. Blumes Behauptung a. a. O. p. 14 „Von der Anwendung der 2. Person Singularis findet sich in den P. L. kein Beispiel..." ist also unrichtig.

M. 341/1 ... *but goo where someuer thou wilt, for I will not go with you.*

ib. 567/7 ... *I haue herd youre complaynte and of thy treason that thow hast owed me so longe.*

Myst. ed. Hone 25
I crye ye mercy and thin' erthe cus; (wenn hier *y* nicht vielleicht das handschriftliche ʒ wiedergiebt?)

Everyman 99
Be you neuer so gay:
Ye think sin in the beginning full sweet,
Which in the end causeth thy soul to weep,
When the body lieth in clay.
Here shall you see how Fellowship and Jollity,
Both Strength, Pleasure, and Beauty,
Will fade from thee as flower in May;

Calisto and Melibaea 76
Ah, ill-tongued wretch, will ye not see?
Thinkest thou, lurden, thou handlest me fair?
Why, knave, wouldest thou put me in despair?

Cambyses 242
Will all expedition, I Murder will take place,
Though thou be a queen, ye be under my grace.

G. G. Needle 241
Chill show you his face, ich warrant thee...

Greene, Looking Glass 86
Sirrah, you, hearest thou, fellow?

Angry Women 345
So ho! I come: where are ye? where art thou? here?

Anm.: Auf solche Weise entstehen wahrscheinlich Fälle von Kontamination wie: New Custom 18
Art you minded on me your anger to wreak...?

Weiterentwicklung.

Inbetreff Shakspere's Sprachgebrauch in dieser Hinsicht cf. Abbot § 231 ff., Deutschbein § 32; *thou* ist jetzt in der Umgangssprache ausser bei Quäkern (Bibel) und in Dialekten geschwunden (Storm 937).

§ 151. Dativus commodi und incommodi.

Es sei konstatiert, dass die Verwendung des Dativs in diesem Sinne wie im Ae., Me., und jetzigem Ne. auch dem

15. und 16. Jahrhundert durchaus geläufig war. Einige wenige Beispiele werden genügen, das zu zeigen:

P. L. 778/164
> ...*it shalle cost me grett mony*...

ib. 839/254 *I have goten me a frende*...

Thersites 398 *Get thee a wallet:*

Disobedient Child 283
> *It hath cost him so much on costly array,*

Marlowe, Jew 1312 *Goe buy thee garments:*

Greene, Looking Glass 99 *it cost me forty pence in ale*...

§ 152. Ethischer Dativ.

Inbetreff seiner Verwendung bei **intransitiven** Verben siehe § 178 ff.

Soweit er bei **transitiven** steht ohne Beziehung auf das Subjekt, ist er eine Erscheinung, die für das 15. und 16. Jahrhundert als vor allem der **volkstümlichen Umgangssprache** angehörig bezeichnet werden muss; wir finden ihn in Denkmälern aller Art, besonders im Drama, dagegen nicht, was sich leicht begreift, in der **Briefkorrespondenz und Tagebuchlitteratur**.

Eine Auswahl von Belegen wird ein klares Bild von der Verbreitung und demzufolge auch von der Bedeutung des dat. eth. im 15. und 16. Jahrhundert geben:

M. 101/20 *Now Merlyn said kyng Arthur, goo thow and aspye me in al this land l knyghtes*...

ib. 353/26 *Thenne sayd sir Tristram here shalle ye abyde me these ten dayes*...

Bale, Kynge Johan 97
> *And marke me thys wele, they never ponnysh for popery,*

Tyndale, Ap. 13/2 (Auth. Vers. und Rev. Vers. ebenso)
> *separate me Barnabas and Saul, for the worke*...

Latimer, Sermons 63
> *Vpon thys the bishop goeth me to the quene Katherin*...

Interlude of Youth 9
> *Sir, I pray you soil me this question*

G. G. Needle 221
> *She stands me gasping behind the door*...

ib. 239 *Call me the knave hither, he shall sure kiss the stocks.*
Lyly, Euphues 381
Which way I should vse thee I know not...
Puttenham 209
Take me the two former figures and put them into one...
Marlowe, Tamburlaine 678
*Thou breakst the law of Armes, vnlesse thou kneele,
And cry me „mercie, noble King"!*
Greene, James IV 127
Now, sir, cut it me like the battlements of a custard, full of round holes: edge me the sleeves with Coventry blue...
Looking Glass 114
*Go, break me up the brazen doors of dreams,
And bind me cursed Morpheus in a chain,*
Sidney, Astrophel and Stella 49/12
He sits me fast how euer I do sturre,
Arcadia 491
But as he was by divers principal young gentlemen, to his no small glory, lifted up on horseback, comes me a page of Amphialus, who... delivered a letter unto him...
Angry Women 274 *No, wife, she plays ye true.*
Mucedorus 224
You have lost me a good occupation by this means.
Der dat. eth. „oft" bei Shakspere (Deutschbein § 47).

§ 153. *to me ward.*

Ohne im übrigen auf die Stellung des Personalpronomens, die in das Kapitel der Syntax des Satzes gehört, eingehen zu wollen, müssen wir der Stellung des Personalpronomens in Verbindung mit *toward(s)* gedenken.

P. L. 125/167 *and in lyke wyse standith Sir Thomas Tudenham his neighburs to hymward* (ib. 727/92 *to hym wardys*), ib. 150/202 *The baly... knewe not at that tyme what myn unkyll was to us ward.*

ib. 506/196 *... I fynd hym, as me symyth, ryght well disposyd to you wards;* (ib. 708/69) ib. 638/395 *And than the Duk of Clarence and the Erle of Warwick harde, that the King was comyng to them warde*...

ib. 660/419 *Therfore I pray you comune with my Cosyn Clere at London, and wete how he is dysposyd to her ward*... (ib. 668/4, 733/104).

ib. 668/4 *Item, I beseche yow... to thanke hym ffor hys goode wyll to me wardes*... (ib. 703/58, 717/79).

Fox 14 ...*ye shal wel vnderstande the very yonste and good wyl that I bere to you ward*...

ib. 87 *They leep and ronne faste fro them ward al that they myghte*...

Tyndale, 2. Cor. 1/12 ...*we haue had our conuersacion in the world, and moost of all to you wardes;* (Auth. Vers. und Rev. Vers. *to you-ward*).

2. Thess. 3/4 *to you warde* (Auth. Vers. und Rev. Vers. *touching you*).

2. Peter 3/9 *The Lorde is not slacke to fulfyll his promes, as some men count slacknes: but is pacient to vs warde*... (Auth. Vers. und Rev. Vers. *to you-ward*).

Sidney, Arcadia 313
She concluded, that there at last I... should be assured to her ward...

ib. 513 ...*who never knew what love meant, but only to him-ward*...

Für M. und Greene vergl.:
M. 720/19 ...*to the world ward.*
Greene, Alphonsus 67 ...*to the temple wards,*
etc. etc.

Wir haben es hier mit einer auf der ursprünglichen Selbständigkeit zweier Kompositionsglieder beruhenden Erscheinung zu thun, die sowohl im Me. (Stratm. 623) als auch schon im Ae. belegt ist und zwar hier auch bei *wið-weard*.

Man vergl.:
* Aelfric, Lives of the Saints ed. Skeat 23 B. 777 f.
þā ongan seo leo fægnian wið þæs ealdan weard.

---

* Diese Belege wurden mir von meinem Freunde MacGillivray freundlichst zur Verfügung gestellt.

ib. 26/118 *wið þæs heofones weard.*
ib. 31/78 *hēt þæt he biheolde to his drihtne werd.*
ib. 23 B. 684 *wið... weardes swā ēode hēo on uppan þā huescan ȳða wið his weardes, gangende swā swā on drȳȝum.*

Aus unseren Belegen des 15. und 16. Jahrhunderts (die der P. L. haben wir nicht sämtlich angeführt) ergiebt sich, dass diese Stellung, *to* + Personalpronomen + *ward (e, y)(s)* (also eine Trennung der beiden Kompositionsglieder von *towards*) eine im 15., in geringerem Masse in der 1. Hälfte des 16. Jahrhunderts volkstümliche Erscheinung war, die sich aber in der 2. Hälfte des 16. Jahrhunderts seltener zeigt.

Weiterentwicklung.

Ebenso vereinzelt bei Shakspere und später (cf. Flügel, Dict. 1577 Sp. 3).

Anm.: Diese Trennung der beiden Kompositionsglieder von *toward* zeigt, nebenbei bemerkt, dass sie noch im 15. und 16. Jahrhundert durchaus als solche im Bewusstsein des Volkes lebten, was wieder für die Verschiebung des Accentes auf das zweite Kompositionsglied nicht ohne Wichtigkeit ist; cf. Morsb., Me. Gr. § 27 Ende.

Possessivpronomen.

§ 154. Ersatz von *its*.

Für *its* (cf. § 23) werden im 15. und 16. Jahrhundert gebraucht:

1. *his* bezw. *her*, z. B.:

Sidney, Ap. 50 ... *euery word hauing his naturall seate*...
Puttenham 274 *euery thing hath his season*...
Joy, Ap. XI *If the text be left vncorrupt, it will pourge hir selfe ... as a sethinge pot casteth vp hir scome*...

2. *of it, therof*, z. B.:

Gorboduc, Vorwort des Druckers 5
...*and neuer intended by the authors therof to be published:*
Peele, David and Bethsabe 37
Unpeople Rabbah, and the streets therof;
Sidney, Arcadia 570
...*I had not virtue enough to despise the sweetness of it*...

§ 155. Possessive Beziehung auf ein unbekanntes Subjekt.

Die possessive Beziehung auf ein unbekanntes Subjekt, auch in verallgemeinerndem Sinne, wird noch bis in das 16. Jahrhundert durch *his*, welches schon im Ae. *sīn* verdrängte, ausgedrückt (z. B. Puttenham 299, Lyly, Endimion 53); daneben kommt aber in der 2. Hälfte des 16. Jahrhunderts schon *one's* vor und zwar in unseren Texten zuerst

Jacob and Esau 213
*I defy that birthright that should be of more price
Than helping of one's self:*

ib. 251
*O God of Abraham, what reason is herein,
That to sle one's enemy it should be made sin?*

G. G. Needle 217
Stand out one's way, that ich kill none in the dark.

Three Ladies 323
Or if 'twere to eat one's meat, then I knew what I had to do.

Ganz besonders häufig bei Lyly, Euphues 242 (282, 288, 293, 330)
...and that were as fond as not to cut ones meate with that knife yat an other hath cut his finger.

Galathea 225
Of all deaths I would not bee drowned, ones clothes will be so wet when he is taken up.

Mydas 14, 39, Campaspe 125, Mother Bombie 118, 137, Marl., Ovid 146, Sidney, Astrophel 86/14, Arcadia 647, 682, 759.

In der 1. Hälfte des 16. Jahrhunderts findet sich für *one's* auch *a man's*:

Tyndale, Mark. 12/33 *...and to loue a man's neyghbour as him selfe, is a greater thing then...* (Auth. Vers. und Rev. Vers. *his neighbour*).

Indem nun *his* anstatt des Genitiv-*s* (nach § 163 f.) eintritt, entstehen die allerdings vereinzelten Fälle:

R. A., Toxophilus 47
To go on a man his tiptoes, stretching out thone of his armes forwarde, the other backewarde, which if he blered out his tunge also, myght be thought to daunce Anticke verye properlye.

ib. 157 *To se the wynde, with a man his eyes, it is vnpossible...*

Analytische Umschreibung des Possessivs durch *of* + Personalpronomen.

§ 156.

(Die Fälle, wo *of* + Personalpronomen in ausgesprochen objektivem Sinne steht, sind hier selbstverständlich ausgeschlossen.)

Dieser Fall musste zuerst da eintreten, wo es wegen der determinativen Bedeutung des Possessivpronomens nicht mehr möglich war, dasselbe anzuwenden (cf. § 166).

Die nächstliegende Umschreibung war die mit *of* + Personalpronomen, die dann weiter auf andere Fälle analogisch übertragen wurde. Begünstigt wurde diese Erscheinung teils durch Fälle, wo ein Substantivum von *of* abhängig ist, z. B.:

Bale, Thre Lawes 1128

A vayle wyll I sprede, vpon the face of Moses,

oder wie unter 2 (s. u.), zu denen wir noch solche wie

P. L. 845

Receyved at Cressingham, the Thirsday nex aftyr Seynt Edmund at the corte ther V li. xs. by the handes of me, John Paston, Sqwyer.

gesellen können, teils durch solche, bei denen ein starker Nachdruck auf dem Pronomen liegt, z. B. Hickscorner 176

Them will I exhort to virtuous living,
And unto virtue them to bring,
By the helps of you, Contemplation.

Diese Fälle können natürlich erst im Me. auftreten, z. B.:

„þe modir of hym seith Joh. 2/5.

Das 15. und das 16. Jahrhundert haben diesen Gebrauch fortgeführt; sein häufiges Vorkommen auch in populärer Literatur beweist für seine Volkstümlichkeit.

Wir geben im Folgenden eine Auswahl von Belegen und knüpfen daran einige speziellere Bemerkungen an.

1. **Das Pronomen ist allein von *of* abhängig.**

P. L. 18/31

For the goode reule ... of the Kynges persone, and draught of him to vertue ...

ib. 317/429 *And haped me, at the fyrste abordyng of us, we toke a schippe...*

ib. 681/23 *...so that a frend of her of late hathe loste better than CCC. marc...*

M. 44/23
Thenne the kyng remeued in to walys, and lete crye a grete feste that it shold be holdyn at Pentecost after the incoronacion of hym at the Cyte of Carlyon...

Fl. (Balladen) 186/88
*By my trouth sayde Adambel
Not by the counsell of me*

Bale, Promises 305
Not one of them shall enjoy the promise of me,

Suppl. of the Poore Commons 82
...they might winne the hertes of vs, your Hyghnes commons...

Interlude of Youth 5
*There may no man saued be
Without the help of me,*

Hickscorner 176
By the help of you, Contemplation.

Lyly, Euphues 376
...I see nowe at length...the faith of thee is to be preferred, before the beautie of Camilla.

Soliman and Perseda 288
*Come Janissaries, and help me to lament,
And bear my joys on either side of me —*

Marlowe, Edward II 204
The life of thee shall salve this foul disgrace.

Introductory Sketch 142
That the Authors of them seemed not to be the professors of Pietie...

Sidney, Arcadia 8
...a galley which came with sails and oars directly in the chace of them;

Anm. 1: Vereinzelt ist das Vorkommen dieser Konstruktion bei *these* und *those*:

Gorboduc 1252
> *Alas, he liueth not, it is to true,*
> *That with these eyes of him a perelesse prince,*
> *Sonne to a king, and in the flower of youth,*
> *Euen with a twinke a senseless stocke I saw.*

Sidney, Arcadia 840
> *... any thing relenting to those tragical phrases of her ...*

Anm. 2: Besonders erwähnenswert ist diese Ausdrucksweise in Ausrufen bzw. Flüchen, die im elisabethanischen Drama keine Seltenheiten sind. Die Reihenfolge unserer Belege stellt zugleich die Entwicklung dar:

Cambyses 222
> *O' the body of me, husband Hob, what, mean you to fight?*

ib. 231 *O' the passion of me!*

Clyomon and Clamydes 509b
> *O the bones of me!*

Trial of Treasure 277
> *By the body of me, I hold best that I walk,*

Appius and Virginia 121
> *Body of me, hold, if ye can!*

Trial of Treasure 280, 290,
Like Will to Like 317
> *Body of me, I was so afraid ...*

ib. 329 *Body of me, Hance, how doth thy belly, canst thou tell?* ib. 350,
Look about You 491
> *Body of me, peace, woman, I prythee, peace.*

Clyomon and Clamydes 513a *bones of me, he is either kill'd or dead!*
Wesentlich gestützt ward diese Ausdrucksweise durch ähnliche Wendungen wie
  New Custom 12 *Body of God ...*
  ib. 32 *Body of our Lord ...*

Weiterentwicklung.

Die Verwendung von *of* + Personalpronomen ist Shakspere nicht unbekannt, im 17. und 18. Jahrhundert vorhanden (Franz 214, 5), heutigentags jedoch fast ausschliesslich auf Ausrufe wie *by the soul of me* etc. beschränkt.

2. Von *of* ist ausser dem Poss. pron. auch noch ein Substantiv abhängig.

P. L. 218/305
> *... I will obeye me, and offre me to abyde the rewle of you and my cosin your brothir,* etc.

ib. 654/412 *... my Lord of Oxynforth shall have the rwyll of them and thers.*

Fox 40
...*alle the mysdedes and trespaces of his fader and of hym also*...
Jacob and Esau 227
The God of my father Abraham and of me
Hath promised, that our seed as the sand shall be.
G. G. Needle 191
God save the lives of them and their wives,
Misfortunes of Arthur 258
Sovereign Lady of our laws and us
Peele, Edward I 170
it is the common good
Of us and of our brave posterity.
Marlowe, Edward II 210 (176)
My lord, I see your love to Gaveston
Will be the ruin of the realm and you,

Das Possessivpronomen in der ursprünglichen Bedeutung als Genitiv des Personalpronomens.

§ 157.

1. Beziehung eines Relativpronomens auf ein vorangegangenes Possessiv.

Diese Spracherscheinung, welche ihre Erklärung in dem Ursprunge des Possessivpronomens als eigentlichem Genitiv des Personals findet, ist dem Ae. fremd, da sie sich erst nach völliger Ausbildung des Relativpronomens entwickeln konnte, dagegen im Me. vielfach zu belegen, z. B.:

Vor her soules, þat þer aslawe were R. of Gl. II, 369.

Für das 15. und 16. Jahrhundert kann diese Erscheinung als ziemlich volkstümlich gelten; wenn auch die Briefliteratur fast gar keine Belege aufzuweisen hat, zeigen uns doch die Denkmäler des 16. Jahrhunderts ihr Vorkommen in Poesie und Prosa:

P. L. 144/191 *Hese name is Thomas Dowce that was slayn;*
Anc. Myst. ed. Hone 37
That evyl langage I her not rowse,
For hese love that all hath wrought.

Fl. 30/28 *Swete is his death, that takes his end by loue.*

ib. (Volksbücher) 204/7
...and God his soule pardon,
That for theyr sake made this foundacyon:

Joy, Ap. 46
For by this text Paule confuteth their heresye, that saye we shal not ryse agene...

Heywood, P. P. 377
What is his name thou wouldst have eased?

Latimer, Sermons 151
...for euen as pytche dothe pollute theyr handes that medle with it:

Gorboduc 283
Nor yet as if I thought there did remaine
So filthie cankers in their noble brestes,
Whom I esteeme (which is their greatest praise)
Undoubted children of soo good a kyng.

ib. 535
Ill is their counsell, shamefull be their ende,
That raysing such mistrustfull feare in you,
...Trauaile by treason to destroy you both.

Conflict of Conscience 47
We Mercurialists...do alter our mind
To theirs that talk with us...

Sidney, Astrophel and Stella 7/12
Shee...gaue him this mourning weede:
To honour all their deathes, who for her bleede.

Marlowe, Edward II 263
Well may I rent his name that rends my heart.

Tamburlaine 844
Direct my weapon to his barbarous heart,
That thus opposeth him against the Gods,

Udall, Demonstr. 74
Therefore admonition...is a necessary and ordinary way, for their amendment that do offend.

ib. 75 *...for their vnderstanding that desire direction in the trueth...*

Udall, State 6
...*what are his quallities, that you dislike so much?* (*that* bezieht sich nicht auf *quallities*).

Peele, David and Bethsabe 48
What happiness or honour may betide
His state that toils in my extremities?

ib. 67
Adding thereto his most renowned death,
And all their deaths, that at his death he judg'd,

Greene, Looking Glass 107
The Israelite of whom I told you last.
Then question we his country and his name,
Who answer'd us, I am a Hebrew born,

Diary of Henslowe 70
Take vergine waxe...and put yt under his head to whom the good partayneth...

Weiterentwicklung.

Auf Grund der Verhältnisse im 16. Jahrhundert erklärt sich nun auch die mehrfache Verwendung dieses Gebrauches bei Shakspere (Abbot § 218). Im Laufe der Zeit ist diese Erscheinung immer mehr auf die Poesie beschränkt worden und findet sich daselbst jetzt nur noch gelegentlich.

§ 158.

2. *both* + Possessivpronomen.

In dieser Verbindung schimmert im 15. und 16. Jahrhundert noch in zahlreichen Fällen, in denen das Pronomen nicht in gleichem Kasus wie das zugehörige Substantiv zu denken ist, beim Possessiv die ursprüngliche Bedeutung als Genitiv des Personalpronomens durch. Der Verlust der Flexion, welche im Ae. und Me. „ihre beiden" und „ihrer beider" genau von einander trennte, erschwert im 15. und 16. Jahrhundert nicht selten eine genaue Unterscheidung, ja macht sie in manchen Fällen, wo sie dann allerdings für den Zusammenhang belanglos ist, sogar ganz unmöglich. Dass im übrigen die zweifellos sicheren Fälle eine noch in der gesprochenen Volkssprache lebendige Erscheinung waren, mögen einige Belege aus verschiedenen Zeiten und Denkmälern veranschaulichen.

P. L. 490/159
and ther was made appoyntment be twen hem by the advyce of bothe ther Conceylis...

M. 439/4 *And so at the laste by bothe their assentes they were made frendes and sworne brethren for euer...*

Joy, Ap. 45
...let all that rede bothe our talis be iuge...

R. A., Schoolemaster 101
A true tochstone, a sure metwand lieth before both their eyes.

Tancred and Gismonda 56
I hope it brings recure to both your pains.

G. G. Needle 195
Well, Hodge, this is a matter of weight, and must be kept close, It might else turn to both our costs, as the world now goes.

Lyly, Mydas 21 *I weepe over both your wits!*

Greene, Menaphon 80
From both their lips hir lips the Corrall drew:

Marlowe, Jew 1590
Now I haue such a plot for both their liues

Sidney, Astrophel and Stella p. XCIII
*Like as the shadowe awnswering by signes
Save comfort somtymes vnto both our myndes*

Arcadia 451
*how much that discord foul hath stain'd
Both our estates...*

Weiterentwicklung.

Ebenso bei Shakspere (Abbot § 219, Deutschbein § 49), jetzt aber nicht mehr üblich.

§ 159.

3. Das Possessivpronomen in Verbindung mit substantivisch gebrauchten Adjektiven.

Schon im Ae. und Me. werden substantivisch gebrauchte Adjektive, die einen Vergleich bezeichnen, mit dem Genitiv des Personalpronomens (= späterem Possessivum) verbunden. Ueber diesen Gebrauch im 15. und 16. Jahrhundert, wo er sich als allgemein üblich fortsetzt, ist nichts besonderes zu sagen. Zuweilen tritt die Genitivbedeutung noch hervor. Z. B.:

M. 579/32 *But in this spyrytuel maters he shalle haue many his better.*

ib. 751/25 ... *there ye proued your self his better.*

Calisto and Melibaea 92 *their inferiors,*

Latimer, Sermons 83
...*but I was called to it, and would be willynge if you mislike me, to geue place to mi betters.* R. A., Toxophilus 33,

Lyly, Euphues 272
...*if thou loue thine equall, it is no conquest: if thy superiour, thou shalt be enuyed: if thine inferiour, laughed at.*

ib. 313 *Doest thou not thinke that hourely shee is serued and sued vnto, of thy betters in byrth, thy equales in wealth, thy inferiors in no respect.*

Greene, James IV 100   *but I teach this knave*
  How to behave himself among his betters.

Pinner 169
  For wherefore have we given us our wealth,
  But to make our betters welcome when they come?

Sidney, Arcadia 555
  you shall find many their superiours...

ib. 786 *Servile, though envious, to his betters:*

Dieser Gebrauch ist bis heute erhalten.

Anm.: Während bei den eben genannten Fällen das Possessivpronomen syntaktisch als Genitiv angesehen werden muss, handelt es sich bei einer Reihe anderer Fälle um blosse Substantivierung des Adjektivs, wie sich chronologisch auch schon daraus ergiebt, dass sie erst seit dem Me. belegt sind. Z. B.:

Marriage of Wit 366
  I warrant thee, do thy best,
Kyd, Spanish Tragedy 21 *let fortune do her worst.*
Marlowe, Tamburlaine 4222 *Do all thy worst,*
Sidney, Arcadia 553 *Thou hast done thy worst, world...*

§ 160.
My (*our*) in der Anrede.

Wie im Ae. und Me. darf auch für das 15. und 16. Jahrhundert *my* bezw. *our* (in der Regel verbunden mit einer Liebe oder Wohlwollen versichernden Apposition) in der Anrede meist mehr als ein Ausdruck der (herzlichen) Zuneigung als (wie meist jetzt) konventioneller Höflichkeit gelten, z. B.:

P. L. 923
To the right worshipfull and my right welbeloved Sir John Paston, Knyght.

Plumpton Correspondence 26
To my right trusty and welbeloved Coussin, Sir William Plompton, knight.

Elizabeth schreibt an James meist *my deare brother* (z. B. 29), in mehr offiziellen Schriftstücken z. B. *right deare brother* (26); umgekehrt James an Elizabeth: *Madame and dearest sister* (20 etc.).

Rein formell ist z. B. P. L. 933 *To the ryght wurshupfull Sir John Paston, Knyght, be this delyvered,*

oder Leycester an seinen Secretär (137)
The Earl of Leycester to Mr. Secretary Walsingham (Ueberschrift), dann *Mr. Secretary...*

Anm.: Dagegen ist *my* + *lord* als konventionell anzusehen, da es thatsächlich schon vielfach zu éinem Begriffe verschmolzen ist, wie z. B. aus folgenden Belegen ersehen werden mag:

Diary of Machyn 12
The VII. day of Desember at Hyd parke a gret muster of men of armes: the furst the kynges trumpeters; [then] my lord Bray, in gylt harnes... The secound my lord Tresorer...

ib. 38 *The XXVI. day of July cam unto the Towre my lord marqwes of Northamton, by and my lord Robart Dudley,* etc. etc.

§ 161.
Your im Sinne eines Dativus ethicus.

Diese Erscheinung ist in charakteristischer Weise von Puttenham ausgebildet:

ib. 30 *Anon after came your secular Priestes as iolly rymers as the rest...*

ib. 133 *For your foote pirrichius ... ye haue these words ... for your feete of three times and first your dactill, ye haue these wordes and a number moe... For your molossus, of all three long, ye haue a member... etc. etc.*
ib. 143 *Of the breaking your bisillables and polysillables ...*
ib. 171 *And that first sort of figures doth serue th'eare onely and may be therefore called Auricular: your second serues the conceit onely ...*
etc. etc.

§ 162.
Stellung des adjectivischen Possessivpronomens.

Während in der Regel das adjectivische Poss. vor ein mit ihm verbundenes Adjectiv tritt, ist das in einigen erst im elisabethanischen Drama (daher auch bei Shakspere, cf. Abbot § 13, Deutschbein § 54) auftretenden aber wahrscheinlich schon früher üblichen Wendungen der Anrede nicht der Fall.

So findet sich zahlreich neben der (selteneren) gewöhnlichen Stellung:

good my lord (Kyd, Span. 156, Peele, Alcazar 110, Marlowe, Tamburlaine 3079, Greene, Pinner 181 etc. etc.);

Mucedorus 215
Thanks, good my lords ...
Look about You 399
Be quiet, good my lords;
diesem haben sich andere angeschlossen:

Marprelate, Epistle 11

Now good your grace you shall haue small gaynes in medling with Margrete Lawson I can tell you.

Greene, Pinner 200
Nay, good my liege, ill- nurtur'd we were then:
Diese Fälle erklären sich dadurch, dass das Possessivum an seiner possessiven Bedeutung verlor und in vielen Fällen mit dem folgenden Substantiv einen zu engen Begriff bildete, als dass noch ein Adjectivum hätte dazwischen treten können.

Vgl. Fl. (Balladen) 175/8
Now good syr abbot be my frende

Angry Women 322
nay, good Sir Ralph Smith, do not so.
Jack Straw 391, Look about You 450 etc. sowie ferner
§ 160 Anm.

§ 163.

Das Possessivpronomen zur Bezeichnung des Genitivs.
Vgl. hierzu Jesp. 248 ff.
Diese auch anderen Sprachen (a. a. O.) geläufige Erscheinung, die im Ae. und Me. bei Possessiven verschiedenen Geschlechts üblich ist, hat im 15. und 16. Jahrh. weiteste Verbreitung gefunden und erweist sich insbesondere durch die zahllosen Belege in der Brief- und Tagebuchliteratur als eine Eigenheit der gesprochenen Volkssprache, doch ist sie auch in der Literatursprache nichts ungewöhnliches, ja selbst die Poesie bleibt nicht frei davon (Sidney, Astr., Peele, Polyh., s. u.). Doch gilt das nur für *his*, bei anderen Pronominibus ist diese Erscheinung ganz vereinzelt (Diary of Dr. Dee 13 (1581)
Dec. 1st, Katharyn Dee her nurse was payd 6 s ...
Wir geben nun im folgenden zur Erläuterung des gesagten eine Auswahl von Belegen aus verschiedenen Zeiten und Gattungen der Literatur unseres Zeitraums:
P. L. 72/92 ... *hit ys the saide Fastolf ys wille ...*
ib. 72/93 ... *after the descece of the saide hys wyf (!) ...*
ib. 125/167 ... *Sir Thomas Tudenham his neighburs ...*
ib. 522/224 ... *the seide Nicholas his fadir ...*
ib. 739/110 ... *John Lee is wyff ...*
ib. 828/242 ... *Sir William Holle his presentacion ...*
M. 126/27 ... *this lord of this castel his name is syr Damas ...*
ib. 220/30 *For the fyrste knyghte his hors stumbled ...*
Egerton Papers 163
An Inventorie of such superstitious thinges as were founde in Sir John Sothworthe his howse ...
Fl. (Geschichte) 276/22
The kyng his armie was domble to all this
R. A., Toxophilus 47
To set backe to backe, and se who can heaue an other his heles highest, with other moche like:

ib. 101 *For that is called vnpossible whych is in no man his power to do.*

Diary of Machyn 105
the penter ys nam was Huw Loveroke...

Diary of Dr. Dee 33
Francys Garland was by, and Mr. Thomas Kelley his wife.

More, Utopia 120 *For when we shewede to them Aldus his print in bookes of paper...*

Trial of Treasure 293
Thou never rememb'red'st Thales his sentence,

Lyly, Euphues 69... *had not womanly shamefastnes and Philautus his presence, stayed his wisedome.*

Sidney, Astr. 24/1
Rich fooles there be...
Damning themselues to Tantalus his smart,

Udall, Demonstr. 47
Musculus his iudgment appeareth in the 6. and 7. reasons...

Marlowe, Massacre 352
I am thy brother, and I'll revenge thy death,
And root Valois his line from forth of France;

Puttenham 76
The Lord Vaux his commendation lyeth chiefly in the facillitie of his meetre...

Peele, Edward I 176
and now since, like one of Mars his frozen knights...

Peele, Polyh. 206
Brave Knowles his offspring, hardy champions.

Sidney, Arcadia 446 *But neither could danger be dreadful to Amphialus his undismayable courage...*

Clyomon and Clamydes 501 b
all are not born to be God Mars his men;

Greene, Alphonsus 6 *Jove his seed,* Leycester Corr. 299
... from the poore souldier his gaine...

Henslowe's Diary 113
... to be payd unto the sayd philippe his heires...

§ 164.

Bemerkungen hierzu:

Inbezug auf die Erklärung stehen wir auf dem Standpunkt Jespersens, insbesondere darin, dass nicht éine sondern eine Reihe von Erscheinungen zur Entstehung dieses Brauches mitgewirkt haben. Dass in überaus zahlreichen Fällen ein Anakoluth vorliegt, davon kann man sich durch die nhd. Umgangssprache überzeugen.

Im Uebrigen müssen wir gerade für das 15. und 16. Jahrh. eine recht enge Berührung von *his* in dieser Funktion mit der Genitivendung konstatieren, besonders da das *h* von *his*, wie die zahlreichen Schreibungen *is, ys* zeigen, in vielen Fällen nicht mehr gesprochen wurde; die Aussprache des *is, ys* war dann, zumal da es bei enger Anlehnung an das Substantiv schwach betont war, thatsächlich vielfach der des Genitiv-*es* gleich; man beachte hierfür besonders Fälle wie:

P. L. 315/426 ... *with God is grace* ...
P. L. 590/324 ... *by Cryst ys sides* ...
etc. etc.

Dass wenigstens im 15. Jahrh. *his* wirklich mit dem Genitiv *s* wechselt, ja vielleicht als aus diesem entstanden gedacht wurde, zeigt die Unterschrift:

P. L. 809/215. *Your ys, M. P.*

Dieses wird weiterhin bestätigt durch P. L. 183/248 *Jon, brynge me my lettre hom with you, and my cosyn Cler is copy of her lettre ...*, wo sich *is* also auf ein Femininum bezieht.

Vgl. hierzu den von Hoelper p. 48 aus Tottels Misc. etc. angeführten Beleg:

upon the deceas of Annes his mother.

Hierin liegt nun aber zugleich die Ursache des (nicht weiter entwickelten) Keimes, *his* zur Bezeichnung des Genitivs auf ein anderes Geschlecht auszudehnen, also eines analytischen Zuges in der Richtung, die Bezeichnung des Genitivverhältnisses nicht mehr durch eine Endung, sondern durch ein eigenes unabhängiges Wörtchen zu bewerkstelligen; vgl. hierzu Jespersens Vermutung p. 327, dem dieser Fall noch nicht bekannt war).

Anm.: Eine besondere Anwendung erfährt der Gebrauch von *his* zur Bezeichnung des Genitivs in der dramatischen Literatur der zweiten Hälfte des 16. Jahrhunderts durch den auf den Titelblättern vielfach wiederkehrenden Zusatz, dass das betr. Stück von der Truppe dieses oder jenes Gönners aufgeführt sei; damit ist für diese spezielle Verwendung zugleich die Chronologie gegeben.

Z. B.: Marlowe, Tamburlaine p. 1
Be the right honorable the Lord Admyrall, his seruantes ...
Peele, Alcazar 82
As it was sundrie times plaid by the Lord high Admirall his servants.
etc.

Bei der Truppe der Königin heisst es dagegen z. B.: Greene, Bacon and Bungay 142 *be her Maisties seruants*, oder es wird in anderer Weise umschrieben.

Weiterentwicklung.

Bei Spenser ganz gewöhnlich (Günther p. 63), bei Shakspere besonders häufig hinter Namen, die auf einen Zischlaut ausgehen (Abbot § 217). Diese Erscheinung nimmt dann ab, wenn sie auch im 17. Jahrh. noch recht üblich ist (Franz 388), und ist jetzt auf Dialekte beschränkt.

Verwendung des substantivischen Possessivpronomens anstatt des adjektivischen.

§ 165.

1. Nur in der Poesie, zur Erzielung eines feierlichen, gehobenen Tons, vornehmlich in der Anrede, aber auch in anderen Fällen, wird im 15. und 16. Jahrh. das substantivische poss. anstatt des adjektivischen verwendet.

Historisch betrachtet stellt sich uns diese Erscheinung als ein Rest der ae. Stellung des Genitivs des Personalpronomens in possessiver Funktion nach dem zugehörigen Substantiv dar: *Joseph mīn* Exon. 11, 1.

Dieser Rest konnte sich erhalten, da *mine*, als sich nach dem Schwinden der Genitivbedeutung im Bewusstsein des Volkes das Possessivum herausbildete, zugleich auch die (in der Stellung nach dem Substantiv allein mögliche) substantivische Form darstellte. Die unter b) verzeichneten Fälle bei anderen Pronominibus sind als spätere Analogiebildungen zu betrachten.

a) In der Anrede.
  Cambyses 212
    O lording dear, and brother mine,
    ib. 213 *Farewell lord and brother mine,*
    ib. 239 *O mighty king and husband mine,*
  Appius and Virginia 145
  O father mine, refrain no whit your sharped knif to take
  G. G. Needle 240
    God 'eild ye, master mine.
  Rare Triumphs 177 (148)
    Now, farewell, master mine...
  Jack Straw 382
    Brethren mine, so might I thrive,

b) In anderen Fällen.
  Bale, Thre Lawes 1649
  Shewe me brother myne, who ded the hyther sende.
  Cambyses 170
    You shall have favour mine.
  ib. 200 *To question mine give 'tentive ear,*
  ib. 227
    Should brother mine have reigned king,
    When I had yielded breath?
  ib. 228 *According to rule of birth you are*
    Cousin-german mine;
  ib. 229
    My meaning is, that beauty yours
    My heart with love doth wound;
  ib. 230 *For counsel theirs I mean not, I,*
    In this respect to go.
  Sidney, Astrophel and Stella 9/13
  Which Cupids selfe, from Beauties mine did drawe:
  Arcadia 710
    So may you never die,
    But pull'd by Mira's hand,
    Dress bosom hers, or head,
    Or scatter on her bed,

ib. 715
A king, in language theirs they said they would:
Sir Clyomon and Sir Clamydes 528 a
Well, my queen, sith daughter ours hath chosen such a make,
ib. 528 b
*My Clyomon in court to have, the nuptial fort to see
Of Juliana sister his!*
ib. 529 b
Let not the loss of lady thine so pinch thy heart with grief
ib. 530 a
With whom I met in travel mine;

§ 166.
2. Pseudo-partitiver Genitiv.

Die mit diesem Namen von Kellner, Hist. Outl. p. 113 ff., belegte Erscheinung ist ebenda erklärt, worauf wir auch für die historische Entwicklung verweisen.

Wir gehen gleich zum 15. und 16. Jahrhundert über:

a) Der unbestimmte Artikel oder andere Indefinita in Verbindung mit dem Possessivpronomen.

Die Entwicklung zu *a frende of myn* (P. L. 745/114) ist durchgeführt.

Anm. 1: Der Fall Sidney, Arcadia 705
*A neighbour mine not long ago there was...
That married had a trick and bonny lass,
As in a summer day a man might see:*
ist eine dichterisch freie Konstruktion in Anlehnung an die unter 1. besprochenen Fälle (Dagegen Nice Wanton 166 *A neigbour of mine*).

b) Bestimmte Pronomina *(this, that, yonder)* in Verbindung mit dem Possessivpronomen.

Im 15. Jahrhundert herrscht der alte Sprachzustand (*this my son*) noch im grossen und ganzen vor, dasselbe gilt für die ersten Dezennien des 16. Jahrh.; Tyndales Bibelübersetzung steht ganz auf dem Boden des Alten, die Auth. Vers. und die Rev. Vers. haben nie geändert, z. B.: Matth. 20/21 *Graunte that these my two sones may syt*... Luk. 15/32, Joh. 3/29 etc. Roger Asham hat den jetzigen Gebrauch durchgeführt, ebenso Mores Utopia. Trotzdem ist der Umwandlungsprozess auch in der 2. Häfte des 16. Jahrh. noch nicht zum Abschluss gekommen; denn ausser dem Drama weisen auch populäre Flugschriften sowie die Briefe Elisabeths und James und die Leycester Correspondence noch zahlreiche Belege der älteren Art auf, ebenso Lylys Euphues und Sidneys Arcadia; eine Ausnahme macht nur Puttenham, für den dasselbe wie für Asham gilt.

Im übrigen ergiebt sich für das ausgehende 16. Jahrh., dass die alte und die neue Konstruktion gleichberechtigt sind.

Anm. 1: Der Fall mit dem bestimmten Artikel ist ganz vereinzelt:
Thersites 421
Now Christ's sweet blessing and mine
Light above and beneath the body of thyne,

Anm. 2: Bei relativer Anknüpfung, die in Verbindung mit dem Possessivpronomen so wie so selten ist, fand sich als Beleg für den alten Sprachzustand nur bei Lyly im Euphues 81 *In token of which my sincere affection, I giue thee my hande in pawne*..., ein Fall, der in Anbetracht des oben über Lyly gesagten nicht auffallen kann.

Dagegen More, Utopia 12
The wiche busie labour, and toyle oftheires...
Sidney, Arcadia 320
Which proceeding of hers I do the more largely set before you...

Anm. 3: Als weitere Folge des fortschreitenden Gebrauches der neuen Konstruktion erweisen sich nur in der Poesie oder poetischen Prosa vorkommende Fälle, bei denen das Possessivum nicht mehr in Verbindung mit irgend einem Pronomen oder dem Artikel erscheint; dies hauptsächlich bei Sidney:

Cambyses 227
Of truth, my lord, in eye of mine
All ladies she doth excel:
Sidney, Arcadia 261
O eyes of mine, where once she saw her face,
ib. 288 *Ah chasted bed of mine*...
ib. 665 *but O wicked mouth of mine, how darest thou thus blaspheme the ornament of the earth, the vessel of all virtue?*
ib. 740 *O mother of mine, what a deathful suck have you given me?*
ib. 775 *O mind of mine! said he*...
ib. 797 *O notes of mine, your selves together tie:*

Weiterentwicklung.

In den Fällen unter a) ist keine Veränderung eingetreten.

In denen unter b) ist die neue Konstruktion allmälich durchgedrungen, die ältere jedoch in poetischer und feierlicher

Sprache (Bibel s. o.) noch möglich. Shakspere (Abbot § 239) verwendet beide.

Wechsel und Verwechselung von Possessiv- und Personalpronomen, sowie von Possessiv und ’Artikel *the*.

§ 167.

1. Verwechselung von Possessiv- und Personalpronomen.

a) *my* für *me* und umgekehrt.

P. L. 175/232 ... *he grantyd my his god lordship* ...
M. 222/11 *And hors ne harneys getest thou none of my, but* ...
Lusty Juventus 48
  Against another time they have taught me wit:
    Copland's Ed. „*my*".
Peele, Arr. 53
  Me thought in beauty should not be excell'd.
    Old copy „*My thought*".
Sir Clyomon and Sir Clamydes 517 b
  a ha driven my sheep above from the flock:
    The 4to „*me*".
Marlowe, Edward II 230 *Pembroke and Lancaster*
  Spake least; and when they flatly had denied,
  Refusing to receive me pledge for him,
  The Earl of Pembroke mildly thus bespake;
So 4tos 1598, 1612; 2to 1622 „*my*"; *me* ist nach p. 221 *My lords, I will be pledge for his return*, erforderlich.
Angry Women 322 ... *and there I'll take my stand.*
    So second edit., first edit. „*me*".

b) *you* für *your* und umgekehrt.

P. L. 702/56 ... *Pekok hath receyvyd of Sir John Stylle by a bylle all suche stuff as he had of you*r.
Heywood, P. P. 384
  Sir, be your sure he telleth you true,
ib. 368 *Now since both ye the truth confess,*
    1 ed. „*your*".

Nice Wanton 174
*You have named me already, if I durst be so bold:
**Your sister Delilah, that wretch I am;
  * Old copy „your"; ** old copy „you".

Marriage of Wit and Science 382
On me *you furies all, on me, have poured out your spite,
Come now and slay me at the last, and rid my sorrows quite.
  * Old copy „your".

Lyly, Euphues 221
If your thinke this Loue dreamed not done, yet mee thinketh you may as well like that loue...

Kyd, Spanish Tragedy 113
  On, then, and hear you, lord ambassador
4 tos of 1618, 1623, 1633 „your" (was unmöglich).

Peele, Edward I 198
  You curled locks, draw from this cursed head:
      Both 4 tos „your".

Marprelate, Epistle 23
And my good L... are you partiall or no in all your actions tell me? yes your are?

Marlowe, Ovid 174
But when she comes, *you swelling mounts, sink down,
      * Old eds. „your".

Soliman and Perseda 260
      Ay, watch you[r] vantages?

§ 168. Bemerkungen zu a und b.

Die grosse Zahl der Fälle aus Denkmälern verschiedener Art zeigt, dass wir es nicht mit zufälligen Schreib- oder Druckfehlern zu thun haben, vielmehr mit einer Verwechselung, die, der Volkssprache angehörig, mehrfach in die Schriftsprache eindrang.

Diese Fälle müssen nun da entstanden sein, wo eine Wechselwirkung zwischen Personal- und Possessivpronomen vorhanden war; eine solche fand nun statt beim Partizipium, wo in der älteren Zeit das Personalpronomen anstatt des späteren und jetzigen Possessivpronomens verwandt wurde, solange das Partizipium als solches und nicht als Verbalnomen gefasst wurde. Im 15. und 16. Jahrhundert sind beide Ausdrucksweisen möglich, z. B.:

P. L. 320 *After my takyng leefe, he called me ageyn,*...
Gorboduc 989
And greadie wormes had gnawen this pyned hart
Without my feeling payne:
Lyly, Euphues 34 ...*at my being there*...
Blades 140 (aus Kellner, Blanchardyn p. 76)
Most humblie beseekynge my...lord to pardon me so presumyng,
ib. 148, (165) (desgl. aus Kellner)
take no displaysir on me so presumyng,
Latimer, Sermons 160
I toulde you what I hard saye, I woulde haue no mans honestye empayred by me tellynge.

Derselbe Wechsel muss natürlich auch bei *you* und *your* stattfinden:

P. L. 36/48 ...*thanckyng God of yowr a mendyng of the grete dysese that ye have hade;*
ein Fall mit *you* fiel uns nicht auf, doch ändert das an der Thatsache nichts.

Dieser Wechsel von Personal- und Possessivpronomen war zweifellos einer der Gründe der Verwechselung.

Weiter mag beachtet werden, dass in einer Reihe der oben angeführten Fälle das Personalpronomen sowohl wie das Possessivpronomen einen Sinn geben, wenn auch für die betr. Stelle nur éine Auffassung möglich ist.

Man vergl. hierzu ferner:
Greene, Pinner 209
Your commission (saith George) I cry your mercy, sir;
gegenüber dem (weit mehr gebräuchlichen) *I cry you mercy* (Digby Myst. 30/92, Heywood, P. P. 331, Bale, Kynge Johan 3, Lusty Juventus 51, Cambyses 181, Trial of Treasure 263, Marriage of Wit 335, Three Lords 399 etc.), sowie *I cry the(e) mercy* (Digby Myst. 89/901, Everyman 126, Bale, Promises 289 etc.).

Beide Konstruktionen auch bei Shakspere.

Ebenso können andere Fälle wie
Plumpton Correspondence 70 ... *who ever preserve you body and soule.*
wo auch *your* (cf. Fl. (Volksbücher) 291/53 ... *to gete and haue my body and soule* ...) einen Sinn geben würde, herangezogen werden.

Es lassen sich also eine Reihe von Erscheinungen zur Erklärung dieser Verwechselung beibringen, die wohl alle — vielleicht waren ihrer noch mehr — zu ihrer Entstehung beitrugen.

Ohne Zweifel hat schliesslich auch noch bei *my, me* sowohl wie bei *you, your* ein nicht geringes phonetisches Moment mitgewirkt (vgl. § 171).

§ 169.
2. Wechsel und Verwechselung von *thy* mit dem Artikel *the*.

Lusty Juventus 53
*O Lord, grant me of thy infinite mercy
The true knowledge of *thy law and will,*
    * Copland's ed. „the".

ib. 55
*Blessed is the man whom thou teachest, O Lord, saith he,
To learn *thy law, precepts, word, or verity.*
    * Copland's ed. „the".

Lyly, Euphues 180
Art not thou one of those, that hauing gotten on their sleeue the cognisance of a courtier haue shaken from thy skirts the regard of curtesie.

ib. 181 *if then the reward bee to be measured by thy merites, what boote canst thou seeke for, but eternall paine, whiche heere lyuest in continuall pleasure?*

ib. 363 *I but Philantus prayse at the partyng, if she had not liked thee, she would neuer haue aunswered thee.*

Kyd, Spanish Tragedy 15
But now, knight marshal, frolic with *thy king
    * Ed. of 1618, 1623, 1633 „the".

ib. 85
> *Confess thy folly, and repent thy fault;*
> *For there's *thy place of execution.*
>   * 4tos of 1618, 1623, 1633 „the".

Peele, Edward I 113
> *Welchman, allegiance, which thou ow'st *thy king.*
>   * 4to of 1599 „the".

ib. 189
>   *but I that prove *the pain*
> *May hear thee talk but not redress my harm.*
>   * Beide 4tos „thy".

Greene, Looking Glass 105
> *When I please, — mark *the words, —' tis a lease parol to have and to hold.*
>   * 4to of 1598 „thy".

ib. 131
> *'Tis I that wrought *the sin, must weep *the sin.*
>   * The 4to of 1598 "thy".

Marlowe, Edward II 227
> *Then tell *thy prince of whence and what thou art.*
>   * Old eds. „the".

Dido 414
> *Carthage, my friendly host, adieu!*
> *Since Destiny doth call me from *thy shore:*
>   * Old ed. „the".

Hero 89
> *No need have wee of factious Day,*
> *To cast, in envy of thy peace,*
> *Her balls of discord in *thy way:*
>   * V. R. „the".

Ovid 107
> *If, reading five, thou plain 'st of tediousness,*
> *Two ta' en away, *thy labour will be less.*
>   * So eds. B. C., ed. A. „the".

ib. 126
> *To beggars shut, to bringers ope *thy gate;*
>   * So ed. B., ed. C. „the".

ib. 165
> *And with thy hand assist *the swelling sail.*
>   * Old eds. „thy".

Three Ladies 319
> But such as thou art, such are *the attenders on thee
> * Old copies „*thy*".

§ 170.

Bemerkungen hierzu:
Diese Fälle finden in ähnlicher Weise ihre Erklärung, wie die in § 168 aufgeführten, nämlich durch solche, wo sowohl *the* als auch *thy* einen guten, wenngleich anderen, Sinn giebt, was zum Teil auch bei den oben angeführten zutrifft; man vgl. (s. o.) insbesondere Kyd, Spanish Tragedy 85 und Peele, Edward I 113, sowie Peele, Edw. I 201
> *And, Mortimer, 'tis thou must haste to Wales, ...*
> *And rid thy king of his contentious foe;*

wo zwar *the* möglich, *thy* aber ungleich wirkungsvoller ist; ähnliche fälle von *my* und *the* sind:

Kyd, Spanish Tragedy 111
> *For I'll go marshal up *the fiends in hell,*
> *To be avenged on you all for this.*
> * 1618, 1623, 1633 „*my*".

Peele, Edward I 143
> *But tell me now, lapped in lily bands,*
> *How with *my queen, my lovely boy it stands,*
> * 4to of 1599 „*the*".

Auch Fälle wie: Three Ladies of London 297
> *Good Simplicity, hold thy peace:*

gegenüber: Three Lords and Three Ladies 459
> *I charge ye keep the peace, and lay down your weapons.*

mögen von einfluss gewesen sein.

Vgl. ferner Lyly, Euphues 407
> *... which is commonly applied to those that witch with the eyes not to those that wooe with their eyes.*

und schliesslich

Heywood, Pardoner and Friar 232
> *I'sh knock thee on the costard...*

Misfortunes of Arthur 272
> *why turn'st thou (mind) thy back?*

wo auch *thy* bezw. *the* möglich wären.

Es ergeben sich also auch hier eine ganze Reihe von Ursachen für die Möglichkeit und das thatsächliche Vorhandensein einer Vertauschung und Verwechselung.

Bei Shakspere scheinen solche Vertauschungen nicht vorzukommen.

§ 171.
3. Andere Fälle.

Unter den Abweichungen der verschiedenen Drucke eines Werkes aus der elisabethanischen Zeit beobachten wir ferner in zahlreichen Fällen einen Wechsel ähnlich lautender Possessivpronomina und anderer, untereinander und mit dem Artikel. Die Frage des in jedem einzelnen Falle notwendigen oder vorzuziehenden ist Aufgabe der Textkritik. Für uns handelt es sich darum, diesen, wie wir sehen, ziemlich weitgehenden Wechsel darzulegen und zu erklären.

a) Personalpronomina untereinander.

me und *thee*: Greene, Alphonsus 52;

thee und *ye*: Marlowe, Dido 372, Look about You 396;

thee und *she*: Angry Women 323;

he und *she*: Sir Clyomon 498b, Marlowe, Hero 43, 54 (zweimal);

he und *ye*: Appius and Virginia 125, Marlowe, Dido 422, Ovid 182, Three Ladies 366, Angry Women 323;

she und *we*: Greene, Verm. 285, Marl., Hero 43, Ovid 181;

thou und *you*: Lusty Juventus 85.

b) Possessivpronomina untereinander.

my und *thy*: Lusty Juventus 68, Appius und Virginia 113, Kyd, Span. 158, Peele, Edward I 110, 175, Old Wives Tale 227, 239, Greene, Orlando 33, James IV 153, Looking Glass 63, 109, Bacon 208, Marlowe, Edward II 193, Dido 416, 431, 437, Ovid 143, 145, 159, 171, Rare Triumphs 149, Angry Women 327, Look about You 499;

our und *your*: Heywood, P. P. 368, 372, Lusty Juventus 94, G. G. Needle 208, Marriage of Wit 350, Kyd, Span. 43, 158, Peele, Edward I 112, Greene, Looking Glass 76.

c) *thy* und *they*.

Lusty Juventus 58, Marlowe, Ovid 134, 137, 145, 187.

d) Personalpronomen und Artikel.

the und *thee*: Marl., Ovid 111, 158, 207, Peele, Arr. 7, Angry Women 296; vgl. § 7;
the und *he*: Angry Women 269;
the und *we*: Heywood, P. P. 378;
the und *ye*: Greene, James IV 104;
the und *they*: Four Elements 29, Marlowe Hero 8.

e) *this* und *his*.

Heywood, P. P. 355, Lusty Juventus 61, 79, 89, 95, Confl. of Consc. 129, Kyd, Span. 14, Peele, Edw. I 129, Marlowe, Hero 23, 33, 88 (zweimal), 96, Ovid 203, Epigr. by J. D. 233, Look about You 469, Mucedorus 243; hierzu Marl., Hero 28 'Tis und This. Dieser Wechsel ähnlicher oder gleichlautender Wörter, der also, wie unsere Belege ergeben, in der Literatur des 16. Jahrhunderts von nicht geringem Umfange ist, erklärt sich sofort durch ihre lautliche Gleichheit oder Aehnlichkeit. Sie lassen uns den in den §§ 167—170 dargestellten Wechsel von *my* und *me*, *thy* und *the*, *you* und *your*, bei denen noch das psychologische Moment hinzukommt, nur um so begreiflicher erscheinen.

Reflexivpronomen.

Bezeichnung des reflexiven Verhältnisses durch Pronomina.

(NB. Gerade für das 15. und 16. Jahrh. genügen die einschlägigen Werke in Bezug auf diesen Punkt durchaus nicht, eine eingehende Darstellung für diesen Zeitraum dürfte daher sehr wohl am Platze sein.)

I. Bei ursprünglichen Transitiven, die reflexiv gebraucht sind.

§ 172.

Da das Ae. keine besonderen Reflexivpronomina besitzt, werden anstatt dessen die Personalia verwandt. Daneben treten jedoch schon, zum Teil veranlasst durch die Abneigung der Sprache gegen die doppelte Funktion eines morphologischen oder grammatischen Elementes (Kellner, Zur Syntax des engl. Verbums, Wien 1885, p. 73), die durch *self*, *silf* verstärkten Formen auf.

Im Me. nehmen die verstärkten Formen in dem (wenn auch geringen) Masse zu, wie die unverstärkten abnehmen, doch sind die letzteren noch immer bei weitem überwiegend. Untersuchen wir nun, wie sich diese Verhältnisse im 15. und 16. Jahrh. bis auf Shakspere weiter entwickelt haben.

NB. Selbstverständlich bleiben bei unserer Betrachtung alle diejenigen Fälle ausgeschlossen, bei denen ein besonderer Nachdruck die verstärkte Form des Pronomens verlangt.

Die Paston Letters weisen durchweg einfache und verstärkte Formen des Pronomens neben- und durcheinander auf. In der ersten Hälfte des 15. Jahrh. bilden die ersteren noch bei weitem die Mehrzahl, in der zweiten Hälfte jedoch treten die letzteren häufiger auf,

z. B.: 68/85 .. *we .. made us redy for to over sayle them;*
111/149 .. *that he must applie hym to execute oure commaundement...*
263/361 .. *that shuld grow and be dewe to hym for the takyng of John, callyng hym Duc of Alauncon ..*
737/108 *Wherefore I woll and desire you .. to dispose you to come ..*
840/255 .. *the Bysshop off Hely, whyche shewyth hymselffe goode and worshyp full;*
883/817 (Prokl. gegen Heinr. Tudor 1485)
.. *Charlys, callyng hymself Kyng of Fraunce ..*
909/353 .. *that ye woll .. prepare youre selfe ..*

Anm.: Das Verbum *to recomaund*, das in einer allgemein üblichen und zahlreich verwandten Brieffloskel vorkommt, wird in den P. L. stets nur mit dem einfachen Pronomen verbunden, z. B.:

P. L. 37/50 ... *the Chief Justice of the Kynggs Benche recommaundeth hym to yow ...*
42/55 *My maistres Garneys ... Berney and my maisteries your sonys ... recommend hem to yow.*
155/208 ... *we comaund us to you ...*
167/224 *Myn awnte recommawndeth her to you ..*

Desgl. Digby Mysteries 133/2072
I recummend me with all vmbylnesse,
On-to my sell 1 woll pretend.
etc. etc.

Den Erklärungsgrund geben uns folgende Belege: P. L. 367/540
Rythe reverent and worchypfwl broder, 1 recomawnde to yow, certy fyyng yow that ...

596/333 ... *with all my servyce moost lowly I recomande unto your gode maistirship, besechyng you* ...

631/387 *Ryght worchepfull sir, I recomand on to you, praying yow that* ...

885/322 *And, nevew, I prey yow recomand to my neese your wyff, whom I wold be glad to se onys a yen in London* ...

886/323 *I pray you, cosyn, that thys byll may recomawnde to myn Lady Brews and to myn cosyn, your wyf.*

(Die beiden letzten Fälle führen wir hier mit auf, weil sie sich durch die vorhergehenden erklären.)

Diese Belege zeigen, dass in der That Tendenzen vorhanden waren, *to recomaund* zum Intransitivum werden zu lassen.

§ 173.

Was nun den Morte Darthure anlangt, so finden sich die einfachen Formen (in überwiegender Anzahl, s. u.) neben verstärkten,

z. B.: 25/8 ... *there he named hym self le chyualer malfet* ...

40/28 .. *I commande .. that ye kepe yow within your chirche* ...

188/29 .. *and there he vnarmed hym* ...

669/11 .. *but sythen he kept hym self so wel in chastyte* ..

778/33 .. *now I put me holy in to your grace* ...

780/16 .. *he was fayne to putte hym self in a charyot* ...

254/27 .. *what knyghte there preneth hym best* ...

823/37 .. *they prened hem self not in the ryght* ...

etc. etc.

Die einfachen Formen werden besonders beim Imperativ bevorzugt, so heisst es immer: *defende the (you)* 199/34, 299/13, 337/22 etc. Der Grund hierfür ist darin zu suchen, dass, da ein Befehl bezw. eine Aufforderung naturgemäss möglichst kurz ist, sich die verstärkten (längeren) Formen hier schwerer einbürgerten; auch ist der Anschluss an die gesprochene Volkssprache hier ein engerer. Ausschliesslich finden sich die einfachen Formen, wenn wir von einigen nur vereinzelt reflexiv gebrauchten Verben absehen, bei:

to betake: 472/2 .. *and so lyghtly he auoyded his hors and bitoke hym to his varlet.* 636/14, 687/30 (angelehnt an Verba der Bewegung § 180);

to bethink: 132/31 *Thenne syre Accolon bethoughte hym and said*... 239/31, 317/31;

to bless: 96/38 .. *he* .. *blessid hym and mounted vpon his hors* 128/10, 650/21;

(diese beiden Verben meist in stehenden ausdrücken);

to lay: 89/23 .. *there he leyd him doune on a paylet to slepe*... 231/21, 338/29 (Berührung mit *to lie*).

Das Umgekehrte ist in auffälliger Weise nur bei to disguise der Fall:

480/30 *Soo thenne Palomydes desguysed hym self in this manere* .. 498/24, 535/18, 769/17.

§ 174.

Was nun den Zeitpunkt betrifft, wo etwa die verstärkten Formen zur Regel werden, so sagt Kellner Hist. Outl. § 299 .. *as early as Caxton's time they seem to be the rule.*

Unsere Untersuchung ergab hierfür Folgendes: Da die P. L. verhältnismässig sehr wenig Belege aufweisen, man vgl. z. B.:

P. L. 1471—1472, p. 1 — 76: 7 einf. : 5 verst.,
1473—1474, p. 76—121: 3 einf. : 0 verst.,
1475, p. 122—168: 4 einf. : 3 verst.,

und daher zu keinem sicheren Resultate führen können, zogen wir zum Morte Darthure noch einige andere Denkmäler dieser Zeit hinzu, die Angaben betr. Blanchardyn entnahmen wir Kellners Einleitung, p. 35:

Tabelle.

Denkmal	Jahr	p.	einf.	verst.
Morte Darthure	1469/70	1/100	36	6
Godeffroy de Bol.	1481	1/30	16	2
Caxton Curial	1484	1/16	3	5
Blanchardyn	1489	1/42	3	27
Eneydos	1490	1/50	5	12

Diese Tabelle giebt ein ziemlich deutliches Bild, wir ersehen hieraus, dass die beiden erstgenannten Denkmäler ein Ueberwiegen der einfachen, die drei letzten ein Ueberwiegen der verstärkten Formen zeigen. Daraus können wir wohl den Schluss ziehen, dass die verstärkten Formen im Laufe der achtziger Jahre im Gebrauch zu überwiegen begannen.

NB. Bei den Zählungen blieben nachdrücklich betonte Formen, sowie *to recomand* unberücksichtigt.

§ 175.

Die erste Hälfte des 16. Jahrhunderts führt zu weiterer Verdrängung der einfachen durch die verstärkten Formen. Roger Asham hat in seinem Toxophilus (1545) nur noch einen Beleg, 119 ... *I shoulde truble me wyth other thinges infinite more:* in seinem (allerdings 1570 erschienenen) Schoolemaster kein Beispiel des einfachen Pronomens mehr.

Sehr wenige Belege bietet auch Tyndale in seinem English New Testament (Matth. 28/12, Luk. 1/2 sowie in seinem Briefe an Frith Pl. 238/19 ... *that ye kepe you alowe by the ground*).

Belege aus anderen Denkmälern.

Fl. (Hawes) 16/22 *Vnto all Poetes, I do me excuse*
ib. (Wyatt) 20/15 (18/30)
Yet can I not hide me in no dark place:
ib. 25/45 *The canses, why that homeward I me draw,*
ib. 28/29; 29/42 *content the then with honest povertie*
ib. (Howard) 31/17, (Skelton 58/48),
ib. 69/30, (69/119) *I cannot me refrayne*
To loke on her agayne:
ib. (Barclay) 92/25
Yet nothynge he hadde to comforte hymin age
94/23 *I count me happy*...
105/19, 106/13, 106/33,
ib. 113/49 (geistl. Volkslied) *I haue ysoghe in many a syde:*
to fynde water to washe me fro woo:
ib. (Liebeslieder) 126/7, 133/29, 134/47
Then as I ought. I me be thought.
ib. (Balladen) 165/5, 168/25, 180/11, 181/104
And arme you well and make you redy
186/24, 187/28, 187/82, 192/42, 196/37, 196/45,
ib. (theol. Schriften), 242/32, 242/36,
ib. (Volksbücher) 291/52 *The fendes of hell be with grete dylygence to applye theym to gete and haue my body and soule*...
ib. (Uebersetzung von Huon de Bord.) 312/53
... she rose and made her redy ...

ib. (Davis) 325/45, ib. (Briefe) 330/55, 333/45, 335/48, 349/51
I must remitt me to mr vawghan...
Four Elements 41 (49)
Then thou hast quit thee like a tall knight!
Everyman 138 *Go, thrist thee into the ground*
Calisto and Melibaea 86, World and Child 269, Hickscorner 175 (160; 161)
Let us amend us we true Christian men,
Joy, Ap. 47 *T. will excuse him be the greke...*
ib. 49 *yet ought he not to auenge himselfe...*
Thersites 398
This sallet I would have to keep me from his ire.
ib. 401, 403, 404, 405,
ib. 427 *Farewell, son, I will go me to prepare.*
Bale, Promises 318
Apply thee apace thine office to fulfil.
Heywood, P. P. 372
But when I bethought me how this chanced,
Suppl. to Henry VIII 30
Doo we, which thinke vs Christen men, esteame spirituall benefyees to be nothinge...
etc.

§ 176.

Wir kommen nun zu der 2. Hälfte des 16. Jahrh.; die zahlreichen Belege für das einfache Pronomen, die wir in den Denkmälern dieses Zeitraums noch finden, zeugen dafür, dass sie in der Volkssprache noch lebendig waren; insbesondere finden wir sie beim Imperativ (s. o. § 173).

Zur Veranschaulichung des gesagten geben wir eine grössere Anzahl von Belegen aus dem gesammelten Material:
Interlude of Youth 37
And to God I me betake;
R. R. Doister 62
Let him keepe him there still...
More, Utopia 117 *... yet against the ayer they so defende them with temperate diete...*

Jacob and Esau 213
I promise with this sale to hold me content.
ib. 236
have I not despatched me quickly?
Disobedient Child 313
To my good neighbours I me report,
Appius and Virginia 133
Prepare thee in haste Virginius unto.
G. G. Needle 197 (215, 216)
Now will I settle me to this gear.
Like Will to Like 337
I will never acquaint me with such...
Marriage of Wit 364 *Bethink you well...*
Conflict of Conscience 91
Have I not plied me...
Damon and Pithias 92 *make you ready.*
Lyly, Euphues 269
...which keepeth him in a dead sleepe...
Lyly, Endimion 23 *Let them to it, and we will warme us by their words.*
Peele, Wives Tale 224 *Hold thee there, friar.*
Briefe Elisabeths 13 (120)
...you wyl shew you uncareful of suche a treason.
Marlowe, Tamburlaine 1993 (3616)
Till we haue made vs ready for the field.
Jew 1130 *Hold thee, wench...*
ib. 2064, Edward II 171 (192)
I can no longer keep me from my lord.
Massacre 342
I'll secrethy convey me unto Blois.

Dido 406 *Then would I wish me in fair Dido's arms,*
Ovid 135 *And soldiers make them ready to the fight.*
Misfortunes of Arthur 293, Marprelate, Epistle 38
Kyd, Jeronimo 365 *we have bethought us,*
Spanish Trag. 14, Cornelia 197, 212
Nor shalt thou bathe thee longer in our blood.

Rare Triumphs 185
> *Go, yield thee captive to thy care...*

Puttenham 152 *wherein I report me to them...*
Three Lords 481 *Tut, hold thee content*:
Introd. Sketch 63 *They... not apply them... to dininity...*
Peele, Arr. 57, Edward I 91
> *So do I hold me well apaid:*

ib. 175 *hang thee, I pray thee...*
David and Bethsabe 16
> *Thus it shall be: lie down upon thy bed,*
> *Feigning thee fever-sick, and ill at ease;*

Polyhymnia 212
> *He would betake him to his orisous,*

Greene, Bacon 149
> *Therefore my wags, we'll horse us in the morn,*

ib. 204 *Prepare thee, Serlsby:*
James IV 121 *What, shall I clad me like a country maid?*
ib. 142 *We will submit us to the English king.*
Look. Glass 96 *Go, let us prostrate us before his feet.*
ib. 121
> *When honour yields him friend to wicked life,*

Menaphon 80 *She... bathde hir in the springs,*
Verm. 250 *The lion laid and stretch'd him in the lawns;*
Sidney, Arcadia 239, 263,
703 *Go snake, hide thee in the dust,*
Soliman and Perseda 295
> *...arm thee from top to toe,*

ib. 301 *... let's make us ready...*
Jack Straw 383 *... I... may hide me in the throng.*
Lodge, Wounds 163 *Rouse thee...*
Henslowes Diary 114
and for the trewe payment herof I bynde me, my eares, exsecutors... by this presente.

Weiterentwicklung.

Shakspere steht in Bezug auf diese Frage nach Abbot § 223, Deutschb. § 46 zu urteilen auf dem Boden des ausgehenden 16. Jahrhunderts. Die einfachen Formen werden im weiteren Verlauf der englischen Sprachgeschichte immer mehr zurückgedrängt, haben sich jedoch in der Poesie zum Teil erhalten.

§ 167.

Im einzelnen ist noch zu bemerken:

1. Das Verbum *to (re)commánd* bewahrt auch in dieser Zeit (16. Jahrh.) fast ausnahmslos den alten Zustand, es findet sich natürlich besonders in der Briefliteratur dieser Epoche, in den Briefen Elisabeths und James (z. B. 9, 35), sowie der Leycester Corr., doch auch sonst R. R. Doister 50, Jacob and Esau 217, bei Kyd, Peele, Greene und anderen.

2. *to advise* wird nur imperativisch in der scheinbar recht populären, besonders der dramatischen Literatur (Dialog!) eigenen Redewendung *advise you (thee)* überwiegend mit dem einfachen Personalpronomen verbunden, was sich durch die Wechselwirkung mit Fällen wie Heywood, Pard. and Friar 230
I advise you all, that now here be —
Disobedient Child 305
Yet I advise thee, thou cullon, make haste.
etc.
erklärt; vgl. hierzu die ähnlichen Fälle bei *to assure* § 167, 3 und Anm.

P. L. 676/14
avyse you I deme ye woll her afftr ellys repent yow.
Everyman 130 (132)
Advise you, will ye go with him...?
J. Juggler 142 *And if you blat me, mistress, avyse gou;*
Kyd, Spanish Tragedy 69 (170; 98 *you*)
Advise thee therefore, be not credulous;
Greene, Alphonsus 66, Lodge, Wounds 113;
Dagegen: Marriage of Wit 349
Nay, Wit advise yourself, and pause a while,

3) *to assure*, mehrfach noch mit dem einfachen Pronomen verbunden, tritt besonders imperativisch in der Redewendung *assure thee (you)* auf, im Sinne von *be assured*, was auch (Greene, Orl. 40, Peele, David and B. 46 etc.), aber bei weitem seltener erscheint.

Kyd, Spanish Tragedy 80 (148)
Assure thee, Don Lorenzo, he shall die,

Peele, David and Bethsabe 43, Marlowe, Massacre 345
Cousin, assure you I am resolute,

Anm.: Diese Fälle könnten auch als Auslassung des Personalpronomens der 1. Person (eine Wechselwirkung mit diesen Fällen ist nicht zu leugnen, cf. § 104 Anm. 2) angesehen werden, doch sprechen dagegen teils Fälle mit verstärktem Pronomen (diese immer in Sidney's Arcadia 256, 402 etc.), z. B.: Kyd, Spanish Tragedy 147
Assure yourself it would content them well.
Soliman and Perseda 301
But this assure yourselves, it must be mine,
Marlowe, Massacre 307 etc. etc.,
teils auch Fälle wie: Kyd, Spanish Tragedy 62
And what we may, let him assure him of.
Marlowe, Tamburlaine 1128 *Yet we assure vs of the victorie.*

4. Das Verbum *to content*, welches in der 2. Hälfte des 16. Jahrh. im Drama eine grosse Rolle spielt, nimmt noch überwiegend das einfache Pronomen zu sich; da es meist in der Form des Imperativs *(content the, you, ye)* auftritt, übten diese Fälle grossen Einfluss aus, auch die Form *content* (z. B. Kyd, Jer. 388 *Content; this is joy mixed with spite,* ib. 389, Marl., Jew 1780, Greene, Bacon 170 etc.) mag zur Erhaltung der einfachen Formen beigetragen haben.

Z. B.: Gorboduc 68 (1106)
Mother, content you, you shall see the end.

Sodann zahlreich bei Peele, Greene, Marlowe, Lodge etc., selten bei Kyd (Span. 5 verst.: 2 einf. Formen).

5. *to bow* (Voges, Anglia VI, 361) meist ohne Pronomen (Tyndale, Rom. 14/11 [Auth. Vers. und Rev. Vers. ebenso], Cambyses 233, Sidney, Arc. 571 etc.).

Nur bei Greene mit einf. Pron. beobachtet:
James IV 185 *Bow thee,*
Looking Glass 109 *Bow ye...*

Verstärktes Pronomen nur Tyndale, Joh. 20/11 *And as she wept, she bowed her self into the sepulcre* (Auth. Vers. und Rev. Vers. *stooped down*),

Marlowe, Hero 101
She bow'd herself so low out of her tower,

6. *to complain.*
Selten und dann nur mit dem einf. Pronomen:
P. L. 961/416
...*I have be confortid to complaine me*...
M. 473/8, 650/2, 664/26, Kyd, Span. 93, Greene, Menaphon 64 *Sometime... he would complaine him to the windes of his woes*...

7. *to endeavour* bisweilen mit dem einf. pronomen.
P. L. 895/335 (942/393)...*that ye have ryght well endevyrd you*...
Plumpton Correspondence 115
...*I shall indevor me for you as farre as I can*...
Interlude of Youth 31 (Kyd, Span.-*you*)
    And endeavour thee, for God's sake,
    For thy sins amends to make
recht häufig dagegen und entschieden **volkstümlich** ist die Verbindung mit dem **verstärkten** Pronomen:
P. L. 890/328 (883/319)...*that ye...endevore your self that*...
Fl. (Roy and Barl.), 84/2, Fl. (theol. Schriften) 218/11, ib. (Hall), 273.10, ib. (Conf. Amantis Vorwort) 303/56, Plumpt. Corr. 27, Egerton Pap. 6, Utopia 58, 135, Euphues 100, Puttenham 25 *Finally, because they did altogether endeuor them selues.*

8. Bei *to lay* nur das einf. Pronomen (Berührung mit *to lie* § 179).
Lyly, Endimion 29...*when thou laidst thee downe to sleepe.*
Peele, Verm. 225, 228 *I laid me down,* (Sir Clyomon and Sir Clamydes 530 b),
Greene Looking Glass 110
    Come, lay thee down upon thy mistress' knee,
Marlowe, Hero 52   *She rose*...
    And laid her down even where Leander lay;
Three Ladies 347...*he may lay him down to rest.*
Sidney, Arcadia 65
    ...*they themselves laid them down*...

9. *to remember.*

In zahlreichen Fällen, wo es im Imperativ gebraucht ist, kann es zweifelhaft sein, ob wir das Pronomen als Acc. oder als Nom. (§ 97) anzusehen haben. So:

P. L. 113/152 (428/73) *And therfor, Sir, remember yow of all these maters.*
 ib. 132/174 *I pray you remembre ye...*
     etc.

Im übrigen kann bei *to remember* das Pronomen nicht besonders auffallen, wenn man erwägt, dass dieses Verb während des ganzen 15. und 16. Jahrhunderts transitiv gebraucht wird. Hieraus erklärt sich dann auch weiter die Neigung, für die einf. die verst. Pronomina einzuführen (s. u.).

  a) Belege für das einfache Pronomen.
P. L. 349/512 ... *as I remembre me and suppose I seyd...*
 ib. 773/156 ... *I remembred me of a persone...*
 M. 132/21 (534/28, 574/23, 740 36)
  Thenne syr Arthur remembrid hym and thoughte...
 M. 289/31 (696/14)
  ... *she remembryd her of a pyece of a swerd...*
  M. 328/30 (463/35) *And soo whanne they were abedde bothe, sire Tristram remembryd hym of his old lady la beale Isoud.*
  M. 381/16 ... *but I shalle remembre me and...*
  M. 567/22 ... *for when I remembryd me of la beale Isoud...*
 Caxton, Eneydos 43/9
  Remembre the of the swete dysportynges
Latimer, Sermons 108 *I remembred me that...*
Fl. (Terenzübersetzung) 98,15
  Then Chremes to rememberhim began
   Of his doughter...
 Kyd, Span. 89 *Nay, nay, now I remember me, let them alone*... (Puttenham 163),
 Sidney, Arc. 767 *But remembring him, that the burthen of the state...lay all upon him: Well, said he...*

  b) Belege für das verst. Pronomen.
 P. L. 622/378 *prayng you therfor, as your frende to remembre wele your self...*

M. 567/3 *Thenne syr Tristram remembryd hym self that*...
Fl. (Caxton) 2/7 ... *I remembryd my self of my symplenes*...
Latimer, Sermons 58
   Kynge Dauid remembryng hym selfe swore...
Marprelate Epistle 23
   ...*I do now remember my selfe another prynter*...
Sidney, Arcadia 354
   But remembring her self, and seing Basilius by... *she turned her call*...
   ib. 611 ...*when he remembred himself to be in danger*...

10. to (*di*)*sport* im 15. und 16. Jahrhundert fast ausnahmslos nur mit dem einfachen Pronomen.

P. L. 318/431
   my Lord of Caunterbury and my Lord Bourgchier shall ...hunte and sporte theym with Sir William Oldhall.
   ib. 357/525 ...*the Kyng is way...to hunt and to sport hym there*... (812/220)
   ib. 573/305 *Hyr men seyd that she had non othyr erend to the towne but for to sport hyr;*
   ib. 824/237 *And if it lyke yow that I may...sporte me with yow*...
   M. 327/8 ...*Tristram yede in to the forest for to disporte hym*...
Sidney, Astrophel and Stella 46/13
   That he so long may sport him with desire
Greene, Bacon 175
   Well, doctors, seeing I have sported me
   With laughing at these mad and merry wags,
Puttenham 249 *Others there be so simple, as they thinke,*
   Because it shines, to sport them in the fire,

Gegenteilige Fälle begegneten erst in der 2. Hälfte des 16. Jahrhunderts:

Cambyses 228
   They sport themselves in pleasant field,
Barnfield, Poems 49
   Sporting our selues to day, as we were woont
   ib. 57 *Diana (on a time) walking the wood,*
   To sport herselfe...

Anm.: An *to (di)sport* hat sich *to play* von ähnlicher Bedeutung angeschlossen, doch ist es nur im 15. Jahrhundert wirklich volkstümlich:

P. L. 36/48 *My fader Garneyss senttee me word, that he xulde ben her the nexch weke, and my emme also, and pleyn hem her with herr hawkys.*
   ib. 703/59 ... *she left hym rome to pleye hym in.*
   M 525/26 *And whanne they hadde played them a grete whyle*...
   ib. 565/19 ...*playe you with me this nyghte* (kann auch Nom. sein).
   ib. 598/10 *And soo at after none dame Elayne and her maydens came in to the gardyn to play them*...
   Peele, Alcazar 115
      And even in Spain, where all the traitors dance
      And play themselves upon a sunny day,
   Sidney, Arcadia 247
      But as the ladies plaid them in the water...
   ib. 699 *so that she might play her as she would*...

11. *to ware.*

Folgender wenn auch einziger Beleg weist auf eine recht populäre Wendung hin (cf. auch Oxf. Dict. unter *beware*):

P. L. 228/317
...*jentylmen, whiche utteryd skornefull language of me, as in thys wyse, with mor, saying: „War the, gosune, war, and goo we to dyner;"*

Im übrigen selten mit (einf.) Pronomen:

Greene, James IV 137
   For many times, if ladies 'ware them not,
   A nine months wound with little work is got.

Dagegen Greene, Looking Glass 68
   the ginger, O ware of that!

II. Bei intransitiven ursprünglich mit dem reflexiven Dativ konstruierten Verben.

§ 178. Vorbemerkung.

Ueber den reflexiven Dativ in historischer Entwickelung siehe Voges, Anglia VI, 317 ff. Indem wir hierauf verweisen, können wir uns eine Wiederholung der historischen Entwicklung ersparen. Im übrigen wird die folgende Darstellung nicht überflüssig sein, da die Uebergangszeit des 15. und 16. Jahrhunderts bei Voges begreiflicherweise zu kurz gekommen ist.

Einzelne Verba, bei denen es zweifelhaft sein kann, ob urspr. Dativ oder Accusativ, schliessen wir hier doch der Uebersichtlichkeit wegen mit ein.

Diese Verben nehmen im Ae. und Me., wenn überhaupt, nur das einfache Personalpronomen im Dativ (Acc.) zu sich.

§ 179.
1. Verba der Ruhe.

to abide: M. 685/38

Thenne wolde he haue rysen to haue departed them, but he had not soo moche myghte to stande on foote, soo he abode hym soo longe tyl Colgreuaunce had the werse...

to lie: in der Regel ohne Pronomen, z. B.: Peele, David and Bethsabe 16, 25, Marlowe, Jew 1774, 1925, Greene, Orl. 43, 44, Sidney, Arc. 681, 696 etc. Dagegen vereinzelte Fälle mit dem einfachen Personale, wo *to lie* in Verbindung mit *down* eine transitive Färbung hat:

Joy, Ap. 39 *As the man that lyeth him down to slepe...*

Peele, Edward I 128

Then, Friar, lie thee down and die:

to rest: wenn überhaupt mit Pronomen, ist das einfache gebräuchlicher als das verstärkte.

a) Belege für das einfache Pronomen.

M. 238/21 *Soo whan they had restyd them a whyle...*

ib. 416/16 *...my lord and I rested vs here...*

Myst. ed. Hone 54

therfore I wole sytt downe and rest me ryght her'

Rutland Pap. 24, Hickscorner 148, Fl. (Caxton) 4/38, ib. (Froissartübersetzung) 308/38, Kyd, Span. 124, Peele, Edward I 104, David and B. 17, 20, Greene, Orl. 50, Menaphon 27, Verm. 318, Marlowe, Tamburlaine 2566, Massacre 323, Edw. II 259 etc.

b) Belege für das verstärkte Pronomen.

Disobedient Child 289

Rest yourself in this little chair.

Lyly, Euphues 233

...who...rested him-self vppon the side of a siluer streame...

Conflict of Conscience 120

O father! rest yourself in God...

Puttenham 88

...he taketh vp his lodging, and rests him selfe till the morrow:

Jack Straw 414
Where we'll repose, and rest ourselves all night.
Anm.: Bei *to rest* hat zweifellos eine Berührung mit *to repose* stattgefunden, das sich ähnlich verhält,
einf. Pron.: M. 201/20 ... *here shal ye repose yow*..., 559/24 ... *as she and I reposed vs* ... 707/31, R. R. Doister 30, Peele, Alcazar 124, Rare Triumphs 151 etc.
verst. Pron.: M. 369/5 *Soo that nyght Kynge Arthur and his knyghtes reposed them self.* Asham, Schoolemaster 43, Lyly, Euphues 233, Conflict of Conscience 120, Puttenham 88, Jack Straw 414.

to sit:
M. 597/9 *Anone with alle there came an old man in to the halle, and he satte hym doune*..., More, Utopia 71 ... *we came unto the same place again, and sate vs downe;* Jacob and Esau 226, Peele, Alcazar 89, Edw. I 81, 92, Old Wives Tale 215, Sidney, Arcadia 126, Greene, James IV 130, Looking Glass 110, Soliman and Perseda 331 etc.
Anm. 1: Zahlreich im Morte Darthure, später vereinzelt findet sich *to set* für *to sit* (schon me. solche Vertauschungen, cf. Morsb., Me. Gr. § 114 Anm. 1), so: M. 215/8, 220/6, 284/15, 319/16, Fox 104, 117, Fl. (Jagdlieder) 151/4, ib. (Balladen) 165/14, Greene, Orlando 13, Peele, Edw. I 92 (eine Lesart) etc.
Anm. 2: Als einziger Fall der passiven Konstruktion mit refl. Bedeutung verbunden mit einem Pronomen fand sich:
P. L. 71/90
Wherfore, cosyn, thynk on this mateer, for sorow oftyn tyme causeth women to be set hem otherwyse than thei schuld do, and if sche where in that case, I wot weel ȝe wold be sory.
ein Fall, der sich leicht durch Kreuzung erklärt.

§ 180.
2. Verba der Bewegung.

to busk:
Fl. (Balladen) 173/50 *Hastely I wyll me buske sayd the knyght Ouer the salte see*
ib. 177/84 *Buske you thyderwarde my dere mayster*
to come: Unzweifelhaft sichere Fälle mit reflexivem Dativ:
Fl. (Balladen) 175/84
He wente hym forth full mery syngynge
Fl. (Balladen) 180/91
Now hath the knyght this leue I take
And went hym on his way

ib. 5/17

Whan the kynge pryant herde the crye, he ... wente hym in to his temple of Appolyn...

Marllowe, Faust II 1604

I went me home to his house, and there I found him asleepe

to get: (Ueber die Frage, ob trans. oder intrans., cf. Voges, Anglia VI, 346).

Es steht überwiegend in Verbindung mit dem einfachen Pronomen:

P. L. 904/344 *... there was 200 of them, that gete them in to a Breten schyppe...*

Fl. (Tyndale) 234/10 *And so I gate me to london...*

Latimer, Sermons 169

He gettes him to the vniuersitie.

More, Utopia 33 *...I wondre greatly, why you gette you not into some kinges courte.*

Greene, Menaphon 35, Marlowe, Hero 31 etc.

Viel seltener werden die verstärkten Formen gebraucht:

Tyndale, Luk. 22/41 *And he gate him selfe from them* (Auth. Vers. und Rev. Vers. *he was withdrawn*) Suppl. of the Poore Commons 84 *...they...gette them selues streyght to the kennel.* R. A., Toxophilus 74, Sidney, Arcadia 55.

etc. etc.

Anm.: Bei imperativischem Gebrauch von *to get*, meist bei stehenden Redensarten des täglichen Lebens, die seit dem Anfang des 16. Jahrhunderts in unseren Texten auftreten, sich aber erst in weitester Ausdehnung im elisabethanischen Drama finden, steht immer nur das einfache Personalpronomen:

Fl. (Weihnachtslieder) 124/54 (325/5 Mem.)

Get the hence what doest thou here

Four Elements 34, Bale, Kynge Johan 9,

Tyndale, Joh. 5/8 (Auth. Vers. und Rev. Vers. *walk*),

Joh. 7/3 (Auth. Vers. und Rev. Vers. *Depart hence*),

Ap. 10/20 *...get the doune and go with them...*

(Auth. Vers. und Rev. Vers. ebenso),

Thersites 397 *Go get thee to my lover Venus*

R. R. Doister 38 *Get you in to your work.*

Jacob and Esau 253, G. G. Needle 203, Cambyses 223, Appius and Virginia 121 *get thee packing*, Peele, Arr. 40 *get thee gone*, ebenso Marlowe, Edward II 186,

Marlowe, Edward II 280, Massacre 349, Jew 1565 *get you away*, Dido 418 *Get you aboard*, Greene, James IV 108, 115 *get you gone* (einmal Look. Glass 98 *I'll get me gone*), ib. 73 *Get the ganging*..., Lyly, Mother Bombie 86, Peele, David and Bethsabe 27 *get thee in*,
Three Lords 454 *Sirrah, get ye packing*,
Astrophel and Stella p. 59, 1
Goe, my Flocke, goe get you hence.
Sidney, Arcadia 92, Three Ladies 262 *get you walking*
etc. etc.
NB. Analogische Bildungen hierzu:
R. R. Doister 64
Auaunt lozell, picke thee hence.
Greene, Alph. 43 *Go, pack you hence*...
Three Lords 434 *Pack you my friend;*
Auch Fälle ohne Pronomen:
Greene, Alphonsus 52
...pack hence, or...
Verm. 293
Pack hence ... thou idle, lazy worm;

to hie, to haste, to speed:
P. L. 504/192 ... *I wyll spede me to send non a awnser ...* (ib. 352/518)
M. 178/9... *yf we hye vs hens*...
Digby Myst. 9/209 (34/196)
I say, hye the hens that thu were goon,
Digby Myst. 107/1384
per-for' hast you forth with gladnesse,
goddes commavddement for to fulfylle.
Fl. (Weihnachtslieder) 117/42
The shepardes hyede them to bedlam
ib. (Balladen) 175/32
Spede the out of my hall
Gorboduc 700 *In secrete I was counselled by my frendes,*
To hast me thence
G. G. Needle 182 *Go hie thee, Tib*...
New Custom 31
...they hied them apace,
Greene, Bacon 171 *I will in post hie me to Fressinfield,*
Pinner 171
Let us hie us to Wakefield...

Peele, David and Bethsabe 15
Urias will haste him, and his own return.
Edward I 186
Bid Mortimer, thy master, speed him fast,
Marl., Tamb. 805 *Haste thee, Techelles;*
Sidney, Arc. 784 *but Philanax... hasted her up to the lodge, where her sister was...*
Barnfield 24, 66.

etc. etc.

Selten sind Fälle wie: Udall, State 23
... we will speed our selues to London...

to kneel: Wir bemerkten nur

Soliman and Pers. 335 *Then kneel thee down,*
And at my hands receive the stroke of death,

to mount, dismount:
Peele, Alc. 140 *Mount thee thereon, and save thyself by flight.* ib. *Mount me I will;*
Polyhymnia 201 *(He) Dismounts him from his pageant, and attonce...*
He mounts him bravely for his friendly foe;
Soliman and Perseda 275, Greene, Alphonsus 45, Marlowe, Faust 807 (Verschiedenheit der Ausgaben).

to return, to turn:
Häufiger verstärkte Formen bei *to turn* (refl. urspr. Acc.; cf. Voges, Anglia VI 353).

M. 46 10 *Soo tho kynge retorned hym to the toure...* 93/30, 115/6, Fox 15, Latimer, Sermons 82, Rutl. Pap. 22, Fl. (Balladen) 193/41, Tyndale, Matth. 9/22 (Auth. Vers. und Rev. Vers. *turning*), Mark. 5/30 (Auth. Vers. und Rev. Vers. ebenso), More, Utopia 30, Peele, Verm. 258, Marl., Tamb. 801, 3590, Puttenham 274, Sidney, Arcadia 698;

Daneben: Tyndale, Ap. 7/42. *Then God turned him selfe and gave them up* (Auth. Vers. und Rev. Vers. nur *turned*), Joh. 20/14 *...she turned herself back...* (Auth. Vers. und Rev. Vers. ebenso), R. A., Toxophilus 97, Lyly, Campaspe 102, Peele, Old Wives Tale 213, Greene, Menaphon 30, Marlowe, Faust 423, Sidney, Arcadia 870.

to ride:
Kyd, Jeronimo 387
    Especially ride thee home so, my son.
to start:
Fl. (Balladen) 175/58
    He sterte hym toa borde a none
    Tyll a table rounde
to stir: G. G. Needle 196
    Come hither then, and stir thee not
    One inch out of this circle plat;
ib. 226
    And as she began to stir her...
Dagegen: Sidney, Arcadia 783 ...*she stirred her self...*

§ 181.
Allgemeine Bemerkungen zu 2.

Bei einer grossen Anzahl von Fällen, wo das Verbum im Imperativ steht, sind wir vor die Möglichkeit gestellt, entweder refl. Dativ oder Nominativ des Pronomens nach § 97 f. anzunehmen; für ersteres lassen sich zum Beweis Fälle mit *thee*, für letzteres Fälle mit *thou* anführen. Eine endgültige Entscheidung ist schwerlich zu fällen.

Greene, James IV 125
    Welcome, ye ladies, and thousand thanks for this:
    Come, enter you a homely widow's house,
    And if mine entertainment please you, let us feast.
Peele Edward I 121
    The gates are open'd: enter thee and thine.
Greene, Looking Glass 116 (Soliman and Perseda 304)
    The devil, mistress! fly you for you safeguard;
Vgl. hierzu Peele, Edward I 103 *Fly thou on them amain!*
Greene, Alphonsus 44
    And march you on, with all the troops you have,
Greene, Looking Glass 59
    So pace ye on, triumphant warriors;
Marlowe, Edward II 216
    Madam, stay you within this castle here.
Marlowe, Massacre 317 *cousin, stay you here,*

Vgl. hierzu: Marlowe, Edward II 200
> *But stay thee here where Gaveston shall sleep.*

sowie: Marlowe, Dido 391
> *Fair child, stay thou with Dido's waiting-maid*:

Heywood, Pardoner and Friar 236
Neighbour, ye be constable; stand ye near,
Take ye that lay knave... (Voges 337 2 sichere Citate m. d.
Nom.)

Greene, Alphonsus 26
> *But, fellow soldiers, wend you back with me,*

ib. 67
> *Meantime, dear Muses, wander you not far*
> *Forth of the path of high Parnassus' hill,*

§ 182.

3. Verba des Affects.

Der Kasus schwankt in seinem Ursprunge zuweilen zwischen Dativ und Accusativ.

to cheer:

Greene, Pinner 174
> *Cheer thee, my boy, I will do much for thee.*

Bacon and Bungay 205
> *Yet, Bacon, cheer thee, drown not in despair.*

Peele, Alcazar 108
> *Good madam, cheer yourself, my father's wife*

Marlowe, Ovid 138
> *Cheer up thyself;*

to doubt:

Heywood, P. P. 384
ye need not doubt ye (also hier nicht nur in der 1. Sg.)

Lyly, Campaspe 122
> *I doubt mee that nature hath overcome art*...

Marprelate, Epistle 42
> *I doubt me whether all the famous dunses be dead.*

Marlowe, Epigr. by J. D. 235
> *I doubt me, he had seen a lioness.*

Anm.: Fälle wie P. L. 514/209 *dowt ye not* M. 75/7, 439/38, Marl., Edw. II 242, Tamb. 601, Peele, Edw. I 103 *doubt you (ye) not*, können auch als Nominative gefasst werden, vgl. Marl., Ovid 122 *But doubt thou not* ...

to dread ist nur im 15. Jahrh. und dann mit dem einf. Pronomen anzutreffen:

P. L. 53/65 ... *thanne he nedyd never to drede hym of* ...
M. 745 29 *I drede me sore*, 729/10, 767/24, 769/12, 829/13;
  M. 224/36 *Nay drede you not* ... wohl Dativ,
  M. 393/1 ... *neuer drede the* ...
  Myst. ed. Hone 47
    I drede me sor' I om be trayd,

Anm.: *to dismay* obwohl urspr. trans. wird mit *to dread* imperativisch nur mit dem einf. Pronomen verbunden:
  M. 38/12 *Desmaye you not said the kyng* ... 350/28, 699/24,
  Fl. (Uebersetzungen) 313/2 *Huon dysmay the not* ...

to fear: Wir müssen nach Verbformen scheiden; in der 1. Sg. Praes. herrscht *I fear me* entschieden vor, z. B.:

P. L. 435/82 *I fere me it is not well with yow* ...
Myst. ed. Hone 14
  I fere me grettly the prest wole me dysspice;
Latimer, Sermons 107
  This I feare me is theyr entente ...
Lyly, Euphues 69, Briefe Elisabeths 115, Marl., Jew 1606.
    etc. etc.

In der 1. Sg. Praet. und Fut. findet sich das Pronomen nur im 15. Jahrh.:

P. L. 371 ... *y ferd me lest they be knowyn* ...
ib. 706/64, 745/114,
M. 840/1 ... *I shal not fere me to do that* ...

Beim Imperativ ist das Pronomen nicht ungewöhnlich:
Tyndale, Matth. 28/3 *The aungel answered and sayde to the wemen, feare ye not.* (Auth. Vers. und Rev. Vers. *fear not ye*)

Trial of Treasure 287 *Fear ye not*, 295 *Fear you not*,
Marlowe, Edward II 188, Jew 1480.

Diese Fälle könnten auch als Nominative aufgefasst werden.

In anderen Verbformen ganz vereinzelt nur in den P. L.:
435,83 *The pepyll feryth hem myche the more to be hurt* ...
Das verstärkte Pronomen begegnet nur
Sidney, Arcadia 281 *Now seeming to fear himself* ...

to repent:
Im 15. und zahlreich auch noch im 16. Jahrh. mit dem verstärkten Pronomen verbunden.
P. L. 56/69 *and all that have done and seyd azens him, they xul sore repent hem.*
ib. 91/122, 146/193,
M. 474/2 ... *thenne he repentyd hym of his othe* ...
ib. 607/22, 701/30, Fox 28,
Everyman 137 *I repent me, that I hither came.*
Jacob and Esau 220, Lyly, Euphues 34, 114, Loves Metam. 236, Briefe Elisab. 55, Jack Straw 411,
Angry Women 370 *I do repent me of my coming forth;*
Dagegen: Latimer, Sermons 127
An vnfaythful Iudge hath fyrste an heauye rekenyge of his faulte, repentynge him self of his wickednes ... (einf. Pron. ib. 90, 137)
Introd. Sketch 168
At the least, I shall not repent myself of the meditation. (einf. Pron. ib. 183)
Sidney, Arcadia 527
But Amphialus might repent himself of his wilful breaking his sword:

to shame:
Im Morte Darthure in Verbindung mit dem einfachen Pronomen gebraucht, sonst fast ausnahmslos ohne Pronomen.
M. 248/23 ... *I shame me not to be with hym* ...
M. 622/6 ... *ye nede not to shame you* ...;
Daneben:
M. 774/2 ... *wolte thow shame thy self* ...
Sidney, Arcadia 489
But Amphialus ... very earnestly dealt with him not to shame himself;

§ 183.

4. **Andere Verba**
haben sich den im § 178—182 besprochenen angeschlossen:

1. *to agree, to assent, to obey, to purpose, to recant* weisen nur im 15. Jahrhundert die Verbindung mit dem einfachen Pronomen auf.

to agree:
P. L. 196/265 ... *as ye do therinne, she woll agre her therto.*
M. 624/8 ... *I ryghte wel agree me therto ...*
ib. 672/14 *Sir sayd he I agree me therto ...*

to assent (cf. me. consenten mit refl. Dativ Voges 362):
M. 71·12 *I assente me said Arthur ...*
ib. 340/5 ... *I assente me wel therto said the kynge.*

to obey (Belege aus älterer Zeit bei Voges 368):
P. L. 218/305
... *I will obeye me, and offre me to abyde the rewle of you ...*
ib. 576/177 ... *and he hathe obeyed hym to yow ..*
M. 575/17 ... *for I haue obeyed me vnto the prophecy ...*

te purpose:
P. L. 7/26 *I purpose me to come homward be London, to lerne ...*
ib. 247 (467/126)
... *I purpose me, as I woll auswer God, to retorne the dieu eleccion ...*
ib. 357/526 ... *and they seythe here, he porpose hym to go to Walys to the Quene.*
ib. 390 ... *Howard purposith hym to make any aray ..*

to recant:
Greene, Friar Bacon 167
    Recant thee, Lacy, thou art put in trust:

Einige andere in unseren Texten nicht belegte siehe Kellner, Blanch. p. 53.

2. *to hark, to hear, to look:*
Peele, Old Wives Tale 230 *But hark you, gammer ...*
Angry Women 381 *Frank, hark ye:*

Mucedorus 212 (214, 217) *But hark you, sir*...
Three Lords 421 *Hark ye, you women*...
Fälle dieser Art fasst Voges 366 als refl. Dativ; doch lässt sich ein absoluter Beweis nicht führen.

to hear: Hierfür gilt das bei *to hark* gesagte.
Marriage of Wit 365
Do so, and, hear you, couch a cod's-head!
Soliman and Perseda 302 *Ay, but hear you, master*...
Greene, Looking Glass 71
Nay, but hear you, master Usurer:
ib. 86
Nay, but hear ye, take me with ye...
Three Lords 421
Marry, but hear ye, motley-beard.
Knack to Know a Knave 530
Hear you, sir, you have a good bargain;
to look: Vergl. die Bemerkung zu *to hark*.
Angry Women 276
Look ye, mistress, now I hit ye.

§ 184.

Rückblick.

1. Im allgemeinen haben die in den vorangegangenen §§ niedergelegten Ergebnisse unserer Untersuchung aufs neue die Thatsache bestätigt, dass das Pronomen bei den **transitiven Verben eine notwendigere Ergänzung bildet als bei den intransitiven**, daher bei ersteren die grössere Verwendung des **verstärkten Pronomens**. Wenn wir nun trotzdem beobachten, dass die einfachen Formen bei transitiven Verben sich auch in der Volkssprache lange behaupten, so liegt das vornehmlich an der steten Wechselwirkung von Fällen, wo ein und dasselbe Verbum bald transitiv bald intransitiv (zum Teil mit verschiedener Bedeutung), also auch ohne Pronomen gebraucht wurde.

Man vergl. hierzu die folgenden Fälle aus dem 15. und 16. Jahrhundert, die sich leicht beliebig vermehren lassen:

P. L. 675/15 (Disobedient Child 301, Marlowe, Ovid 116)
... that they dysport not with noon other yonge peple ...

M. 244/25 (Appius and Virginia 126)
We wille goo to dyner, and soo they wasshed and wente to mete ...

M. 480/14 (Latimer, Sermons 108, Marlowe, Edward II 209)
... there came a damoysel to the haute prynce and complayned that there was a knyghte ...

M. 483/32 (Lyly, Euphues 302, Sidney, Arcadia 9)
... but at the laste he recouerd well be good surgyens.

Four Elements 28 (R. R. Doister 80, Sidney, Arcadia 389)
And that is Scotland that joineth him near,

Thersites 410
Will there none of you in battle me oppose?

Bale, Thre Lawes 967 (Sir Clyomon 498a, Sidney, Arcadia 290)
I wyll not bowe sure, to soch a folysh face.

Lyly, Euphues 193 (Sidney, Arcadia 279, Leyc. Corr. 332)
... she endeauoreth to set down good lawes ...

Kyd, Cornelia 246 (Sidney, Arcadia 96)
They 'gan retire, where Iuba was encamp'd;

Peele, Arr. 19 (Greene, Verm. 215, Lodge, Wounds 137)
but sith my cunning not compares with thine,

Peele, Alcazar 102 (Edward I 190, Sidney, Arcadia 166)
And now draw near ...

Rare Triumphs 169 (Jack Juggler 128)
My lord, I make no challenge with offence;
But first I will prepare for my defence.

Greene, James IV 156 (Tancred and Gismonda 72)
Guid knight, I grant thy suit. First I submit,
And humble crave a pardon of your Grace.

Greene, Menaphon 36 (Misfortunes of Arthur 337)
thus did the poore shepheard bathe in a kinde of blisse ...

Marlowe, Tamburlaine 445
We yeeld vnto thee, happie Tamburlaine.

ib. 2873
Arme, dread Soueraign, and my noble Lords!

Marlowe, Faust II 756
Keepe further from me O thou illiterate, and vnlearned Hostler.
Sidney, Arcadia 225
And so Pyrocles taking his time... separated somewhat from the rest...
Three Ladies 260 (Damon and Pithias 53)
therefore make ready.
Three Lords 419 *Ladies, unmask!*
ib. *Unveil, I say...*
ib. 431 *Unmask, Love.*
etc. etc.

Dass im Einzelnen noch Gründe mancherlei Art hinzukommen, ist bereits oben bei gesondert betrachteten Verben hervorgehoben, so bei *to content, to recomand* und anderen.

Man vergl. auch Fälle der Aufforderung wie:
New Custom 41
Content, in faith, thither with speed let us hie.
Lyly, Euphues 142
... let vs endeauour euery one to amend one...
Greene, Looking Glass 128
Come, ladies, come, let us prepare to pray.
Jack Straw 408
Let me now to your counsel recommend,
wo ein in der älteren Zeit erfordertes doppeltes *us (me)* als euphonisch unschön vermieden wurde.

2. Die intransitiven ursprünglich mit refl. Dativ konstruierten Verben zeigen gegenüber den transitiven im 15. und 16. Jahrhundert in der Regel keine Verbindung mit einem Pronomen, zeigen sie eine solche, was je nach dem betr. Verbum seltener oder häufiger ist, so ist es meist mit dem einfachen, ungleich seltener mit dem verstärkten Pronomen.

Der Haupterklärungsgrund ist darin zu suchen, dass bei den intransitiven Verben das Pronomen weniger als Reflexiv empfunden wurde und entbehrlich war.

Ein weiterer Einzelgrund liegt auch in der Vermeidung des Zusammentreffens zweier Pronomina, ein Fall, der beim Imperativ (cf. § 97 f.) leicht eintreten konnte; vgl. z. B.:

Digby Mysteries 103/1279 *Dawth ʒe nat, my lord…*
Heywood, P. P. 382
    But doubt you not I will now do
Peele, David and Bethsabe 34
    Fair Bethsabe, sit thou, and sigh no more;
Marlowe, Edward II 181
    Here, Mortimer, sit thou in Edwards's throne;
Mucedorus 232 *Then lie thou down and die.*

Bezeichnung des reciproken Verhältnisses.
Vorbemerkung.
§ 185.

Von den untersuchten Quellen erweisen sich besonders ergiebig für das reciproke Pronomen im 15. Jahrhundert der Morte Darthure, nicht allein wegen seines Umfanges, vielmehr vor allem deshalb, weil die Schilderung zahlloser Rittereinzelkämpfe der Ausbreitung des reciproken Pronomens weitesten Spielraum gewährte. Es darf also nicht auffällig erscheinen, wenn gerade dieses Denkmal, das daher die verschiedenen Spielarten des reciproken Pronomens am besten repräsentiert, ein grosses Contingent unserer Belege liefern wird.

§ 186.
I. Entwickelung des reciproken Pronomens seit dem Ae.

Im ae. und me. werden *ǣlc* bezw. *ǣghwaeđer*, *ǣgþer* in Verbindung mit *ōđer* zur Bezeichnung des reciproken Verhältnisses verwandt und zwar in den syntaktisch erforderlichen vollen Formen; jedoch verliert *ōđer* seine Flexion seit dem Frühmittelenglischen.

Die Art der Bezeichnung kann nun eine zweifache sein:

Fall 1: Der Satz wird durch ein beliebiges im Plural stehendes Subjekt eingeleitet und die beiden Pronomina folgen nach dem Verb, *ǣlc* im Nominativ, *ōđer* in dem entsprechenden Casus obliquus.

Das Verbum richtet sich entweder nach dem den Satz einleitenden Subjekt im Plural, z. B: ae. *Hi cwǣdon ǣlc tō ōđrum*, Mark. 4/41.

me. *Thei swēren ēch to ōther* B. Gen. 26, 31;
oder, indem dieses absolut vorangestellt wird, nach *ǣlc:*
ae. *þā cnyhtas behēold heora ǣlc ōđerne* Joh. 13/22.

Fall 2: *ǣlc (ǣghwaeđer, ǣgþer)* beginnt den Satz als einziges Subjekt und *ōđer* folgt im Casus obliquus,

Z. B.: ae. *ǣghwaeđer ōđerne earme beþehte* An. 1017.
me. *Elk man rēuede ōđer* Laȝ. 4038.

II. Fortentwickelung im 15. und 16. Jahrhundert.

1. Im 15. Jahrhundert.

§ 187.

a) Erster Fall.

Die P. L. weisen nur einen Beleg auf:

601/341 .. *for we be eyther of us werye of other.*

Dagegen zeigt der Morte Darthure durch mannigfache Variationen, welche Möglichkeiten zum Ausdruck des reciproken Verhältnisses in damaliger Zeit vorhanden waren. Für *each* bez. *either* tritt einzeln auch *eueryche* und *one* ein.

α) *other* ist Objekt des Verbs:

M. 25/22 ...*how they smote eche other*...

83/17 ...*I wil wel said Balan that we do and we wil helpe eche other*...

142/31 ...*and they brysed their helmes and their hauberkes and wounded eyther other*...

238/35 ...*they graunted eyther other to rest*...

97/20 *Soo they went vnto bataille ageyne and wounded eueryche other dolefully*...

etc. etc.

β) *other* ist von einer Präposition abhängig:

Diese Fälle zeigen, dass die beiden das reciproke Verhältnis ausdrückenden Pronomina noch nicht zu éinem Begriffe verschmolzen sind, weil sonst die Präposition vor beide treten würde:

M. 14/17 (besonders charakteristisch)

How syr gawayn and syr Gareth fought eche ayenst other, and how they knewe eche other...

M. 48/32 ... *so they took them in theyre armes and made grete ioye eche of other.*

M. 704/18 ... *thenne lete they renne eche to other* ...

M. 70/38 ... *they met so hard either in others sheldes* ..

M. 561/23 ... *Jhesu send yow Joye eyther of other* ...

M. 301/14 ... *and soo they took theyr leue one fro thother* ...

Anm.: Einige Male zeigt sich auffallender, doch leicht erklärlicher, Weise nur *other* für *each (either* etc.) *other;*

M. 51/36 *And how they sware that for wele nor woo they shold not leue other* ...

M. 60/15 ... *they wold neuer faille other* ...

M. 97/8 ... *they smote other in the sheldes* ...

M. 337/14 *Soo they rode to gyder, and vnhorsed other, and torned theier sheldes* ...

M. 479/20 *So bothe the kynge Bagdemagus and the kyng of Northgalys party hurled to other, and thenne* ...

Diese Fälle sind durch Contamination entstanden, wir können sie uns durch folgende Gleichung veranschaulichen:

$$\frac{\textit{They vnhorsed eche other}}{\textit{Eche vnhorsed other}}$$
$$\textit{They vnhorsed other}$$

Im Reynard wird nur *eche (to, of* etc.) *other* gebraucht 34, 109 etc.

§ 188.

b) Zweiter Fall.

Er bietet nichts besonders auffälliges. Die verschiedenen Möglichkeiten mögen durch einige Beispiele erläutert werden:

M. 24/59 ... *how they faught and eche had almoost slayne other* ...

M. 116/23 ... *and eyther salewed other* ...

M. 688/14 ... *and eueryche comforted other* ...

M. 53/26 *Soo on the morn whan eyther hoost sawe other* ...

M. 238/25 ... *they were so amased that eyther took others swerd in stede of his owne.*

P. L. 747/118 ... *iche off yowe is moche beholten to other;*

M. 68/20 ... *and eyther wepte vpon other.*

2. Im 16. Jahrhundert.
§ 189.
a) **Erster Fall.**

Das 16. Jahrh. charakterisiert sich dadurch, dass *either* in dieser Verbindung mit *other* selten wird (z. B.: Egerton Pap. 231, Marl., Fragm. 302), dass dafür aber das im M. nur einmal (301/15 als *one thother*) belegte *one + other* (*the other, another*) ausserordentlich an Ausdehnung gewinnt und gleichwertig mit *each other* gebraucht wird, gleichwertig auch insofern, als nicht etwa ein Unterschied zwischen *each other* (2 Personen) und *one another* (mehr als 2 Personen) gemacht wird, was von zahlreichen Beispielen folgende besonders frappant beweisen:

Marlowe, Hero and Leander 37
> *Both in each other's arms chain'd as they lay.*

ib. 53
> *Two constant lovers being join'd in one,*
> *Yielding to one another, yield to none.*

ib. 100
> *They (the waves) lov'd Leander so, in groans they brake*
> *When they came near him; and such space did take*
> *'Twixt one another, loath to issue on,*
> *That in their shallow furrows earth was shown,*

ib. 101 *Where tears in billows did each other chase;*

Präpositionen treten, wie im 15. Jahrh., unmittelbar vor *other*, doch in der zweiten Hälfte schon häufig vor *one another*, *each other*:

Lyly, Euphues 296
> ... *yet will they not meddle in each other office.*

Peele, David and Bethsabe 54
> *That nestle close in one another's neck:*

Zahlreiche belege bei Marlowe, Hero 26, 37, 53 etc. Wie sich hieraus ergiebt, begann man also, die beiden Pronomina zu éinem Begriff zu verschmelzen.

Anm.: Ueber die Frage, *other* mit oder ohne bestimmten oder unbestimmten Artikel, ist folgendes zu bemerken:

In der Verbindung *each, everych, either + other* ist der Artikel im Ac. wegen der Flexionsendungen unnötig, ist später nicht eingeführt und steht auch im 15. und 16. Jahrh. nicht, bis auf zwei Fälle in Sidney's Arcadia:

220 ... *and so for a time parted those friends, each crying to the other;*

451 *how much that discord foul hath stain'd*
Both our estates, while each the other did deprave,

die sich aber als spätere Analogieformen zu denen von *one* + *the other* erweisen;

In der Verbindung *one* + *other* zeigte sich schon im M. 301/14 der bestimmte Artikel, doch ist seit der 1. Hälfte des 16. Jahrhunders, wo *one* + *other* eine grössere Verbreitung fand (s o.) unbestimmter Artikel + *other* also *another* durchaus vorherrschend, *the other* erscheint z. B.: R. A., Schoolemaster 68, Damon and Pithias 24, Marprelate Epistle 25, Leycester Correspondence 361, besonders häufig und mehr als *anŏther* nur im Euphues, z. B.: *As they wer thus pleasauntly conferring the one with the other* ... ib. 43, 46 etc.;

Relativ häufig in Sidney's Arcadia, z. B.:

10 ... *the nightingales striving one with the other* ... ib. 11, 87 etc.

One + *other* ohne jeden Artikel fand sich niemals; zur Erklärung cf. Abbot § 88.

§ 190.

b) Zweiter Fall.

Auch hier dringt *one* + *other* auf Kosten von *either* + *other* vor; doch nimmt dieser Fall überhaupt stark ab:

G. G. Needle 193 *The puddings cannot lie still, each one over other tumbleth.*

Marlowe, Hero 51
   Each limb help'd other to put on disgrace:

Fl. (Balladen) 196/31
   The Perssy and the Dowglas mette
   That ether of other was fayne

Gorboduc 1729
   One kinsman shall bereaue an others life;

Sidney, Arcadia 220 ... *and so for a time parted those friends, each crying to the other;*

Anhang.

§ 191.

Ersatz des reciproken Pronomens durch *together*.

Vielfach im Morte Darthure, vereinzelt in einigen Denkmälern des 16. Jahrh., bietet sich uns die auf den ersten Blick auffällige Erscheinnng, dass *together* die Stelle des reciproken Pronomens vertritt:

M. 82/36 (308/18, 336/11, 707/25)
   ...they putte of her helmes and kyssed to gyders...

M. 338/11
   And thenne they sware to gyders that none of hem shold neuer fyghte ageynst other...

M. 725/19 (771/33, 854/13)
   ...and so they loued to gyder more hotter than they did to fore hand...

M. 763/13 *...and there they aduysed to gyders to make a party...*

M. 401/20 *...they encountred to gyders with grete speres...*

Calisto and Melibaea 74
   And thus they meet and embrace together.

Tyndale, Joh. 15,17
   This commaunde I you, that ye loue to gether.
   (Auth. Vers. und Rev. Vers. *one another*)

Diese Verwendung von *together* war also bis in die erste Hälfte des 16. Jahrh. gebräuchlich: sie wird erklärlich, wenn man erwägt, dass thatsächlich in manchen Fällen sowohl *each other* wie *together* denkbar ist, da die Begriffe der Gegenseitigkeit und des Zusammens sich teils berühren, teils in einander übergehen, vgl. M. 412/11 *thenne shalle ye and I doo bataille to gyders...* (dann werdet ihr und ich zusammen d. h. gegen einander kämpfen).

Weiterentwickelung.

Shakspere steht in Bezug auf Fall 1. auf dem Standpunkt der 2. Hälfte des 16. Jahrh. (Abbot § 88).

Im weiteren Verlauf der engl. Sprachgeschichte (noch nicht im 17. Jahrh., cf. Franz 400 sowie Oxf. Dict. unter *each*) sind *each other* und *one another* zu éinem Begriff geworden, so dass Präpositionen vor *each* bez. *one* treten; *either + other* ist noch 1677 und 1867 im Oxf. Dict. belegt.

§ 192.

Verstärkung von *my self* etc. durch *own*.

Schon seit ae. Zeit (Koch § 323, vgl. auch Wülfing § 253) können die Possessiva durch Hinzusetzung von *own* in ihrer Bedeutung gesteigert werden; es ist daher nicht zu verwundern, dass diese Verstärkung alsbald auch auf *my self* etc. übertragen wurde.

Diese Erscheinung, die wir in unseren Texten des 15. Jh. nur vereinzelt beobachteten (Fox 118... *I haue ynowh to doo with myn owne self.*), gelangt erst erst im 16. Jahrh. in der Literatur zu weiterer Verbreitung und muss, wie folgende Auswahl von Belegen auch zeigen wird, als besonders der Volkssprache angehörend bezeichnet werden; in hervorragendem Masse findet sie sich in Tyndale's Bibel, wenn wir sie dann weiter häufig in theol. Schriften und Predigten bemerken, so ist das aus dem mächtigen Einfluss der Bibelsprache heraus erklärlich.

Fl. (Volksbücher) 289/1
Wherfore it is good for euerye man to helpe hys owne selfe in tyme of neede...

ib. 326/20 ...*and the gentlewoman his wyf did anoynte his legges her owne selfe...*

Tyndale, Vorwort zu Matth. (Vorwort zu Rom. p. 5)
Fyrst Matthew... was one of Christes Apostles... and heard his owne selfe all most all that he wrote.

Joh. 5/30 *I can of myne owne selfe do nothyng:* (Auth. Vers. und Rev. Vers. *of myself*)

2. Cor. 8/5 *but gaue their owne selues fyrst to the Lorde..* (Auth. Vers. und Rev. Vers. ebenso)

1. Peter 2/24 *which his own selfe bare our synnes in his body* (Auth. Vers. und Rev. Vers. *Who his own self..*)

Joy, Ap. 36 *our own selues*,

ib. 50 *my nown selfe*,

Latimer, Sermons 32 *his owne selfe*

R. A., Toxophilus 164 ... *excepte the faulte be onely in youre owne selfe* ...

Jacob and Esau 208 *mine owne self*, ib 260 *thine own selfe*, ib. 263 *his own self*,

G. G. Needle 255 *mine own self*,
J. Juggler 135
He is even I mine own self without any fail!
ib. 148 *Even mg very own self it was.*

R. R. Doister 16, Lyly, Euphues 232, Sidney, Astrophel and Stella 38/7, Arcadia 144, 543, Puttenham 286, Marlowe, Ovid 121, Jack Straw 410, Leycester Correspondence 417 *my none selfe*, Barnfield, Poems 36 *thine owne selfe*.

Weiterentwickelung.

Shakspere ist diese jetzt veraltete (nur in der Bibel, s. o.) Konstruktion noch ganz bekannt (Schmidt Sh. Lex. unter *self*),

§ 193.

Self als Substantivum.

Muss schon in den Fällen, wo zwischen *my* (*thy* etc.) und *self* ein *own* zur Verstärkung eingeschoben wird, *self* als Substantiv (dieses schon me., cf. Mätzner I, 321) gefasst werden, so ist das auch da der Fall, wo

1. Ein oder mehrere andere Wörter zu näherer Bestimmung zwischen *my* (*thy* etc.) und *self* treten. Dieser Gebrauch ist bei Shakspere ganz gewöhnlich (Abbot § 20 p. 30) und noch heute üblich (cf. Flügel, Dict. unter *self*).

Kyd, Jeronimo 356 *my dear self*, Spanish Tragedy 31 *your gracious self*, ib. 93 *thy conquer'd self*, ib. 128 *my dying self*, Cornelia 179 *your so worthy self*, ib. 180 *my poor self*,

Greene Menaphon 51 *your sweete selfe*,

Marlowe, Ovid 166 *their drunken selves*,

Marlowe III, 4 Dedication of Richard Blunt.

... *I present the same to your most favourable allowance, offering my utmost self now and ever to be ready at your worship's disposing*:

Sidney, Arcadia Dedication *Your dear self*, ib. 162 *her dear self*, ib. 466 *our mortal and corruptible selves*, ib. 711 *Their sugred selves*, Apologie 47 *his inward selfe*

etc

2. Bei der Verbindung Substantiv + *self* ersteres in den Genitiv tritt.
   Jacob and Esau 190
   Sometimes Esau's self will faint fordrink and meat,
   Misfortunes of Arthur 336
   Yea, fortune's self in this afflicted case
   Exacts a pain for long-continned pomp.

   Sidney, Astrophel and Stella 9/13 *Cupids self,* ib. 35/6 *Reasons self,* ib. 38/7 *Loues owne selfe,* ib. 52/10 *Stellas selfe,* ib. 73/14 *Angers selfe,* ib. 103/14 *honours selfe,*
   Sidney Arcadia 50 *Parthenia's self,* ib. 140 *a man's self,* ib. 145 *a man's own self,* ib. 551 *Philoclea's self,* Kyd, Jeronimo 372 *Andrea's self,* Marlowe, Hero 80 *Love's self;*
   vgl. auch noch: Barnfield, Poems 40
And her selfe more worth than all the wealth shee possessed;
Selfe? indeed such a selfe, as thundring Joue ... could finde in his hart to be husband.

3. Einige andere Fälle der substantivischen Verwendung von *self* ohne nähere Bestimmung erklären sich durch die Umgebung:
   Kyd, Jeronimo 373
   Bel.: *Welcome, my life's self-form, dear Don Andrea.*
   Alc.: *My words iterated give thee as much:*
   Welcome, my self of self.
   Angry Women 288
   You are myself! when self sees fault in self,
   Self is sin-obstinate, if self amend not:

Anm. 1: Dass auch in *my self, thy self* etc. *self* noch als Substantiv gefasst wurde, geht abgesehen von der (wenn auch traditionellen) Schreibung in zwei Worten auch noch aus Beispielen wie:
   Bale, Promises 290
   Sweet Lord, the promise that thyself h a t h made me
   Bale, Kynge Johan 59
   Cum hether, my frynde; stand nere: ys thy selfe he?
   Lyly, Galathea 241
   Thou hast told what I am in uttering what thyselfe is: hervor.

Anm. 2.: Hierher gehören eine Anzahl von Fällen, die in der verschiedenartigsten Weise vermittelst des Reflexiv- und auch des Personalpronomens das deutsche „Ich" in Verwendungen wie „mein zweites ich, mein anderes ich, etc. wiedergeben:

Kyd, Jeronimo 354
>*Whither in such haste, my second self?*

Spanish Tragedy 49
>*No, he is as trusty as my second self.*

Knack to Know a Knave 526
>*...I loved thee as my second self*

Damon and Pithias 45
>*A my Damon, another myself, shall I forego hee?*

Sapphisches Gedicht von Studenten ed. Flügel, Anglia XIII, 458
>*Nowe my selfe euer to my selfe auoucheth*
>*That thi self euer is an other my selfe*
>*To thy selfe therfore as an alter Idem*
>   *I do comande me.*

Dass man hierbei zum Teil an das lateinische dachte, zeigen die Briefe Elisabeths, wo p. 15 direct auch *alter ego* gebraucht ist;

Sidney, Arcadia 236 ... *I needed envy no farther for the chief comfort of mortality, to leave another ones-self after me...*

Fälle mit dem Personalpronomen.

Jack Juggler 144
>*I shrew me, if I drank any more than twice to-day,*
>*Till I met even now with that other I.*
>*And with him I supped and drunk truly;*

ib. 147 *But the other-I knave had me by the pate;*

ib. *Until that other I was gone,*

ib. 150   *I have had beating enough for one day:*
>   *That a mischief take the other-me Careaway!*

ib.   *But I marvel greatly, by our Lord Jesus,*
>   *How he-I escaped, I-me beat me thus;*
>   *And is not he-I an unkind knave,*
>   *That woll no more pity on myself have?*

Lyly, Euphues 48
>*...that a frend is...at al times an other I.*

§ 194.

his self, their selves.

1. his self.

Das analogisch zu *myself, thyself,* wo man *my* für das Possessivpronomen hielt, gebildete (und noch heute nicht blos in der Vulgärsprache übliche [cf. Franz, Engl. Stud. XII, 225, Zupitza, Archiv 84, 181, Baumann XCVII,]) *his self* ist im 15. und 16. Jahrh. mehrfach zu belegen, war also recht gebräuchlich.

P. L. 617/365
...because of the sadnes and good dysposysion of his sylfe and hys wyfe...
Rutland Papers 22
...and after the Cardinall hath comoned his self, he... shall turne hymself to the King...
Bale, Kynge Johan 98
Of that he hath tolde hys selfe is the very grounde.
Three Lawes 1629
Hys selfe maye do that...
ib. 1761 *Where Christ hys self is...*
Marlowe III, 4 Dedication of Edward Blunt
for, since his self had been accustomed thereunto, it would prove more agreeable...
Marprelate, Epistle 14
...if he doth not but alloweth it, and his selfe practized it:
ib. 15 *Now the question is, whom Sir Peter his selfe nowe alloweth to be this bounsing priest?*
ib. *And brother John, did Sir Peter his selfe in deede practize this authoritie?*
Ueber *his own self* cf. § 192.

2. *their selves.*

Analogische Formen nach *myself, thyself, his self* weisen unsere Texte des 15. Jahrh. nicht auf, dagegen manchmal im 16. Jahrhundert:

Tyndale, Luk. 1/2 *...euen as they declared them vnto vs, which from the biginnyng sawe them theyr selues, and were ministers at the doyng:* (Auth. Vers. und Rev. Vers. überhaupt andere Wendung).

Suppl. to Henry VIII. 30
...yet they their selfe will, by their fryndes, make importunate sute...

R. A., Toxophilus 44 (69, 101)
...I maruell that you do not remember howe that the IX muses their selfe... wer put to norse to a lady called Euphemis...

R. A., Schoolemaster 97
...but liking it well their selues, they thought...

§ 195.

Ersatz von *one's self*.

Die reflexive Beziehung auf eine unbekannte Person wird, bevor *one's self* auftritt, teils durch *himself*, z. B.:

R. A., Schoolemaster 111
But do dwell in Epitomes and bookes of common places, and not to binde himselfe dailie by orderlie studie, to reade with all diligence ... maketh so many seeming, and sonburnt ministers as we haue ...

teils durch *a man's self* ausgedrückt:

Tyndale, Vorwort p. 5 ... *submittinge of a mans selfe vnto the congregacion of Christ.*

Sidney, Ap. 30
... *which stands, (as I thinke) in the knowledge of a mans selfe ...*

Arcadia 140
Tush, tush, said nature, this is all but a trifle, a man's self Gives haps or mishaps, even as he orsereth his heart.

§ 196.

Myself etc. als Subjekt.

Seitdem sich die Formen *myself, thyself* etc. als Verstärkungen fesgesetzt hatten, konnten sie auch als Vertreter der Personalpronomina gebraucht werden, z. B.:

Laʒ. B. 5990 *Heom self nōmen hire lónd.*

Dieser Gebrauch ist noch im 15. und 16. Jahrh. erhalten, wenn auch in letzterem die Fälle mit beigefügtem Personalpronomen überwiegen, z. B.:

P. L. 159/214 ... *and hymselff had non deserved ...*

ib. 465/124 *hym self is clerk convicte ...*

Bale, Promises 293 ... *thyself cannot say nay.*

Joy, Ap. 19
... *sith himselfe is not so exquysitely sene thereyn.*

Gorboduc 1525
Yea though them selues haue sene depe death and bloud

Lyly, Galathea 231 ... *because myselfe am a virgine ...*

Campaspe 141 ... *I know not what my selfe am!*

Udall, State 17 ... *because your selues cannot so doe ...*

Demonstr. 21 ...*and themselues confesse that he is*...
Marlowe, Dido 378
Myself will see they shall not trouble ye:
Peele, Arr. 46 ...*myself thy bail will be;*
Misfortunes of Arthur 268
Fronia: *What rage is this?*
Guenevera: *Such as himself shall rue.*
etc.   etc.

§ 197.

self für himself etc.

Im 15. und 16. Jahrhundert ist als Nachklang ae. und me. Brauches (Koch § 334) auch noch das einfache *self* für *himself* etc. üblich. Zur Erhaltung dieser Ausdrucksweise im 15. und 16. Jahrh. haben vor allem die zu dieser Zeit zahlreichen Fälle beigetragen, in denen *self* als Substantiv zu dem zugehörigen im Genitiv stehenden Substantiv zu fassen ist (cf. § 193, 2), und wo das Genitiv-*s* und das von *self* in der Umgangssprache in einander übergingen und phonetisch thatsächlich zu einem einzigen *s* wurden.

P. L. 97/130 *And if the comyng thider of our persone self shuld be to plesir of hir*...

Fl. (Th. More) 219/7 ...*wer it not that the matter selfe of reason doeth require it.*

Latimer, Ploughers 36
...*but the deuyll ...broughte the people to worshyp the serpente self*...

ib. *none be so folishe to do it to the flocke or stone or to the Jmage selfe*...

R. R. Doister 83
Roister Doister selfe your wower is with hym too.

Jacob and Esau 236
God Almighty self may wet his finger therein.

Sidney, Astrophel and Stella 102/5
How doth the coullour fade of those vermillion [d]ies
VVich Nature self did make and self engra[u]e the same?

Marlowe, Lucan 290
> *The fathers selves leap'd from their seats...*

Sidney, Arcadia 707
> *Th'epistle self such kind of words it had;*

Leycester Correspondence 335
> *...yet am I content to be judged herin by her highnes self...*

Barnfield, Poems 13
> *With Cyparissus selfe thou shalt compare*
> *For gins and wyles, the Oozels to beguile;*

Diese Ausdrucksweise noch zahlreich bei Spenser (Günther 64).

Demonstrativpronomen.

§ 198.

self im Sinne von *same*.

Self im Sinne von *same* war im 15. und 16. Jahrhundert üblich, wenn auch nicht sehr verbreitet.

Rutland Papers 4
> *...which is called the evyn or the vigill of the coronacion, and the self daye of coroncion...*

Tyndale, Matth. 8/13
> *And his servaunt was healed the selfe houre.* (Auth. Vers. und Rev. Vers. *selfsame*).

Heywood, P. P. 345
> *Wherefore I went myself to the self thing*

Joy, Ap. 11
> *..and so the selfe sacrifice offred vp for the synne..*

Lyly, Euphues 129
> *...euen in the selfe said moment it is borne...*

Marlowe, Faust II 2068
> *At which selfe time the house seem'd all on fire,*

Anm.: Auch *self* wird verstärkt:

Tyndale, Rom. 2/3
> *For thou that iudgest doest euen the same selfe thinges...* (Auth. Vers. und Rev. Vers. nur *the same*)

R. A., Toxophilus 126
> *For that shafte whiche one yeare for a man is to lyghte and scuddinge, for the same selfe man the next yeare may chaunce to be to heue and hobblynge.*

Fl. (Vorwort zur Conf. Amantis) 303/54
...*he and Gower were bothe of one selfe tyme*...
Gorboduc 411 *In one selfe purpose do I still abide.*
Marlowe, Faust 560
*Hell has no limits, nor is circumscrib'd
In one selfe place*...
Marlowe, Hero 19
*And, like a planet moving several ways
At one selfe instant, she, poor soul, assays*...
Sidney, Arcadia 162
Where by his words his self-like case he knew.
Puttenham 209
...*when one and the selfe word doth begin and end many verses in sutc*...

Weiterentwicklung.

Dieser Gebrauch von *self* findet sich noch bei Shakspere (Abbot § 20), stirbt dann aber aus.

§ 199. *this* für *these*.

Die Erklärung ist schon von Mätzner III, 247 gegeben (vgl. auch Morsbach, Schriftsprache p. 128 f.). *This* ist eine schon me. belegte, wenn auch seltene, Pluralform und fand dadurch eine besondere Verbreitung, dass vielfach Plurale als Kollektivbegriffe aufgefasst wurden. Im 15. und 16. Jahrhundert finden sich zahlreiche Beispiele für diesen daher sehr populären Gebrauch, und zwar steht *this* weitaus am meisten vor Zahlwörtern und hier wieder meist vor Zahlwort + Zeitbestimmung, welche ja sehr leicht als éin Begriff zu fassen sind und noch heute zum Teil (vgl. *twelvemonth, Twelfthnight, fortnight* etc.) so gefasst werden. Den Gebrauch von *this* hat ohne Zweifel auch die vielfach nicht konsequent durchgeführte **Pluralbildung mit** *s* (s. Belege), sowie der Umstand begünstigt, dass manche Substantive im **Plural Singularbedeutung** hatten (vgl. *means, pains* u. a., cf. § 200 Anm.). Auch mögen wendungen wie *this ten day's space* (Marlowe, Edward II 282) verglichen mit (Misfortunes of Arthur 280) *Hail, native soil, these nine years' space unseen!* oder *this XX yeares payment* (Henslowe's Diary 80) nicht ganz ohne Einfluss gewesen sein.

Auswahl von Belegen.
§ 200.
1. *this* vor Zahlwörtern.
a) *this* vor Zahlwort + Zeitbestimmung.

P. L. 462/118
...*and they say thys III. wyks came there neythyr shyp nor boot out of Irelond*...

ib. 491/161 *this II. ycre,*

M. 232/16 *this two yeres,* ib. 250/35 *this XXX wynter,*

ib. 397/20 *this twelue moneth,*

ib. 777/31 *within this two myle,*

ib. 789/17 *of alle this seuen yere,*

Digby Mysteries 132/2051

þe *wych I never save* þis *XXX wynter and more;*

Fl. (Balladen) 182/106 *This seuen yere by dere worthy god*
      Ne yede I so fast on fote

Bale, Kynge Johan 67

This V dayes I wyll kepe this crowne in myn own hande

World and Child 247
  But, sirs, when I was seven year of age,
  I was sent to the world to take wage,
  And this seven year I have been his page,

Jack Juggler 119 desgl.

Lyly, Euphues 251 ...*where now with-in this two houres, we shall finde them in Caunterbury.*

ib. 344 ...*he hath liued this three monethes carefully*...

ib. 455 ...*whose dore hath not bene opened this twentie yeares*...

Udall, State 10 *some of which bookes haue beene extant this dozen yeres*...

Greene, Friar Bacon 145
  So frankly dealt this hundred years before:

James IV 114 *I shall estramp your guts*...*that you no point manage this ten ours.*

Looking Glass 66 ...*thou shalt not be worth a horse of thine own this seven year.*

Marlowe, Faust 1204
  I tell thee he has not slept this eight nights.

Jew 269 *To what this ten yeares tribute will amount,*
(Stützbeleg!, s. o.)

Three Ladies 331
Me shall a content your debt within this two or three day.

Leycester Correspondence 68
This VI wekes can I gett no reckoning...
ib. 218 *...what graces she hath shewed him this IIII monethes.*
ib. 226 *this C yeres there was never man soe weakly assisted.*
ib. 370 *I haue bin here this XV dayes for monie...*

Jack Straw 379
And yet I have been officer this seven year and more.
ib. 396 *Myself was not so scared this seven years:*

Anm.: Hierher sind auch folgende Fälle mit *few* zu rechnen:
P. L. 695/44 *thys fewe days,*
Tyndale, Ap. 1/5
but ye shalbe baptised with the holy goost, and that with in this feawe dayes (Auth. Vers. und Rev. Vers. *not many days hence*).
Appius and Virginia 136
There might one (quoth he) within this few days
With a cast-net had given four knaves great essays,
Briefe James 21 *Your ambassadouris present dispatche hath mouitt me to wryt this few wordis...*

etc.

b) *this* + Zahlwort + anderes Substantiv.

M. 626/2
Soo on a day this two (sc. knyghtes) mette to doo bataill.

Decay of England 99
Furthermore it is to be consydered what thys twelf hundreth quarters of corne is able to do...

Thersites 429 *By this ten bones,*
She served me once.

§ 201.
2. In anderen Fällen.

P. L. 264/367 *Item, overe all thys grete debtes dew...*
P. L. 612/357 *Contrary to thys maters, and all the comfort...*
M. 579/32 *But in this spyrytuel maters he shalle haue many his better...*
(Die Ausgabe von 1529 hat *these*).

Four Elements 32
> *But this new lands found lately
> Been called America...*

Marriage of Wit 354
> ...**these fellows will undo it,*
> * Old copy: *this.*

Epigrams by J. D. (Marl. III) 239
> *Yet this new-fangled youth, made for *this times,*
> * So M. S. eds. „these".

Briefe James 101
> ...*I consider this strainge effectis*...

Henslowe's Diary 113
> *Be yt knowne unto all men by this presents, that*...

(vgl. ib. 114 *by these present, by thes presentes, by this presente,* 150 *these presents* etc.).

Anm.: Bei manchen Wörtern, die schon im Plural Singularbedeutung angenommen haben, kann *this* nicht auffallen, so: means, *by this means* Fl. 251/43, More, Utopia 135, Greene, Pinner 182, Leyc. Corr. 172, Sidney, Arcadia 70. (Marlowe, Mass. 296 *a means*, Leycester Correspondence 174 *by an nother meanes*, Greene, Alphonsus 36 *A readier means*).

news, (Greene, Bacon 157 *But, Thomas, what's the news?*)
Disobedient Child 294
> *This news to me was so great pain.*

Greene, Alphonsus 50 *What news is this!*

pains, Introductory Sketch 67 *But they are far from taking this small pains.*

tidings, (Plumpton Correspondence 49 [50] *Sir, other tydings is none here as yett.*), P. L. 225/314 *This is the tydinges that I have*; ib. 452/104 *Thes is the last tydyngs that I knowe.* (zweideutig nach § 45 und § 46), ebenso P. L. 937/358 *Thes is such tydynges as*...

Tyndale Matth. 24/14
And this glad tydinges of the kyngdom shal be preached in all the world... (Auth. Vers. und Rev. Vers. *this gospel* bezw. *these good tidings*). Hierzu auch *this many*: Peele, Edward I 167 (Latimer, Ploughers 28 *a greate meanye of wardes*).

Weiterentwicklung.

This für *these* ist Shakspere sehr geläufig (Deutschbein § 66, Schmidt, Sh. Lex. 1212), allmälig jedoch aus dem mustergültigen Schriftenglisch geschwunden und jetzt nur noch in der Umgangs- und Dialektsprache üblich (Franz 392 sowie Engl. Stud. XII, 226).

§ 202.

Wechsel und Verwechslung von *this* und *thus*.

Für die Möglichkeit eines Wechsels und damit zugleich auch einer Verwechslung von *this* und *thus* sind zwei Erklärungsgründe gegeben, ein **phonetischer** und ein **psychologischer**.

Was den **phonetischen** anlangt, dem wir jedoch nur eine geringere und bedingte Berechtigung zuerkennen können, so haben wir schon me. mehrfach Reime von $u : i$ bei den satztieftonigen Wörtchen *thus* und *vs* (cf. Heuser, Die me. Legenden von St. Editha und St. Ethelreda, Erlangen 1887 p. 11 f. *thus : this, thus : wys, thus : ys, thus : blys* etc.).

Diese Reime finden sich fast ausnahmslos in jenem äusserst frei reimenden Denkmal, sodass wir daraus nicht den Schluss auf eine gleiche Aussprache von *this* und *thus* ziehen möchten.

Greene, Looking Glass 127

Thus saith the Lord, the mighty God of hosts:

gegenüber: New Custom 27

This saith it in words, but he thinketh it not in deed.

Marlowe, Edward II 186

In saying this, thou wrong'st me, Gaveston:

Man vergl. ferner: Udall, Demonstr. 45 (Kapitelüberschrift) *The second proposition that they hold is thus.* (Die zweite These, welche sie aufstellen, heisst folgendermassen). Setzen wir *this* = „ist folgende",
sowie Lusty Juventus 54

The True Knowledge of God's Verity, this my name doth hight,
(dem Gedanken nach = *this is my name*, eine andere Lesart hat *thus*; vgl. auch § 220 Anm.).

Zu diesem phonetischen Moment kommt ein **psychologisches**:

In vielen Fällen ist sowohl *this* wie *thus* möglich, und es thatsächlich also gleichgültig, welches von beiden verwandt wird, indem nur eine den Zusammenhang nicht störende Modifikation des Sinnes eintritt, z. B.:

Digby Mysteries 187/467

Ye promesit me ye wold not do thus.

gegenüber: New Custom 27
This he doth for my mistress his wife's sake, by the rood,
sowie Interlude of Youth 9
> *That witnesseth Holy Scripture, saying thus:*

Peele, David and Bethsabe 30
Dav.: *But what saith Nathan to his lord the king?*
Na.: *Thus Nathan saith unto his lord the king:*

Lusty Juventus 71
> *You are to blame this me to challenge;*

ib. 93 *I marvel, why you do this reprove me;*
ib. 97 *Thus Saint Augustine doth them define,*
> (eine andere Lesart hat *this*).

Cambyses 211
> *If that wicked vice he could refrain,*
> *From wasting wine forbear,*
> *A moderate life he would frequent,*
> *Amending this his square.*

ib. 231 *O God, forgive me, if I do amiss;*
> *The king by compulsion enforceth me this.*

Jack Juggler 143
> *I was never this canvassed and tossed:*

Appius and Virginia 142
> *Lo, Rumour, this I run.*

§ 203.

Dieser mögliche Wechsel von *this* und *thus* führt nun weiter zu einer Verwechslung beider:

Heywood, P. P. 379
> **This in effect he told for truth.*
> * *Thus* ed. 1569 (eine spätere).

Thersites 408 **This passeth my brains;*
> * Original hat *thus*.

Lusty Juventus 48
> *I beshrew their hearts for serving me this,*
> *I will go seek them, whether I hit or miss.*

ib. 69 *This will I convey*
My matter, I say,
Somewhat handsomely;
Conflict of Conscience 60
The conclusion of my reason is this inferred;
Sidney, Astrophel and Stella 98/6
... but wretch I am constrained,
Spurd with Loues spurr, this held and shortly rained
With Cares hard hand, to turne and tosse in thee,
Marlowe, Edward II 216
That *thus, your army, going several ways,
Might be of lesser force ...
* Old eds. „this".
Dido 428
Welcome, sweet child! where hast thou been this long?
ib. 432 *Ah, foolish Dido, to forbear this long! —*
Hero 103
And *this true honour from their love-death sprung, —
* V. R. „thus".
Epigr. by J. D. (Marl. Bd. III) 254
*This Orpheus to such hearers giveth music,
And Philo to such patients giveth physic.
* So M. S. Eds. „thus".

Anm. 1: Die Erklärung von *thus much* (z. B.: Latimer, Sermons 113, Trial of Treasure 276, Angry Women 297) durch *this much* (vgl. Mätzner III, 121), welche durch vorstehende Erörterung ernente Bestätigung erhält, wird schliesslich noch gestützt durch folgende Belege:

Sir Clyomon and Sir Clamydes 533 a
Indeed, my queen, this much he told, he lov'd a lady since he went,
Briefe Elizabeths 34
although I must say for myselfe this muche, that the pithe and effect of all you receiued before;

Anm. 2: Das in § 202 f. gesagte wirft zugleich ein interessantes Streiflicht auf die Funktion von *thus* als Pronomen und Adverb in nördlichen Dialekten (cf. Mätzner III, 12).

§ 204.

this many a hundred year, this many a day.

Diese Konstruktion, für die, soweit wir sehen, bis jetzt noch keine Belege bekannt waren, scheint erst in der 2. Hälfte des 16. Jahrhunderts aufzutauchen.

Greene, Alphonsus 32
Then bend with speed unto the darksome grove,
Where Mahomet, this many a hundred year,
Hath prophesied unto our ancestors.
ib. 51
Call to your mind your predecessors' acts,
Whose martial might, this many a hundred year,
Did keep those fearful dogs in dread and awe,

Diese Fälle stellen sich als eine Contamination der durch *this hundred year* und *many a hundred year* ausgedrückten Gedanken dar.

Die folgenden scheinen analog dazu gebildet:
Peele, Edward I 142
We have not seen the man this many a day.
The 4to of 1599 omits *a*.
Like Will to Like 310
... it is my godfather Lucifer,
Whose prentice I have been this many a day.

§ 205.
such + like.

Die pleonastische Verbindung von *such* mit *like* lässt sich für das Ae. und Me. noch nicht nachweisen (Mätzner III, 382).

In unseren Texten fand sie sich erst im 16. Jahrhundert, häufiger in der 2. Hälfte, scheint aber in der ersten doch schon recht verbreitet gewesen zu sein, z. B.:

Bale, Kynge Johan 77
... and suche lyke myrye trickes,

Joy, Ap. 38
... as yt is the comon phrase of scripture to saye spiritus sanctifiationis ... with many siche lyke.

Latimer, Sermons 50
... and such lyke vnreasonable exactions ...
ib. 89 *... these, or suche other lyke were hys wordes ...*
R. A., Toxophilus 87 *Such lyke battel ...*
Schoolemaster 156
I could be long, in reciting many soch like ...
More, Utopia 104 *These and such like opinions ...*

New Custom 28 *Beads, and such like:*
Udall, State 10, Kyd, Spanish Tragedy 34, Greene, James IV 113, Puttenham 47, 97, Sidney, Astrophel and Stella 47/10, Arcadia 766, Leycester Correspondence 26, 182.
etc. etc.
Shakspere macht von dieser Verbindung, die noch heute üblich ist, reichlichen Gebrauch (Schmidt, Sh. Lex. 1148).

§ 206.
Gebrauch von *same*.

1. Ausser in der eigentlich demonstrativen Bedeutung wird *same* während des ganzen 15. und 16. Jahrhunderts in Poesie und Prosa jeder Art massenhaft in abgeschwächter Bedeutung, d. h. im Sinne eines einfachen Personalpronomens verwandt, z. B.: P. L. 852/271 im Inventory of Plate:

VI. soketes, with branches to remeve.
III. wherwilles to the same.

Plumpton Correspondence 257, Egerton Papers 9,
Fl. (W. Lily) 299/26
An Introduction of the Eyght Partes of speche, and the construction of the same ...
Tyndale, Joh. 4/46
Assone as the same herde that ...
(Auth. Vers. und Rev. Vers. *When he heard ...*).
Sidney, Astrophel and Stella 19/1
On Cupids bowe, how are my hart strings bent?
That see my wracke, and yet imbrace the same:
Briefe Elizabeths 129, Marprelate, Epistle 1, Puttenham 309, Marlowe, Tamburlaine 2.

Diese Verwendung von *the same* hat sich jetzt nur noch im Kurial- und besonders im kaufmännischen Briefstil erhalten; vgl. hierzu Koch, Archiv 91 p. 13.

2. Wenn so *the same* von seiner ursprünglichen demonstrativen Kraft sehr viel eingebüsst hatte, war es natürlich, dass hierfür ein Ersatz geschaffen werden musste, der sich in der Verstärkung durch ein anderes Demonstrativ oder ein Adverbium einstellte.

a) Am meisten verbreitet ist die Verstärkung durch *self*, z. B.:

Fl. (Skelton) 55/36 *He were idem in numero*
The selfe same samuele
Joy, Ap. 46
...*our bodyes shulde not ryse the selfe same ageyn:*
Tyndale, 1. Cor. 12/11
...*And there all worketh euen the selfe same sprete...*
(Auth. Vers. und Rev. Vers. *the one and the same*).
More, Utopia 103
...*which selfe same wol...a shepe did ones weare:*
R. A., Toxophilus 158, Schoolemaster 64,
Jack Juggler 144 ...*I shall take the self-same weed*
Lyly, Euphues 231 *with the selfe same waxe,*
Kyd, Cornelia 187, Peele, Arr. 46,
Greene, Menaphon 49
...*it is either a selfe same or another Sephestia.*
Marlowe, Ovid 147, Puttenham 129, Three Ladies 259, Leycester Correspondence 220, Sidney, Sonn. and Transl. 165. Jetzt nur noch in dichterischem Gebrauche (Koch § 334).

b) Seltener ist die Verstärkung durch *very*.
Tyndale, Joh. 8/25
Then sayde they unto him: who arte thou. And Jesus sayd vnto them: Euen the very same thynge that I saye vnto you.
(Auth. Vers. und Rev. Vers. *Even that*).
Egerton Papers 154
This was don the very same day...
G. G. Needle 246
Diccon, whom all men knows, it was the very same.
Marlowe, Jew 2058 *The very same, my Lord:*
Angry Women 382
O, that same very name
Hath in it much variety of shame! (Stellung!)

c) Vereinzelt andere Arten der Verstärkung.
Joy, Ap. 27 ...*whiche worde...haue but one and euer the same significacion...*
Lyly, Euphues 235
Yet as out of one and the selfe-same roote...
Sidney, Astr. and Stella (Vorrede vom Drucker Nashe) p. C.

but Religion ... bids me looke back to the house of honor, where from one and the same root of renowne, I shal finde many goodly branches deriued ...

Interrogativpronomen.
§ 207.
Who im Sinne von *any one*.

Schon das ae. *hwā* hat ganz allgemein die Bedeutung „irgend einer"; zahllose Beispiele bieten die ags. Gesetze, z. B. Legal Code of Aelfred (ed. Turk) 72, 18 *ʒif hwā on cēase ēacniende wīf ʒewerde, bēte þone ǣwerdlan swā him dōmeras ʒereccen.* (cf. auch Wülfing § 326).

Ebenso me. *whō*:
The nāme as yet of her Among the pēple, as whō seyth, halwed is. Chaucer, Troil. and Cr. III, 268;
Suilk ribaudie þei led, þei gaf no tāle of whām Brunne p. 220 (aus Sturzen-Becker p. 56).

Im 15. und 16. Jahrhundert ist diese Bedeutung (irgend einer, man, auch = unserem unbestimmten „einen", franz. vous) noch nicht erloschen, ja darf wohl sogar als mehr der volkstümlichen Umgangssprache angehörend gelten; sie ist am häufigsten in dem zur festen Formel (= unserem sozusagen) gewordenen *as who should (would) say.*

Eine relative Bedeutung des *who*, die von Abbot § 257 vermutet, von Ritzenfeldt p. 18 behauptet wird, ist nicht anzunehmen, da sich erstens Fälle finden, bei denen das Antecedens eines Relativsatzes nicht ergänzt werden kann, und zweitens der Accussativ *whom* in indefiniter Bedeutung noch im 16. Jahrhundert (s. u.) zu belegen ist; damit soll nicht bestritten werden, dass ähnliche Fälle mit *who* nur in relativer Bedeutung aufzufassen sind, vgl.:

More, Utopia 135
But they in this behalfe thinke themselfes muche prayse woorthy, as who lyke wyse men by this meanes dispatche greate warres withoute anny battell or skyrmyshe.

Das lateinische Original hat hier:

...*crudele facinus illi magnae sibi laudi ducunt, tanquam prudentes, qui maximis hoc pacto bellis, sine ullo prorsus proelio defungantur...*
Sidney, Arcadia 383

But Erona, sad indeed, yet like one rather used, than new fallen to sadness; as who had the joys of her heart already broken, seemed rather to welcome than to shun that end of misery;

Im übrigen vergleiche man als Parallelen ·in der nhd. Umgangssprache die Bedeutung von „wer" in Sätzen wie: „*Es soll mir nur wer kommen, ist wer da?, er hatte das Buch von Carl oder sonst wem, ich warte noch auf wen*" etc.

Belege für das 15. und 16. Jahrhundert.
§ 208.
1. Für *who*.

P. L. 702/57

Sir Jamys is evyr choppyng at me, when my modyr is present, with syche wordys as he thynkys wrathe me, and also cause my modyr to be dyspleased with me, evyn as who seyth he wold I wyst that he settyth not by the best of us;

Digby Mysteries 178/189

He lukyd on that maide, his moder, rewfully,
And with a tender cowntenaunce,
As who say, modere! the sorow of your harte
Makes my passion mor bitter and more smarte,

ib. 214/1298

All ye shall suffer sclaunder for me,
Os who say ye shall forsak me a-lonly;

Heywood, The four P. P. 373

And I from thence to hell that night,
To help this woman, if I might;
Not as who saith by authority,
But by the way of entreaty.

Calisto and Melibaea 65,

Bale, Kynge Johan 92

He wyll do thys acte to the popes most hygh displeasure:
As who sayth I woulde for pleasure of my persone,
And not for Gods truthe have such an enterpryse done.

Latimer, Sermons 27
...*where he saith: whan thou shalt come in to the lande,
etc. As who should say. O ye children of Israel*...

R. A., Toxophilus 154
This boye is fit for nothynge els, but to set to lernyng and make a prest of, as who would say, yat outcastes of the worlde ...be good ynough to make those men of...

More, Utopia 35
As who should sai, it were a very daungerous matter...

New Custom 7 *As who should say in short time*...

Jack Juggler 109
*For the mind... must needs be soon wearied,
And (as who should say) tried through continual operation*

Kyd, Spanish Tragedy 83
Will't not be an odd jest for me to stand and grace every jest he makes, pointing my finger at this box, as who would say, Mock on, here's thy warrant?

Puttenham 88 (46)
The shortest pause or intermission they called comma as who would say a peece of a speach cut of.

ib. 154; ib. 223
...*the Greekes call it Sinonimia, as who would say, like or consenting names:*

ib. 226 (235)
As who would say her owne ouermuch lenitie and goodnesse, made her ill willers the more bold and presumptuous.

ib. 288
...*when will he vse it, that now at this yeares is seeking after it, as who would say it is not time to talke*...

Marlowe, Jew 1694
Curt.: *And what said he?*
Pil.: *Not a wise word, only gaue me a nod, as who shold say: Is it euen so?*

Edward II 177
*And, when I come, he frowns, as who should say,
Go whither thou wilt, seeing I have Gaveston.*

Peele, Polyhymnia 200
>   *Knight of the crown, in rich embroidery,*
>   *And costly fair caparison charg'd with crowns,*
>   *O'ershadow'd with a wither'd running vine,*
>   *As who would say, my spring of youth is past;*

ib. 201
>   *And having by this trounchman pardon crav'd,*
>   *Vailing his eagle to his sovereign's eyes,*
>   *As who should say, stoop, eagle, to his sun,*
>   *Dismounts him from his pageant...*

ib. 205, 210, 220,

Three Ladies of London 344 (Sidney, Arcadia 87)
But, fellow Simony, I thank you heartily, for comparing the tailor to me.
As who should say his knavery and my policy did agree.

§ 209.

2. Für *whom*.

P. L. 56/69

I fell hym so disposyd that he wold asold and asett to morgage all that he hath, he had nowth rowth to qhom, so that he myth an had mony to an holpyn hym self wyth;

P. L. 275/377

and no man knoweth or can sey that ony prefe may be hadde by whom, for men thinken verily there is no man able to take ony suche enterprinse.

Latimer, Sermons 48

...and wrathe shall be poured from heauen vpon our vngodlynes. He (God) is long a commyng but when he comes he wil paye whome and (as Lactancius sayeth) recompense his long sufferaunce wyth greuous repunishmentes.

Fl. (Briefe) 352/47 *I cannot perrsuad myself that your maistershipp hateth in me or elswhom, any thyng excepte vices.*

G. G. Needle 232

Doctor Rat: *What good news, Diccon? fellow, is mother Chat at home?*

Diccon: *She is, sir, and she is not; but it please her to whom:*

Unerklärlich bleibt More, Utopia 19 in der Vorrede des Druckers, dem daher auch kein lateinisches Original zur Seite steht:

Thou shalte vnderstande gentle reader that thoughe this worke of Utopia in English, come nowe the seconde tyme furth in Point, yet was it neuer my minde nor intente, that it shoulde euer haue bene Imprinted at all, as who for no such purpose toke vpon me at the firste the translation thereof:

Es liegt vielleicht ein Versehen des Druckers vor; *I* für *who* eingesetzt würde die Schwierigkeit heben.

Weiterentwicklung.

Fälle wie unter 1 sind mehrfach bei Shakspere zu finden (Abbot § 257) und vereinzelt noch in ne. Prosa, z. B. bei Dickens (cf. Koch § 368 Anm., wo auch Belege aus Tennyson), vgl. ferner Koch, Archiv 91, 3 f.; solche wie unter 2 finden sich schon bei Shakspere nicht mehr.

who für *whom* und umgekehrt.
NB. Das Relativum ist mit eingeschlossen.

§ 210.

1. *whom* für *who*.

Dieser Fall ist entschieden auffälliger, weil vor allem seltener, als der umgekehrte.

P. L. 591/326 (1468 Anonymus)

And I shall be hastyly with you by the grace of God, whom have yow in kepyng.

ib. 609/6 (1471 The Earl of Oxford)

...I schall brynge my purpose abowte now by the grace of God, Qwhome have yow in kepyng.

ib. 824/238 (1478 Wylliam Paston)

...by the grace of God, Whom have yow in Hys kepyng.

ib. 896/337 (1487 or later Dame El. Brews)

...Jesu, Hom haff zow and zowyr in Yss keppyng.

Diese vier Fälle dürften, wenn ihnen auch zahlreiche grammatisch korrekte Fälle gegenüberstehen, doch nicht nur zufällige Schreibfehler sein. Sie zeigen uns zunächst, dass in der zweiten Hälfte des 15. Jahrhunderts schon eine Unsicherheit zwischen *whom* und *who* herrschte.

Zur Erklärung gerade dieser Fälle können wir folgende Beispiele heranziehen:

Aus dem 15. Jahrhundert:

P. L. 416/51

...*our Lord Jesu, whom I besech save and sende you a gode ende*...

ib. 596/334 *I have grete myst of it, God knows, whom I beseche preserve you from all adversite.*

ib. 670/8

...*with Godys grace, Whom I beseche preserve you*...

Aus dem 16. Jahrhundert:

Briefe Elizabeths 117

...*as God best knowes; whom I beseech inspyre you ever the best.*

Hier konnte *whom* wie als **Objekt** zu *I beseche* so auch zugleich als **Subjekt** zu *preserve* aufgefasst werden.

Unsere Belege mit *whom* als Nominativ gingen nun hervor aus einer Contamination dieser Fälle mit solchen grammatisch korrekten wie:

P. L. 132/175 ...*God...who have you in hys kepyng.*

ib. 587/320 ...*God...who preserve you*...

etc. etc.

§ 211.

Ein weiterer frappanter Beleg von *whom* für *who* aus dem Ende des 16. Jahrhunderts ist:

Henslowe's Diary 110

Lent W^m borne, the 19 of desembr 1597, in Redey money, to be payd me agayne at crysmas eve next comynge, thirten shillinges. Wittines Thomas Dowtons bigcr boye, whome feched yt for hime.

whome ist hier zweifellos Nominativ. Die Annahme eines Schreibfehlers ist in diesem zur Gruppe II (cf. § 1) gehörigen Diary nicht ungerechtfertigt, doch ist wohl in Anbetracht der anderen Fälle von *whom* für *who* hiervon abzusehen; der

Erklärungsgrund läge dann in der allgemein eingetretenen Unsicherheit der Unterscheidung von *who* und *whom*. Hierzu ferner: Marlowe, Hero 37

> *Again, she knew not how to frame her look,*
> *Or speak to him, who in a moment took*
> *That which so long, so charily she kept;*

wo eine Lesart *whom* hat.

§ 212.

Durch Attraktion sind zu erklären:
P. L. 58/71
he hathe seyd that he woold lyfte them whom that hym plese...
Jacob and Esau 262
> *Whom pleaseth thee, thou dost choose or reprobate,*

Greene, Friar Bacon 174
> *Doctors... know that I am Edward Plantagenet, whom if you displease, will make a ship...*

Sidney, Arcadia 769
> *Whom as soon as they saw turned towards them...*

Attraktion an das als Praeposition behandelte *but* liegt vor:
Jack Juggler 129
J. J.: *Who art thou? now tell me plain.*
Car.: *Nobody but whom please you, certain —*
vgl. demgegenüber ib. 128
> *By my troth, sir, whosoever please you:*

Dagegen erklärt sich durch Ergänzung von *to reject* (elect) nach *thee*:
Jacob and Esau 248
> *Of thy justice, whom it pleaseth thee, thou dost reject;*
> *Of thy mercy, whom it pleaseth thee, thou dost elect.*

§ 213.

who für whom.

a) 1. P. L. 78/112 ... *that thei wost ho I ment.*
   2. Tyndale, Mark. 14/44
   > *who so ever I do kysse, he it is.*

(Auth. Vers. und Rev. Vers. *Whomsoever I shall kiss...*).

3. G. G. Needle 246
But he that heard it told me, who thou of late didst name:
4. Cambyses 183
with who this night wilt thou lie?
5. Greene, Alphonsus 18
The father dead, the son is likewise slain
By that man's hand who they count as dead,
6. Marlowe, Ovid 162
He's happy who Love's mutual skirmish slays;
7. Sir Clyomon and Sir Clamydes 522
But stay, who do I here espy?
8. Look about You 434 *tell me who you seek.*
9. Greene, Friar Bacon 150
Espy her loves, and who she liketh best;

b) Lusty Juventus 63
Sancti amen, who have we there?
Damon and Pithias 69
But who have we here?
Marlowe, Tamb. 4190 *Uuho have ye there, my Lordes?*
Massacre 314 *Who have you there?* Edward II 207,
Greene, Pinner 190 *Soft, who have we there?*
Peele, Edward I 97 *What now? Who have we here?*
Old Wives Tale 213 *Soft, who have we here?* ib. 224, 231 (2 mal),
Knack to Know a Knave 568
How now, Perin; who have we here? Mucedorus 239,
Look about You 438
But, Gloster, look about, who have we yonder? (zur Erklärung ib. 439 *Who's yonder,* im übrigen s. u.).

Bemerkungen hierzu.

Fälle dieser Art erklärt Jespersen § 171 durch den Einfluss des überwiegend am Anfang des Satzes auftretenden *who*. Für die unter a. aufgeführten Fälle trifft das wohl zu, wenn auch für Fall 1/8 die damals allem Anschein nach überhaupt schon herrschende Unsicherheit besonders in der Volkssprache, deren Einfluss auf die Literatursprache gerade durch das elisabethanische Drama ein sehr grosser gewesen ist,

vielleicht massgebend war, für Fall 9 an Vermengung mit einem
„*and who her liketh best*" gedacht werden kann, da *to like*
noch Ende des 16. Jahrhunderts zahlreich unpersönlich gebraucht wurde (Greene, Friar Bacon 161 *this motion like me
well*, im übrigen siehe Anhang I § 271).

Dagegen lässt sich für die Fälle unter b mit *who have we
(ye* etc.) *here* (*there*) noch ein anderes wesentliches Moment anführen: *who have we (ye* etc.) *here* (*there*) entspricht dem Sinne
nach einem *who is here?* (Greene, Pinner 193), *who is there?*
(Mysteries ed. Hone 46, Marlowe, Edward II 173, 200, 207, 266,
Angry Women 324, 328, 329 etc.), *who comes here?* (Peele, Old
Wives Tale 213, Three Lords 414, 437, Knack to Know a Knave
547, 550, 558, 585, Angry Women 339), *who goes there?* (Angry
Women 362), *who walketh there?* (Marlowe, Edward II 238) oder
ähnlichem. Contamination einer dieser Wendungen mit *whom
have we here?* (Hickscorner 179, 188, Like Will to Like 310
Sancte benedicite, whom have we here?) unter Einfluss von
Fällen wie G. G. Needle 199 *Who have we there maketh such
a din?* ist doch recht wahrscheinlich.

§ 214.

P. L. 5/20

*...ye lyke to sende me redes lettres of alle the seyd malicv,
and the circumstances ther of, and* [sc. *of*] *who ye wil I be
governed in this mater.*

scheint angelehnt an Fälle wie:

P. L. 631/388

Send my modyr and me word who ye wyll that have the rwyll...

§ 215.

Im allgemeinen waren schliesslich auch noch Fälle wie
die folgenden dazu angethan, das Gefühl für Kasusunterscheidung zu trüben:

Joy, Ap. X

*It is lawfull for who will, to translate and shew his mynde,
although a thousand had translated before him.*

Soliman and Perseda 365

It was and shall be, maugre who says no.

Greene, James IV 112
But he, injurious man, who lives by crafts,
And sells king's favours for who will give most,
Hath taken bribes of me...

Friar Bacon 174
...I am Edward Plantagenet, whom if you displease, will make a ship...

Alphonsus 53
And as for Mars whom you do say will change,
He moping sits behind the kitchen door,

Sidney, Ap. 27
and this Poesie must be vsed, by whosoever will fellow S. James his counsell...

Ferner:
Damon and Pithias 47
I have talk'd with Damon, whom though in words I found very witty,
Yet was he more curious than wise...

Lyly, Mydas 44
blame not Apollo, whom being god of musicke thou didst both dislike and dishonour;

Marlowe, Ovid 128
And who thou never think'st should fall down, lies.

Bei alle dem darf auch ein erhebliches phonetisches Moment nicht ausser Acht gelassen werden: thatsächlich ist der lautliche Unterschied zwischen *who* und *whom* nicht so bedeutend, als dass nicht in der Umgangssprache, und auf die kommt es hier ja besonders an, eine Verwechselung schon dadurch möglich oder doch wenigstens begünstigt wäre.

Weiterentwicklung.

Schon Shakspere (cf. Schmidt, Sh.-Lex.) weist überaus zahlreiche Belege von *who* für *whom* auf; *whom* wird mehr und mehr verdrängt, sodass *who* jetzt, selbst in der gebildeten Umgangssprache, fast schon als gemeinsamer Kasus gilt (cf. Jesp. § 172); vergl. ferner Franz, Engl. Stud. XII, 227, Zupitza, Archiv 84, 181, Storm 211.

§ 216.
what für *who*.

Das nach dem Namen fragende *what*, für das seit dem 14. Jahrhundert (Kellner, Outl. § 325) *who* einzutreten beginnt, ist im 15. und 16. Jahrhundert noch ganz allgemein üblich, z. B.:

P. L. 466/126
Also on Thursday... was a man slayn, by whom no man woot, nor what he is that was slayn no man knowe, his face is so mangled.

M. 66/25 *Also I knowe what thow arte...*

Tyndale, Mark. 1/24
I knowe the what thou arte (Auth. Vers. und Rev. Vers. *who*)

R. R. Doister 14
What he is that durst haue put me in that heate?

Lyly, Endimion 24
but what is yonder formall fellow?

Dass *what* und *who* nebeneinander üblich waren, zeigt vortrefflich Marlowe, Faust 787

F.: *What are you mistresse Minkes?*
Lechery: *Who I sir? I am one that...*

Weiterentwicklung.

What für *who* ist Shakspere geläufig (Abbot § 254, Deutschbein § 60), kommt im 17. Jahrhundert (Franz 401) noch vor, ist aber jetzt nicht mehr möglich.

§ 217.
what als Ausruf.

Das schon im Eingang des Beowulf (in allerdings etwas modifizierter Bedeutung) belegte *what* als Ausruf war besonders im 16. Jahrhundert entschieden populär; es ist natürlich nur da anzutreffen, wo die Rede sich belebt, besonders im Dialog der dramatischen Literatur, z. B.:

Digby Mysteries 73/493
what! wene ʒe, syrrys, þat I were a marchant,

Anc. Myst. ed. Hone 32
Whath, Joseph!

Thersites 402
What, should such a fisher keep good fellows out?
Latimer, Ploughers 31
what sir are ye so priuie of the deuils counsell that ye know al this to be true?
R. R. Doister 18
What if Christian Custance will not haue you what?
Udall, State 24
what and if the matter which our friend preacheth be false ...?
Lyly, Women 204
What! dost thou mocke us?
Sir Clyomon and Clamydes 496 b
What, what, sir?
Greene, Friar Bacon 162, Peele, Edward I 97 etc. etc.

Bei Shakspere und noch jetzt ganz gewöhnlich (Schmidt 1354).

§ 218.

what a.

Hierüber ist für das 15. und 16. Jahrhundert nichts besonderes zu sagen. *What* in Verbindung mit *for* (das sich bei Spenser und anderen findet, s. Morris § 200) wurde in unseren Texten nur beobachtet bei Peele, Edward I 97 *What's he for a man?*

Anm.: Bemerkenswert sind die Fälle
Gorboduc 595 *what one is he that dare*
Be minister to such an enterprise?
Marriage of Wit 378 *What one art thou?*
Kyd, Cornelia 198
What one he is that in this broil hath been,
Rare Triumphs 164
Say to me straight, what one hath done this deed?
wo *what one* in verächtlich geringschätzigem Sinne verwandt ist.

§ 219.

what im Sinne von why.

Dieser auch bei Shakspere (Schmidt, Sh.-Lex. 1353) zahlreich zu findende Gebrauch ist in unseren Texten seit der ersten Hälfte des 16. Jahrhunderts zu belegen.

Fl. (Roy and B.) 76/31
>And what dost thou their names call...?

Heywood, Pardoner and Friar 211
>Marry, what standest thou there...!

Soliman and Perseda 282 *what are you crying?*
Greene, James IV 122
>What should I wear a sword, to what intent?

ib. 147 *What blush you...?*
Sidney, Arcadia 365 *what shall we curse the sun...?*
ib. 743 *What stay ye shepherds, whose great shepherd is gone?*

§ 220.
what im Sinne von how.

What im Sinne von *how* ist seit dem 15. Jahrhundert in unseren Texten zu belegen:

M. 153/30 ... *thenne this lord asked hym what he hyghte*...
Latimer, Ploughers 23
>I can not tel what to call it...

Latimer, Sermons 111 *Call it what you will.*
ib. 161 *What should I call it? a preueledged place for whoredome.*

Calisto and Melibaea 56
Sem.: *What hight she?*
Cal.: *Melibaea is her name.*

Lyly, Euphues 316 ...*I know not what to terme it*...
Marlowe, Dido 427
>But what shall it be call'd? Troy, as before?

Introductory Sketch 47, Three Ladies 254.

Anm.: Auf Grund des in § 220 gesagten ergiebt sich die Erklärung von Fällen wie Sir Clyomon and Sir Clamydes 499b (502b, 517a) *Well, what hight thy name?* leicht durch Contamination.

§ 221.
what (etwas).

Das ae. und me. recht verbreitete (Koch § 368) *what (hwaet)* in indefinitem Sinne ist noch im 16. Jahrhundert nicht ungewöhnlich.

1. In der auch Shakspere (Schmidt 1855) geläufigen Redewendung *I'll tell thee (you) what*, z. B.:

Greene, Looking Glass 85 *I'll tell you what, ale is ale*...
Marlowe, Faust II 766 *I'le tell thee what*.
Sir Clyomon and Clamydes 518a *But chill tell you what*...
2. Für *else what* fand sich nur:
Sidney, Sonn. and Transl. 147
For why should I, whom free choice slave doth make,
Else-what in face than in my fancy bear?
3. Ebenso für ein analog zu *somwhat* gebildetes *muche what*:
R. A., Toxophilus 114 ...*whan the back and the bellye in workynge be muche what after one maner*.

§ 222.
what — what (what — and).

Die sich aus der in § 221 erörterten Bedeutung von *what* ergebende, seit ae. Zeit vorhandene (Koch § 259), konjunktionale Verwendung von *what* darf für das 15. und 16. Jahrhundert als durchaus volkstümlich gelten. Folgende Auswahl von Belegen möge das zeigen:

P. L. 368/542
For he seyd ye had moche good of the dede to dispose, what of your fader ... what of Berney, and what now of his good Mayster Fastolfe.

P. L. 711/71 ...*I truste be Ester to make of money, what with the barke and with the asshe, at the leest l. marke*...

M. 101/9 ...*and so they rode fresshly with grete royalty, what by water and what by land*...

M. 805/5 *Thenne there felle to them what of Northwalys and of Cornewaile*...

Fl. (Geschichte) 266/30, Latimer, Sermons 205, Introductory Sketch 165 und besonders häufig in More's Utopia, z. B.: 15
...*he had at ye laste, what by ye force of his pitthie argumentes and strong reasons, and what by hys authority so persuaded me*...

ib. 28
but in reasonynge, and debatyng of matter that by his naturall witte, and what by daily exercise... ib. 30 etc.

Diese Verwendung von *what* ist bei Shakspere (Schmidt, Sh.-Lex. 1355) und noch heute üblich.

§ 223.

Gebrauch und Verbreitung von *whether*.

Als Interrogativ und Relativ, das wir der Uebersicht halber mit einschliessen.

In unseren Texten wird *whether* nur von zweien gebraucht, eine Verwendung von dreien wie bei Spenser ist nicht zu belegen. Was seine Verbreitung anlangt, so findet es sich in den P. L. nicht, in M. 87/22, Fl. (Briefe) 338/6, besonders zahlreich bei Tyndale, Matth. 21/31, 22/27, 23/17, 27/21 etc. (Auth. Vers. und Rev. Vers. ebenso), R. A., Toxophilus 39, 97, Lyly, Euphues 49, Kyd, Spanish Tragedy 18, Greene, Friar Bacon 211, Sidney, Ap. 70, Astroph. and Stella p. 54, 55, Arcadia 506, 692, 834, Like Will to Like 334, Lodge, Wounds 192 etc.

Es war also im 16. Jahrhundert recht volkstümlich. Einige ganze Belege:

Tyndale, Luk. 22/27

For whether is greater, he that sitteth at meate or he that serueth. (Auth. Vers. und Rev. Vers. ebenso).

R. A., Toxophilus 97

... *the Mayre of London or Yorke, I can not tel whether* ...

Lodge, Wounds 192

Sirrah, whether is better good ale. or small-beer?

Weiterentwicklung.

Whether stirbt im 17. Jahrhundert aus (Franz 402). Nur die Bibel (s. o.) hat es bewahrt.

§ 224.

who so, what so.

Im 15. und 16. Jahrhundert ist *who so* noch ziemlich verbreitet, wie sich aus folgendem ergiebt:

P. L. 371/546, 696/46, M. 40/25, Fox 65, Fl. (Wyatt) 28/34, (More) 40/15, (Hist. Volkslieder) 157/389, (Geogr. Werke) 284/19, (Anekdoten) 329/7, Heywood, P. P. 385, More, Utopia 77, 79, Lyly, Euphues 185, 384, Endimion 30, Galathea 217, Greene, Looking Glass 122, Peele, Edward I 180, Sir Clyomon 530 b, Puttenham 33, Sidney, Arcadia 719 etc.

What so ist seltener:

P. L. 733/103, M. 654/3, Fl. (Skelton) 57/34, (Balladen) 170/17, Lyly, Euphues 230, Conflict of Conscience 135, Rare Triumphs 228, Briefe Elizabeths 116, Greene, Friar Bacon 203, Marlowe, Edward II 172, Sidney, Arc. 140

etc. etc.

Weiterentwicklung.

What so hat Shakspere nicht mehr, wohl aber *who so* (Schmidt 1365), beide, im 17. Jahrhundert nur sporadisch, sind jetzt auf Dialekte und Poesie beschränkt (Franz 206).

§ 225.
who that, what that, which that.

Diese seit me. Zeit vorhandenen Verbindungen waren im 15. Jahrhundert noch überaus volkstümlich, was besonders durch zahlreiche Belege in den P. L. bewiesen wird, z. B.:

who that:

P. L. 486/152 ... *or to som othyr man, who that ye wole* ... ib. 670/7, M. 43/29, 60/6, Fox 23, Digby Mysteries 12/287, 47/536;

whose that: P. L. 181/243 *Itt is to remembre under hos rule that the gode lord is at this day* ... ib. 376/308;

whom that: P. L. 58/71

... *he hathe seyd that he wold lyfte them whom that hym plese* ... ib. 705/63, M. 449/9, 812/14;

what that: P. L. 175/233

And what that I may do be your comaundment shall be redi with the grace of God ... ib. 224/313, Fox 36;

P. L. 68/85 ... *to go with me in what port that me lust and my felawys;* ib. 506/195, M. 645/33;

whiche that:

P. L. 402/28 ... *whech of them that had fewest to geve* ... ib. 784/171;

whether that: (Koch § 357 am Ende) wurde nicht mehr beobachtet.

Im 16. Jahrhundert sind diese Verbindungen selten: Four Elements 12 *who that,* Heywood, P. P. 355 (386) *And who that list sing after me,* World and Child 250,

Jacob and Esau 208 (244)
Take all that I have for meat, help who that can.
Heywood, P. P. 352
Devise what pastime that ye think best,
Damon and P. 100 ...*which that you may plainly see.*

§ 226.
whichsoever.

Es lässt sich schon im 15. Jahrhundert in den P. L. belegen, war also in der Volkssprache schon vorhanden, doch ist es auch im 16. Jahrhundert noch recht selten zu belegen:
P. L. 332/449 (1459)
...*in whiche sum ever counteez or townez*...
ib. 793/184 *but which of these soo ever hit be, hit hevyeth me.*
Lyly, Euphues 301
...*which waye so-ever one cast his eye, she alwayes behelde him:*
ib. 365 ...*or as Aristotles Quadratus, which way soever you tourne it, is alwayes constant:*
Conflict of Conscience 94
For I am but dead, whichever side I take:
Sidney, Arcadia 217 (Tancred 77)
...*which way soever it went.*
Shakspere scheint es nicht zu haben.

§ 227.
Whatso(m) ever, what that ever, which so ever in adjektivischer Funktion.

Da das erst im Me. zu *what so* etc. tretende *ever* einen selbständigen Bestandteil bildet und daher frei beweglich ist, kann das hierzu gehörige Adjektiv + 1 bezw. mehrere Substantiv(e) ursprünglich sowohl zwischen *what* und *so (that) ever* als auch hinter *what so (that) ever* treten. Die Tendenz der Sprachentwicklung geht nun, wie bei *each other* und *one another* (§ 189 Ende), dahin, die einzelnen Bestandteile von *whatsoever* etc. zu einem Ganzen zusammenzuschliessen, ein Prozess, der heute vollkommen durchgeführt ist.

Im 15. und 16. Jahrhundert gehen beide Konstruktionen auch bei demselben Schriftsteller noch nebeneinander her. Eine

Konstruktion allein konsequent durchgeführt hat, abgesehen von einigen Autoren, bei denen sich in Anbetracht der nur vereinzelt vorkommenden Belege kein sicherer Schluss ziehen lässt, nur Puttenham, der in seiner Arte of English Poesie nur die jetzt allein noch übliche verwendet (cf. ib. 34, 82, 159, 310).

Im übrigen zeigen Beispiele wie:

P. L. 114/154
... of what astatte, degre, or condicion so euer thei be ...

ib. 239/328
... of what degre, or state, or condicyon that evere he be ....

Disobedient Child 310,
oder Fälle, wo das Substantiv mit einem Adjektiv verbunden ist, wie

Gorboduc 1673
O by what other meanes so euer it be,

Sidney, Arcadia 429 ... *and what other delights soever your mind esteems delights;*

wie sehr die einzelnen Bestandteile noch als solche im Bewusstsein des Volkes aufgefasst wurden.

§ 228.

whosoever, whatsoever in erweiterndem Sinne.

Die nachgestellten *whosoever, whatsoever* werden von Koch § 355 als verkürzte Sätze aufgefasst und entstammen ohne Zweifel der Umgangssprache. Sie treten in unseren Texten erst in der zweiten Hälfte des 16. Jahrhunderts auf, dürfen aber, nach unseren Belegen aus Denkmälern mancherlei Art zu schliessen, als recht gebräuchlich angesehen werden.

Greene, Alphonsus 56 ... *to see Alphonsus fly the field From any king or keisar whosome'er:*

Marlowe, Tamburlaine p. 3
Gentlemen, and curteous Readers whosoever:

Introductory Sketch 58 ... *their godly Prince, in whom they do claim more interest then the rest of hir subiects whosoeuer.*

Disobedient Child 305
I will do your commandements whatsoever.

Lyly, Euphues 432
Heere shall you see ... all other vertues whatsoeuer ...

Udall, Demonstr. 9,
Egerton Papers 242,
Introductory Sketch 62, 65, 110, 111,
Marlowe, Faust 538
Thirdly, that Mephastophilis shall do for him, and bring him whatsoeuer.

Peele, Alcazar 131
And (we) will resist his forces whatsoe'er.

Knack to Know a Knave 525
So there is no man whatsoever without some fault:

Relativpronomen.
§ 229.
Auslassung des Relativs.

Auf diese Frage, für die unser Material keine neuen Gesichtspunkte bietet, gehen wir daher nicht näher ein.

Die sogenannte Auslassung des Relativs als Nominativ und Akkusativ ist im 15. und 16. Jahrhundert in allen Literaturgattungen gleichmässig verteilt anzutreffen, also eine überaus volkstümliche Erscheinung.

Einige bemerkenswerte Belege der Auslassung des Relativs als Nominativ mögen hier Platz finden:

P.L. 386/7 ... *that Herry the sext is in a place in Yorkschire is calle Coroumbr;*

ib. 621/374 ... *I hope of a goode dyreccion schall be hadde.*

M. 420/1 *Thenne was he ware of a semely knyght came rydyng ageynst him ...*

ib. 729/4 *For they wyste not what to saye consydcrynge Quene Gueneuer made the feest and dyner ...*

Digby Mysteries 164/712
ye! who is hym shall hem offende?

Introductory Sketch 28
Thirdlie, that the other Bishoppes, are called Lords, haue domination.

Greene, Orlando 15 *But who is this comes here?*

James IV 84 *'Tis Ida is the mistresse of your heart,*

Alphonsus 20 *It is not words must recompense my pain, But deeds.*

Marlowe, Ovid 168
*On labouring women *thou dost pity take,
My wench, Lucina, I entreat thee favour;*
* i. e. thou that dost.

Lodge, Wounds 115
What fire is this is kindled by thy wrath?

§ 230.
Relative Anknüpfung.

Die relative Anknüpfung ist eine Erscheinung, die, wie im Altfranz. (cf. Jung, Syntax des Pronomens bei Amyot p. 43), schon im 15. Jahrhundert weite Verbreitung gefunden hat und im 16. ihren Höhepunkt erreicht, in der ganzen Zeit jedoch in allen Literaturgattungen gleichmässig vertreten ist. Inbetreff des Einflusses des Lateinischen ist es bemerkenswert, dass schon im 15. Jahrhundert gerade die P. L. zahlreiche Belege aufweisen (vgl. hierzu die Bemerkung von Franz p. 208, 7). Eine endgültige Entscheidung über den Anteil des Lateinischen an der Ausbildung der relativen Anknüpfung kann erst nach Vornahme von Untersuchungen über die frühere Zeit getroffen werden.

§ 231.

Wir geben im Folgenden eine Auswahl von Belegen aus verschiedenen Zeiten und Gattungen der Literatur, die das oben gesagte genügend illustrieren werden.

1. **Relative Anknüpfung vermittelst eines Pronomens.**

a) Das Relativ im adjektivischer oder substantivischer Funktion an der Spitze des Satzes.

P. L. 132/174
Whych lettre J woll ye breke to undrestand my wrytyng...
  ib. 392/15 *...weche answere Sothwel tolde me was...*
  ib. 491/161 *Weche suerte is taken, and a letter wreten to...*
  ib. 797/190 *all which concyderyd, and the necessary relyffe that my brother most have, I mervayle the lesse...*
Fox 6
...a puddyng, wyche puddyng reygnard the foxe had taken away from hym.

Tyndale, Ap. 16/36
Which iaylar when he had receaued suche commaundement thrust them into the inner preson ... (Anth. Vers. und Rev. Vers. *And the jailer* ...)

Joy, Ap. 21
... that T. himself wil put it forth more perfait and newly corrected, which if he do, yours shalbe naught set by nor neuer solde.

Latimer, Sermons 22
which when he is at schole, wyl chose a lesson...

R. A., Toxophilus 48
whiche when they be shoters gyue it over...

ib. 63 *Whiche matter to entreate at large, were ouerlonge at this tyme to declare...*

More, Utopia 10
Whom though I knew to be a men in dede...

R. R. Doister 79
Which when I hearde and sawe I would none to you bring.

G. G. Needle 184 *Which thing when thou hast done,
There shalt thou find...*

Damon and Pithias 52
Which merciful justice if you would follow, and provident liberality;

Lyly, Euphues 348
... the plant Latace, which who so hadde, shoulde haue plentye of meate and money...

Introductory Sketch 41
... and asked me my name, which when I had told him, he asked me...

Puttenham 207
For to say truely, what els is man but his minde? which, whosoeuer haue skil to compasse, and make yeelding and flexible, what may not he commaund the body to perfourme?

Greene, Pinner 190
Which George but hearing, fell'd them at his feet,

Greene, Menaphon 70
Which said, the teares gusht from her eyes ...

Marlowe, Tamburlaine 2681
Twise twenty thousand valiant men at armes,
All which haue sworne to sacke Natolia.

Sidney, Arcadia 410
Pamela only casting a seeking look, whether she could see Dorus (who poor wretch wandred half mad for sorrow in the woods, crying for pardon of her who could not hear him)...

ib. 719 *Which whoso wants, half of himself doth miss.*

b) Das Relativ in adjektivischer oder substantivischer Funktion ist von einer Präposition abhängig.

P. L. 4/13 *Aftyr which pleynte affermyd...*

ib. 76/104 *In proof of the wich treson...*

ib. 241/334 *and as for what rule we shall have yit I wote nett...*

ib. 274/376 *and for whate rewarde competant to be yeven uppon the same, I wolle agree it.*

Heywood, P. P. 356
Before which death he saith indeed,
No soul in heaven can have his mede.

Fl. (Philos. Schriften) 254/33
In which time childhode declineth...

Fl. (More) 264/16
At which worde the prince sore abashed, began to sigh and said:

More, Utopia 19
To the meanesse of whose learninge I thougte it my part to submit...

ib. 107 *Of whose goodnes it is that we be...*

Latimer, Ploughers 10
In the which his painfull trauayles, he continued...

John Knox 45
For anoiding of which it was commanded by Moses...

R. A., Schoolemaster 20
For whose bringinge vp, I would gladlie... vse speciallie your good aduice.

Lyly, Galathea 255
... a faire daughter, then the which none was more beautiful.

Greene, Alphonsus 37
In recompense of which my good intent,
I have recived this woeful banishment.

Marlowe, Faust 1060
> *Amongest which kings is Alexander the great,*

Sidney, Arcadia 567
> *In wich piteons plight when she saw him ...*

Leycester Correspondence 107
For the removinge of which hard conceite that the world may iustlyc take ... you shall let him understande ...

ib. 108 *After the delivery of which messuage to thearle, we thincke ...*

2. Relative Anknüpfung vermittelst relativer Adverbien.

Relative Anknüpfung vermittelst relativer Adverbien hatte im 15. Jahrhundert, aber weit mehr noch im 16. eine sehr grosse Verbreitung, wie zahllose Belege aus Werken aller Literaturgattungen erweisen.

Wir heben, um das zu zeigen, einige hervor:
P. L. 392/15 *Wherfor he comaunded me ...*
ib. 762/139 (M. 3/28) *wher in I spake to my brother John ...*
ib. 192
In performmyng wherof the berer of this shal enforme you ...
ib. 177/235 (M. 2/9) *wherto he answered ...*
Fl. (R. and Barl.) 75/33
> *Wherby they had gret confidence,*

Heywood, P. P. 377
> *Whereby what time thy pleasure is,*
> *I shall requite any part of this,*

More, Utopia 24
> *Wherfore I moste earnestly desire you ...*

ib. 50 (Marlowe, Tamburlaine 2173)
> *Wherein what humanitie is vsed ...*

ib. 117
> *Wherin whether they beleue well or no ...*

Fl. (More) 264/27 (ib. [Hall] 271/19, Sidney, Arcadia 809)
For the execucion wherof, he appointed Miles Forest ...

More, Utopia 27
For the debatement and final determination wherof ...

Fl. (Briefe) 342/5 (Heywood, P. P. 385)
Wher to I answerd...

Latimer, Sermons 206
...wherto whether he suffered, or wrastled with the spirites ... I wyl not desier to knowe...

Fl. (Anecdoten) 327/5
Wherunto my L. Cranmer made answer...

ib. (theol. Schriften) 234/22
Wherevppon my lorde answered me...

Heywood, P. P. 376 *Wherewith they played so prettily,*
Kyd, Cornelia 179
Wherein what grace that excellent Garnier hath lost...

Egerton Papers 102
For the better dispatch wherof this bearer .. is to attend on you.

Lyly, Euphues 442
...and that which followeth I saw, where-of who so doubteth, I will sweare...

Sidney, Arcadia 585
Guided wherewith, though he did not with knowlege, yet he did according to knowlege...

Leycester Correspondence 157
...whearein what to awnsweare your lordship at this time I knowe not...

Henslowe's Diary 53
In wyttnes wherof I the sayd John grygges have sette my hand and seale...

Pleonastisches Relativum.
§ 232.

P. L. 747/118
He tellythe me off hyr delyng and answers, whyche iff they wer acordyng to hys seyng, a ffeynter lover than ye wolde, and weell aghte to, take therin greet comffort...

ib. ... in thees werkys, whyche iff they be browte abowte iche off yowe is moche beholden to other;

Joy, Ap. (11), 26

... *which yf yt had not be done at that time, ther had bene printed and solde two. M. mo falser bokis then euer before*:

Latimer, Sermons 30

Who yf they shulde mary with straungers, what should ensue God knoweth.

Lyly, Euphues 53

... *the graces of the one are to be prefered before ye gifts of the other, which if it be so ... then doubtlesse women either do or should loue those best whose vertue is best*...

ib. 151, 197, 225, 357, 396,

ib. 405 ... *which how repugnant it is to our common experience, there is none but knoweth*...

ib. 410 *Which how idle a thing it is, and how pestilent to youth, I partly knowe, and you I am sure can gesse.*

Briefe Elizabeth's 50

wiche, what a stain hit wer in a princis honor, you yourselfe in jugement can wel deme.

Briefe James 148

quilk as it is ... so will we pray you to be persuadit that ...

Sidney, Arcadia 286

who though she hated Amphialus, yet the nobility of her courage prevailed over it...

ib. 402 *Which when at the first it made that unexpected bliss shine upon Dorus, he was like one frozen extremity of cold*...

Angry Women 310

  And then some one will fall to argument,
  Who if he over-master her with reason,
  Then she'll begin to buffet him with mocks.

§ 233.

Bemerkungen hierzu.

Aus den in § 232 angeführten Belegen ergiebt sich, dass die Verwendung des an vorhergehendes anküpfenden aber nicht fortgeführten und daher pleonastischen Relativs (*which* selten *who*) im 15. und 16. Jahrhundert üblich war, sich aber in besonders markanter Weise in Lyly's Euphues ausgeprägt findet, wo *which* thatsächlich zur satzverbindenden Kopula geworden ist.

Zur Erklärung: Die Möglichkeit der Entstehung wird durch die im 15. Jahrhundert schon weit verbreitete, im 16. Jahrhundert zu höchster Blüte gelangende relative Anknüpfung (cf. § 230 f.) angebahnt (Erste Stufe!)

Die nähere Veranlassung geben Fälle, wo das Relativ zwar fortgeführt, zugleich aber durch ein Personalpronomen wieder aufgenommen wird und daher in Wirklichkeit schon entbehrlich geworden ist (Zweite Stufe!), z. B.:

Fl. (Barcl., Sallustübersetzung) 308/1

whiche after he had obtayned victory ouer Jugurth with greate glorye, triumph and fauoure of the commentie, he supported them in suche wyse agaynst the noble men:

Tyndale, Ap. 17/10

Which when they were come thyther, they entred into the synagoge of the Jewes. (Anth. Vers und Rev. Vers *who-went*).

Damon and Pithias 25

Which when it is spied, it is laugh'd out with a scoff,

Sidney, Arcadia 261

... that virgin wax,
Which while it is, it is all Asia's light.

etc.

Als dritte Stufe ergeben sich alsdann die oben verzeichneten Fälle (Anakoluth!)

Weiterentwicklung.

Fälle der in § 232 verzeichneten Art kommen bei Spenser und Shakspere nicht selten vor, schwinden aber in der zweiten Hälfte des 17. Jahrhunderts aus der Schriftsprache, sind jedoch noch heute in der Dialekt- und Vulgärsprache anzutreffen (Franz 208 sowie Engl. Stud. XII, 228, Zupitza Archiv 84, 182, Storm 278).

Indefinita.
§ 234.

Bezeichnung des unbestimmten „*man*".

1. In der Regel wird das unbestimmte „*man*" im 15. und 16. Jahrhundert durch *they* wiedergegeben, besonders in Sprichwörtern oder sprichwörtlichen Redensarten, z. B.:

a) **Bei Sprichwörtern oder sprichwörtlichen Redensarten.**

Four Elements 9
> *So they say that man occupied is*
> *For a commonvealth ...*

New Custom 9
> *Youth is rash, they say, but old men hath the knowledge.*

ib. 20 *They say better to be idle than to do harm.*

Conflict of Conscience 60
> *Inter amicos omnia sunt communia, they say.*

ib. 96   *but yet, as they say,*
> *One bird in the hand is worth two in the bush;*

Lyly, Mother Bombie 74
> *they say, if ravens sit on hens' egges, the chickens will be blacke, and so forth.*

Peele, Old Wives Tale 244
> *Jack, they say it is good to go cross-legged, and say prayers backward;*

Puttenham 211
> *An ape wilbe an ape, by kinde as they say,*
> *Though that ye clad him all in purple array.*

Rare Triumphs 223, Angry Women 306, 320, 351, Look about You 459.

b) **In anderen Fällen.**

P. L. 357/526
> *And the Duc of Somerset he is in Depe ... and they seythe here, he porpose hym to go to Walys to the Quene.*

ib. 711/71 ... *ther is a man of Carbroke, they calle hym Saunders ...*

M. 770/8 ... *and the pryce was gyuen vnto syr Launcelot, and by herowdes they named hym, that he had smyten doune fyfty knyghtes ...*

Latimer, Sermons 160
> *I harde saye syns of a nother murder, that a Spanyarde shoulde kyll an Englisheman, and ronne hym thorowe wyth hys swerde: they say he was a tall man.*

More Utopia 35
> *These things (say they) pleased our forefathers and auncestours:*

R. A., Toxophilus 164
The body both blood and bone, as they say, is brought out of his ryght course by anger:
Diary of Machyn 35
The VI day of July, as they say, dessessyd the nobull Kyng Edward the VI...
Lyly, Mother Bombie 98
Sil. *They say you are a witch.*
Bom. *They lie, I am a cunning woman.*
Greene, James IV 138, Marlowe, Dido 417, Three Ladies 253, Knack to Know a Knave 513.
Puttenham 227
They say it is a ruth to see thy louer neede,
Sidney, Arcadia 460
as they say, the Cranes overthrow the whole battles of Pigmeys...
etc.
Diese Konstruktion ist bei Shakspere (Mätzner II, 10) und noch heute üblich.

2 Durch *one*, dass sich in dieser Bedeutung erst in der 2. Hälfte des 16. Jahrhunderts weiter verbreitet, z. B.
Fl. (Lieder) 147/27
Pastymes ther be I nought trewlye
Whych one may vse and vice denye
And they be plesant to god and man,
Heywood, Pardoner and Friar 207
Ay, by the mass, one cannot hear —
Jacob and Esau 218
Ah, sir, when one is hungry, good meat is much worth.
Lyly, Euphues 435
...wher-by it seemeth so populous, that one would scarse think so many people to be in the whole Island...
Lyly, Campaspe 117
I meane, I must crie; not as one would say crie; but crie, that is make a noyse.
Greene, Orlando 28
... the Count Orlando... rends him, as one would tear a lark!

Puttenham 296
But generally to weepe for any sorrow (as one may doe for pitie) is not so decent in a man:
Sidney, Arcadia 729
... in the very anatomy of her spirits one should have found nothing but devilish disdain ...
Anm.: Kreuzung der beiden möglichen Konstruktionen zeigt folgendes Beispiel:
Lyly, Euphues 289
I knowe Nature hath prouided, and I thinke our lawes allow it, that one maye loue when they see their time, not that they must loue when others appoint it.

Weiterentwicklung.

Die Verwendung von *one* im Sinne von „*man*" ist wie bei Shakspere (Schmidt, Sh. Lex. 809) auch noch heute üblich.

3. Durch *who*, cf. § 207 ff.

4. Seltener auf andere Weise, z. B.:
Conflict of Conscience 31
If long unworn you leave a cloak or gown,
Marlowe, Hero 36
Love is not full of pity, as men say,
But deaf and cruel where he means to pray.
ib. 97   *as when you descry*
A ship ...
Greene, Friar Bacon 173
I am, father doctor, as a man would say, the bell-wether of this company:

§ 235.
no als Negation.

Die im Ae. angebahnte, me. weit verbreitete und zum Teil noch jetzt übliche Verwendung von *no* als Negation neben *not* (Mätzner II, 135 f.) ist im 15. und 16. Jahrhundert überaus volkstümlich und in denkmälern aller Art zu belegen.

a) **Im 2. Gliede eines disjunktiven Satzverhältnisses.**

In einem Verhör (Egerton Papers 167 ff.) finden sich zwei *not* gegen sechs *no*.

P. L. 838/253 ... *whether she be buried or noo...*

Everyman 112
>   *Whether ye have loved me or no,*

Latimer, Sermons 180
>   *he could not tell whether it were so or no.*

Lyly, Euphues
>   *But whether these be true or no, I wil not say:*

Greene, Orlando 47   *Thou tell me,*
>   *Whether thou wrong'dst Angelica or no?*

Marlowe, Tamburlaine 2126
>   *See, se, Anippe, if they breathe or no.*
>   etc.   etc.

Vgl. hierzu: Knack to Know a Knave 514
>   *Whether she be resolved to love me, yea or no.*

ib. 556
>   *Speack, Osrick, shall I have her, ay or no?*

b) Desgl. natürlich vor Komparativen, *no more, no less, no farther, no better, no worse, no longer* etc.

c) Zuweilen in anderen Fällen.

Tyndale, Rom. 4/2
If Abraham were iustifyed by dedes, then had he wherin to reioyce: but no with God... (Auth. Vers. und Rev. Vers. *not*)

§ 236.
Stellung von *none* am Ende des Satzes.

Die schon dem Ae. geläufige, jetzt seltenere (Mätzner III, 261) Stellung von *none* in prädikativer Beziehung am Ende des Satzes, die im Me. grosse Ausdehnung gewonnen hat, ist im 15. und 16. Jahrhundert noch weit verbreitet, z. B.:

P. L. 75/97
>   *... and other cause he had non to him...*

ib. 140/186 (241/334, 315/426 etc.)
>   *Other tydings as yett can I non tell you:* (Stehende Redensart).

ib. 365/538
>   *... but othyr answer have I none yet of hym.*

M. 367/26
>   *... I wille not haue adoo with yow for cause haue ye none to me.*

Four Elements 17
That the earth is so deep, and bottom hath none,
Fl. (Balladen) 173/82
Fynde a better borowe sayd Robyn
Or mony getest thou none
Joy, Ap. X ... *and other resurreccion shall there none be.*
More, Utopia 12
for other dwellynge place wold he haue none.
Lyly, Euphues 438 ... *wildfo[u]le and fish they want none.*
Damon and Pithias 42 *other cause there is none.*
Greene, Looking Glass 95
for other remedies have we none...
Puttenham 45
temples or churches or other chappels then these they had none at those dayes.
Sidney, Arcadia 753 ... *for other cause I see none...*

§ 237.
none in neutralem Sinne.

none in neutralem Sinne ist schon seit ae. Zeit belegt.
Ae. Caedm., Genesis 1400 *þem ... wæs nān tō gedāle,*
Me. P. Ploughm. B. XV 95 (Skeat) *Some bowes bēn lēved, and some bereth nōne.*

Im 15. und 16. Jahrhundert scheint es, nach unseren Belegen zu schliessen, in diesem Sinne besonders vor *other* recht gebräuchlich gewesen zu sein, was formelhaft war.

P. L. 312/423 *and thynke veryly non other but that ȝe haue it...*

M. 95,32 ... *god knoweth I dyd none other but as I wold ye dyd to me...*

Egerton Papers 33
... *it was none other but agreable to the meanynge of the statute...*

Fl. (Weihnachtslieder) 119/70
yet none the lesse I wyll not cess

Tyndale Vorr. zu Hebr.
that is to saye, soche malicious vnkyndnes which is none nother then the blasphemynge of the holy goost...

ib. *he meaneth none other ... then ...*

Diary of Machyn 14
... they thought no nodur butt that they shuld ...
R. R. Doister 63
*And ywis this letter if ye woulde heare it now.
I will heare none of it.*
Damon and Pithias 25
I duly obey, I can do no other.
Kyd, Spanish Tragedy 21
O no, she envies none but pleasant things;
ib. 172
*This hand shall hale them down to deepest hell,
Where none but furies, bugs, and tortures dwell.*
Die späteren Drucke von 1618, 23, 33 haben *nought*.

Sidney, Arcadia 155, 507, Leycester Correspondence 172
... that the states durst doe noe other but to satysfye the people allso with that oppynion;

Weiterentwicklung.

Das neutrale *none* findet sich bei Shakspere (Abbot § 53, Deutschbein § 83) und ist im 17. und 18. Jahrhundert (Franz 396) wie noch heute bisweilen vor einem partitiven Genitiv gebräuchlich.

§ 238. *both*.

a) Stellung von *both*.

Die Stellung von *both* ist in der Volkssprache des 15. und 16. Jahrhunderts eine recht freie gewesen, wie sich im folgenden zeigen wird; wir bemerken jedoch, dass wir nur charakteristische Fälle hervorheben, und verweisen im übrigen auf den gut orientierenden Artikel im Oxf. Dict.

1. **Stellung von *both* nach dem Substantiv.**
P. L. 939/390 *Mastyrs bothe, I recomand me to yow ...*
M. 815/11 *... my lordes bothe wete ye wel ...*
Hickscorner 178 *Now, brethren both, I thank you.*
Damon and Pithias 26
These gentlemen both ... have all the fruition:
Peele, Alcazar 88
This traitor king hales ... his younger brethren both.

Greene, Friar Bacon 205
See, friar, where the fathers both lie dead.
Diese Stellung zur besonderen Hervorhebung des *both* war also recht üblich.

2. *both* + Personalpronomen.

Analog der Stellung *all* + Personalpronomen erscheint, abgesehen von den Fällen, wo die auch im 16. Jahrhundert bei weitem seltenere Umschreibung mit *of* eingetreten ist, die Stellung *both* + Personalpronomen nur selten:

Lyly, Euphues 77
both they vnfaithfull of their promises.
Lyly, Mydas 12
Let us go further, Licio, she hath both us in the wind.
Marlowe, Tamburlaine 381
Both we wil walke vpon the lofty cliffes,
ib. 385 *Both we will raigne as Consuls of the earth,*
ib. 3415 *Death, whether art thou gone, that both we liue?*
ib. 3705
Twill please my mind as wel to heare both you
Sidney, Arcadia 158
Imprison her who both them did possess

3. *both* in Verbindung mit dem Artikel oder Demonstrativpronomen.

Abgesehen von den seltenen Fällen der Umschreibung gilt die Stellung *both* + Artikel oder Demonstr. als Regel; die umgekehrte Stellung ist selten:

P. L. 233/322 ... *the right of thes bothe patentes* ...

M. 593/20 ... *and thenne syre launcelot took hym by the bothe sholders* ...

Rutland Papers 50
... *the tentes, where the bothe Kinges after their meeting may common to guyder* ...

Suppl. of the Commons 34 *These bothe causes* ...

4. *both* + Relativ.

Als Regel gilt im 15. und 16. Jahrhundert die Stellung Relativ + *both*, z. B.:

P. L. 281/384 *in whiche bothe,*
Latimer, Sermons 54 *which both,*

R. A., Schoolemaster 130 *who both, liued in one tyme:*
Damon and Pithias 26
Which both are in virtue so narrowly laced,
Sidney, Arcadia 146
Whom both nature seems to debar from means to be helped,
etc. etc.

Daneben tritt die Stellung *both* + Relativ besonders häufig seit der 2. Hälfte des 16. Jahrhunderts auf, z. B.:

Lyly, Euphues 396
...both which, with little suite being obteined, I may lyue with loue.

Introductory Sketch 131 *both which nombres of Bookes,* Puttenham 168, Greene, Alphonsus 62, Marlowe, Lucan 280, Hero 66, Leycester, Correspondence 449.

§ 239.
b) *bothe two.*

Das ae. m. f. *bā twā* (n. *bū tū, butwu*) = beide zwei, wofür me. oft *bōthe twō* erscheint, ist im 15. und 16. Jahrhundert als *both(e) two, both(e) twain* recht geläufig, z. B.:

Fox 71 *...they durste not speke but pyked and stryked them out of the court bothe two.*

Fl. (Lee) 38/5 *I dyde intende...to refus both twayne to hold my selffe contente*

Four Elements 16
Leaving you together here both twain;
Hickscorner 176
I think, they will come hither again,
Freewill and Imagination, both twain:
Heywood, P. P. 358
For both you twain shall wait on me.
R. A., Schoolemaster 155
bothe two, by vse of life, were daylie orators...
R. R. Doister 23 *...here I leaue both twaine.*
ib. 28 *Hence both twaine.*
Jack Juggler 150
Now mercy that I ask of you both twain:
Marriage of Wit 365
Both twain on either side assault him...

Nice Wanton 180
>That they died so shamefully both two:

§ 240. nothing als verstärkte Negation.

Diese schon bei Orrm (Koch § 378) sich findende Verwendung von *nothing* ist im 15. und 16. Jahrhundert überaus populär, z. B.:

P. L. 776/161
> I was noo thynge gladde off thys jornaye ...

Digby Mysteries 36/234
> be nothyng a-drad ...

Fl. (Skelton) 62/12
> Her lothelye lere
> Is nothynge clere
> But vgly of chere.

More, Utopia 48 ... *their life is nothing hard* ...
Lyly, Euphues 96 ... *although I nothing fear your malice* ...
Puttenham 41 ... *who mounted nothing so high* ...

Ebenso bei Shakspere (Abbot § 55, Deutschbein § 81), jetzt veraltet.

Anm.: In ebendemselben Sinne ist auch *no whit* seit der Mitte des 16. Jahrhunderts zahlreich zu belegen, z. B.:

G. G. Needle 255
> I am not whit sorry to see you so rejoice.

Peele, Alcazar 110
> I doubt no whit but I shall live, my lord.

Nur in Briefen Elizabeths 27 (53, 161)
> my los of honor be no whit repaired ...

§ 241. few.

1. *In few.*

Das bei Shakspere zahlreich zu belegende (Schmidt 413) *in (a) few* = *in (a) few words* fand sich nur bei Marlowe, Jew 1364
> In few, the blood of Hydra, Lerna's bane ...
> Breake from the fiery kingdome;

Sonst *in few words* (Fl. [Briefe] 334/47, John Knox 58, Disobedient Child 317, Damon and Pithias 78) oder *in the fewest words* (Heywood, P. P. 367).

2. *fewer* und *fewest.*

fewer ae. und me. nicht belegt fand sich in unseren Texten zuerst in Barclay's Bearbeitung von Seb. Brandts Narrenschiff

(1508) Fl. 105/35 *But fewe I rede and fewer understande* und scheint daher erst nach 1500 volkstümlich zu werden.

Fl. (Vorwort zur Conf. Amantis) 303/52

... *that very fewe men knewe, and fewer hadde them* ...

Suppl. of the Commons 51

... *moche fewer of these matters of contencyon shalle in vre and experience* ...

Decay of England 96

The more shepe, the fewer egges for a peny.

Latimer, Sermons 19

... *I had XX. mens wittes, and no fewer handes to wryte with all.*

R. A., Toxophilus 140 *fewer shooters,*

Schoolemaster 33

but a greate deale fewer of them cum to shewe ...

More, Utopia 75

Now howsholde or ferme in the countrey hath fewer then xl. persones ...

(Das lat. Original hat beide Male *pauciores*).

Misfortunes of Arthur 36

They had been none, or fewer at the least,

Leycester Correspondence 40

... *and then the nombers may be the fewer afterward.*

ib. 246

yet are we many fewer than he ...

Sidney, Ap. 60 *with fewer Laurels.*

fewest seltener als *fewer* ist in unseren Texten zuerst zu belegen:

P. L. 402/28 ... *whech of them that had fewest* ...

Heywood, P. P. 367 *And in the fewest words thou can.*

R. A., Schoolemaster 37 ... *that number of men is fewest* ...

ib. 61 *And verily they be fewest of number* ...

Three Ladies 284 *the fewest shall laugh me to scorn.*

Das Oxf. Dict. hat für *in few* schon Belege von 1526 und 1565, von *fewest* 2 aus dem Alexander (1400—1450).

Weiterentwicklung.

Fewer und *fewest* sind wie heute auch bei Shakspere ganz gewöhnlich (Schmidt, Sh.-Lex. 413).

§ 242. *many*.

Many im Singular ohne folgenden unbestimmten Artikel nur vereinzelt noch im 15. Jahrhundert:

P. L. 517/213 ... *that it was payd many day a goon.*

M. 823/7 *Wete yow well thenne was there many bold knyghte ther with kynge Arthur* ...

Anm.: Nur *many one* ist auch im 16. Jahrhundert noch üblich, wenngleich in der 2. Hälfte vereinzelt.

Fox 33, Fl. (Roy and B.) 76/34, 169/15 (Balladen), 137/61 (Liebeslieder), Four Elements 7, Latimer, Ploughers 26, Peele, Vermischtes 257.

Der Genitiv ist sehr selten: Bale, Thre Lawes 282 *To many ones decaye.* Schon Shakspere kennt diesen Gebrauch nicht mehr.

Desgl. der Plural Sidney, Arcadia 465.

For this word, one being attributed to that which is all, is but one mingling of many, and many ones;

§ 243. *each* und *every*.

Zwischen *each* und *every* wird während des 15. und 16. Jahrhunderts kein Unterschied gemacht. So noch Ende des 16. Jahrhunderts:

Kyd, Spanish Tragedy 114

I pry through every crevice of each wall,

Lyly, Woman 155

Each fish that swimmeth in the floating sea,
Each winged fowle that soareth in the ayre,
And every beast that feedeth on the ground,
Have mates of pleasure to upholde their broode:

Greene, Vermischtes 284

The silent shade had shadow'd every tree,
And Phoebus in the west was shrouded low;
Each hive had home her busy labouring bee,
Each bird the harbour of the night did know:

Ebenso bei Shakspere (Deutschbein § 77, 79).

§ 244. *all*.

Bei der Verbindung von *all* mit einem Personalpronomen ist, soweit nicht die im 16. Jahrhundert noch seltene Umschreibung mit *of* verwandt wird, ausser der gewöhnlichen Stellung Personalpronomen + *all* auch die umgekehrte im 15., seltener im 16. Jahrhundert üblich.

Unsere Belege mögen die Verbreitung veranschaulichen:

P. L. 720/82 ...*it encomberthe hym evyll...and alle us hys frendys here;*

M. 26/9 (63/4) ...*how all they auowed the enqueste*...

M. 45/7 ...*it was grete shame to all them*...

Fox 47 *alle them of the court,*

Thersites 397 *She hath sallets enough for all us:*

R. A., Schoolemaster 67 *and all they together,*

Greene, Menaphon 78
All you that heare;

Marlowe, Tamburlaine 3592
Nay, when the battaile ends, al we wil meet.

Schlussbetrachtung und Folgerungen.

§ 245.

Die Mannigfaltigkeit der in der vorangegangenen Untersuchung behandelten Erscheinungen verhindert uns, eine Aufzählung der gewonnenen Resultate in der dortigen Anordnung vorzunehmen, da diese unvollständig sein würde, wollte sie nicht durch genaueres Eingehen überflüssige Wiederholungen veranlassen. Es soll daher, indem wir in allem übrigen auf die Abhandlung selbst verweisen, in diesem Abschnitte teils der Versuch gemacht werden, die Ergebnisse unserer Untersuchung soweit als angängig nach grösseren allgemeinen Gesichtspunkten kurz zusammenzufassen, teils eine Reihe von Folgerungen verschiedener Art daraus gezogen werden.

Verfasser knüpft daran zugleich die Hoffnung, auf diese Weise dem Vorwurf einer schematischen Einteilung, die sich nach reiflicher Ueberlegung aus praktischen Gründen doch als empfehlenswert herausstellte, am wirkungsvollsten begegnen zu können.

§ 246.
I. Dialektisches (zur Entwicklung der ne. Schriftsprache).

In der Flexionslehre trafen wir eine grosse Anzahl von dialektischen Formen an, die sich nach Massgabe ihres Ursprungs in drei Kategorieen sondern lassen.

1. **Allgemein in der Schriftsprache vorhandene (dialektische) Bestandteile.**

In wie weit sich die zahllosen dialektischen Formen in den Paston Letters durch ihre allgemeine Geltung oder durch die besondere Heimat des Briefschreibers erklären, müsste durch eine mit historischen Studien verbundene Untersuchung festgestellt werden, falls nicht ein zum Mindesten zweifelhaftes Resultat sich ergeben soll. Wir sehen also hiervon ab und gehen gleich zu den übrigen dialektischen Formen über:

Das auf das ae. *þā* zurückgehende *tho* (§ 48 Anm.) sowie *ilk* (§ 51) sind bis in die erste Hälfte des 16. Jahrhunderts hinein, wenngleich letzteres meist nur in der gehobenen Dichtersprache, erhalten; ebenso lassen sich *siche* (§ 49) und *miche* (§ 76) noch mehrfach in dieser Zeit belegen.

Die Frage nach der Bedeutung des auch noch im 16. Jahrhundert belegten *at* liessen wir offen (§ 65); *ether* und *nether* wurden noch vereinzelt in der 1. Hälfte des 16. Jahrhunderts, *owther* und *nother* nur noch im 15. Jahrhundert beobachtet. Das nördliche *mickle* bildet noch das ganze 16. Jahrhundert hindurch einen festen Bestandteil der Schriftsprache (§ 76 Anm.). Dasselbe gilt in gleichem Masse für das südliche *ha*, *a* (§ 10 Anm.). Von den südlichen Formen *hem* (§ 16 Anm. 1) für *them* und *her* (§ 26 Anm. 4) für *their* finden sich bei den Dramatikern der 2. Hälfte des 16. Jahrhunderts nur vereinzelte Reste, die wir aber als in der gesprochenen Volkssprache noch lebendig ansehen müssen. *Hemself* war schon in der 2. Hälfte des 15. Jahrhunderts bis auf wenige Spuren geschwunden (§ 43 Anm. 1). *Everychone* (§ 80 Anm. 2) schwindet um die Mitte, *everich* (§ 80 Anm. 1) in der 2. Hälfte des 16. Jahrhunderts. *Wother* dringt in der 1. Hälfte vorübergehend in die Schriftsprache ein (§ 83 Anm. 4).

Im Anschluss hieran mag bemerkt werden, dass die noch im 15. Jahrhundert häufige Schreibung *y*, *i* für *I* in der 1. Hälfte des 16. Jahrhunderts nur mehr vereinzelt anzutreffen ist.

2. **Dialektische Formen, durch die Heimat des Verfassers bedingt.**

a) Nördliche Formen (inkl. nördl. Mittelland).

Sho (§ 12 Anm.), *thai* (§ 15), *yender* (§ 54 Anm. 2) in den Digby Mysteries, letzteres auch in dem Gedicht auf die Schlacht bei Otterburn Fl. 194/13; *whilk*, *quilk* (§ 60 Anm. 1) in der Plumpton Correspondence, einem Briefe Jacobs V. von Schottland (Fl. 331/21), bei John Knox und in Briefen James VI.; *qwo*, *quho* (§ 55 Anm. 4) und *quhom* (§ 57 Anm. 1) bei Wedderburn

(Fl. 131 ff.) und in Briefen James VI, *quhat* (§ 58 Anm. 1) in den Digby Mysteries, einem Schäferkalender (Fl. 95/9) und in Briefen James VI, *quhich* bei Barclay (Fl. 94/35) und in Briefen James, in letzteren auch *qwatsumever* (§ 62 Anm. 2); *na, nane* (§ 68 Anm. 1) bei Wedderburn, *every ylkc* (§ 80 Anm. 3) in einer Proklamation (P. L. 918/362).

b) Südliche Formen.

Hur als pers. pron. (§ 13) in den Mysteries ed. Hone, den Digby Mysteries, sowie in einem Liebeslied (Fl. 138/II), *hur* als pron. poss. nur an den beiden letztgenannten Stellen.

3. Beabsichtigte Dialektformen — Bühneneffektmittel.

Ueber die Verwendung von Dialektformen als Mittel zur Erregung von Komik ist schon an den betr. Stellen der Flexionslehre ein Wort gesagt.

Es kommen hier in Betracht teils nördliche: *day* (Mischform, § 15 Anm. 1), *thea* (§ 15 Anm. 2), *tham, theam* (§ 16 Anm. 2), *may, thay* (§ 20 Anm. 6), *awer, awr, aur, awre* (§ 24 Anm. 2), *ilk* (§ 51), *sike* (§ 49 Anm. 1), *whe* (§ 55 Anm. 5), *whese* (§ 56 Anm. 2), *whilk, quilk* (§ 60 Anm. 4), *nething* (§ 72 Anm.);

teils südliche:

ich (§ 2 Anm. 2) in ausgedehntem Masse und *vat* (§ 56 Anm. 2).

Um eine Gesamtübersicht über die zur Erzielung einer komischen Bühnenwirkung verwandten Mittel, soweit sie in unsere Untersuchung einschlagen, zu ermöglichen, schliessen wir diese anderen hier an:

ick (§ 2 Anm. 3), *dy* (§ 2 Anm. 4), *dee* (§ 7 Anm.), *dey, day* (Mischform, § 15 Anm. 1), *dem* (§ 16 Anm. 3), *dy* (§ 20 Anm. 5), *dis* (§ 45 Anm. a), *dese* (§ 46 Anm. 1), *dat* (§ 47 Anm.), *sush, shush* (§ 49 Anm. 2), aus der Syntax die Verwendung von *me* für *I* (§ 133).

Die Dramen, in denen wir grössere oder kleinere Dialektstellen antrafen, sind folgende:

Cambyses, G. G. Needle, Damon and Pithias, Sir Clyomon and Sir Clamydes, Like Will to Like (diese schon von

Panning¹)), Trial of Treasure 280, Greene, James IV 73 ff., Conflict of Conscience 71 ff., Rare Triumphs 200 ff., Three Ladies of London 303 ff., Knack to Know a Knave 547 (hier nur *cham*).

§ 247.
II. Analytische Tendenzen.

Bei einer Reihe von Erscheinungen unserer Untersuchung können wir die analytische Tendenz der englischen Sprache deutlich erkennen:

Ist so die Umschreibung des Possessivs durch das Personalpronomen (§ 156) ein Zug in dieser Richtung, so können wir weiter die Ausbildung des pseudo-partitiven Genitivs (§ 166) sowie die Umschreibungen von *them both* (§ 238, 2), *both which* (§ 238, 4) und *us all* (§ 244) durch *both of them, both of which* und *all of us* hierher rechnen. Vor allem aber bildet die Bezeichnung des Genitivs durch das Possessivpronomen (§ 163 f.) eine analytische Tendenz, der, wie in § 164 näher ausgeführt ist, dadurch eine erhöhte Geltung zukommt, dass *his* auch vor Femininen verwandt wurde.

§ 248.
III. Kürze des Ausdrucks — Sparsamkeit.

Für die Oekonomie im sprachlichen Ausdruck bot sich uns in der Auslassung des Personalpronomens (§ 89—104) ein charakteristisches Beispiel. Wir hatten es hier teils mit Ueberresten eines alten Sprachzustandes, die vielfach durch den Einfluss der Umgangssprache (Drama!) lebenskräftig erhalten wurden, zu thun (§ 90—102), teils mit Neubildungen, die wieder absichtlich geschaffen (in Inhaltsangaben und Protokollen § 103, sowie Bühnenanweisungen § 103 Anm.), oder aus der Umgangssprache in die Schriftsprache eingedrungen sein konnten (§ 104). Zu den letzteren waren insbesondere eine Reihe von Redensarten des täglichen Lebens (*I pray, prythee,*

---

¹) Es ergiebt sich also hieraus, dass die Zahl der von Panning untersuchten und von ihm p. 7 f. aufgezählten Dramen mit Dialektstellen eine sehr unvollständige ist, besagte Arbeit also, auch abgesehen von den zum Teil unzuverlässigen Ausgaben der untersuchten Dramen, die er benutzt hat, ein endgültiges Ergebnis schwerlich darstellen kann.

I would § 104 Anm. 1, *advise you, assure you* § 104 Anm. 2) zu rechnen. Besonders begünstigt wurde die Auslassung da, wo die alte Flexionsendung erhalten war (cf. § 92).

§ 249.
IV. Verschwenderische Züge der Sprache (Fülle des Ausdrucks).

Der Zug der Verschwendung von sprachlichen Ausdrucksmitteln zeigte sich in hervorragendem Masse in unserer Untersuchung beim Personalpronomen (§ 105—112), das entweder in bewusster Absicht (Nachdruck!) dem Subjekte pleonastisch beigefügt wurde (§ 107 f., § 109 f. zum Teil), oder aber seine Existenz einer Eigentümlichkeit der Umgangssprache (Anakoluthe) verdankt (§ 109 f. zum Teil, § 111 f.); man vergleiche hierzu auch Anhang II Zur Bildung der Relativsätze im 15. und 16. Jahrhundert, insbesondere die Bemerkungen zu a und b § 302.

Eine andere Art der Fülle des Ausdrucks entsteht durch das Verblassen des ursprünglichen Bedeutungsgehaltes eines Wortes. So veranlasst der Bedeutungsverlust bei *same* (§ 206, 1) eine pleonastische Verstärkung durch *self* etc. (§ 206, 2), umgekehrt bei *self* eine solche durch *same* (§ 198 Anm.); in gleicher Weise ist die Entstehung von Verbindungen wie *ylk same* (§ 51) und *such like* (§ 205) gegeben. Auch der Verlust an Bedeutung beim Possessivpronomen und seine dadurch bedingte Verstärkung durch *own* (§ 192) kann hierher gerechnet werden.

Schliesslich mag auch noch auf die durch missverständliche Auffassung entstandenen Verdoppelungen *I cham, cham I* (§ 2 Anm. 2 Ende) sowie *pleasyt it* und *lckit it* (§ 17 Ende) hingewiesen werden.

§ 250.
V. Contaminationen.

Wie das psychologische Moment der Contamination in jeder Sprache eine Rolle spielt, so hatten auch wir mehrfach Gelegenheit, diese psychologische Kraft in Thätigkeit zu sehen.

So stellten sich *I would God* (§ 104 Anm. 1), *if it please it you* (§ 108 Anm. 2), *art you minded* (§ 150 Anm.), *other* im Sinne von *each other* (§ 187 Anm.), *this many a hundred year, this many a day* (§ 204), *what your own lust* (Anhang I § 272

Anm.), *meseem* (ib. § 282 Anm.) und *methink* (ib. § 281 Anm.) als Contaminationen dar. Sie gaben uns ferner den Erklärungsgrund ab für eine ganze Reihe von Kasusvertauschungen beim Personalpronomen sowohl (§ 116—126), wie beim Relativ (§ 210) und bieten uns so schon auf einem verhältnismässig kleinen Gebiete ein Bild von der eminenten Bedeutung dieses Momentes.

§ 251.
VI. Einfluss des Traditionellen.

Wie gross und weitgreifend der konservative Einfluss des traditionell Hergebrachten bei der Entwicklung grammatischer Erscheinungen ist, wurde im einzelnen an den betr. Stellen unserer Untersuchung bereits erörtert.

Wir hatten es hierbei teils mit Redensarten des Briefstiles zu thun, wie den ständig wiederkehrenden Glück- und Segenswünschen in den Paston Letters (Konstruktion ἀπὸ κοινοῦ § 96 Ende) oder den üblichen Empfehlungsfloskeln (*to recomand* § 172 Anm., § 177), die natürlich sämtlich auch in Werke anderer Art eindringen, teils mit Höflichkeitswendungen (*to please* § 99b NB. sowie Anhang I § 279, *to like* Anhang I § 271), teils auch endlich mit formelhaften Redensarten anderer Art (*wete ye well, be ye sure, know ye, farewell* § 98, 1, *how chance* § 99b Anm., *mayhap* § 100, *sufficeth* § 100 Anm., *if so be* § 101 Anm. 1, *as who should say* § 207—209).

§ 252.
VII. Einwirkung fremder Sprachen.

1. Einfluss des Französischen.

Schon in § 89 nahmen wir Gelegenheit, die Ansicht Einenkels inbetreff des altfranzösischen Einflusses auf die Auslassung des Personalpronomens zurückzuweisen.

Ebensowenig wollen wir die auf p. 66 zu dem Belege aus Greene, Looking Glass 74 gemachte Bemerkung auf einen Einfluss des Französischen bezogen wissen.

2. Einfluss des Lateinischen.

Ueber den Einfluss des Lateinischen auf die Entwicklung der relativen Anknüpfung im Englischen wollten wir (§ 230 f.) kein endgültiges Urteil fällen. Jedenfalls ist die Bemerkung von Franz p. 208, 7 „Dass die Dialekte grade diese Eigentümlichkeit der älteren Sprache noch bewahren und auch sonst noch eine Neigung für relativische Anknüpfung zeigen, spricht einigermassen gegen die Annahme der Beeinflussung des Englischen von Seiten des Lateinischen in diesem Punkte" kein Beweis gegen den Einfluss des Lateinischen; denn wir können in zahlreichen Fällen die Beobachtung machen, dass eine Erscheinung, gleichviel welchen Ursprungs, in Dialekten noch lebendig ist, während die Schriftsprache keine Spur mehr davon aufweist.

§ 253.
VIII. Erscheinungen,
die im 15. bezw. 16. Jahrhundert aufhören oder entstehen.

Gerade der Zeitraum des 15. und 16. Jahrhunderts charakterisiert sich wie jede Verbindungszeit zweier Sprachepochen als eine Periode des Uebergangs. Dieser Uebergang kann sich sprachlich entweder so darstellen, dass schon vorhandene Erscheinungen unter mehr oder minder grossen Veränderungen zur nächsten Sprachperiode übergeleitet werden oder andererseits so, dass grammatische Erscheinungen in dieser Zeit teils ihr Ende nehmen, teils neu entstehen. Diese beiden letzteren Fälle sind für uns hier von besonderem Interesse. In vielen Fällen bedingt das Aufhören einer Erscheinung den Anfang einer anderen.

Wir beginnen mit den Erscheinungen, deren Existenz im 15. oder 16. Jahrhundert erlischt:

Die Verbindung der Verba *to agree, to assure* etc. mit dem (einfachen) Personalpronomen zur Bezeichnung des reflexiven Verhältnisses gehört nur dem 15. Jahrhundert an (§ 183). Die Verwendung von *myne* und *thyne* (§ 20 Anm. 1) sowie von *none* vor Konsonanten hört (ausser der Verbindung *none such*) mit der 1. Hälfte des 16. Jahrhunderts auf (§ 68 Anm. 3).

Die Formen *ourselfe, yourselfe, themselfe* (§ 41—43) sind anscheinend im 16. Jahrhundert noch nicht gänzlich den Formen mit dem Plural-*s* gewichen.

Die Bezeichnung der possessiven Beziehung auf ein unbekanntes Subjekt durch *his* hört auf (§ 155).

Von der alten Ausdrucksweise *that am I* für späteres *it is I* begegneten im 16. Jahrhundert nur noch spärliche Reste (§ 134 Anm. 1).

Die Verbindungen *who that, what that, which that* (§ 225) scheinen die 1. Hälfte des 16. Jahrhunderts nicht zu überdauern.

Eine besondere Erwähnung verdienen hier diejenigen Verba, die ihre unpersönliche Konstruktion völlig zu Gunsten der persönlichen aufgegeben haben (Anhang I). So ist der Uebergang zur persönlichen Konstruktion vollzogen schon im 15. Jahrhundert bei den Verben:

to forthynk (§ 265), *to lack* (§ 270), *to marvel* (§ 274), *to owe* (§ 277), *to shame* (§ 283), sowie bei *to be better, to be lief* und *to be loth* (§ 289);

in der 1. Hälfte des 16. Jahrhunderts bei:

to fortune (§ 266), *to long* (§ 273), *to need* (§ 276), *to pity* (§ 278), *to rue* (§ 281) und *to think* in Verbindung mit anderen Pron. als *me* (§ 284);

in der 2. Hälfte des 16. Jahrhunderts:

anscheinend bei *to list* (nur bei Peele unpersönlicher Gebrauch, cf. § 272) und *to repent* (§ 280), das Shakspere nicht mehr unpersönlich gebraucht. Wahrscheinlich verschwinden auch die in § 285 besprochenen unpersönlichen Ausdrücke, von denen nur Peele noch *it saith* hat.

Im Anschluss hieran muss bemerkt werden, dass *to seme* im Laufe des 16. Jahrhunderts seinen persönlichen Gebrauch wieder verliert.

Hieran schliessen wir die Erscheinungen, die im 15. oder 16. Jahrhundert ihren Anfang nehmen:

Die Kasusvertauschungen beginnen bei *ye, you* schon im 14. Jahrhundert (vgl. für *ye* als Akkus. auch den Beleg aus Chaucer im Nachtrag), Belege für andere Pronomina zeitigte erst das Drama des 16. Jahrhunderts.

Fewer konnte vereinzelt schon im 15. Jahrhundert, *fewest* erst in der 1. Hälfte des 16. Jahrh. belegt werden (§ 241, 2).

Ebenso tritt *whichever*, wenn auch mit nur wenig Belegen, mit dem 15. Jahrhundert auf (§ 226).

Die pleonastische Verbindung *such like* scheint vor 1500 entstanden zu sein (§ 205).

Für die Verwendung von *he* und *she* zur Bezeichnung des

Geschlechts weist erst die 1. Hälfte des 16. Jahrhunderts Belege auf (§ 113).

Erst in der 2. Hälfte finden wir die possessive Beziehung auf ein unbekanntes Subjekt durch *one's* ausgedrückt (§ 155), wie auch die Bezeichnung des unbestimmten „man" erst in dieser Zeit durch *one* geschieht (§ 234, 2).

Jetzt treten auch *whosoever* und *whatsoever* in erweiterndem Sinne auf (§ 228).

Dagegen konnten wir für das zuerst 1598 belegte *its* aus unseren Quellen keinen Beleg nachweisen (cf. § 23 sowie Nachtrag). Für älteres *his self, a man's self* zeigte sich erst bei Sidney *one's self* (§ 40).

Erste Fälle persönlicher Konstruktion bei ursprünglich unpersönlichen Verben stellten wir zum Teil unter Zuhülfenahme des Oxf. Dict. fest.

So finden sich zuerst persönlich im 15. Jahrhundert:
to chance (§ 262), *to ail* (§ 261), *to please* (§ 279), *to forthynk* (§ 265), *to happen* (§ 268);
in der 1. Hälfte des 16. Jahrhunderts: *to fortune* (§ 266); in der zweiten: *to grieve* (§ 267).

Obwohl eigentlich nicht hierher gehörig, mag doch an dieser Stelle wiederholt werden, dass die relative Anknüpfung im 16. Jahrhundert ihren Höhepunkt erreicht (§ 230 f.).

§ 254.
IX. Eigentümlichkeiten einzelner Schriftsteller.

Bei der grossen Anzahl von Schriftstellern, deren Werke den Stoff zu unserer Untersuchung geliefert haben, war es vorauszusehen, dass wir bei manchen, vielleicht bei vielen ein gerade für sie charakteristisches Merkmal finden würden.

So war Malory's Morte Darthure charakteristisch für die reiche Entfaltung des reciproken Pronomens (cf. § 185). Weiter Tyndale in orthographischer Beziehung durch die sonst nur bei Roy (Fl. 76/49) belegte Schreibung *feawe* (cf. § 75 Anm.). Als sprachfortschrittlich erwiesen sich im 16. Jahrhundert vor allem die englische Uebersetzung von More's Utopia, für die auch *the self* im Sinne von *its self* charakteristisch ist (§ 39 Anm.), und Asham durch die Verwendung des pseudo-partitiven Genitivs (§ 166 b), ersterer allein auch noch durch den vorwiegenden Gebrauch der verstärkten Formen des Reflexivpronomens (§ 175) und die meist persönlich konstruierten Verba *to like* (§ 271) und *to list* (§ 272).

Demgegenüber ist der unpersönliche Gebrauch von *to list* für Peele charakteristisch, der von *to happen* (§ 268) für Lyly, der ebenso wie Sidney an Stelle des pseudo-partitiven Genitivs die ältere Konstruktion bevorzugt (§ 166 b). Lyly's Euphues zeichnet sich ausserdem durch die zahllosen Fälle von $I = aye$ in Antithesen aus (§ 2 Anm. 5) sowie durch das zur satzverknüpfenden Kopula herabgesunkene *which* (§ 232).

Puttenham bevorzugt wie Asham und More's Utopia den pseudo-partitiven Genitiv (§ 166 b) und charakterisiert sich weiter durch den Gebrauch von *your* im Sinne eines Dativus ethicus (§ 161) sowie der Erklärungsformel „*and is*" (§ 101 Anm. 2).

In den zahlreichen Kasusvertauschungen, die sich in dem früher Peele zugeschriebenen Sir Clyomon and Sir Clamydes fanden (§ 131), hatten wir (wie übrigens schon mit Recht Kellner, Engl. Studien XIII, 193 f.) einen sprachlich syntaktischen Grund gegen die Verfasserschaft Peele gesehen.

Greene entwickelt einen Plural *noughts* (§ 71) und Barnfield erweist seine volkstümliche Art zu dichten durch zahlreiche, der Umgangssprache entsprungene und ihr vornehmlich angehörende Verschmelzungsformen des Personalpronomens mit dem Verbum (cf. § 17).

§ 255.

X. Eigentümlichkeiten einzelner Literaturgattungen.

Das Drama. Wie gross im 15. und 16. Jahrhundert der Einfluss der Umgangssprache auf die Schriftsprache, den wir schon bei verschiedenen Gelegenheiten betonten, gewesen ist, lässt sich am besten an der Sprache der Dramatiker erkennen, die in Anbetracht der dialogischen Form ihrer Erzeugnisse die Umgangssprache am treuesten wiederspiegeln und in der 2. Hälfte des 16. Jahrhunderts überdies die Hauptrolle in der englischen Literatur spielen.

Hier finden wir die zahllosen Belege für die Verschmelzung des Personalpronomens mit dem Verbum (§ 17) sowie andere der Umgangssprache entsprungene Verstümmelungen (*God b' w' ye* § 9 Anm., *by m'fay, bum troth* etc. § 20 Anm. 4, *by'r Lady, by Lady* § 24 Anm. 1).

Hier begegnen uns vor allem die vielen Fälle der Auslassung des Personalpronomens (insbesondere § 92 und 104), die aus der Volkssprache hervorgegangenen Kasusvertauschungen des Personalpronomens (§ 116 ff.) und des Interrogativs bezw. Relativs (§ 210—215), hier auch ist die pleonastische Verwendung des Personalpronomens in charakteristischen Belegen anzutreffen, insbesondere die rhetorische Wiederholung von *I* bezw. *we* (§ 108 Anm. 4), die erst vom Drama aus in andere Literaturzweige eingedrungen ist, und schliesslich auch die Verwendung des Possessivpronomens zur Bezeichnung des Genitivs (§ 164), besonders auf Dramentiteln (§ 164 Anm.).

Die Poesie. Die gehobene Sprache der Poesie zeichnete sich aus durch das pleonastische Personalpronomen, wenn es dem Nomen vorangeht (§ 106), teils auch, wenn es von seinem Beziehungsworte durch einen oder mehrere Satzteile getrennt ist (§ 108).

Ferner fand die Verwendung des substantivischen Possessivpronomens anstatt des adjektivischen zur Erzielung eines feierlichen Tons nur in der Poesie statt (§ 165). Als dichterische Freiheiten bezw. Weiterbildungen mussten wir Fälle wie *a neighbour mine* (§ 166 Anm. 1) und *o eyes of mine* (§ 166 Anm. 2) bezeichnen.

Der Briefstil. Traditionelle Eigenheiten des Briefstils sind unter VI. § 251 übersichtlich zusammengestellt.

Der Kurialstil. Characteristica für den Kurialstil fanden sich in dem Nom. c. Inf. (p. 118) sowie der bewussten Auslassung des Personalpronomens zwecks Erzielung eines gedrungenen Stils (§ 103).

§ 256.

XI. Umgangssprache des 15. und 16. Jahrhunderts.

Ueber die Umgangssprache des 15. und 16. Jahrhunderts giebt unsere Untersuchung, insbesondere die Flexionslehre eine Reihe von Aufschlüssen, die zum Teil schon unter X. bei den Eigentümlichkeiten dramatischer Ausdrucksweise erörtert sind.

Wir können dem an dieser Stelle folgendes hinzufügen: Abfall des *h* bei *ym, im* (§ 11), *ym self* (§ 37), *yr seylff* (§ 38), *is, ys* (§ 21 und Anm. 1), *my nown* (§ 20 Anm. 2), *whose* für *who is* (§ 55 Anm. 2), *that at* für *that that* (§ 65), *the tone, t'one, tone, th'one, thone* (§ 67), *the tother, th'other, thother* (§ 83 Anm. 3), *no nother* (§ 68 Anm. 2), *a nother, nodur* (§ 83 Anm. 5), alles das giebt uns die Möglichkeit zu sicheren Rückschlüssen auf die Umgangssprache des 15. und 16. Jahrhunderts.

§ 257.
XII. Stellung Shaksperes und Spensers zur Sprache des 16. Jahrhunderts.

1. Shakspere.

Den sprachlichen Standpunkt Shaksperes in den von uns behandelten Erscheinungen haben wir nach Massgabe der in der Einleitung ausgesprochenen Absicht unter der Rubrik „Weiterentwicklung" auf Grund der darüber vorhandenen genaueren Untersuchungen (Abbot, Deutschbein [und Schmidt]) angedeutet. Wir geben uns jedoch keiner Täuschung darüber hin, dass die Untersuchungen der beiden erstgenannten für ein entscheidendes Urteil nicht genügen können und müssen daher eine eingehende Vergleichung von Shaksperes Sprachgebrauch mit dem seiner Zeit und der vorhergehenden vorerst ablehnen und einer besonderen Untersuchung vorbehalten, die, wenn gegründet auf ein erschöpfendes Material, sichere Schlüsse auch nach anderer Richtung hin gestatten wird.

Wir beschränken uns also darauf, zusammenfassend zu bemerken, dass wir im allgemeinen eine Fortführung des in der 2. Hälfte des 16. Jahrhunderts geltenden Sprachgebrauchs, insbesondere des der Dramatiker, konstatieren konnten (wozu wir in schriftsprachlicher Beziehung auch die Verwendung von *ha, a* [Schmidt 3], *hem* [Schmidt 1207] und *mickle* [Schmidt 718] zu rechnen haben), dass jedoch die Zahl der Kasusvertauschungen bei Shakspere eine verhältnismässig höhere ist, als bei den vorhergehenden Dramatikern, dass er *its* verwendet (worüber jedoch Zweifel herrscht), während er andrerseits *what so* (§ 224) nicht mehr kennt, und auch Verwechselungen von *your* und *you, my* und *me* (§ 167f.), *thy* und *the* (§ 169f.) sowie von *this* und *thus* (§ 202f.) bei ihm nicht vorzukommen scheinen.

Dagegen hat sich Shakspere die im elisabethanischen Drama so überaus beliebte Verwendung von Dialektstellen zum Zwecke der Komik (Aufzählung der in unseren Quellen sich findenden Dramen mit Dialektstellen siehe § 246, 3) nicht entgehen lassen; cf. Panning p. 7 f.

2. Spenser.

Auf die Sprache Spensers haben wir an verhältnismässig nur wenigen Stellen der „Weiterentwicklung" hingewiesen, da hier vornehmlich Archaismen von Interesse waren, die sich als Eigentümlichkeiten dieses Dichters darstellten.

Hierzu gehören die Verbindung von *thilk* (§ 50, Günther p. 63), *ilk* (§ 51, Günther p. 63) von *none* vor Konsonanten (§ 68 Anm. 2, Günther p. 69), und von *to list* als unpersönliches Verbum (Anhang I § 272, Günther p. 38).

Die Verwendung von *self* für *himself* (§ 197, Günther p. 64 f.) sowie einige andere Erscheinungen wie die Auslassung des Personalpronomens (§ 89 ff., Günther p. 18 ff.), *his* als Genitivbezeichnung (§ 164, Günther p. 63) *none* in neutralem Sinne (§ 237, Günther p. 68), die Wiederaufnahme des Relativs durch ein Personalpronomen (Anhang II § 300 f, Günther p. 17) sowie die Apposition statt eines partitiven Genitivs (Anhang IV § 306, Günther p. 63 f.) können nicht eigentlich als Eigentümlichkeiten[1]) Spen'sers gelten, da sie zu seiner Zeit noch mehr oder weniger allgemein im Gebrauch sind.

§ 258.
XIII. Bibelsprache.

1. Verhältnis von Tyndale's English New Testament zu der Auth. Vers. von 1611 und der Rev. Vers. von 1881.

Aehnlich wie bei der „Weiterentwicklung" im Grossen, haben wir jedesmal bei den Belegen aus Tyndale's English New Testament im Kleinen die Fassung der Auth. Vers. und der Rev. Vers. beigefügt. Die Sprache der Bibel ist bekanntlich sehr konservativ — unsere Untersuchung hat das aufs neue dargethan. Trotzdem ist doch manches alte geschwunden: So ist *tho* in *those* bezw. *the* geändert (§ 48 Anm.), desgleichen *whomsoever* in *whom* (§ 61 Anm. 2), das Personalpronomen in

---

[1]) Demgemäss ist auch der Titel der Günther'schen Untersuchung inkorrekt, denn was G. behandelt, ist weit mehr als blosse **Eigentümlichkeiten Spensers**.

der Anrede vor dem Vocativ ist jetzt weggelassen (§ 98, 4), desgl. das pleonastische Personalpronomen bei relativer Anknüpfung (§ 110, 2 Anm.), und auf orthographischem Gebiete ist das schon bei Tyndale merkwürdige *feawe* (§ 75 Anm.) durch *fewe* ersetzt.

In anderen Punkten ist die Modernisierung auf halbem Wege stehen geblieben:

So ist das ältere *myn, thyn* (§ 20 Anm. 1) teils beibehalten teils nicht, desgl. das Pronomen beim Imperativ (§ 98, 3), *to turn* und *to return* werden nur zum Teil noch mit reflexivem Pronomen verbunden (§ 180).

Demgegenüber sind nun eine ganze Reihe von Archaismen in die Auth. Vers. und in die Rev. Vers. übergegangen:

So die formelhafte Redensart *if so be*, allerdings nur in einem Falle (§ 101 Anm.), die Verwendung des pleonastischen Personalpronomens in gewissen Fällen (§ 107, 110), der Gebrauch von *thou* als gegenseitige Anrede (§ 150), die in § 153 behandelte Trennung der Kompositionsglieder von *toward*. *His* als possessive Beziehung auf ein Neutrum ist nicht durch *its* ersetzt worden (Wright 317), ebensowenig ist *his* zur Bezeichnung des Genitivs geändert worden (Wright 318). Die ältere Ausdrucksweise *this my son* (§ 166 b), auch *him* zur Bezeichnung des reflexiven Verhältnisses in einigen Fällen (Wright 316), desgl. *his own self* und *their own selves* (§ 192) sowie *what* im Sinne von *why* (§ 219, Wright 650) sind beibehalten worden.

Ebenso ist in der Bildung der Relativsätze keine wesentliche Aenderung eingetreten (cf. Anhang II 2 b § 299).

2. Einfluss der Bibelsprache auf andere Werke.

Dass die Sprache der Bibel auf Werke, die ihren Stoff im wesentlichen aus dieser schöpfen oder sich mit religiösen Angelegenheiten beschäftigen, von nicht geringem Einflusse ist, dürfte an und für sich schon keinem Zweifel unterliegen und ist von uns insbesondere bei der Verwendung von *thou* in der Anrede bemerkt worden (cf. § 143, 144, 145, 3).

§ 259.

XIV. Textkritisches.

Als schliessliche Folgerungen schliessen wir an unsere Untersuchung eine Reihe von Betrachtungen textkritischer Art:

1. Jack Straw 394
*He promised us to meet us on the water,
And by [our] Lady, as soon as we came to the waterside,
He fair and flat turns his barge...*

Diese Aenderung ist unnötig und die Ueberlieferung wiederherzustellen; die Verbindung *by Lady* mit Unterdrückung des Possessivpronomens ist in der 2. Hälfte des 16. Jahrhunderts im Drama gebräuchlich (cf. § 22 Anm.).

2. Marlowe, Tamburlaine 3102
Die von Wagner verteidigte Lesung *other* anstatt des von neueren Herausgebern eingesetzten *others* wird durch unsere Erörterung ein für allemal festgelegt (cf. § 83 Anm. 2).

3. Paston Letters 36/48
I pray yow hertely that [ye] wol wochesaf to sende me a letter as hastely as ȝe may...

Da das Personalpronomen als Subjekt fehlen kann, wenn es sich aus einem vorhergehenden Kasus obliquus ergänzen lässt (cf. § 96), so ist die Conjectur ungerechtfertigt.

4. Peele, Edward I 176
Bind fast the traitour and bring him away, that the law may justly pass upon him, and [he] receive the reward of monstrous treasons and villainy...

Die Einsetzung von *he* ist hier ebensowenig zwingend wie die von *ye* unter 3.

5. Damon and Pithias 81
Go to, then; since you begun, do as [it] please ye.

Diese Conjectur ist unmotiviert, da die Auslassung des *it* in unpersönlichen Sätzen in der 2. Hälfte des 16. Jahrhunderts noch möglich ist (cf. § 99 b und als nächste Parallelen Jacob and Esau 226 *if please you*, ib. 261 *as pleaseth you*), und ferner keiner der alten Drucke *it* hat.

6. Soliman and Perseda 360
*A matter not unlikely: but how chance[th]
Your Turkish bonnet is not on your head?*

Die Aenderung von *chance* in *chanceth* ist ungerechtfertigt; § 99 Anm. erklärt das formelhafte *how chance*, das sich in unserem Falle wie bei Shakspere (cf. Abbot § 37) auch bei der 3. Person findet.

7. Marlowe, Edward II 230
Well, and fortunes it that he came not?

Die Einsetzung von *it* ist sprachlich nicht gerechtfertigt; *it* kann noch im 16. Jahrhundert fehlen (§ 100) auch bei Marlowe, cf.

Massacre of Paris 349
But what availeth that this traitor's dead...?

8. Marlowe, Dido 432
Ah, foolish Dido, to forbear this long! —

Eine Aenderung in *thus* (cf. ib. die Fussnote) ist nach § 202 f. zurückzuweisen, um so mehr, als wir in demselben Drama p. 428 *this long* haben.

9. Flügel (Lieder Wedderburns) 131/48
[Whome Christ had ransomit on the Rude].

Für das von Flügel fälschlich ergänzte *Whome* ist nach Zeile 30 *quhome* einzusetzen.

Anhang I.
Zum Uebergang von unpersönlichen Verben in persönliche.

§ 260.
Vorbemerkung.

Obwohl es ursprünglich nicht in unserer Absicht lag, auf diese Frage einzugehen, machten doch einzelne Punkte der vorangegangenen Untersuchung eine Nebensammlung hierfür notwendig, und da wir nun vollends bei weiterem Fortschreiten thatsächliche Unrichtigkeiten und Ungenauigkeiten in Kellners Darstellung (Einleitung zu Blanchardyn and Eglantine § 17) konstatieren mussten, stehen wir nicht an, die Ergebnisse hier folgen zu lassen. Aus praktischen Gründen wurde alphabetische Reihenfolge gewählt.

§ 261.
1. Eigentliche Verben.

a) Verba im Activum.

to ail: Der persönliche Gebrauch ist schon aus dem Jahre 1425 (Oxf. Dict.) nachgewiesen worden, doch ist er im 15. Jahrhundert schwerlich sehr gebräuchlich gewesen. Die P. L. bieten keinen Beleg, dagegen

M. 858/37 ... *and therwyth al the felyshyp awoke and came to the bysshop and asked hym what he eyled.*

Darnach ist auch wohl persönlich zu fassen: ib. 859/8 ... *I doubte not syr Launcelot ayleth no thynge but good.*

Im übrigen unpersönlich z. B.: ib. 407/2 ... *what eyleth you...*, 508/29, 531/2, 546/10, 731/5 etc., Fox 21, 68, 69,

Digby Mysteries 34/197 *O mercyfull god, what aylyth me?* ib. 113/1545.

Im 16. Jahrhundert ist die unpersönliche Konstruktion vorherrschend, da es, wie schon Jespersen § 179 hervorhebt, meist in der Wendung *what ails him (her* etc.) gebraucht ist, z. B.:
Four Elements 41
> *Why, man, what aileth thee so to blow?*

Damon and Pithias 27 *What aileth them?*
Sidney, Arcadia 647
...Dorus...gave Mopsa occasion...to ask her lover Dorus what ailed him...

etc. etc.

Doch zeigen folgende Belege, dass auch die persönliche Konstruktion, besonders in der Umgangssprache des 16. Jahrhunderts, durchaus volkstümlich war.

G. G. Needle 174
> *I marvel in my mind what the devil they ail.*

ib. 221
See, gammer, gammer, Gib our cat, cham afraid what she aileth,
Lyly, Galathea 241 ...*tell mee what thou aylest...*
Peele, Edward I 138
> *Nor ask questions, what I ail,*

Marlowe, Jew 1193
> *Why, what ayl'st thou?*

Faust II 1205 *What a deuill ayle you two?*
Knack to Know a Knave 559
> *Alas, poor Piers Plowman! what ailest thou?*

Three Ladies 358 *Tell me, sweet wench, what thou ailest...*
Look about You 475
> *How now, what ail'st thou?*

Bei Shakspere persönlich und unpersönlich (Schmidt 26).

§ 262.

to chance: Erster Beleg für persönlichen Gebrauch aus dem Jahre 1400 (Oxf. Dict.). Es tritt in unseren Texten erst im 16. Jahrhundert auf, persönliche und unpersönliche Konstruktion nebeneinander, erstere überwiegt in der 1. Hälfte, wenn auch nicht sehr.

Vgl. z. B.: Latimer, Sermons 3 unpers. (71, 97, 106), 2 pers. (84, 175), More, Utopia 4 pers. (73, 87, 140, 142), 1 unpers. (47).

In der 2. Hälfte, besonders bei den Dramatikern, überwiegt
der persönliche Gebrauch bei weitem, z. B.:
  Kyd, Spanish Tragedy 87
    I may chance to break your old custom.
  Peele, Edward I 73
    But afterwards she chanc'd to pass
    Along brave London streets,
  Peele, Verm. 257, Marlowe, Tamburlaine 1144, Jew 1136,
Edward II 274, Greene, James IV 91, Bacon 159 etc. etc.
  Dagegen unpersönlich, z. B.:
  New Custom 35
    If it had chanced me in those days in thy hands to have fell,
  Disobedient Child 295
    When he shall wish that to him it may chance,
  Shakspere verwendet beide Konstruktionen (Schmidt 186).

§ 263.

to delight: Aus dem 15. Jahrhundert keine Belege; im
16. Jahrhundert herrscht der persönliche Gebrauch bei weitem
vor, z. B.:
  Fl. (Wyatt) 25/44   *sins ye delite to know*
    The causes why that homeward I me draw,
  Everyman 127
    Also thou delightest to go gay and fresh;
  Bale, Kynge Johan 73, Lusty Juventus 72, Cambyses 202,
Conflict of Conscience 141, Tancred and Gismonda 35, Marlowe,
Dido 413, Sidney, Arcadia 319.
  Demgegenüber unpersönlich:
  Conflict of Conscience 124
    Sith to forgive and do us good it chiefly him delights?
  Soliman and Perseda 316
    A man whose presence more delighted me;
  Marlowe, Hero 27, Ovid 179, Lodge, Wounds 181, Sidney,
Arcadia 305 etc.

§ 264.

to desire: Einziger Beleg für unpersönlichen Gebrauch
  Fox 84
    ...al thynge that me wold desire to wyte and knowe...

§ 265.

to forthynk: Me. nur unpersönlich (Stratmann), doch vgl. Kellner, Blanchardyn p. 47.

In unseren Texten nur in M. (dafür später *to repent, to rue*, s. d.)

M. 82/2 ...*that me forthynketh*...
ib. 324/17 ...*for me forthynketh of that I haue done*...
ib. 330/15 *That forthynketh me*...
ib. 643/12 ...*hit sore forthynketh me*...

Einmal persönlich: ib. 712/31 ...*for that he forthoughte hym ryzte moche that he had broken his promyse*...

Shakspere hat es nicht mehr (Schmidt).

§ 266.

to fortune (mysfortune): Im Me. nur unpersönlich (Stratm.); desgl. im 15. Jahrhundert, z. B.:

P. L. 58/71 *Yt fortunyd hym to be a spyed*...
M. 304/21 ...*hit fortuned me that I was a slepe*...
ib. 842/35 ...*it mysfortuned me to be stryken vpon thy stroke*.

Im 16. Jahrhundert wird es durch *to chance* und besonders durch *to happen* (s. d.) verdrängt.

Unpersönliche Konstruktion ward nur noch in der 1. Hälfte bemerkt: Fl. (Hall, Chr.) 236/14

Shortly after, it fortuned one George Constantine, to be apprehended by sir Thomas More...

Fl. (Paget an Heinrich VIII.) 350/50

...*if it shuld fortune Him to here.*

Dagegen persönlich:

Bale, Thre Lawes 1538

Els maye they fortune, to be of their purpose wyde.

R. A., Toxophilus 25 ...*I fortuned to come*...

Egerton Papers 32 (a. d. 1559)

...*if they should fortune to perishe for lake of one thing or of another*...

New Custom 13 *If ye fortune to come*...
ib. 26 ...*whatsoever we fortune to crave,*

Bei Shakspere nicht mehr in diesem Sinne (Schmidt 448).

§ 267.

to grieve: Im 15. und 16. Jahrhundert vorherrschend unpersönlich.

M. 444/16 ... *hit greued hym sore* ...
ib. 453/30 ... *the whiche shold greue yow moche more* ...
Tyndale, Phil. 3/1 *It greueth me not to write* ...
New Custom 10, Conflict of Conscience 75, Lyly, Euphues 328, Greene, Bacon 194, Introductory Sketch 57, Sidney, Arcadia 621 etc.

Persönliche Konstruktion erst in der 2. Hälfte des 16. Jahrhunderts, doch nicht überwiegend.

Kyd, Cornelia 186
  For one man grieveth at another's good,
Spanish Tragedy 164
  And griev'd I, think you, at this spectacle?
Peele, Edward I 198, Greene, James IV 77, Menaphon 36
  ... *how she grieued at his misfortune* ...
Marlowe, Ovid 153
  I grieve lest others should such good perceive,
Lucan 284
We grieve at this thy patience and delay (lat. conquerimur).
Sidney, Arcadia 258
  For who grieves not, hath but a blockish brain,
Lodge, Wounds 156 etc.

Shakspere hat persönliche und unpersönliche Konstruktion (Schmidt 497).

§ 268.

to happen (myshappen): Im Me. nur unpersönlich (Stratm.). Im 15. Jahrhundert noch vorwiegend desgl.

P. L. 58/71 *Yt happyd hym to have a knavys loste* ...
ib. 317/429 *And haped me ... we toke a schippe* ...
ib. 933/383 ... *yf it had not happyd me to have seyne them* ...
M. 80/15, 200/2, 242/25, 243/32, Fox 73,
M. 673/22, (811/6, Fox 33)
  Soo hit myshapped he loued a gentilwoman ...

In M. nicht einmal (Kellner, Blanch. 48), sondern mehrfach unzweideutig persönlich:

306/21 (356/15, 369/20, 443/33, 587/17, 726/23)
...*wel may he happen to smyte me doun*...
Fox 104 ...*I wold be sory yf ye myshapped.*

Im 16. Jahrhundert gehen unpersönliche und persönliche Konstruktion gleichberechtigt nebeneinander her. Die Wahl derselben hängt zum Teil von der Eigenart des Schriftstellers ab; so hat Asham wie More's Utopia niemals unpersönliche Konstruktion (pers. z. B.: Toxophilus 26, 89, Utopia 20); bei den elisabethanischen Dramatikern sowie bei Sidney und Puttenham ist die persönliche Regel. Bevorzugt wird dagegen die unpersönliche von Lyly, Euphues 35, 51, 101 etc. Im allgemeinen lässt sich sagen, dass die persönliche schon in der 1. Hälfte des 16. Jahrhunderts durchgedrungen ist.

Shakspere hat beides (Schmidt 511 nur je 1 Beispiel).

§ 269.

to joy: Schon Me. persönlich (Stratm.).

Fast ausnahmslos persönlich konstruiert, z. B.:
Damon and Pithias 24, Conflict of Conscience 40, Sidney, Astrophel and Stella 62/5, Greene, Friar Bacon 195, Marlowe, Edward II 171 etc. etc.

Dagegen unpersönlich nur:
Greene, Bacon 190
> *It joys me that such men of great esteem*
> *Should lay their liking on this base estate,*
Sir Clyomon and Sir Clamydes 517a
It joyeth me at the heart that I have met thee in this place.
Bei Shakspere persönlich und unpersönlich (Schmidt 606 f.).

§ 270.

to lack: Seit dem 15. Jahrhundert fast nur persönlich.
M. 238/18 (586/20, 688/15) ...*they lacked wynde bothe*...
Fl. (Book of St. Albans) 14/2
Si tibi deficiant medici...*Yf a man lacke leche or medicyne*...
Everyman 121, More, Utopia 118, R. A., Toxophilus 29, Tyndale, Phil. 4/10 (Auth. Vers. und Rev. Vers. ebenso), Bale, Kynge Johan 70, R. R. Doister 14, Damon and Pithias 38, Peele, Alcazar 107, Greene, James IV 87, Marlowe, Faust II 1554, Puttenham 282, Leycester Correspondence 257 etc. etc.

Dagegen: M. 115/15 ... *but now me lacketh an hors*...
Bei Shakspere nur persönlich (Schmidt 623).

§ 271.

to like (*dislike, mislike*): Ursprünglich persönlich und unpersönlich. Im 15. und 16. Jahrhundert persönlich und unpersönlich.

P. L. 70/88 ... *he lyked wel*... 215/301, 275/379, 332/456, 440/90, 502/186 etc.

M. (Kellner, Blanch. p. 48 unrichtig) 690/24
... *and he wold folowe there as she lyked.*

Die Fälle unpersönlicher Konstruktion überwiegen jedoch bei weitem; vgl. z. B. P. L. 715/76—830/246 (a. d. 1472—1479) 14 unpers. : 5 pers.

Was das 16. Jahrhundert anlangt, so ziehen Asham, Bale, Latimer und Tyndale die persönliche Konstruktion vor, die dann, wie das elisabethanische Drama zeigt, ständig auf Kosten der unpersönlichen vordringt. Doch weisen gerade die Dramatiker noch zahlreiche Fälle der letzteren auf, z. B.:

Lyly, Galathea 239, Greene, Friar Bacon 161, James IV 110, Marlowe, Faust 1078, 1256 ... *if it like your grace*... (formelhafte Höflichkeitswendung!), Edward II 227 etc. etc.

Also, die persönliche Konstruktion gewinnt gegen Mitte des 16. Jahrhunderts die Oberhand über die unpersönliche (doch nicht in dem Masse wie bei *to list*, s. d.).

Bei Shakspere beide Ausdrucksweisen.

§ 272.

to list: Ursprünglich unpersönlich, schon bei Gower persönlich. Im 15. Jahrhundert ist die persönliche Konstruktion nichts ungewöhnliches, die P. L. weisen schon zahlreiche Beispiele auf, z. B.: 179/238 ... *as long as thei lyst*...

318/431 ... *he list not to be commynd*...
besonders in der 2. pl.: 502/188 ... *yf ye luste*..., 505/193, 570/300, 706/66, 792/182, 933/377, M. 61/20, 114/32, 146/24, 206/35, Digby Mysteries 192/602 etc.

Daneben die unpersönliche noch in der Ueberzahl, z. B.:
P. L. 68/85 ... *to go with me in what port that me lust*...
ib. 201/278 ... *and kepte hym as long as them lyst*...

ib. 502/184, 668/4, 839/254, M. 71/34, 90/27, 148/21, 230/15, Rutland Papers 23, Fox 16, Caxton, Mirrour of the world and thymage of the same (Originaldruck der Göttinger Universitätsbibliothek) Ende des Vorworts
..*it liste hym of his most bounteous grace to departe with vs...*
Digby Mysteries 17/421 etc.

Der Sieg der persönlichen Konstruktion fällt direkt in den Anfang des 16. Jahrhunderts; sowohl Flügels Texte wie die sonstigen Denkmäler verschiedener Gattung dieser Zeit zeigen das, sogar die Poesie, z. B. Fl. (Wyatt) p. 18—29 6 pers : 3 unpers.

Erstere noch: Latimer, Sermons 202, Tyndale, Bibelvorwort p. 1, Bale, Thre Lawes 1264, Fl. (Volkslieder) 114/11, ib. (Skelton) 48/43, ib. (theol. Schriften) 243/1, ib. (Briefe) 333/6, Calisto and Melibaea 79, R. A., Schoolemaster 20, R. R. Doister 12 etc.

So nehmen nun im Laufe des 16. Jahrhunderts die Fälle der persönlichen Konstruktion stetig zu.

Im elisabethanischen Drama gehören die Fälle der unpersönlichen Konstruktion schon zu den Seltenheiten, Marlowe und Greene scheinen nur die persönliche zu gebrauchen; dagegen zeigt Peele noch häufiger die unpersönliche, man vgl. Arr. 17, 22, 28, 43, Verm. 175, 249, desgl. Jack Juggler 130, Marriage of Wit 333, Tancred and Gismonda 59.

An sich zweideutige Fälle aus dieser Zeit dürfen daher als persönliche Konstruktion aufgefasst werden, z. B.:

Greene, James IV 140 ...*what pretty triumph you list*... (nach ib. 97 *Even as he list:* etc.),

Like Will to Like 357

Virtuous Life, do what you list: (nach ib. 344 *who so list* etc.).

Begreiflich ist es natürlich, wenn in sprichwörtlichen Redensarten die unpersönliche Konstruktion gebraucht wird, vgl. Lyly, Euphues 189

Aristotle must dine when it pleaseth Philip. Diogenes when it listeth Diogenes...

Bei Shakspere nur persönlich (Schmidt 858), dagegen bei Spenser mehrfach unpersönlich (Günther p. 38).

Anm.: Der Fall Lusty Juventus 77
Do what your own lust, and say as they say;
ist eine Contamination aus *Do what you lust* und *Do your own lust*, was aus folgendem Beleg ersichtlich wird:

Four Elements 29
>Which would take no pains to sail farther
>Than their own list and pleasure;

§ 273.

to long: Ursprünglich unpersönlich, persönlich zuerst bei Laȝamon, begegnete in unseren Texten noch unpersönlich:
Fl. (Balladen) 185/126 *Me longeth sore to bernysdale*
ib. (desgl.) 192/24 *Me longeth sore her to se.*

Sonst persönlich: Joy, Ap. 41, Nice Wanton 166, Conflict of Conscience 108, Peele, Edward I 186, Greene, Verm. 273, Marlowe, Edward II 179, Sidney, Arcadia 353, Leyc. Corr. 142 etc.
Bei Shakspere nur persönlich (Schmidt 664).

§ 274.

to marvel: Schon me. persönlich. Fälle unpersönlicher Konstruktion begegneten nur im 15. Jahrhundert.
P. L. 521/223
Me mervelyt gretly off the certificat off Mr. Robert...
M. 221/33 *...that merueylled me sayd the black knyghte...*
ib. 665 1 *...one thynge merueilled me said syre Ector...*
ib. 666/18 *...the whiche merueylled them gretely.*
Digby Mysteries 76/567
>*me mervellyt sore þei be not here,*

Anc. Myst. ed. Hone 47
>*Me merveylyth, wyff!*

Sonst persönlich: P. L. 855/276, 865/293, 866/295, M. 74/10, 576/28, Digby Mysteries 37/248, 105/1325, Fl. 41/13, Bale, Thre Lawes 744, Jack Juggler 146, G. G. Needle 174 etc.
Bei Shakspere nur persönlich (Schmidt 697).

§ 275.

to myster cf. Kellner, Blanch. p. 49; weitere Fälle fielen uns nicht auf.

§ 276.

to need: Im Me. unpersönlich, desgleichen vorwiegend im 15. Jahrhundert, z. B.:

P. L. 255/348 ... *I have not usid to meddel with Lordes maters meche forther than me nedith;*
M. 101/1 ... *hym nedeth none...,*
ib. 216/35, 278/15, 412/13, 419/2,
Digby Mysteries 162/664
    We haue that nedith vs, so thryve I.
    etc.

Demgegenüber schon oft im M. (Kellner ungenau) persönliche Konstruktion:
M. 254/3 ... *that shalle ye not nede...,*
ib. 278/8, 715/8, 727/35, Fox 24.

Die persönliche Konstruktion dringt gleich nach 1500 durch, da sich nur noch wenige Fälle der unpersönlichen Konstruktion finden:
Suppl. of the Poore Commons 74
    ... *what neadeth them to seke any further?*
Fl. (More, Gedichte) 41/27
    Me nedeth not to bost.
Fl. (Balladen) 195/38
    It nedes me to layne.

Sonst persönlich in Poesie und Prosa:
Fl. (Roy and B.) 72/34, ib. (Barclay) 94/15, ib. (Balladen) 171/9, ib. (Briefe) 336/16, Tyndale, Luk. 22/71 (Auth. Vers. und Rev. Vers. andere Wendung), Heywood, P. P. 360, Latimer, Sermons 80, R. A., Toxophilus 29, R. R. Doister 34 etc. etc.

Bei Shakspere nur persönlich (Schmidt 763).

§ 277.
to owe: Me. persönlich und unpersönlich.

Im M. (Kellner ungenau) persönlich neben zahlreicheren unpersönlichen Fällen.

M. 1/37 *Affermyng that I ougt rather tenprynte his actes and noble feates...*

Dagegen ib. 242/16 ... *as me oughte to doo...,* 337/24, Fox 13, 47 etc.

In späterer Zeit wurde kein Fall des unpersönlichen Gebrauches mehr bemerkt.

Bei Shakspere nur persönlich (Schmidt 826).

§ 278.

to pity: Fälle persönlicher Konstruktion:
Bale, Kynge Johan 20
We pety yow now consyderyng yowr repentante modes,
Sidney, Arcadia 559
Alas how I pitied to hear thy pity of me;
Fälle unpersönlicher Konstruktion:
Bale, Kynge Johan 19
S. O. *Yt pyttyth me moche that ye are to them so harde.*
K. J. *Yt petyeth me more that ye them so myche regarde.*
ib. 44
It petyeth my hart to se the controvercye.
Bei Shakspere nur persönlich (Schmidt 865), unpersönlich bei Spenser, F. Qu. 4, 11, 1.

§ 279.

to please: Ursprünglich nur unpersönlich, ist es auch im 15. Jahrhundert noch fast ausschliesslich Impersonale. Belege in den P. L. und M. fast auf jeder Seite. Fälle persönlicher Konstruktion bemerkten wir P. L. 440/90 (1462)
...ye may excuse yow by me if ye please...
wo aber *ye* nach § 136 f. auch Accusativ sein könnte.
Digby Mysteries 192/625
He pleside to be born, and sowked my pape.
Doch sind sie auch in der 1. Hälfte des 16. Jahrhunderts noch selten und werden erst bei den elisabethanischen Dramatikern häufiger, wenn auch die unpersönliche Konstruktion noch überwiegt.
Da nur die Fälle persönlicher Konstruktion grösseres Interesse beanspruchen können, geben wir nur dafür Belege:
Plumpton Correspondence 154 (1501)
...insomuch as ye pleased not to content me...
Fl. (Hist. Volkslieder) 163/5
And yf your grace wold pleas to here
R. R. Doister 19
In the meane time sir, if you please, I wyll home,
Egerton Papers 58
so as here Matie may delyver if shee please...

Jacob and Esau 231 ... *if thou please*...
Nice Wanton 167 ... *preaching as she please!*
Marriage of Wit 373
    Dance you, sir, if you please...
Damon and Pithias 17
Therefore to a trimmer kind of mirth myself I apply:
Wherein though I please, it cometh not of my desert,
Lyly, Campaspe 124 (Sidney, Criticisims 29)
    your majestie may beginne where you please;
Rare Triumphs 150
    And if I please to smile...
Greene, Orlando 14
    That you may safely pass wher'er you please,
Looking Glass 105 *When I please*...
Bacon and Bungay 157
    Then let our fathers prize it as they please.
ib. 191 *try me if thou please.*
James IV 97
    I with my needle, if I please, may blot
    The fairest rose within my cambric plot:
Marlowe, Tamburlaine, Prolog 8
    And then applaud his fortunes as you please.
Edward II 201 (Faust 152)
    A trifle! we'll expel him when we please.
ib. 266 (Jew 753)
Who now makes Fortune's wheel turn as he please,
Faust 106
    Shall I make spirits fetch me what I please,
Dido 410
    That can call them forth whenas she please,
Ovid 156
    The parrot, into wood receiv'd with these,
    Turns all the godly birds to what she please.
Leycester Correspondence 161
    ...*and that*...*you wold please to dyrect one large better unto the boddy of the councell, as unto pryvate frendes.*

Der Grund, dass dieses Verb seinen unpersönlichen Charakter langsamer als andere verliert, liegt zweifellos zum grossen Teile darin, dass sein hauptsächlichstes Gebiet eine zur festen Formel gewordene, traditionell sich fortschleppende Redensart bildete.

Bei Shakspere persönlich und unpersönlich (Schmidt 872).

§ 280.

to repent: Me. unpersönlich und persönlich.

In den P. L. verhältnismässig nur wenige Fälle persönlicher Konstruktion:

P. L. 56/69 ...*they xul sore repent hem.*, ib. 146/193, 818/231 etc.

In den anderen untersuchten Denkmälern des 15. Jahrhunderts, insbesondere in M., beide Konstruktionen neben einander unter vorherrschen der unpersönlichen.

Unpersönlich: M. 96/33 *Me repenteth sayd balyn*...,
 ib. 106/34, 117/29, 185/25, Fox 28, 53;

Persönlich: M. 59/7 ...*but some of them may sore repente thys.* ib. 117/31, 224/26, 245/27, Fox 28, 34, Digby Mysteries 192/611.

Im 16. Jahrhundert sind die Fälle unpersönlicher Konstruktion selten:

Bale, Promises 293 *For it repenteth me*...

Tyndale, Bibelvorwort p. 5
 I repent peniteor, it repenteth me pacnitet me.

Rom. 11/29
 ...*it cannot repent him of them*... (Auth. Vers. „not repented of", Rev. Vers. „are without repentance").

Lyly, Euphues 186
...*it shal not repent thee of thy labour, nor me of my cost.*

Greene, Bacon and Bungay 205
 I tell thee, Bungay, it repents me sore,

Three Ladies 303
 it repents me I have let it so reasonable.

Bei Shakspere nur persönlich (Schmidt 962).

§ 281.

to rue (*rew*): Schon me. persönlich (Stratm.).

Mit vereinzelten Ausnahmen persönlich konstruiert im 15. und 16. Jahrhundert.

Unpersönlich: Fl. (Balladen) 179/125
> *Nay for god sayd the monke*
> *Me reweth I cam so nere*

ib. 193/16 *Full sore it rewyth me*
Interlude of Youth 12
> *If I fight, it will thee rue*

Persönlich: Digby Mysteries 14/343 (108/1414)
> *ye shuld it rue;*

Bale, Promises 298, World and Child 256, Conflict of Conscience 40, Misfortunes of Arthur 317, Peele, Arr. 31, Greene, Pinner 167, Marlowe, Dido 440, Lodge, Wounds 137 etc. etc.
Bei Shakspere nur persönlich (Schmidt 992).

§ 282.

to seme: Me. nur unpersönlich.
Belege persönlicher Konstruktion im 15. und 16. Jahrhundert:
P. L. 155
> *...wheder ye seme best to come your self...*

ib. 164/222
Item, I beseche yow if it may be...that ye wole take it to suyche on as yow seme best...

ib. 291/398
> *...as ye seme it shulde profite to be knowen...*

ib. 332/449 (links)
...as my seyd executores...shal seme best to plese God...

ib. 332/450 *...as they shall seme beste to the plesure of God.*
ib. 729/97 *...as ye shal seme gode.*
ib. 847/264 *...men seme it wer good...*
ib. 915/360 *...such as ye seme necessary.*
M. 76/12 *...as they semed best...*
ib. 442/5
Why sir sayd the knyght, seme ye that I am weyke and feble...

ib. 682/25
For a lady soo ledde the where thow semyd thy broder was slayne...

Godeffroy de Boloyne ed. Colvin, E. E. T. S. No. LXIV 29/30
But after, they chaunged theyr counseyl, and semed better, that they shold charge them with suche tributes...

Digby Mysteries 160/601
*these thynges be now so conuersaunt,
we seme it no shame.*

Fl. (geschichtliche Werke) 275/22
And afterward, as it was sayd he had a terrible dreame in his slepe semyng that he sawe horrible deuilles appeare vnto him...

Gorboduc 321
Nor which yourselfe haue seemed best to lyke.

Lyly, Euphues 420
For you seeme you beare good will to the game you cannot play at...

Aus unseren Belegen ergiebt sich, dass die im Laufe des 16. Jahrhunderts wieder aufgegebene Tendenz von to seme nach persönlicher Konstruktion doch einen ziemlich starken Rückhalt in der gesprochenen Volkssprache des 15. Jahrhunderts hatte; die Fälle im 16. Jahrhundert sind vereinzelte Ausläufer.

Bei Shakspere nur unpersönlich.

Anm.: Analog *me think* (§ 2·4 Anm.) erklärt sich *me seem* durch Contamination aus *I* (*ye you*) *seem* und *me seems*:

Damon and Pithias 79
Me-seem my head doth swim.

§ 283.

to shame: Schon me. persönlich. Im 15. Jahrhundert vorwiegend unpersönlich; aber in M. mehrfach persönlich (Kellner, Blanch. p. 50 unrichtig), cf.:

M. 248/23 ...*I shame me not*...
ib. 324/6 ...*for me shameth of that I haue done.*
ib. 622/6 ...*ye nede not to shame yow*...
ib. 774/2 ...*wolte thow shame thy self*...

Im 16. Jahrhundert nur persönlich:

Bale, Kynge Johan 88
I shame to rehearce the corruptyons of your state.

Kyd, Spanish Tragedy 129
*Then shamest thou not, Hieronimo, to neglect
The sweet revenge of thy Horatio?*

Greene, Orlando 12 *Shame you not...?*
Looking Glass 89, Verm. 303, Marlowe, Jew 342 etc.
Bei Shakspere nur persönlich.

§ 284.

to think:

Die unpersönliche Konstruktion ist im 16. Jahrhundert fast ausschliesslich auf *methinks* und *methought*, die durchaus volkstümlich sind, beschränkt.

Beispiele sind unnötig, man vergl. jedoch

Greene, Looking Glass 136

1. Search. *But stay, methinks I feel a smell of some meat or bread about him.*
2. Search. *So thinks me too.*

Im 15. Jahrhundert ist ausser diesen auch die unpersönliche Verbindung mit anderen Personalien ganz gebräuchlich (im 16. Jahrhundert fiel uns nur auf Fl. [Balladen] 189/116 *Them thought they herd a woman wepe*):

P. L. 18/34 *him thenketh*, ib. 100/139 *hym thought*, ib. 502/185 etc., M. 65/25, 71/22, 620/4 *hem thought*, 806/20 *vs thynketh* etc.

Daneben auch im 15. Jahrhundert persönlich:

P. L. 196/269 *...she thynkyt right strange...*
ib. 763/141 *Do as ye thynk best;*
ib. 916/362 *wherfor I thynke best that...*
M. (Kellner, Blanch. p. 50 unrichtig) 478/30
   ...as he thought best.
ib. 597/25 *And when they beheld hym...they thought they sawe neuer so goodly a man.*

Anm.: Das schon von anderen (auch von Jespersen § 177) durch Contamination aus *me thinks* und *I think* erklärte *me think* ist im (15. und) 16. Jahrhundert ausserordentlich verbreitet, man vergl. nur:

Plumpton Correspondence 30 (1475)
   ...me think it nott necessary so to do...
Bale, Kynge Johan 30
   By the mas, me thynke they are syngyng of placebo.
R. A., Toxophilus 100
   ..me thinck this is the wisest counsel...
Interlude of Youth 17
   Methink it were best therefore,

Jacob and Esau 222, Damon and Pithias 83
Me-think ich am lighter than ever ich was.
Udall, State 13, Greene, Looking Glass 129 (Lesart), James IV 118 (Lesart).

§ 285.
as it reherceth, sheweth, telleth etc.

Fand sich vornehmlich im M. (Aufzählung bei Kellner, Blanch. p. 50, zu denen für *it reherceth* noch die Belege 75/21 und 75/27 nachzutragen sind.

Im 16. Jahrhundert bemerkten wir nur 2 Belege:

Fl. (Odyssee XI, 362—366) 100/7
And that thy mynde ist good, it sheweth in thy face.
(Original „οἷς ὅτ' ἀοιδός".)

Peele, Vermischtes 237
Ill be to him, it saith, that evil thinks.

Vgl. im übrigen Kellner a. a. O.

§ 286.
b) Verba im Passivum.

Es handelt sich hier um die von Jespersen, dessen Einteilung wir übernehmen, in § 181 f. besprochenen Fälle. Es ist in diesem Abschnitte keine erschöpfende historische Darlegung und Erklärung beabsichtigt, sondern lediglich eine Darstellung des Zustandes im 15. und 16. Jahrhundert. Für die historische Entwicklung vergleiche man auch Koch § 147 ff.

α) Das Verb regiert ursprünglich den Dativ, hat aber kein Accusativobjekt.

Im 15. Jahrhundert haben wir die unpersönliche Konstruktion neben der persönlichen, die überwiegt, im 16. herrscht die persönliche entschieden vor.

αα) Belege für den unpersönlichen Gebrauch.
P. L. 460/112 (M. schon Kellner, Blanch. p. 55)
... *but thus it was told me, and desyryd me to kepe it secret;*
ib. ... *that it is informyd me thys day* ...
ib. 591/324 ... *it was warnid hym that my Lady Suffolk wolde entyr* ...
ib. 754/129 *it was never desyryd of me* ...

Calisto and Melibaea 64
And it was told me I should have found him here.
Hickscorner 161, Interlude of Youth 14,
Soliman and Perseda 276
And, when it was ask'd him where he had that musk,
He said all his kindred smelt so.
Leycester Correspondence 302
...and so was it informed me...

ββ) Belege für den persönlichen Gebrauch.
P. L. 283/389
It was not desired to write unto you of no on persone...
ib. 770/151 *wherfor if I mygh be pardond...*
M. (Kellner, Blanch. p. 55 nur 463/5, also unrichtig) 585/2
(597/4, Fox 77) *...and yet he shall be wel holpen...*
ib. 820/14 *For they were alle holpen...*
Digby Mysteries 38/277
for as I was commaundyd by hys gracyos sentens,
Plumpton Correspondence 161
...I am promysed suerly they will appere...
Fl. (Hall) 274/22 (Tyndale, Ap. 26/1 [Auth. Vers. und Rev. Vers. ebenso]) *And although you be permitted to reade...*
ib. (Briefe) 341/19 *I was offred to sitte downe...*
World and Child 254 (Disobedient Child 292)
To maintain manner ye were never taught;
Gorboduc 700
In secrete I was counselled by my frendes,
To hast me thence...
Jacob and Esau 235 (Marlowe, Edward II 280)
As I was commanded to fet herbs for the pot.
G. G. Needle 233 *Well, if ye will be ordered...*
Udall, Demonstr. 22 (Sidney, Arcadia 88)
...the prieste of God is not obeyed...
Tancred and Gismonda 70 *...as we were foretold...*
Sidney, Arcadia 38 *And he was answered by a man...*
Jack Straw 405 *...as I am given to understand,*
ib. *You are too many to be talked withal;*

§ 287.

β) Das Verbum ist mit einer Präposition verbunden.

Die passivische Konstruktion in diesem Falle ist durchaus nichts ungewöhnliches, jedoch gebräuchlicher im 16. Jahrhundert als im 15.

P. L. 18/34 (Sidney, Arcadia 54)
...he hath be stured by summe from his lernyng, and spoken to of diverse materes not behovefull...

M. (siehe auch Jesp. a. a. O.) 15/17
...how he was fougten with

Latimer, Ploughers 19 (Look about You 393)
...they geue not any iust occasion to be sclaundered and yll spoken of by the hearers...

Latimer, Sermons 25
...all preachers are to be eschewed, and in no wyse to be harkened vnto.

R. A., Schoolemaster 36 *...he is...little looked vnto...*

Udall, Demonstr. 39
...but they may bee otherwayes prouided for;

Puttenham 193 *...they be...much looked vpon...*

§ 288.

γ) Das Verbum regiert einen Accusativ und einen Dativ.

Wir bemerkten nur wenige, aber charakteristische Fälle.

P. L. 262/357
...and ye schall be paied hit truly at London...

Appius and Virginia 116
...and she was paid her hire.

Lyly, Euphues 143
They must nowe be taunted with sharpe rebukes, straight wayes admonished with fayre wordes, now threatned a payment, by and by promised a reward, and dealt withal as nursses do with the babes...

M. 626/15 (Verbindung von 2. und 3.)
And soo it befelle that a man of Kynge Euelaks was smyten his hand of...

§ 289.

2. *to be* in Verbindung mit einem Adjektiv.

to be better (best):

Jespersen § 180. Die im 15. Jahrhundert noch übliche unpersönliche Konstruktion (Kellner, Blanch. p. 47) findet sich im 16. Jahrhundert nicht mehr; dagegen die persönliche:

Lusty Juventus 75
  Whether were I better to be ignorant and blind,
Interlude of Youth 16 *He were better to bide still;*
Jacob and Esau 239
  I were best also to get me into the tent.
Disobedient Child 270 (314)
  What thing I were best to take in hand,
Cambyses 184 ... *she were better be hanged*...
Jack Juggler 139
  Yet were I better ... to turn home again,
Conflict of Conscience 97
  But you were not best to trust to his courtesy:
G. G. Needle 176, Damon and Pithias 64, Greene, Pinner 198, Marlowe, Massacre 306, Lodge, Wounds 131, Three Ladies 351, Look about You 503 *You're best be quiet;*
  etc. etc.

Bei Shakspere pers. und unpers. bei *best* (Schmidt 106), bei *better* nur einmal unpers., sonst pers.

to be lief:

Unpersönliche Konstruktion wie im 15. Jahrhundert bei *be leuer* (Kellner, Blanch. p. 48) ist in unseren Texten des 16. Jahrhunderts nicht mehr anzutreffen; dagegen persönliche:

Hickscorner 180
  Thou shalt abide, whether thou be lief or loth;
Appius and Virginia 151
  As lief I were near in Limbo bands.
Peele, Edward I 138, Arr. 31, 60.
Bei Shakspere anscheinend nicht mehr (Schmidt 649).

to be like(ly):

Bis ins 16. Jahrhundert, obwohl hier überwiegend persönlich gebraucht, gilt die unpersönliche Konstruktion.

Unpersönlich: P. L. 415/50
...and it is like to be a fowle noyse...
Peele, Edward I 145
Then, niece, 'tis like that you shall have a husband.
Marlowe, Ovid 109
Were Love the cause, it's like I should descry him;
Leycester Correspondence 381 etc.
Persönlich:
P. L. 389/11 ... *bribery is like to be usid*...
M. 745/18, Digby Mysteries 42/394, Bale, Promises 297, Kynge Johan 23, Thre Lawes 854, G. G. Needle 204, Peele, Arr. 58, Marlowe, Verm. 306, Sidney, Arcadia 750 etc.
Dasselbe gilt für Shakspere (Schmidt 653).

to be loth:
Seit Chaucer Fälle persönlicher Konstruktion; cf. Kellner, Blanch. p. 49.
Im 15. Jahrhundert unpersönlich (M. 420/26, 422/24) und persönlich (M. 418/16, Digby Mysteries 6/135).
Im 16. Jahrhundert nur persönlich: Heywood, P. P. 359, Greene, Pinner 183, Marlowe, Dido 429.
Bei Shakspere nur persönlich (Schmidt 662).

to be well:
Persönliche Konstruktion bemerkten wir nur in den von uns sonst nicht untersuchten
Pansies from Penshurst and Wilton 32 (Sidney)
Well was I, while vnder shade
Oten reedes me musike made;
(gegenüber Jacob and Esau 287 *well is me!*)
Dieser Fall erklärt sich durch Anlehnung an ähnliche Verbindungen wie *to be woe* sowie Fälle wie
Marlowe, Edward II 185 *Happy were I!*

to be woe:
Im 15. und 16. Jahrhundert beide Konstruktionen nebeneinander, z. B.:
Unpersönlich: Digby Mysteries 196/747
O swete, swetist child! woo be vn-to me!
World and Child 269 *Alas! alas! that me is woe!*

Persönlich: Digby Mysteries 15,366
I am wo for the wrokyng of this worke wylde,
Hickscorner 147 *Though she was woe...*
Heywood, P. P. 347
But be ye sure I would be woe,
Greene, Verm. 219 *He was glad, I was woe,*
Desgl. bei Shakspere (Schmidt 1386).
Zur Erklärung des Uebergangs in persönliche Konstruktion dienen Fälle wie:
Heywood, Pardoner and Friar 217
Woe be that man, saith our Lord, that giveth no audience,
Bale, Kynge Johan 56
Naye, wo ys that peple that hathe so cruell rewlars.
ib. 74
Woo is that persone whych is undreneth your lawe.
     etc. etc.
 Anm.: In dem Fall Appius and Virginia 133
  By her I live, by her I die, for her I joy or woe,
ist *woe* als (persönliches) Verbum gefasst.

§ 290.
Zur Erklärung des Uebergangs unpersönlicher Verba in persönliche.

Jespersen (§ 173 ff.) hat es bereits unternommen, die hier besonders in Betracht kommenden psychologischen Gründe dieses Uebergangs in übersichtlicher Weise darzulegen. Indem wir darauf verweisen, wollen wir versuchen, Jespersens Ausführungen nach mehreren Richtungen hin zu ergänzen.

1. Unklarheit, ob persönliche oder unpersönliche Konstruktion.

a) Jesp. § 175. Diese Unklarheit musste bei Verbindung von ursprünglich unpersönlichen Verben mit Substantiven seit dem Verfall der Substantivflexion eintreten.

Im 15. und 16. Jahrhundert, die, im ganzen gerechnet, den Umschwung vollendet haben, ist dieser Prozess so gut wie vollzogen, und da unpersönliche Verben wie mit Pronomen ebenso mit Substantiven verbunden wurden, mussten diese Fälle, die kein äusseres Merkmal in der Unterscheidung der Person boten, einen nicht geringen Einfluss ausüben und das Gefühl für die ursprüngliche unpersönliche Konstruktion trüben.

Solche an sich zweideutigen Fälle sind, falls die Ermittelung der Konstruktion wünschenswert oder erforderlich ist, auf Grund der allgemeinen sprachlichen Zeitverhältnisse unter Berücksichtigung etwa vorhandener individueller Verschiedenheiten nach den zweifellos sicheren zu beurteilen.

b) So sind wohl **unpersönlich zu fassen** die Fälle mit *to ail* in der Frage, z. B.:

R. R. Doister 26 *What ayleth thys fellowe?*
Peele, Edward I 125 *What ails my Nell?*
Greene, Looking Glass 112
What ails the centre of my happiness,
Marlowe, Dido 408 *What ails my queen?*
etc. etc.

c) In § 99 haben wir gesehen, dass die **Auslassung von** *it* in unpersönlichen Sätzen, wenn das Verbum mit einem Objekt verbunden ist, im 15. und (doch weniger, cf. ib.) 16. Jahrhundert eine ganz gewöhnliche Erscheinung war. Dieser Umstand, verbunden mit der **Flexionslosigkeit der Substantiva** bringt nun ferner Fälle hervor, deren Konstruktion nur schwer oder gar nicht ohne Berücksichtigung anderer ermittelt werden kann.

Man vergl. z. B.: P. L. 234
... to whom your good grace lyke to yife credence.
Misfortunes of Arthur 283
The laws do licence as the sovereign lists.
P. L. 150/204
And also please your greet wisdams to conceyve...
Plumpton Correspondence 28
And please your good maistershipp to witte...
Egerton Papers 318
...whereof your Lo. may please to informe your selfe...
(vielleicht unpersönlich wegen der sonst hier überwiegenden unpersönlichen Konstruktion).

Peele, Verm. 183
And now the Greeks, and now the Troyans may,
As pleaseth Fortune, bear away the day.
Marlowe, Edward II 240
So pleaseth the queen my mother, me it likes:
etc. etc.

Solche und ähnliche Fälle mussten das Gefühl der Unsicherheit mit erzeugen oder wenigstens erhöhen, also **direkter Einfluss**.

d) Demgegenüber können wir jedoch in den Fällen mit *ye* bezw. *you* nur von einer Wechselwirkung sprechen, da beide im 15. und 16. Jahrhundert als Nominativ und als Accusativ vorkommen (§ 135 ff.).

Solche Fälle sind z. B., um aus der grossen Zahl nur zwei herauszugreifen:

P. L. 870/303 ...*demeane it as you list,*
Jack Juggler 126 *At the devil, if you lust:*
etc. etc.

§ 291.
2. Einfluss begrifflich gleicher oder ähnlicher Verben und Wendungen.

a) Begrifflich gleiche oder ähnliche Verben.

Ein ganz bedeutendes psychologisches Moment für den Wandel in die persönliche Konstruktion bilden Verben, die von gleicher oder ähnlicher Bedeutung mit unpersönlichen sind, z. B. für *to like* und *to list*:

to laugh: Bale, Kynge Johan 76
By the messe, I laugh to see thys cleane conveyaunce:
Greene, Verm. 263
Iris and Aeol laugh within a while
To see this glee.

to love: Everyman 116 *She loveth to go to feasts...*
R. A., Toxophilus 98 ...*yf I loued you neuer so ill...*
Marlowe, Edward II 239
'A loves me better than a thousand Spensers.

to will: Lyly, Woman 209
Go where thou wilt, so I be rid of thee.
Marlowe, Edward II 184 *Live where thou wilt...*

Für *to marvel*:
to wonder: Bale, Kynge Johan 19
I wonder that yow for such veyne popych baggage
Can suffyr England to be impoveryshed.

§ 292.

b) Verbindung ursprünglich unpersönlicher Verben mit persönlichen.

P. L. 752/127
Yf ye lyk be the prys of them, and ye wol have them, send me word.
Calisto and Melibaea 80
    Say what thou wilt, and for whom thou lest.
    R. A., Schoolemaster 63 ... *I both like and loue...*
    ib. 150 ... *I like and loue best...*
Lyly, Euphues 395
I loue the company of women well, yet to haue them in lawfull Matrimony, I lyke much better...
Sidney, Astrophel and Stella 2/5
    I sawe and lik'd, I lik'd, but loued not,
Peele, Arr. 53
    Then, as I look'd, I lov'd and lik'd attonce,
Greene, Verm. 278
    Ah, but had Coridon now seen the star that Alexis
    Likes and loves so dear...
ib. 279
Once was she lik'd and once was she lov'd of wanton Alexis:
Marlowe, Dido 409
    Whiles Dido lives and rules in Juno's town, —
    Never to like or love any but her!
Disobedient Child 281
    We marvel and wonder to see them so lean;
Jack Juggler 146
    Nay, I marvel and wonder at it more than ye;
Die Bedeutung solcher Verbindungen für das Durchdringen der persönlichen Konstruktion bedarf keiner weiteren Erläuterung.

§ 293.

c) Begrifflich gleiche oder ähnliche Wendungen.
Mit *to be*:
    M. 427/14 ... *Kynge Marke was ashamed...*
    Fl. (Volksbücher) 292/27 ... *the emperour that was ashamed...*
    Bale, Kynge Johan 88
    Ye are not ashamed to fynde fyve priestes to synge,

Peele, Old Wives Tale 227 *You be ashamed...*
Marlowe, Jew 17 *I am asham'd to heare such fooleries.*
Marriage of Wit 373 *...whereat you were so griev'd,*
Mit *to have*:
Cambyses 243 *Wherein I had delight;*
Marriage of Wit 341
Should I have joy to think of marriage now, trow ye?
R. A., Schoolemaster 49
We haue lacke in England of soch good order,
P. L. 403/29 *...as he had lyst...*
M. 146/10 *...ye haue no luste to helpe hym.*
ib. 461/35, ib. 610/30 *...I haue no grete luste...*, Fl.(Balladen) 171/42,
P. L. 456/108 *I have nede of it now.*
M. 305/3. *...now haue I grete nede of you...*
ib. 442/4, Fox 68, Fl. (Skelton) 59/18, Greene, Menaphon 47.
Mit *to take*:
Marriage of Wit 343 *...in whom she taketh delight,*
Conflict of Conscience 109
But those...Do take delight to live therein;
Andere Wendungen:
R. A., Toxophilus 43 *...they that stande mooste in nede...*
Lyly, Euphues 62 *...shee must needes coniecture so...*
Greene, James IV 134
Of evils needs we must choose the least:
Marlowe, Jew 242
That you will needs haue ten yeares tribute past,.

Dass auch Wendungen dieser und ähnlicher Art von Einfluss waren, dürfte keinem Zweifel unterliegen.

Anm.: Umschreibende Wendungen in unpersönlicher Konstruktion fallen demgegenüber nicht ins Gewicht. Häufiger ist nur:
Kyd, Spanish Tragedy 145
It was my chance to write a tragedy,
Peele, Alcazar 145, Knack to Know a Knave 562, Mucedorus 209 etc.
Andere sind viel seltener, z. B.:
Sidney, Astrophel and Stella XCVII
It was my fortune...to light vpon the famous deuice...
Angry Women 392
Because it was my hap so long to tarry,
Sidney, Arcadia 322 *...so it fell out, that this Zelmane...*

§ 294.

3. Verbindung ursprünglich unpersönlicher Verben mit anderen persönlichen.

P. L. 91,122
and be them shal ye never be deseyved, ner repente you off.
Gorboduc 1066
We like and praise this spede will in you,
Lyly, Euphues 449
This aunswer Alexander both lyked and rewarded…
Conflict of Conscience 40
At first, therefore, you did lament and rue
The misery of these our days, and great calamity,
Marlowe, Edward II 172
What so thy mind affects, or fancy likes.

Die Zahl der Fälle dieser Art, die auch das ihrige beigetragen haben, lässt sich leicht vermehren.

Anhang II.
Zum Bau der Relativsätze im 15. und 16. Jahrhundert.

§ 295.
Vorbemerkung.

Dieses Kapitel, das der Syntax des Satzes angehört und daher nicht in den Rahmen unserer Untersuchung fällt, wenn es auch zum Teil in unser Gebiet übergreift, behandeln wir daher gesondert. In der äusseren Einteilung schliessen wir uns der durch die Natur der Sache sich ergebenden Einteilung Kellners (Outl. § 112 ff., Blanch. 41 ff.) an.

§ 296.

1. Der ganze Hauptsatz geht voran, der Relativsatz folgt.

a) Das Relativum steht im Nominativ.

Als Regel gilt die heutige Konstruktion.

Dagegen haben wir seltene Fälle mit pleonastischem Personalpronomen; den von Kellner, Blanch. p. 41 aus M. (330/24, 334/2, 407/21) mit me. Parallelen (aus Koch § 349) angeführten Belegen können wir hinzufügen:

P. L. 306/418

... *declare hym his dewte, wheche, as myn reccyvore seyth, hit wole drawe to the summe of XLV li.*

Fl. (Balladen) 166/35

All þat folowt my lyne
And to my favour they did enclyne
they may well bane the tyme

Damon and Pithias 12

The matron grave, the harlot wild, and full of wanton toys.
Which all in one course they no wise do agree;

Sidney, Arcadia 326
...his launces, which though strong to give a launcely blow indeed, yet so were they coloured with hooks near the mourn...

Diese Fälle bilden nur eine besondere Art derjenigen, wo das Subjekt überhaupt durch ein Personalpronomen wiederaufgenommen wird (§ 108, 110).

Anm.: Schon me. (Mätzner II, 22) zeigt sich nach *what* ein pleonastisches *it*, z. B.:

C. d. L. 1084 *Kyng Richard bethought hym that tyde, What it was best.*

Fälle dieser Art erklären sich durch den Einfluss derjenigen, wo *it* berechtigte Geltung hat, und stellen sich demnach als eine Contamination von *what was best* und *it was best* dar.

Das 15. und das 16. Jahrhundert führen diesen Gebrauch fort.

P. L. 829/245
Qwhat it shal lyke yow to commande me yn this or eny odir, ye shal have myn service redy.

M. 309/12 ...*to doo with her what it please you...*

ib. 654/2 ...*now shal ye doo with me what soo hit please yow...*

ib. 751/32 ...*I maye not warne syr Gawayne to say what it pleased hym.*

ib. 802/9 ...*and thenne may ye doo with me what it lyketh yow.*

Fox 32
...*ye wille doo on me what it shal plese yow...*

Fl. (Volksbücher) 289/31
Men alsoo worke by me and dryue me in lengthe and bred and forge of me what it pleasith them...

Appius and Virginia 128
I do what it please me within this my realm.

Introductory Sketch 32
...*and what soeuer it pleaseth the ordinairie.*

ib. 148 ...*by opening what it is, on either part, that keepeth the wound green;*

Puttenham 281
...*whatsoeuer it might become king Alexander of his regal largesse to bestow vpon a poore Philosopher vnasked...*

Sidney, Arcadia 291
...*he was nothing but what it pleased Zelmane;*

§ 297.

b) Das Relativum steht in einem Kasus obliquus.

Die jetzt allein übliche Fügung gilt als Regel. Daneben erscheinen (schon ae. und me., Kellner, Blanch. p. 41) statt der einfachen Relativa

im Genitiv : Relativ + *his (her), their,*
im Dativ u. Acc. : Relativ + *him (her, it), them.*

Ebenso im 15. und 16. Jahrhundert:

P. L. 817/227

...*with other dyveres that I know not ther names;*

• M. 393/34 (andere aus M. schon bei Kellner a. a. O.)

And that olde knyght had fyue sones at the turnement, for whom he prayed god hertely for their comyng home.

P. L. 68/84 (72/93)

...*ever deseryng to her of yowr wurshupfull ustate, the whyche All myghte God mayntayne hyt, and encrese hyt on to hys plesans:*

ib.

Mo over, mayster, I send yow word, by Rauly Pykeryng, of all maters, the whyche I be seche yow yeve hym credens, as he wyll enforme yow of all;

ib. 96/129

...*Sir Thomas Tudenham had a joynte patent with the Duke of Suffolk, which, if it be resumed, Sir Thomas Stanley hath a bille redy endossed therof.*

ib. 839/254

...*bothe the wynter sale and the somer sale, wherof the veker of Sporle and William Halman have the other parties of them...*

Fox 115

...*ye be one of them that oweth me homage, whiche I wyl that ye allway so doo. (!)*

Fl. (Caxton) 6/30

For I fynde many of the sayd bookes, whyche wryters haue abrydgyd it many thynges left out.

Joy, Ap. 45

...*I changed some wordis and sentencis, which T. aftir me was compelled euen as I did, so to change and correcke them himselfe.*

More, Utopia 60

...*and also by sellinge priuileges and licenses, whyche the better that the prince is forsothe, the deerer he selleth them:*

Damon and Pithias 23
But which, into one trip or other, I might trimly them catch,
Lyly, Euphues 416
... the Diall, which though it go, none can see it going ...
Puttenham 54
... with other things autentike, which because we are not able otherwise to attaine to the knowledge of, by any of our sences, we apprehend them by memory ...
Peele, Alcazar 146
Whom by the heels I dragg'd from out the pool,
And hither have him brought thus fil'd with mud.
Marlowe, Dido 404
Mean time Ascanius shall be my charge;
Whom I will bear to Ida in mine arms,
And couch him in Adonis' purple down.

Aus den angeführten Belegen ersehen wir, dass diese im 15. Jahrhundert weiter verbreitete Konstruktion im 16. Jahrhundert an Boden verloren hat. In den beiden letzten Fällen wird das Relativum durch ein Personalpronomen im zweiten koordinierten Satze fortgeführt.

§ 298.

2. Der Hauptsatz wird durch den Relativsatz in zwei Hälften geteilt.

Als Regel gilt im 15. und 16. Jahrhundert der heutige Zustand. Doch wird (was im Ae. geradezu Regel ist, cf. Kellner, Blanch. p. 43) in zahlreichen Fällen das Korrelativ als Subjekt oder Objekt wieder aufgenommen.

a) Das pleonastische Personalpronomen steht im Nominativ, wenn das Beziehungswort Subjekt des Hauptsatzes ist. Diese Fälle sind bereits beim Personalpronomen (§ 110, 1) erörtert worden. Zu den dort angeführten Fällen tragen wir noch nach:

World and Child 274
All they that hath kept God's service
They shall be crowned in heaven bliss,
Sir Clyomon and Sir Clamydes 509 b
The knights that here were captives kept, they are by me at liberty,

§ 299.

b) Das pleonastische Personalpronomen steht in einem Kasus obliquus, wenn das Beziehungswort (direktes oder indirektes) Objekt des Hauptsatzes ist.

Fl. (theol. Schriften) 217/1
More over these that are in the same dignities the moost parte of them doth go...

P. L. 349/513
He or they that hafe infoormyd the Lordes wele of me, I am behold to hem;

Tyndale, Joh. 1/12
But as many as receaued hym, to them he gaue power to be the sones of God (Auth. Vers. und Rev. Vers. ebenso).

P. L. 311/422
and the that be bar, late hem be reysyd.

ib. 466/126
...and confessed over that the same dager he slewe hym with, he kest it in sege...

M. 274/32
But the sorou that the kyng made for his quene that myghte no tong telle.

ib. 503/33
Thenne said Palomydes he that oweth that sheld, lete hym dresse hym to me...

Fox 27
They that were wonte to sytte there, I haue than a waye...

Mysteries ed. Hone 41
He that gaff this co'nsell, lete hy' geve the comforte a lon,

Heywood, P. P. 388
    And all that hath scaped us here by negligence,
    We clearly revoke and forsake it;

Latimer, Sermons 86
And that which is here spoken of wine, he meaneth it of al actes in the cytye...

Fl. (Wyatt) 27/19
    And he that sufferth offence withoute blame
    Call him pitefull...

ib. (theol. Schriften) 217/8
but he that is greatter amonge you, let him be minister.

R. A., Toxophilus 58
Therfore they that wyll not go to farre in playing, let them folowe this counsell of the Poete.

More, Utopia 87
So that which he myghte haue vpholden wyth lytle coste, hys successoure is constreyned to buylde yt agayne...

G. G. Needle 183
A hundred things that be abroad cham set to see them well:
ib. 210, 232, Udall, Demonstr. 24, Kyd, Jeronimo 383,

Greene, Orlando 28
You that are the rest, get you quickly away;

Puttenham 182
...for so many of them as be notoriusly vndecent, and make no good harmony, I place them in the chapter of vices...

Briefe Elizabeth's 84
The small token you shall receave from me I desire yt may serve to make you remember the tyme...

Sidney, Arcadia 856
Those that judge him, let them execute me.

Diese Konstruktion ist, wie unsere Belege zeigen, im 15. und 16. Jahrhundert durchaus volkstümlich und in allen Literaturgattungen vertreten. In zahlreichen Fällen haben wir ein wirkliches Anakoluth anzunehmen.

§ 300.

3. Der Relativsatz geht dem Hauptsatz voran.

Die Verwendung des pleonastischen Personalpronomens ist dieselbe wie unter 2.

a) Das Personalpronomen im Nominativ.

P. L. 122/163
It is apoynted that who shall sue any bille in the Parlement, thei must be put into the Commone Hous...

ib. 349/512
Who so ever sey that of me, he lyeth falsly in hise hede...

ib. 371/546
What ever ye have of me, ye may sey it is found in the stywardes boks...

Mysteries ed. Hone 42
Yet who hath grace he needeth kepyng sor',

M. 378/22 (123/36, 176/35)
...who þat may fyrst mete ony of these two knyghtes they shold torne hem vnto Morgan...

Fox 84
...and what man loked in the glasse had he ony dissease ...he shold be anon heled of it.

Fl. (Briefe) 338/23
And what soeuer should mishappc me, it laye not in my power...

Latimer, Sermons 155
Who beareth wyth other folkes offences, he communicateth wyth other folkes synnes.

Jack Juggler 117
*And whatsoever she to my mistress doth say,
It is written in the gospel of the same day.*

G. G. Needle 234
*Whoever it wrought, and first did invent it,
He shall, I warrant him, erc long repent it.*

Lyly, Euphues 220 (Endimion 30 *who so -- he*)
What-soeuer he hath written, it is not to flatter, for he neuer reaped anye rewarde by your sex...

Marprelate, Epistle 9
Whosocuer therefore clayme vnto themselues pastorall authoritie ouer those Christians, with whome they cannot possiblie at any time altogether in the same congregation sanctify the Sabboth: they are vsurping prelats, Popes and pettie Antichrists:

Peele, Edward I 185 ...*whate'er king Edward hears,
It lies in God and him to pardon all.*

Greene, Looking Glass 85 *Who — he,*
Sir Clyomon and Sir Clamydes 501a *whosoever — he,*
Puttenham 287 *whatsoever — it,*
Briefe Elizabeths 17
...you wyl remember, that who seaketh two stringes to one bowe, the may shute strong, but neuer strait;

Sidney, Arcadia 855
My Lords, what you will determine of me, it is to me uncertain ...

etc. etc.

§ 301.
b) Das Personalpronomen in einem Kasus obliquus.

M. 314/15
...that was a shameful custome that what knight came there to aske herborouh his lady must nedes deye...

Heywood, P. P. 386
For who so wresteth, his work is vain;

Fl. (Liebeslieder) 137/57
Who so that wyll for grace sew.
Hys entent must nedys be trew

Lyly, Euphues 403
...whosoeuer serued vs, we should aunswere his suite...

Kyd, Spanish Tragedy 77 *Who — his,*

Puttenham 276
...and whom we honour we should also reuerence their appetites...

Sidney, Ap. 27
which who mislike, the faulte is in their iudgements...

Arcadia 396
Which who doth miss, his eyes are but delusions,

P. L. 42/54
and what so ever ye do... in my maister Cleris name, he shall avowe it...

ib. 176/234, 224/313 *what — it,*

M. 43/29 (Fox 66)
And who that holdeth ageynst it we wille slee hym.

ib. 226/3 *...who is aferd lete hym flee...*

Tyndale, Mark. 6/23
...whatsoeuer thou shalt axe of me, I will geue it the...
(Auth. Vers. und Rev. Vers. ebenso).

Tyndale, Matth. 12/32
And whosoeuer speaketh a worde agaynst the sone of man, it shalbe forgeuen him (Auth. Vers. und Rev. Vers. ebenso).

More, Utopia 120 *Whosoeuer — him,*
G. G. Needle 185 *whatsoever — it,*
Lyly, Euphues 72
... *of Lucilla: Whom finding in place conuenient without company, with a bold courage and comely gesture, he began to assay hir in this sort.*

ib. 219 (323) ... *in the behalfe of Euphues, who framing diuers questions and quirkes of loue, if by some more curious then needeth, it shall be tolde him that...*

Peele, Arr. 25 *Whoe'er — him,*
Greene, Orlando 51 *What — it,*
Marprelate, Epistle 37, Puttenham 34 *whatsoeuer — it.*
etc. etc.

§ 302.
Bemerkungen zu a und b.

Unsere Belege ergeben ein deutliches bild von der grossen Verbreitung dieser Konstruktion im 15. und 16. Jahrhundert. Hier sowohl wie in den unter 1. und 2. besprochenen Fällen haben wir es mit einer vor allem der Umgangssprache angehörenden, ihrem verschwenderischen Zuge entsprungenen Erscheinung zu thun.

Anhang III.

Einzelne andere Kapitel aus der Syntax des Satzes.

§ 303.

Rückbeziehung auf das im Singular stehende Subjekt vermittelst eines Personal- oder Possessivpronomens im Plural.

Diese Konstruktion nach dem Sinne, die sich erst seit dem Me. belegen lässt (cf. Mätzner II, 149 f., woselbst auch Erklärung), ist im 15. und 16. Jahrhundert sehr verbreitet gewesen, wie folgende Auswahl von Belegen zeigen möge:

1. *each.*

P. L. 332/447 rechts

... *aud iche othyr prist or monk [of the said co]llage X. marks yeerly for here sustenaunce and fynding* ...

M. 149/22

... *soo eche one plyghte their trouthe to other* ...

Fl. (Poesie) 17/5

Eche byrde under boughe drewe nye to theyr nest

Bale, Thre Lawes 708

These two wyll hym so vse,
Ich one in their abuse,

Kyd, Spanish Tragedy 7

When this eternal substance of my soul
Did live imprison'd in my wanton flesh,
Each in their junction serving other's need.

2. *either.*

M. 106/21 ... *thenne eyther dressid her sheldes and smote to gyders* ...

ib. 238/12 ... *and eyther gafe other suche buffets vpon their helmes* ...

ib. 258/15 ... *and eyther of hem brake their speres to their handes* ...

ib. 417/17 ... *and so eyther told other their names* ...
ib. 818/26 ... *thenne eyther party made hem redy* ...
More, Utopia 124
For if either of them finde themselfe for any such cause greued: they maye by the license of the counsel chaunge and take another.
Sidney, Arcadia 586
But like two contrary tides, either of which are able to carry worlds of ships ...
NB. Die grosse Zahl der Belege aus M. erklärt sich nach § 185.

Anm.: So erklärt sich *knyghtes* in
M. 384/1 *And so eyther knyghtes made hem redy* ...

3. *neither.*

John Knox 20
... *that nether of both haue power ouer their owne bodies.*
Lyly, Euphues 436
... *but that neither of them haue their equall* ...
Anm.: So erklärt sich *partyes* in
P. L. 709/193 ... *yt wer non honoure to neyther partyes* ...

4. *every man (body).*

P. L. 94/127
for now every man that hath any, they put theme now inne ...
Latimer, Sermons 18
Therfore, it shal become enery man, which do intende to lyue godly ... to prynte heauenly documentes in their hertes.
R. A., Toxophilus 36
And that euery bodye shoulde learne to shote whan they be yonge ...
ib. 56 *euery man — theyr,* ib. 57 *euerye man — them,*
Lyly, Euphues 278
For eucrye of them haue Venus by the hand, and they are all assured and certaine to winne hir heart.

5. *who.*

P. L. 122/163
It is apoynted that who shall sue any bille in the Parlement, shei must be put into the Commone Hous by for Seint Edmunds day atte ferthest, etc.

M. 378/22
... who þat may fyrst mete ony of these two knyghtes they shold torne hem vnto Morgan...

Mucedorus 218   so who comes first,
Let them abide the happy meeting of us both.

Weiterentwicklung.

Im 17. und 18. Jahrhundert (Franz 399) wie noch heute üblich (vgl. auch Willert, Anm. zur ne. Gramm. Progr., Berlin 1892), wenn auch von Grammatikern eifrigst bekämpft.

§ 304.

Zur Kongruenz des Prädikats mit dem einfachen Subjekt, wenn dieses ein Relativum ist.

Unsere Beobachtungen bestätigen im Wesentlichen die Angaben Mätzners (II, 155 f.).

Doch haben wir im 15. und 16. Jahrhundert Fälle, wo anstatt der zu erwartenden 1. bezw. 2. Person die 3. Sg. eintritt.

Henslowe's Diary 113
Be yt knowne unto all men by this presents, that J, Willame Birde, and gabrell spencer, and Thomas Dowton dothe aknowlege our seallves...

M. 390/2 ... *what arte thou ... that holdeth me soo...*

ib. 691/34 *Thow man whiche shalls entre in to this shyp beware thou be in stedfast bileue...*

Fl. (Wyatt) 28/10 ... *I thowght fortwith to write*
Brian, to the who knows...

Peele, Old Wives Tale 245
How now, what man art thou, that sits so sad?

Peele, Edward I 191
Poor soul, guiltless art thou of this deceit,
That hath more cause to curse than to complain.

Marlowe, Tamburlaine 1496
Dar'st thou, that neuer saw an Emperour ... thus abuse his state ...

Wie weit die Erklärung solcher und ähnlicher Fälle sich ohne weiteres aus den im 15. und 16. Jahrhundert ziemlich verworrenen Flexionsverhältnissen ergiebt, muss einer näheren Untersuchung dieser vorbehalten bleiben.

Man vgl. z. B.:
G. G. Needle 213
Was not thou afraid, Hodge, to see him in this place?
Marriage of Wit 385 *remember, how*
Thou was subdned of Tediousness right now.

Im Uebrigen giebt uns der vielfach auf sehr feinen Unterschieden beruhende Wechsel von Fällen, wo die 1. bezw. 2. oder die 3. Person verwandt wird, die Erklärung an die Hand.

§ 305.
Kongruenz des Prädikats in Beziehung auf mehr als ein Subjekt.

Mätzner II, 165 f. Haben verschiedene grammatische Personen, die in kopulativem Verhältnis zu einander stehen, ein gemeinsames Prädikat, so steht das Verbum im 15. und 16. Jahrhundert in der Regel im Plural, z. b.:

P. L. 36/48 ... *my moder and I wer nowth in hertys es*...
Four Elements 35 *Yet I had liever she and I*
Were both together secretly
Heywood, P. P. 374
This devil and I were of old acquaintance;
Peele, Edward I 135
And you and I are left alone;
Greene, Bacon 200
What say the lord of Castile, and the earl of Lincoln...?
The 4 tos „*says*".
Marlowe, Dido 398
This man and I were at Olympia's games.

Bisweilen richtet sich das Verb in Person und Zahl nach dem nächsten Subjekt:
Plumpton Correspondence 167
Sir, ye, and I, and my sone, was content at your departing, that my sone should talse the farmes at Martingmas of his tenaunts...
Sir Clyomon and Sir Clamydes 501a
For he and I am both of one consanguinity,
ib. 503b
He'll beat a hundred such as you and I am down nat one stroke.

Greene, James IV 155
>   Ah mighty prince! this king and I am one;

Marlowe, Edward II 216
>   How comes it that the king and he is parted?

Look about You 421
>   And she and I am not to be divorced.

Diese letztere Stellung meist bei disjunktivem Verhältnis, z. B.:

Greene, Orlando 12
>   Nor he, nor thou shouldst have Angelica.

Marlowe, Lucan 270
>   Fierce Pyrrhus, neither thou nor Hannibal

Art cause; (Original: *Non tu, Pyrrhe ferox, nec tantis cladibus auctor Poenus erit.*)

Dagegen: Marlowe, Hero 14
>   Nor heaven nor thou were made to gaze upon:

Durch Anlehnung erklären sich:

P. L. 483/146
>   therfor, worsschipfull cosyn, I, a brother ... mekely besechyth you ...

Soliman and Perseda 287
>   It is not meet that one so base as thou
>   Shouldst come about the persone of a king.

In einer grossen Zahl von Fällen ist die Unterscheidung von Person und Zahl infolge der gleichen Flexionsformen unmöglich, z. B.:

Digby Mysteries 193/654
>   He and I com both of your kyn,

Bale, Kynge Johan 5
>   Off that thow and I wyll common more at leyser.

Greene, Verm. 274
>   He and she did sit and keep
>   Flocks of kids and folds of sheep:

Auch in Fällen wie R. A., Toxophilus 159
>   ... where one of the markes or both stondes a lytle short of a hye wall ...

denn man vgl. dazu:
>   what are they that comes here?

sowie Kellner, Outlines § 89.

Anhang IV.
§ 306.
Apposition statt partitiver Genitiv.

Vgl. hierzu Kellner, Outl. § 174 ff., für das Ae. auch Schrader, Studien zur Aelfric'schen Syntax § 83.

Kellner sagt a. a. O. § 175:

„From the Old English down to the Elizabethan age, indefinites and numerals followed by adjectives in the superlative degree, appear as attributes, instead of governing a partitive genitive as in Modern English."

Wir können dies bestätigend weiter dahin formulieren, dass diese Erscheinung im 15. und 16. Jahrhundert noch sehr verbreitet war, wie sich aus der unten angeführten Auswahl von Belegen ergeben wird. Bei den Belegen mit *other* lässt sich nicht immer mit Sicherheit feststellen, ob der Gedanke „meine (deine etc.) anderen" oder „andere von meinen (deinen etc.)" vorliegt, eine Einschränkung, die auch für Kellners Belege § 176 gilt. Man vgl. dazu die Stellung von *other* in Fällen wie:

P. L. 309/420 ... *other the Kynges Juges* ...

Latimer, Sermons 24 ... *Jeroboam with other many* ...

Marprelate, Epistle 21
... *you and I will answere the matter before his grace (or other the high commiosioners)* ...

Marlowe, Hero 87
    A painted box of confits in her hand
    The matron held, and so did other some.

Belege:
P. L. 76/100 ... *and other your enemeys, subgettes and ambassiators* ...
ib. 238/326 (493/168)
... *to put ws yn as diligent and hertye devoyr and dewtee as onye your lyege men on lyve to that at may avaunce* ...
ib. 343/503 ... *as weell as by other his lettres to dyvers persones directed* ...
ib. 603/344 ... *sertayn hys servaunts felleth wode* ...
ib. 883/816
... *with other dyvers his rebelles and traytours* ...
Plumpt. Corr. 105 ... *with other his master frynds* ...
ib. 162 ... *and such others your adversaries;*
Fl. (Wyatt) 25/34
  Hens fourth my poyn[y]s this shalbe all and some
  These wretched fooles shall have nought els of me
ib. (Philos. didact. Schriften) 255/9
... *your hyghenesse in the presence of dyuers your noble men* ... *affirmed that* ...
Joy, Ap. 39 ... *emong so many his friuole notis and gloses* ...
Egerton Papers 140
And where also in other our Letters Patentes ... *yt is conteyned* ...
Gorboduc 319
  Althoug the same do not agree at all
  With that which other here my lordes haue said,
Lyly, Euphues 295
... *she accompanied with hir gentlewomen and other hir seruaunts* ...
Introductory Sketch 117
as by a collation of such their writinges ... may appeare.
ib. *The stile of it and spiritt of the man ... doth alltogether resemble such his writinges as he hath published* ...
Sidney, Arcadia 235 ... *by other his unnatural dealings* ...
ib. 672 ... *for the performance of certain her country devotions* ...

Briefe Elizabeths 37
... *wherin his case is common with many other your subiects* ...
Leycester Correspondence 5
... *I dypached ... above IIe lettres to my servaunts, and sondry my frends* ...
ib. 81
The enymye offeryng any revenge to any hir majesties domynions she might be depryved also of such helps ...

Sachregister.

Es wird nach Paragraphen zitiert.

Accentverschiebung bei *toward* 153 Anm.
all + Personalpronomen 244.
Analytische Tendenzen — Zusammenfassung 247.
Anrede vor dem Vocativ, Pronomen in der, 98, 4.
any thing adverbiell 77 Anm.
Apposition statt partitiver Genitiv 306.

Bibelsprache 258.
both + Possessivpronomen 158.
both, Stellung von, 238.
Bühnenanweisungen, Pronomen in, § 103 Anm.
Bühneneffektmittel — Zusammenfassung 246, 3.

Contaminationen 250.

Dativus comm. und incomm. 151.
Dialektisches — Zusammenfassung 246.

each und *every*, Gebrauch von, 243.
Eigentümlichkeiten einzelner Literaturgattungen 255.
Eigentümlichkeiten einzelner Schriftsteller 254.
Erscheinungen, die im 15./16. Jh. aufhören bezw. entstehen 253.

Französischen, Einfluss des, 252, 1.

get, to, analogische Bildungen zu, 180 Anm.
Gruppe I und II, Einteilung in 1.

he und *she* zur Bezeichnung des Geschlechts 113.

I am he 134 Anm. 2.
ich, mein zweites (anderes) 193, 3 Anm. 2.
Imperativ praet. ohne Pronomen 98, 2.
Imperativ, Pronomen beim, 97 f.
it als Objekt bei intr. Verben 112.
it is I 134.
it pleonastisch nach *what* 296 Anm.
its, ersatz von, 154,

Kasusvertauschungen in Sir Clyomon 131.
Kasusvertauschungen beim Personalpronomen 115—140.
Kongruenz des Praedikats in Beziehung auf mehr als ein Subjekt 305.
Kongruenz des Praedikats mit dem einfachen Subjekt 304.
Kürze des Ausdrucks — Zusammenfassung 248.

Lateinischen, Einwirkung des, 252, 2.

Majestätsplural des Personalpronomens 114.
Majestätsplural des Reflexivpronomens 44.
„man", Bezeichnung des unbestimmten, 234.
me für *I* in bewusster Absicht 133.
my in der Anrede 160.
myself etc. als Subjekt 196.
my self etc. verstärkt durch *own* 192.
my und *mine*, Gebrauch von, 20 Anm. 1.
no als Negation 235.
none in neutralem Sinne 237.
no oder *none* in attributiver Beziehung 68 Anm. 3.
none, Stellung von, am Ende des Satzes 236.
nothing als verstärkte Negation 240.
no vor Komparativen 235, b.
no whit als verstärkte Negation 240 Anm.

one's self, Ersatz von 195.
Orthographie, allgemeines zur, 1.
other für *each* (*either* etc.) *other* 187 Anm.
other, Pluralbildung von, 83 Anm. 2.
our in der Anrede 160.
own verstärkt *my self* etc. 192.

Personalpronomen, Anlassung des, 89—104.
Personalpronomina grossgeschrieben 18.
Personalpronomen, pleonastischer Gebrauch des, 105—112.
Personalpronomen, pleon. als rhetorisches Hilfsmittel 108 Anm. 4.
Personalpronomina, Verschiebung im Gebrauch der, 19.
Personalpronomen, Verschmelzung des, mit anderen Wörtern 17.
Poss. Pron., analytische Umschreibung des, 156.
Possessive Beziehung auf ein unbekanntes Subjekt 155.
Possessivpronomina grossgeschrieben 27.
Poss. Pron. in urspr. Bedeutung als Genitiv des Pers. Pron. 157 ff.
Poss. Pron., Stellung des adj. 162.
Poss. Pron. + subst. Adjectiv 159.
Poss. Pron., subst. anstatt des adj. 165 f.
Poss. und Pers., wechsel und Verwechselung von, 167 f.
Poss. Pron. zur Bezeichnung des Genitivs 163 f.
Pronomina, Wechsel ähnlich lautender, unter einander und mit dem Artikel *the* 167 ff.
Pseudo-partitiver Genitiv 166.

Reciprokes Pronomen, Ersatz durch *together* 191.
Reciproken Verhältnisses, Bezeichnung des, 185—191.
Refl. Verhältnisses, Bezeichnung des, bei intr. Verben 178 ff.
Refl. Verhältnisses, Bezeichnung des, bei trans. Verben 172 ff.
Relativa grossgeschrieben 66.
Relative Anknüpfung 230 f.
Relativsätze, Bau der, im 15./16. Jh. Anhang II § 295 ff.
Relativs, Auslassung des, 229.
Relativs, Beziehung eines, auf ein Poss. 157.
Relativum, pleonastisches, 232 f.
Rückbeziehung auf das Subjekt im Sg. durch ein Pron. im Pl. 303.

same, Gebrauch von 206.
same verstärkt *self* 198 Anm.
self als Substantivum 193.
self für *himself* etc. 197.
self im Sinne von *same* 198.
self verstärkt 198 Anm.
Shaksperes Stellung zur Sprache des 16. Jh. 257, 1.
Spensers Stellung zur Sprache des 16. Jh. 257, 2.
sundry auf dramentiteln 85 Anm.

Textkritisches 259.
that am I 134 Anm. 1.
the und *thy*, Wechsel und Verwechslung von, 169.
they Uebersetzung von „man" 234, 1.
this für *these* 199—201.
this und *thus*, Wechsel und Verwechslung von, 202 f.
thou (*thee, thy, thine*) und *ye* (*you, your*), gebrauch von, 142 ff.
thy und *thine*, Gebrauch von, 20 Anm. 1.
together anstatt des reciproken Pronomens 191.
Traditionellen, Einfluss des, 251.

Umgangssprache des 15. und 16. Jh. 256.
Unconnected Subjekt 141.
Unpersönlichen Verben, Uebergang von, in persönliche Anhang I 260 ff.

Verba der Bewegung 180.
Verba der Ruhe 179.
Verba des Affects 182.
Verschwenderische Züge der Sprache — Zusammenfassung 249.

what als Ausruf 217.
what = etwas 221.
what für *who* 216.
what im Sinne von *how* 220.
what im Sinne von *why* 219.
whatsoever erweiternd 228.
whatso(*m*) *ever* in adjektivischer Funktion 227.

what that ever in adjektivischer Funktion 227.
wether, Gebrauch und Verbreitung von, 223.
whichsoever in adjektivischer Funktion 227.
who für *whom* 213 ff.
whom für *who* 210 ff.
who im Sinne von „any one" 207 ff.; 234, 3.
whosoever erweiternd 228.

ye für *you* 136 f. (138 f.).
you für *ye* 135 (138 f.).
your im Sinne eines Dativus ethicus 161.

Wortregister.

Es wird nach Paragraphen zitiert.

a, 'a § 10 Anm.
abide, to 179.
advise, to 177, 2.
advise you 104 Anm. 2.
ah 130, 5.
æghwaeder, ægþer 186.
ælc 186.
agree, to 183, 1.
ail, to 261, 290 b.
alas 130, 5.
all 84; 244.
all thing 84 Anm.
and is 101 Anm. 2.
another 83 Anm. 5.
any 77.
any one, — *body,* — *man,* — *thing* 77 Anm.
as 124.
assent, to 183, 1.
assure, to 177, 3.
assure you 104 Anm. 2.
at 65.
aught 70.
aur, awer, awr, awre 24 Anm. 2.
ay 2 Anm. 4.
aye 130, 5.

betake, to 173.
bethink, to 173.
be ye sure 98, 1.
bless, to 173.
bom 20 Anm. 4.
both 69; 158; 238.
bothenerys 69 Anm.
bothes 69 Anm.
bothe two 239.
bow, to 177, 5.

bum 20 Anm. 4.
busk, to 180.
but 121.

certain 87.
chance, to 262.
cheer, to 172.
come, to 180.
complain, to 177, 6.
content, to 177, 4.

dat 47.
day 15 Anm. 1.
dee 7 Anm.
delight 263.
dem 16 Anm. 3.
dese 46 Anm. 1.
desire 264.
dey 15 Anm. 1.
dis 45 Anm.
disguise, to 173.
dismay, to 182 *to dread* Anm.
disport, to 177, 10.
divers 86.
doubt, to 182.
dread, to 182.
dy 20 Anm. 5.

each 79; 243; 303, 1.
each body, — *man,* — *one* 79 Anm.
each other 187 ff.
each thing 79 Anm.
either 81; 187 ff.; 303, 1.
else what 221, 2.
'em 16 Anm. 1.
endeavour, to 177, 7.
enough 74.

eueryche 187.
everich 80 Anm. 1.
everychone 80 anm. 2.
every 80.
every body 80 Anm. 4, 303, 1.
every man, — one, — thing 80 Anm. 4.
every ylke 80 Anm. 3.
except 123.

farewell 98, 1.
fear, to 182.
feawe 75 Anm.
few 75; 241.
fewer, fewest 75; 241, 2.
forthynk, to 265.
fortune, to 266.

get, to 180.
godamercy 104 Anm. 3.
gramercy 104 Anm. 3.
grieve, to 267.

ha 10 Anm.
happen, to 268.
hark, to 183, 2.
haste, to 180.
he 10; 113.
hear, to 183, 2.
hem 16 Anm. 1.
hem self 43 Anm. 1.
her Pers. 13.
her Poss. 22.
her = *their* 26 Anm. 1.
her für *hers* 33, 1.
hers 29.
hers für *her* 22 Anm.
herself 38.
hie, to 180.
him 11.
himself 37.
his Adj. Poss. 21.
his Subst. Poss. 28.
hise Plural von *his* 21. Anm. 2.
his nown 20 Anm. 2.
his self 194.
how Schreibung für *who* 55 Anm. 1.

I 2.
I Schreibung für *aye* 2 Anm. 5.
i Schreibung für *I* 2 Anm. 1.
ich(e) 2 Anm. 2.
ick 2 Anm. 3.
if so be 101 Anm. 1.
ilk 51.
I'll tell you what 221, 1.
in few 241, 1.
is Schreibung für *his* 21 Anm. 1.
it 14; 112; 226 Anm.
its 23; 154.
itself 39 und Nachtrag.
joy 269.

know ye 98, 1.

lack, to 270.
lay, to 177, 8; 173.
lie, to 179.
lief, to be 289.
like 125.
like, to 271; 290 c.
like (ly), to be 289.
list, to 272.
long, to 273.
look, to 183, 2.
loth, to be 289.

m' für *my* 20 Anm. 4.
many 78; 242.
many (a) one 78 Anm.; 242 Anm.
many ones (Gen. u. Pl.) 242 Anm.
marvel, to 274.
may Schreibung für *my* 20 Anm. 6.
me 3; 133.
means 201 Anm.
me seem 282 Anm.
me self 35 Anm. 2.
me think 284 Anm.
mickle 76 Anm.
mine Adj. 20.
mine Subst. 28.
misfortune, to 266.
mishappen, to 268.
much 76.
muche what 222, 3.

my 20; 160.
myght' für my ryght 20 Anm. 3.
my lord 160 Anm.
my nown 20 Anm. 2.
myn self 35 Anm. 1.
myself 35; 192; 196.
myster, to 275.

na, nane 68 Anm. 1.
naught 71.
need, to 276.
neither 82; 303, 3.
nething 72 Anm.
news 201 Anm.
no 68; 235.
no body 68 Anm. 4.
noddy 68 Anm. 5.
nodur 83 Anm. 5.
none 68; 236; 237.
no nother 68 Anm. 2.
no one 68 Anm. 4.
nother für no other 83 Anm. 1.
nothing 72; 240.
not one 68 Anm. 4.
nought 71.
noughts 71 Anm.
no whit 240 Anm.

obey, to 183, 1.
öder 186.
one 67; 234, 2.
one another 189 f.
one's self 40; 195.
other 83; 187 Anm.
other wayes, -wise 83 Anm. 5.
ought 70.
our 24; 160.
ours 30.
ourselfe 41; 44.
ourselves 41.
owe, to 277.
own 192.

pains 201 Anm.
pity, to 278.
play, to 177, 10 Anm.
please, to 279.

(I) pray 104 Anm. 1.
prythee 104 Anm. 1.
purpose, to 183, 1.

quha 55 Anm. 4.
quhat 58 Anm. 1.
quhich 60 Anm. 2.
quilk, quilkes 60 Anm. 1.
quho 55 Anm. 4.
quhom 57 Anm. 1.
quhomby 57 Anm. 2.
quhomto 57 Anm. 2.
qwat som ever 62 Anm. 2.

'r für our 24 Anm. 1.
recant, to 183, 1.
recomand, to 172 Anm.; 177, 1
reherceth, as it 285.
remember, to 177, 9.
repent, to 182; 280.
repose, to 179 Anm.
rest, to 179.
return, to 180.
rew, to 281.
rue, to 281.

same 53; 198 Anm.; 206.
save 122.
self 52; 193; 197; 198.
selfsame 206, 2 a.
seme, to 282.
set, to 179 Anm. 1.
several 88.
shame, to 182; 283.
she 12; 113.
sheweth, as it 285.
sho 12 Anm.
shush 49 Anm. 2.
sike 49 Anm. 1.
sit, to 179.
some 73.
some body, -one, -thing, -times, -what
   73 Anm. 2.
speed, to 180.
sport, to 177, 10.
such 49.
such like 205.

summe 73 Anm. 1.
sundry 85.
such as 124.
sush 49 Anm. 2.

telleth, as it 285.
tham 16 Anm. 1.
than 126.
thanks 104 Anm. 3.
(*I*) *thank you* 104 Anm. 3.
that (Dem.) 47.
that (Rel.) 64.
thay 20 Anm. 6.
the 169.
thea 15 Anm. 2.
theam 16 Anm. 2,
thee 7.
their 26.
their für *theirs* 33, 3.
theirs 32.
theirs für *their* 26 Anm. 2.
their selves 194.
them 16.
them seluen 43 Anm. 2.
them selves 43.
these 46.
the self für *thy self* 36 Anm.
the self für *its self* 39 Anm.
they 15; 234, 1.
thilk 50.
thine (Adj.) 20.
think, to 284.
this 45; 199—201; 202—203.
thise Pl. zu *this* 46 Anm. 2
this many a day 204.
this many a hundred year 204.
this much 203 Anm.
tho 48 Anm.
those 48
th'one, thone 67 Anm.
th'other, thother 83 Anm. 3.
thou 6; 142 ff.
thus 202—203.
thus much 203 Anm.
thy 20; 169.
theyself 36.
tidings 201 Anm.

together 191.
to me ward 153.
t'one, tone, the 67 Anm.
tother, the 83 Anm. 3.
turn, to 180.

us 5.

vat 58 Anm. 2.

ware, to 167, 11.
we 4.
well, to be 289.
wete ye well 98, 1.
what 58; 216; 217; 219; 220; 221.
what a 218.
what one 218 Anm.
what so 224.
what so, what(so)ever 62.
whatsomever 62 Anm. 1.
what that 225.
what that ever 227.
what what 58 Anm. 3.
what — what (and) 222.
whe 55 Anm. 5.
whese 56 Anm. 2.
whether 59; 223.
whethersoever 59 Anm.
whether that 225.
which 60.
which(so)(m)ever 63.
whichsoever 226; 227.
which that 225.
whilk 60 Anm. 1.
who 55; 207; 213 ff.; 234, 3; 303, 5.
who Schreibung für *how* 55.
whom 57; 210 f.
whosoever 228.
whomsoever 61 Anm. 2.
whomewyth 57 Anm. 2.
whose 56.
whose Schreibung für *who is* 55 Anm. 2.
whose whose 56 Anm. 1.
who so 224.
who so, who(so)ever 61.
whosomever 61 Anm. 1.
who that 225.

who who 55 Anm. 3.
woe, to be 289.
wother 83 Anm. 4.
(*I*) *would* (*to God*) 104 Anm. 1.

y Schreibung für *I* 2 Anm. 1.
ye 8; 136f., (138f.); 142ff.
ye für *your* 25 Anm. 2.
yender 54 Anm. 2.

yon, yond, yonder 54.
you 9; 135, (138f.).
your 25; 161.
your für *yours* 33, 2.
yours 31.
yours für *your* 25 Anm. 1.
yourselfe 41, 44.
yourselves 41.
ys 21 Anm. 1.

Nachträge und Berichtigungen.

Einleitung p. 2 Z. 12 von unten lies „Spenser"; — p. 3 Z. 6 von unten: Die Ausgabe von Logemann (cf. Engl. Stud. XXI, 449) ist mir entgangen. p. 5 Z. 15 von unten ist zu tilgen; p. 6 Z. 6 lies „1558—1594 (?)"; — p. 9 Z. 10 lies „das" anstatt „dass"; — p. 15 Z. 10 von unten lies „*beʒʒm*" für „*beʒm*";

p. 16 § 17. Auf eine briefliche Anregung des Herrn Professor Max Foerster hin bemerke ich, dass es mir in § 17 vor allem ankam, eine orthographische Uebersicht über die Fälle zu geben, in denen das Personalpronomen durch unbetonte Stellung verändert erscheint, oder wo es mit anderen Wörtern zusammengeschrieben wird; ich gebe zu, dass eine genaue äusserliche Trennung dieser die Uebersicht erleichtert hätte.

p. 20 § 23. Die inbetreff *its* gemachte Bemerkung „In den etc." ist zu streichen, da *its* (*it's*) *self* eine modernisierte Schreibung ist; die Ausgabe von Sidneys Arcadia, London 1633 hat (p. 144 und 429) *it selfe*; —

p. 37 Z. 9 lies „Me. *ěni*, *ǎni*, *ǒni*"; — p. 40 Z. 13 von unten füge hinzu „*sendry* (621/374)"; —

p. 44 § 91. Der Beleg aus Sidney, Astrophel and Stella 6/1 ist in § 104, 2 zu übertragen; — ib. füge hinzu: Greene, Looking Glass 66

whereupon, my friend, in their defence, I give thee this curse, thou shalt not be worth a horse of thine own this seven year.
* Not in the 4to of 1594.

p. 48 Z. 3 lies „3" statt 2; — p. 53 Z. 16 lies „Tyndale"; — p. 64 Z. 3 von unten lies „*Percyuale*"; —

p. 66 Z. 8 von unten füge hinzu „Belege aus Sir Clyomon siehe p. 94; —

p. 76 Z. 2. *They* kann auch demonstrativ als im Gegensatz zu *he* stehend aufgefasst werden; —

p. 107. Das in § 137 über die Verbreitung von *ye* als Akkusativ in der 1. Hälfte des 15. Jahrhunderts wird noch glänzend bestätigt durch einen sogar durch den Reim gesicherten Beleg, den ich nachträglich noch in Chaucers Troilus and Criseyde p. 153 (Complete Works ed. Skeat Bd. II) finde, und den ten Brink in seiner Chaucer-Grammatik nicht erwähnt:

The double sorwe of Troilus to tellen,...
That was the king Priamus sone of Troye,
In lovinge, how his aventure fellen
Fro wo to wele, and after out of joye,
My purpos is, er that I parte fro ye.

Ye könnte allerdings auch ein lautlich geschwächtes *you* darstellen.

p. 107 Z 5 von unten lies § 135.

p. 126 Z. 4 lies „*hnescan*"; —

p. 148 füge bei § 168 hinzu:

Anm.: Vielleicht ist hierher zu rechnen:

Peele, Old Wives Tale 213

Gods me bones, who comes here?

das eine Contamination aus *Gods bones* (Sir Clyomon 516a) und *God me* (= *my* nach § 167, 1a) *bones* darstellen könnte. Vergl. hierzu das Shakspere'sche *God's my life* sowie *God's me, my life* (Schmidt unter *God*); —

p. 155 füge zu § 173 hinzu:

Anm.: Im Morte Darthure 695/36 fand sich auch ein reflexiver Dativ bei passivischer Konstruktion:

Soo there with entryd a spere where with he was smyte hym thurgh bothe the thyes ...

p. 155 Z. 7 von unten füge hinzu „Ausgabe der E. E. Text Soc. No. LVII"; — ib. Z. 9 von unten „Ausgabe der E. E. Text Soc. No. LIV"; — ib. Z. 10 von unten „Ausgabe der E. E. Text Soc. No. LXIV"; — p. 160 Z. 4 lies „§ 177"; —

p. 166 nach Z. 8 füge hinzu „*to be*:

Greene, Looking Glass 63

Be *thou vicegerent of his royalty,

* The 4tos „*thee*".

p. 182 Z. 5 füge ein nach z. B.: „Fl. (Balladen) 196/32".

p. 186 füge bei § 192 hinzu:

Anm.: Verstärkung des Poss. durch *self* liegt vor in *my self oaths* in dem Beleg Marlowe, Ovid 158

Thou, goddes, dost command a warm south blast,
My self oaths in Carpathian seas to cast.

wo das lateinische Original hat (Amores II, 8, 19):

Tu, dea, tu iubeas animi periuria puri
Carpathium tepidos per mare ferre notos ...

oaths übersetzt *periuria* und *self* im Sinne von „*pertaining to one's self*" (cf. Schmidt, Sh.-Lex. unter *self* pronom. adj.) giebt das lateinische „*animi*" wieder; —

p. 194 f. In den unter 1 mitgeteilten Fällen ist *this* doch wohl als Singular aufzufassen, da diese Zeitbestimmungen in Verbindung mit Zahlwörtern schon zu Kompositen geworden waren. Vergl. *a twelvemonth* etc. p. 207 Z. 7 „*as who*" ist wohl als „der ich" zu fassen und als freie Satzbildung in relativem Anschluss an „*yet was it neuer my minde or intente* ..."

Druck von Ehrhardt Karras, Halle a. S.

www.ingramcontent.com/pod-product-compliance
Lightning Source LLC
Chambersburg PA
CBHW021208230426
43667CB00006B/613